A BORDERS

Also in Arrow by Lavinia Derwent

BEYOND THE BORDERS
GOD BLESS THE BORDERS!
A MOUSE IN THE MANSE
LADY OF THE MANSE

A BORDERS OMNIBUS

Lavinia Derwent

Illustrated by Elizabeth Haines

Containing

A Breath of Border Air
Another Breath of Border Air
A Border Bairn

ARROW BOOKS

Arrow Books Limited
20 Vauxhall Bridge Road, London SW1V 2SA

An imprint of the Random Century Group

London Melbourne Sydney Auckland Johannesburg
and agencies throughout the world

Omnibus edition first published in 1991

Printed and bound in Great Britain by
Cox & Wyman Ltd, Reading

ISBN 0 09 985100 8

A BREATH OF BORDER AIR

LAVINIA DERWENT

A Breath of Border Air

Illustrated by Elizabeth Haines

To Jessie

Contents

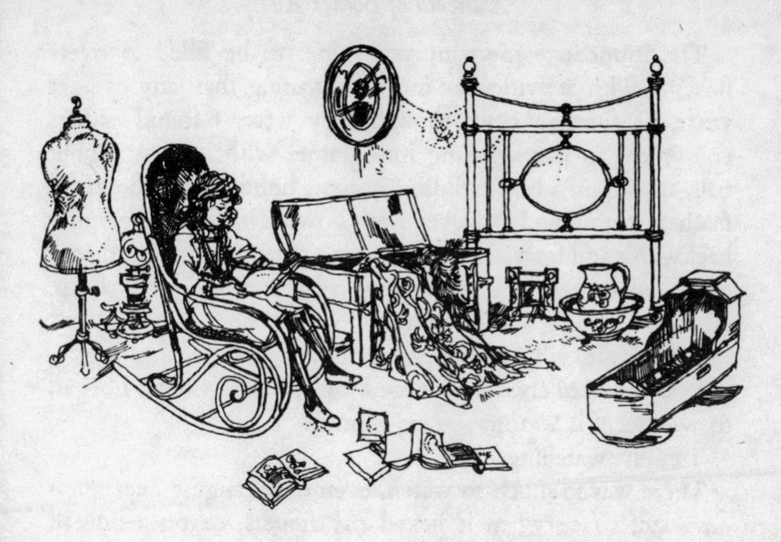

1. Gaol in the Garret

I was thoughtless enough to be born in a snowstorm. February-fill-the-dyke. Think of the trouble it caused the doctor who had to plough seven long miles through snowdrifts just for the purpose of bringing me into the world.

'An' him wi' better things to do,' Jessie often told me. 'Fashious bairn! Ye micht hae waited.'

I had to wait long enough for my first outing. Six weeks or more, and then I was carried high above the hedgerows in a world that was still snow-white. The drifts lay long on that windswept hillside. The farmhouse, the cottages, and the fields seemed locked for ever in the icy grip of winter; and I used to wonder in later years if I would ever see the black earth again or the ripe corn standing in stooks in the fields.

Yet, looking back, it is the long sunny days of summer that I remember best, stretching into eternity, like the for-ever-and-ever in the Bible, when I ran barefoot all over the farm and never thought of yesterday or tomorrow.

The immediate moment was mine, to be filled to overflowing with activities far more engrossing than any of later years, profitless pursuits though they were. I found endless enjoyment in playing long lone games with a burst rubber ball, spying on a bird building its nest, hunting for pheasants' feathers, tumbling head-over-heels down a haystack, swinging backwards and forwards on a creaking gate, listening to the cry of the whaup, watching the shepherd rounding up the sheep. Always watching and listening.

'Man-lassie, what are ye glowerin' at?'

Jock-the-herd always addressed me as Man-lassie till I began to wonder if it was maybe my name.

'I'm just watching.'

There was so much to watch, even the changing expression on a calf's face when it licked my fingers, or on a human being's, though there were few enough of them around. The only crowd I ever saw was a flock of sheep, and the word passer-by had no meaning for me.

The farm was hidden away from the main road, with no signpost to say where the steep track led to, lost amongst trees and hills as if it had been dumped down and forgotten. The farmhouse itself was like a child's drawing, stark and bare, with walls three feet thick, which had withstood hundreds of years of rough wind and weather. The Big Hoose, the cottagers called it.

The outhouses nearby – the cart-shed, the barns, the stables, the byre, the bields for sheep and cattle – were happy hunting-grounds for a young explorer. Frightening, too, with cocks and hens flying out from dark corners, great workhorses stamping their giant feet, pigs grunting and squealing, the bull bellowing and pawing the ground, rats rustling under the straw. The ceaseless sounds were as unconnected as an orchestra tuning up. And as exciting.

There seemed no end to the restless activity of animal-life. Tails whisked, heads tossed, feet stamped, beaks pecked.

Turkeys fluffed out their feathers, roosters spread their wings, and the sheep munched from morning till night. I used to wonder if they were chewing gum and if their jaws never grew tired. Only the scarecrows stood still and quiet in the fields. The tattie-bogles, Jessie called them.

The fields themselves were full of surprises, changing their names depending on the rotation of crops. The corn-field would suddenly become the turnip-field, or the tattie-field change its identity when sown with barley. But others had more permanent names. The three-cornered field was called the Cockit Hat; there was the Lang Field, the Heathery-Hill, and the Cow-gang where the cows used to go and chew up everything they could find. Buttercups, daisies, clover, marsh-marigolds, primroses – everything was grist to their gullets. I used to imagine when drinking their milk that I could still smell the fragrance of honeysuckle or wild violets.

The whole farm was my playground. There were no Keep Off signs, but it was an unwritten law that gates must never be left open. 'Shut that yett!' the men would shout after me. And it was the blackest of sins to traverse a corn- or turnip-field instead of using the pathway that had been left at the edge, the heidrig where one could cross in comfort without damaging the crops.

There were sturdy stone walls round many of the fields, drystone dykes built patiently, stone upon stone, by some old dyker in the past, a craftsman in his own right, and kept in repair by the shepherd who was Jack-of-all-trades and master of many. I thought him the cleverest man in the world. He could make and mend a clothes-horse or a hen-house, lend a hand at haytime and harvest, catch moles, kill pigs, fell trees, and act as midwife to the cows. But his greatest accomplishment, to my mind, was whistling through his fingers and commanding instant obedience from his collies by a few terse words.

''Way by, Jed! In ahint! Doon, Jess!'

When I tried it, they just turned tail and went their own ways.

'Man-lassie,' said Jock-the-herd, shaking his wise head at me, 'there's a knack in't. I doot ye'll never lairn it.'

I doubted it, too, but I still tried. Alas! to this day 'whustlin' ' is not one of my accomplishments.

The farm had once been a battlefield, and lay in that debatable no-man's-land betwixt two warring countries. Only a short distance away stood the range of Cheviot hills with a winding old coach-road leading to the Border. The Carter Bar. Beyond lay enemy territory. England, where the Sassenachs lived.

> Fee-fi-fo-fum,
> I smell the blood of an Englishman.

I pictured them as a wild tribe who crept across the frontier to steal our cattle, plunder our houses, and burn our abbeys. The Scottish reivers, engaged in similar pursuits, were not to be blamed. They were merely retaliating!

When I had mastered the magic art of reading, I filled my head with bloodthirsty ballads.

> When Percy and the Douglas met,
> I wat he was fou fain.
> They swakkit swords til sair they swat,
> And the bluid ran doon like rain.

It was not easy to forget the old fighting days, for the ruins of a Border keep still stood on our hillside, though the sheep and cattle now grazed peacefully enough around it. It was here that the Scots kept a look-out in the old days, ready to light a warning bonfire when the English raiders were sighted creeping across the Border; and here I played houses as a child, with a ready-made castle at my command.

The surrounding farms had strange and fascinating names. Bloodylaws I liked best, because of its wicked sound. Our own,

Overton Bush, was plain in comparison. It was known locally as the Bush, or merely the Buss, in the old Scottish manner. Stotfield marched on one side, Falla on the other. Nearby were Dolphinston, Dovesford, Mervinslaw, and Oxnam; and away down country we could see the Eildon Hills 'cleft in twain' by Michael Scott the Wizard.

But these were far-away and out-of-reach places for a child. It was the immediate surroundings that mattered. The farm itself was a world of its own. The men who worked in the fields were called hinds and the women bondagers, in the old feudal fashion, but they were no mere hirelings; they were our friends.

The hinds wore rough jackets, corduroy breeks, tackety-boots, and leggings which they called nicky-tams. Sometimes they were tied round with binder-twine, or even with straw twisted into rope. Often the scarecrows looked better-dressed, for the men seemed to spend more time grooming their horses than bothering about their own appearance, and were for ever brushing and combing the Clydesdales' tails or plaiting their manes.

The bondagers, too, wore coarse serviceable garments, kilting up their long skirts and fastening them with safety-pins over striped petticoats. But it was their headgear, the distinguishing mark of their trade, that fascinated me and made me determined to become a bondager when I grew up. Big black straw hats shaped in Dolly Vardon fashion which shaded their weather-beaten faces from wind and sun. Sometimes they wore red-and-white spotted kerchiefs underneath, tied under their chins and half-covering their faces. It was difficult to tell who was who unless one peered closely enough under their hats. In wet weather both men and women flung empty sacks over their shoulders to protect them from the rain, making them look more than ever like tattie-bogles. But what did appearances matter? Under their trappings they were all honest, loyal and hard-working. The farm was as much theirs as ours.

Like Lucy Gray, that solitary child in the poem, I was a lone bairn. Not because I was bereft of brothers and sisters, but because I was an in-between, far beneath the regard of a superior sister four years older – a lifetime to a child – and of a brother some eight years my senior. Destined for the kirk, no less. He seemed a lordly creature who rode away each day on a spirited pony to the Grammar School in Jedburgh, mounting from the big stone at the kitchen door. The loupin'-on stane. What happened at the other end I never knew; but I often watched him cantering down the farmroad with his school-bag bobbing on his back, and wondered how on earth I would get off and on the pony when my turn came.

Later he disappeared from my ken to attend college and university at a far-off place called Edinburgh, the capital of Scotland, reappearing for the holidays more of a stranger than ever. What could he, who was learning Latin and Greek, have in common with a mere toddler? To my elders and betters I was less than the dust.

Later on, there were younger ones who came, after a gap, to fill the nest. But during these formative years I remained Number Three. Nobody in particular. A nuisance, as I was often told. It was best, I found, to get on with my own ploys and keep out of everyone's way. Except maybe Jessie's.

Jessie! How can I describe her? For many years she was the most important influence in my young life. I still think of her often, remembering her wise saws and wishing I could still turn to her for advice when in difficulties.

'What should I do, Jessie?'

'Och! juist bide your time an' things'll sort themsel's oot.'

The first sounds I can recall are the clip-clop of her clogs as she went to and fro on the stone kitchen floor. Jessie always seemed to be coming or going, never sitting still with folded hands. Her hands, indeed, were seldom empty. She was always carrying kettles or milk-pails or an apronful of kindling. Or, if she was working outside, a sheaf of corn or a forkful of hay.

Jessie was the odd-job woman on the farm, who worked as a bondager when she was needed, and at other times lent a hand in the Big Hoose. At any time of stress and trouble the cry went up, 'Fetch Jessie!' I used to run helter-skelter out to the fields where she was singling turnips or spreading dung calling breathlessly, 'Jessie, you're wanted!'

We had a succession of servant-lasses in the kitchen. Raw young slavies straight from school. Daughters of herds or hinds from neighbouring farms, they clattered clumsily about the place, dropping dishes and tumbling over pails. But they, poor things, were dim creatures compared with Jessie, and, in her opinion, had little rummlegumption.

Rummlegumption was Jessie's word for commonsense, which she herself possessed in abundance. Upright in every way, straight as a ramrod, she knew the difference between black and white but none of the subtler shades in between. A thing was either right or wrong, full stop.

Jessie had a handsome, nut-brown, gypsyish look about her, with a hawk nose, beetling black brows, and a firm mouth. The kind of face a sculptor would have enjoyed hewing out of some hard material. She made no pretence at fancying-herself-up. Her strong black hair, streaked with grey, was combed back into a firm bun and fixed with fearsome-looking hairpins which never left their moorings. She wore long skirts, high-necked blouses, and a stout apron which she called a brat. Except on Sundays when she put on 'ma good costume'.

Though her whole body seemed so stiff and unyielding and there was nothing soft in her looks or speech, I instinctively felt a sense of security when I gripped her rough hand. The Scots word lippen – to depend on – must surely have been invented for Jessie. If she gave her word, threat or promise, she would carry it out.

She used to call me 'the peerie-top' because I was so seldom still.

Although she belonged to me, I thought, Jessie had another

life. She lived with her brother, the shepherd, and her sister Joan (whom she called Joo-anne) in a cottage some distance from the others, set down by the roadside. The herd's hoose. Joo-anne sometimes emerged in her big straw hat to work as a bondager, but was more often a stay-at-home, looking after the cottage and cooking the meals. Everything was as neat as ninepence inside. 'Ye could tak' your meals aff the flair,' was Joo-anne's boast; but I was glad to see that they had a table. I also remember seeing a string of salt fish hanging outside the door and the herd's long drawers blowing in the breeze.

It was a rare treat to visit the herd's hoose and find him sitting with his stockinged feet on the fender, while Joo-anne knitted on one side of the hearth and Jessie mended his socks on the other. And never a word spoken. Once, late at night, I had to take a message to them, and was amazed beyond measure when Jessie came to the door in a long white goonie, with her hair in a pigtail tied with blue wool.

Looking back, it is Jessie who stands out most clearly in all my childhood memories; and it was she, above anyone, who did most to mould my character. Indeed, my goal was to grow up to be as good as her, and with as much rummle-gumption. It is a goal, alas! that I have never reached.

It surprised me to learn that Jessie had had a previous existence. Sometimes she would speak of her younger days when she was in service in a great house in the town, and of what the parlourmaid and 'the mistress' had said or done. It had been the one adventure of her life, away from the fold; but I had a feeling that she must have pined under all the restrictions and was happier now that she could come and go more freely on the farm.

Certainly her life was varied enough, both indoors and out. Like her brother the shepherd, she could turn her hand to a hundred tasks. I have followed her about while she singled turnips, stooked corn, fed the hens, or turned the hay; and watched her milking the cows, churning the butter, doing the ironing, baking scones, making mealy puddings after the pig-killing, or sitting with a mouthful of pins putting a patch on a pair of breeks.

Jessie was the most complete person I have ever known. In a way, she was my first encyclopedia. Certainly my first story-teller. And, though she never knew it, it was because of her that I became a story-teller myself in later years.

I used to follow after her, pleading, 'Tell me a story. Go on, Jessie!'

'Hoots! I've yell't ye them a' afore.'

'Never mind! Tell me again.'

I could have listened to Jessie's stories for ever and never wearied. Especially when she was milking the cows. I still have the little red creepie-stool on which I sat in the byre, watching her milking and listening to her tales. I often stare at it today when searching for inspiration for my own stories; and I seem to hear her voice saying, 'A'weel, there was ance a wee black-an'-white pownie . . .'

Jessie's stories were all about animals. 'Beasts', she called them; and she told them in the broad Border dialect which seemed to add breadth, depth and colour to them. Tales about cows and pigs, which she called coos and soos; and about the bubblyjock, which was Jessie's name for the turkey-cock.

She had no sooner finished one story than I begged for another.

'Tell me more, Jessie.'

'Hoots, lassie, your heid's fou' o' beasts already.'

But in the end she always gave in; and sometimes, to humour me, she would say, 'I'll gie ye a guess.' I had heard her 'guesses' so often that I always knew the answer, but I pretended to puzzle them out.

Tammy Riddle, Tammy Riddle, Tammy rot-tot-tot,
A little wee man wi' a red, red coat.
A staff in his hand an' a stane in his throat.
Tammy Riddle, Tammy Riddle, Tammy rot-tot-tot.

After pondering for a while I would hazard a guess. 'Is it a cherry?'

'Ay, that's it!'

Jessie had certain rituals which never varied. She would not give me anything without first holding it behind her back and saying, 'Nievie-nievie-nick-nack; which hand will ye tak'?' I had to choose the right or the left, and if I chose the empty hand, I got nothing!

Though Jessie used words sparingly, they were always to the point. She had a rich turn of phrase and could conjure up an old saying to suit any occasion. Often she described me as being 'as daft as a yett on a wundy day' or 'like a hen on a het girdle'. I could see myself flapping about in the wind or jumping up and down on the hot girdle beside the scones.

But she was not one for speaking for speaking's sake. I never heard her address her brother if their paths happened to cross on the farm. Occasionally they might exchange grunts or nods, but that was as far as they would go. I used to wonder what their conversation was, if any, when they sat by the fire in the herd's hoose at night.

One way and another I spent much of my early life in prison. I was a 'bad bairn', so I was told; yet, strangely enough, it was my good deeds that most often caused my downfall. I had a great desire to be helpful, but my acts of kindness directed towards human beings were seldom appreciated. So, in the end, and with no better results, I directed them towards the animals.

There were more of them around, anyway; and on the whole I felt they had an unfair deal. The bull, for example, bellowing with boredom at a closed gate. What was wrong with letting him out for a change of scenery? Or brightening up the sow's life by inviting her into the garden to smell the flowers? Or, for that matter, bequeathing my Sunday hat to the scarecrow? Not entirely out of kindness! I hated the brown straw with its tight elastic band. In any case, it looked better on the tattie-bogle than on me.

I never knew how long my sentence would last. I was just pushed through the door leading up the rickety stairs to the garret and firmly locked in, with an admonition to: 'Bide there till you behave better.'

Sometimes I sat on the stairs and considered my sins, but not for long. I could never see why I was guilty. Besides, there were so many fascinating things to see and do in the gaol. Far from being a punishment, I looked forward to my sentences of solitary confinement.

The garret was as full of junk as an Old Curiosity Shop. It had a strange musty smell till I let in the fresh air by scrambling on top of a decrepit dressing-table to prop up the skylight window. It was a precarious perch, but if I clung on and poked out my head, I could look down the slated roof and see the contents of the rone where many odd objects were stuck. Rubber balls which I had tossed up and lost for ever, arrows fired into the air from my brother's bow, hair-ribbons blown sky-high in the breeze. I was too far up to be able to reach them, but at least I knew where they were, and if ever I had wings I could fly up and retrieve them.

If I leaned far enough out I could gaze down, like God, on the whole world. It looked like a toy farm, with miniature sheep dotted about the fields and haystacks as small as thimbles. Even Jock-the-herd was reduced to a dwarf. If he came near enough I sometimes called down to him.

'Hullo-o-o, Jock!'

He would gaze up, wrinkle his brow, and call, 'Man-lassie, are ye in again? What is't this time?'

'Nothing!'

But the herd knew better. He would shake his head at me and pass by, with Jed and Jess at his heels. I could sense that, like Jessie, he was muttering, 'Nae rummlegumption!' Grown-ups never seemed to give one the benefit of the doubt.

Sometimes a cushy-doo would alight near my head and give a friendly 'Prrrrr' before flying off to freedom, leaving me to thole my sentence as best I could. Though it did nothing to reform my character, the household gaol enlarged my outlook in many ways, and certainly taught me to content myself with my own company; though I was never really alone. There was the other me inside, with whom I held long conversations and who, thank goodness, never scolded or considered I was lacking in commonsense. We got on a treat and never once quarrelled.

Time never dragged in the gaol; there were so many treasures to be discovered in the dusty corners. Discarded toys, an old wooden cradle, a pensioned-off rocking-horse, a battered banjo, a chest full of feather-boas and faded finery. Best of all, a pile of old books with their batters hanging off. Bound volumes of the *Quiver*, *Sunday at Home*, *Spurgeon's Sermons*, and a *Medical Dictionary*, with yellowed pages and f's for s's.

I used to sit for ages in a creaking rocking-chair, shoogling backwards and forwards while poring over the old print. The words were difficult, but at least I could look at the pictures of goitre, diseased livers, and floating kidneys.

One day I came across a musty old Bible and tried to decipher the spidery writing on the margins. The sacred, I discovered, was mixed up with the secular. A reminder that: 'Today I gave the clocker a setting of brown eggs' was side-by-side with a comment on a sermon. 'The minister preached a good discourse. Seek and ye shall find.'

I sought and found treasure-trove between the pages. There were cuttings from old newspapers announcing births or deaths, recipes for making parkins, cures for the toothache, how to take stains out of tablecloths, a photograph of some bygone Sunday-school picnic, an envelope containing 'Baby's first hair-clipping'. And in Revelations I found a half-written letter. 'Dear Thomas, No, it must not be. My mother says we are not to meet again. So . . .'

So what? I wondered. It was like turning the pages of the past, trying to piece the jigsaw together and bring old stories to light. The hours of my imprisonment ticked quietly away and I felt no sense of loneliness.

In spite of the farmhouse being so old, there was nothing eerie or spooky about the gaol. The only thing that disturbed me, if daylight began to fail, was the presence of 'the body'. Mother and Jessie occasionally did dressmaking for the family and kept the dummy in the garret when not in use. Sometimes it stood straight, like a naked lady with no legs; at other times the body lent sideways against the wall. Once it slithered down and landed with a clatter at my feet, startling me out of my skin. But on the whole it was pleasant enough in prison, and and peaceful except for the squeaking of mice in the skirting-boards, which I found friendly rather than frightening. Sometimes they came out and played a kind of jing-a-ring amongst themselves, paying no attention to me. I just watched them and let them get on with it.

In winter the skylight window was often frosted over, and sealed so tightly with icicles that it let in little light, and I could not see to read. In any case, the garret was so perishing cold that I had to keep on the move. I blew on my fingers, waved my arms about, and ran races with myself. Sometimes I burrowed in the old chest to find a shawl or a moth-eaten fur cap to drape over my shoulders. Riding the rocking-horse helped to keep my circulation going, till one day it creaked to a standstill and refused to move either backwards or forwards.

When all else failed I could try to pluck out a tune on the banjo. On the back, some dreadful old jokes had been scribbled out.

BONES: Say, Boss, what am de difference between an optimist and a pessimist?

BOSS: De difference, Bones? De difference am that an optimist

he look after de eyes, and a pessimist he look after de feet.
(laughter)

There was no means of telling the time so far away out of earshot of the grandfather clock in the hall, and no knowing when my gaolers would remember to let me out. If it grew pitch dark, I went down the rickety stairs and thumped on the bolted door, calling: 'Let's out!' to anyone who happened to pass. Usually they had forgotten, as I had, why I had been put in prison. But one thing was sure, I would be back again.

The best place to make for as soon as I was free was the kitchen rug. I would sit there eating a jammy-piece and getting warmed through while the stir of the house went on around me. Usually I shared the rug, and the bread-and-jam, with a dog or cat or a bantam-cock, sometimes even with a pet lamb. Often I could hear a cheep-cheep from inside the oven, where a chicken – the weakling of a brood – had been put to recover, wrapped in a piece of flannel. When it showed signs of becoming lively, it was taken out of its makeshift incubator and delivered back to the protection of its mother's wings.

I had to keep a wary eye on the big black kettle which hung on the swey over the fire. Sometimes it would boil over and spit out at me till I hastily swung it to the side. Often there was a pan of stovies bubbling away, or a dumpling being boiled in a cloth, or an outsize pot of food for the pigs. Great quantities of potatoes in their jackets. The soos'-meat, Jessie called it.

The pigs'-pail always stood in the back-kitchen ready to receive any left-overs. What a strange hotch-potch of a menu the soos ate! Stale gingerbread mixed up with apple-peelings, crusts, carrots, treacle-pudding, cabbage-leaves, cheese-rinds; even bits of bacon, which I felt reeked of cannibalism, though Grumphy and Co. did not seem to mind and appeared to thrive on such an unbalanced diet. When the pail was full it was carried out to the pigsty and the contents poured into the trough where eager snouts were soon routing in the mixture till every morsel disappeared.

The stone-flagged kitchen seemed a vast place to a child. The big dresser, where the lamps stood ready for lighting, contained all the dishes and platters needed for the household, as well as drawers full of cutlery. There were other odd drawers where aprons, dusters and dishcloths were kept, and where anything lost could be found. 'Look in the dresser drawer' was an everyday cry when a key was missing or someone was searching for scissors.

A great bin with a sloping lid held sacks of meal, flour, salt, and sugar, enough to see us through a snow-siege; and a long wooden table stood in the middle of the floor at which a dozen or more men could feed at clipping-time or threshing. Six could sit on the old gaol-stool which was shoved under the table when not in use. Where it came from I never knew; it was just part of the household, as familiar as Jessie herself.

Great hams hung from the ceiling and strings of onions from a hook on the wall. There was no other adornment except a calendar advertising sheep-dip. It had splendid coloured pictures for each month. The Blue Boy, Buckingham Palace, snowscapes in the winter months, and seaside scenes for summer.

The back-kitchen was a utilitarian place, full of pots, pans and basins, a rough wooden table, and a sink at the window where the washing-up was done. The window looked out over the untidy back garden and away down the fields towards the shepherd's cottage. Many a time I stood there on tiptoe to peer out and see if the postie was coming. He left his bicycle at the road-end before traversing the fields and climbing the fences with his mail-bag bobbing up and down on his back. What a welcome sight he was, coming as he did from the big town and bringing with him not only newspapers and letters, but, better still, all the gossip of the countryside.

From the back kitchen a door opened into the dairy which Jessie called 'the milk-hoose'. It was a cool place with wire-mesh at the window which could be left open so that the air, but not the flies, could get in. Here the milk was sieved when it was brought in from the byre and poured into shallow dishes. When the cream gathered it was skimmed off into an earthenware crock, to await churning. Eggs, butter and cheese were also kept in the milk-hoose, and sometimes trifles and cold puddings. Little wonder the cat was always sniffing at the door.

'If ye leave the milk-hoose door open, ye'll no' hae your sorrows to seek,' Jessie used to warn me.

The nearest thing we had to a refrigerator was the meat-safe which hung outside and was reached through the back kitchen window. Here the butcher-meat or sausages were kept and our own mutton if the herd had been killing a sheep.

We had never heard of deep-freezes or, indeed, of any of the mod. cons. taken for granted today. Jessie sprinkled tea-leaves on the carpet to lay the dust before starting to sweep with a besom. She went down on her knees to scrub the kitchen floor, and spent hours blackening the grate and polishing the fire-irons with emery-paper. Sometimes she used pipe-clay to make fancy patterns of whirls and whorls on the doorstep as a finishing-touch.

Going 'ben the hoose' meant opening a door in the kitchen which led to the hall, the staircase and the front door, with the two main rooms opening off. The drawing-room and the dining-room.

The drawing-room would have been better-named the parlour, though it had bits of grand furniture. A buhl cabinet, the piano, a large mirror taking up the full length of one wall, various nick-nacks on the mantelpiece, a beaded footstool, and a white sheepskin rug. Yet, it was small enough just to be a ben-end and could look homely when the fire and the lamps were lit. The shabbier it became the less drawing-room-y it looked.

What I recall most about the best room were the two cushions plumped up on the sofa, one in each corner. They were made of dark purple velvet, with words and pictures worked on them in bright colours. On one a langorous lady, bedecked with jewels and wearing a lovely evening-gown, lay asleep with a beatific look on her face. The words read: *I slept and dreamt that life was beauty.*

On the other cushion the same lovely lady had awakened to reality. She was now wearing a ragged dress and an apron, and in her hand she held a broom with which she was wearily sweeping the floor. The words now read: *I woke and found that life was duty.*

It had a sobering effect on me. I tried to puzzle over the meaning of it. Was life always to be like that, I wondered? And was it only in dreams that one could find beauty? I felt so sorry for the lady that I turned the awake picture wrong way round every time I came into the room, and left her to her happy slumbers.

Life must have seemed very real and earnest to the older generation, judging by a sampler hanging on the wall, painfully cross-stitched by my mother when she was a girl.

A youth who would in life excel
Must study, plan, and toil as well.

Could one not have a little fun thrown in, I wondered, and never mind the excelling?

The most lived-in room was the dining-room, the biggest, brightest, and untidiest, with everyone's clutter lying around on the sideboard, table, and chairs. Father's desk was here, and the safe which he opened with a key kept hanging on his watch-chain.

Inside were mysterious papers and bills over which he pored now and again with a puzzled brow. But he had no love for 'business', and sometimes pushed the papers aside, opened another drawer and brought out a strange musical instrument. An ocarina. Father had the ability to coax a tune from anything – a Jew's harp, a tin whistle, even a paper-and-comb. Sometimes he sat at his desk, ignoring the bills and playing the ocarina, oblivious to all else.

I liked trying out the stamping-machine on his desk. If I pressed it down firmly enough on a piece of paper, the magic address came up: Overton Bush, Jedburgh, Roxburghshire. Long before I could read, I knew the shape of the letters by feeling them with my fingers.

My mother's sewing-machine was here as well as the big bookcase and the wall-cupboard – the press – where the best china was kept: the gold-patterned wedding-cups and the good dinner-set with its great ashets, soup-tureens and vegetable-dishes. The damask tablecloths were kept in the sideboard drawer along with the lace-edged teacloths to be brought out when company came.

At mealtimes the cry went up: 'Clear the table!', and there was a great shifting of ludo, snakes-and-ladders, stamp-collections, knitting, newspapers, the cat, or anything else that had landed there. A thick undercloth protected the polished surface, and a leaf at each end could be pushed in or pulled out, depending on the number of diners.

I remember the day a French polisher came to furbish up the table and how disappointed I was when he spoke in a Jedburgh accent. I had been hoping to meet my first foreigner.

The sideboard groaned under the weight of tureens, ashets, and great jugs of cream, especially when visitors were present. The food was mostly home-produced. Chickens or whole sides of mutton, if a sheep had been killed. There was always plenty of game, too, to be had on the farm. Pheasants, indeed, were so often on the menu that I used to envy folk who ate sausages and thought how rich they must be. They were a treat to us who saw butcher's-meat so rarely.

The divinity students from Edinburgh who sometimes came home with my brother for the holidays used to wallow in the homely fare, licking their lips and asking for second or third helpings of everything. It used to surprise me to see them drooling over the cream. What was so special about it? There was always heaps of it in the milk-hoose.

I was not an eater myself, except of 'rubbish'. Sweeties, if I could get them, or anything I could find for myself and eat between meals. Sitting in to a set meal, which seemed to go on for ages, I considered nothing but a nuisance, and had to be forced with many a dire threat. Usually it was, 'The bubbly-jock'll get you.' He was the creature who terrified me most – the great gobbling turkey-cock who flew at me with out-stretched wings and pecked at my bare legs.

If I failed to finish my porridge Jessie would lower her brows and say, 'Mony a stervin' heathen wad be gled o' them.' She always referred to porridge in the plural, and indeed the kind she made were so thick that they stuck to the ribs. 'Eat them up. They'll pit a guid linin' on your stamoch.'

My stomach was well enough lined with the extras I foraged for myself. Raw turnips howked out of the field and hacked into slices with the gully, stolen for the purpose. Hips, haws, and many other fruits of the hedgerows helped to ease my hunger, as did the young garden peas which tasted far sweeter from the pod than when they were cooked. Brambles, blae-berries, wild rasps and crab-apples (which we called scrogs) formed part of my outdoor diet; and I daresay I was lucky not to poison myself by eating the juicy stalks of reeds, nibbling 'soorocks', by sampling the little red barberries which grew on a bush by the burn, as well as chewing ears of corn, docken-leaves, and anything at all that looked faintly edible.

I can recall many happy hours spent sitting on a heap of bean-locusts, intended for the beasts and not for me, eating my way steadily through them. They tasted vaguely of squashed dates, and had a kind of compulsiveness about them so that I kept on eating long after they had filled me to bursting-point. Perhaps that was the way the cows ate, without knowing when to stop. Small wonder I had no appetite when faced with a plate of cockieleekie soup or a helping of stovies.

Jessie, who was never one for compliments, used to say, 'Ye're a peelly-wally object, an' nae wunner! Eatin' a' the rubbish. Wait an' see! Ye'll puzzen yoursel', an' naebody'll greet.'

2. Elders and Betters

Like the Rhode Island Reds and Minorcas who were provided with cosy enough hen-houses but seldom stayed in them, I had a great urge to get away from restricting walls. Freedom was the thing, and freedom lay outside.

Not that I wanted to be a hen. I had seen too many of them having their necks wrung, poor things. It was a higher price than I was willing to pay for being free; but if I could escape from Them, the grown-ups, I was out of the door like a shot.

If it rained, I never noticed it. Through the rose-coloured spectacles of childhood the sun was always shining. Whenever I got the chance I discarded shoes and stockings and ran barefoot all over the farm.

Run was the word. Strange how children, with all the time in the world before them, feel impelled to rush helter-skelter at everything, urging themselves to run fast and faster, to jump high and higher, to turn bigger and better somersaults. *Wait* is not a word that figures in any child's mind.

I rushed all over the place, clambering on to roof-tops and daring myself to jump down from terrifying heights. 'Go on, fearty!' One-two-three and off I went. Jessie was right. Like a peerie-top, I was seldom still; unless there was something special to watch.

Running barefoot had its pains as well as its pleasures. I was seldom free from scars. The bubblyjock and the bantam-cock pecked at my bare fetlocks, thistles and nettles reached out to sting me, prickly thorns and whin-bushes scratched at me as I ran by. But what did a few wounds matter? The pleasure was well worth the pain.

It was a wonderful feeling, climbing trees barefoot without fear of tearing stockings or scuffing shoes. My feet were soon as tough as leather, and I could scramble up like a monkey, curling my toes round the branches and digging my heels into the bark. Certainly I was nearer to nature when I could feel the good earth beneath my feet and the long grasses swishing against my legs. And it was bliss to walk into the burn and guddle in the cool water, knowing that I could walk out again without bothering to dry my feet. I grew more and more like a wraggle-taggle gypsy and kept well out of sight of any prim visitor, for I was no show-piece.

As for cuts and bruises they were only occupational hazards to be taken in one's barefoot stride. I soon learned how to doctor myself by rubbing soothing docken-leaves on my stings, washing my wounds in the burn and tying wet handkies round the worst of them. I knew better than to complain about them, especially to Jessie who taught me, above all else, to be stoical. Indeed, I felt it was wicked to be ill.

If anyone asked me – which was seldom enough – how I was feeling, I just said 'Fine' and left it at that. Never mind the raging toothache, ignore the bumps and bruises, forget the thumping headache. Unless a limb was actually broken, there was nothing the matter with me. Minor ailments were not to be discussed.

It was no use running to Jessie and saying, 'I've got a pain.' Her only reply would be, 'Weel, what aboot it? Stop girnin', an' it'll get better.' Pain was something to be borne alone, not passed on to other people. True enough, the less one thought about it, the sooner it disappeared as if discouraged through lack of attention.

Jessie did not approve of pills and potions which, according to her, sent people 'oot their minds'. Her chief remedy was a spoonful of treacle which she administered with a fine disregard for the locality of the ailment. 'Fetch the trykle tin,' she would say. Then, 'Open your mooth,' and over it went. At least, if it did no good it did no harm, and was more palatable than the greasy castor-oil which tasted worse than poison.

Sometimes, if I could not hide the fact that I had succumbed to a severe chill, I was given a concoction called toddy, made up of whisky, lemon, sugar and hot water, which I was forced to drink to the last drop before being sent to bed feeling pleasantly tipsy. I remember the bed floating round the room and the ceiling revolving. Then nothing else till I awoke with the shivers gone.

As for feeling ill herself, Jessie would never admit to such a weakness, though it was known that she suffered from a recurring ailment known as 'the bile', but she never gave in to it. When an attack came on she went about with tighter lips, took occasional sips of boiling-hot water and gave an angry thump to her stomach. Bodies were nuisances when they were not running smoothly, but the less one thought about them the better.

A tattered volume entitled *Till the Doctor Comes* was kept in the dresser drawer and consulted when anyone broke out in spots. The advice given was usually, 'Keep the patient quiet', which Jessie interpreted as 'Haud your wheesht!'

Getting the doctor was an enormous step not to be taken

lightly since he had to travel over seven miles to attend to us. He was sent for only in the most stringent cases: to remove tonsils or set a broken arm. Even then it was the doctor who received all the attention. The patient was of little moment compared with such a grand personage who arrived in a big motor-car, driven by a chauffeur, and wearing a long coat with a fur collar.

In Jessie's eyes he was equal to, if not above, royalty. A fire was lit in the bedroom for his benefit, not the patient's, and the best towels laid out. A tray was set with a lace cloth and the good china, in case he might fancy a cup of tea.

'Lie still,' Jessie warned me when he appeared carrying his wee black bag, 'an' dinna daur open your gab.'

I was much too awed to tell him my symptoms, even if I knew them myself. When he sat down by the bedside with his stethoscope slung round his neck and asked how I was feeling, I just gave the usual answer. 'Fine!' It was up to him to find out whether I had pneumonia or a broken toe.

Minor operations were performed on the kitchen table, specially scrubbed for the occasion and with cats, dogs, hens and pet lambs banished outside. The smell of chloroform mingled with the aroma of mutton roasting in the oven, and the patient floated into oblivion to the familiar sound of the herd shouting to his collies as they passed by the kitchen door.

Being kept in bed was the worst fate in the world to me. I would not have minded the measles so much or the mumps and the whooping-cough if only I could have stayed up a tree or been left in the Cockit Hat. It was the bedroom that seemed sickly, as if it was suffering from an illness. The window was tightly closed and the door firmly shut to 'keep the patient quiet'. A shoogly wee table was set by the bedside on which was placed the dreaded bottle of medicine and the equally hated glass of hot milk.

I had nothing to do but stare at the ceiling, count the colours on the patchwork quilt, listen to the muted sounds of the household, and strain my ears to hear the grandfather clock in the hall chiming the slow hours. I read my bound volume of *Chatterbox* from cover to cover though I already knew it inside-out, and even studied the uplifting text-for-the-day on the wall-calendar. 'Blessed are the meek for they shall inherit the earth.' What nonsense, I thought; they never would!

Years seemed to pass before the current servant-lassie came clattering up the stairs carrying a tin tray – no fancy lace d'oileys for me – containing a bowl of beef-tea or a plate of milk-pudding.

'What's going on?' I asked her eagerly, as if I had been marooned for months on a desert island. But she could seldom think of anything better to say than: 'Nothing!'

I liked best when Jessie mounted the stair. She would sit straight as a poker on the edge of the chair by the bedside and tell me that the cow had calved or that the corn was ripening. Once she brought me a sprig of southernwood from the garden (which she called appleringie). I lay still for ages afterwards, holding it in my hand and smelling its clean sharp fragrance. It seemed to bring the outdoors into the stuffy bedroom and did me more good than all the shake-well medicines in the bottles.

I tried to detain her on all manner of pretences, that I needed a drink of water, that I had lost my book (I was hiding it under the patchwork quilt), that the stone hot-water-bottle – the pig – was cold. Jessie saw through my wiles and her ministrations were rough and ready. Yet, though she wasted no sympathy on me, I liked just to look at her and clutch at her hard hand. She would plump up my pillows and say briskly, 'Stop whinin'. There's mony a deid body wad envy ye.'

I lay like a deid body listening to her receding footsteps and longing for the day when I could get up and follow her out to the byre at milking-time.

Sometimes Jessie sang to the cows, or, at least, crooned a tuneless little ditty.

Katy Beardie had a coo,
Black an' white aboot the moo.
Wasn't that a denty coo?
Dance, Katy Beardie.

The cows looked round at her with their large limpid eyes, mooing for more. Jessie declared they gave more milk when she sang to them. Maybe so, but it was her stories I liked best.

'Tell me the one about the wee pig with the curly tail. Please, Jessie.'

'Toots! I tell't ye that ane yesterday. Can ye no' gang awa' an' lairn to mak' up stories for yoursel', lassie?'

So I did.

Well, at least I tried; but they were poor shadows of Jessie's. All the same, it was Jessie who started me off, unknown to her, on my writing career.

I made up my first stories in the gaol and kept them in my head, since I had not yet mastered the art of writing or spelling. They were all about beasts and tattie-bogles, and when I recounted them to Jessie in the byre, as a kind of swap, she looked at me with great suspicion and said, 'Ma certies! sic an imagination ye've got. Mind! I'm warnin' ye; it'll lead ye into trouble some day.'

Maybe she was right, but I did not heed her warning. She had started me off and there was no going back. Ever since then I have been making up stories, dipping into the rag-bag of my mind and pulling out any of the tangled tales I can find there. Sometimes I come across some half-remembered saying of Jessie's and try to recall its meaning. In the course of one of her stories she described someone who 'jumped aboot like a cock at a grosset.'

'What's a grosset, Jessie?'

'A grosset? Wumman, d'ye no' ken it's a gooseberry?'

I was by no means the only audience in the byre. Some cocks and hens wandered in at intervals, and a semicircle of cats sat on their tails with cracked saucers in front of them, awaiting their share of the milk. They were of all shapes and sizes: black-and-white, tortoiseshell, ginger, None of them had names. Jessie just called them all 'Cheetie-pussy', take it or leave it.

My own favourite was the lame white kitten who always sat next to me and had a special way of mieowing up at me as if she was talking. I would answer her by mieowing back, and many an animated conversation we held about goodness-knows-what.

'Ye're a daft pair,' Jessie used to scoff, digging her head into the cow's side in disgust.

One dreadful day the little lame one went missing at milking-time. The others were all in their usual places: the tortoiseshell, the black tabby, the ginger tom, and the rest. But not a sign of my favourite. I ran all over the place hunting for her, up haystacks, in the granary, under the reaper, even in the hen-houses. But she was not to be found and my heart was broken.

'There's plenty mair,' Jessie told me with cold common-sense. But none like the little lame kitten.

It was the next day when I was still hiccupping with grief that Jessie said briskly, 'Stop mumpin', wumman. Open that drawer an' bring me oot a duster.'

I listlessly pulled open the drawer – and out jumped the lost kitten with a duster clutched in her claws. What a reunion we had! I gave her a saucerful of milk and she looked up at me between sips, mieowing out her story. She had jumped into the drawer when someone had left it half-open, fallen asleep amongst the dusters and been imprisoned when the drawer was shut.

Farm bairns, of course, cannot afford to become too sentimental over animals, or squeamish about the realities of life and death. I had enough gumption to realize that pigs were fattened to be killed, that lambs would be made into chops, and that even the proud bubblyjock would end up on an ashet at

Christmas. All the same, I could never bring myself to join in the chase of a young cockerel due for execution, and always looked the other way when its neck was wrung. It was terrible to think of it alive one moment and dead the next.

'Ay, but ye'll help to eat it, nae doot,' Jessie would say as she was plucking off the feathers.

Yes! I would eat though I would not kill. There was nothing consistent about my feelings. But somehow roast mutton or boiled fowl bore so little resemblance to the live beasts that I could forget my finer feelings when the creatures were cooked.

Pet lambs were a different matter, and caused me much heart-rending when the shepherd took them away to the slaughter. Often I had fed them like babies from a bottle. They were usually the weaklings of the flock, with a lame leg or a wry neck. I remember one that looked over its shoulder all the time, a black curly creature who followed me wherever I went, always looking backwards.

Like the cats, none of them had names. I played with them like toys, but suddenly they would shoot up to an alarming size, big enough to knock me over when I was a toddler. I used to sit astride one of them and ride it round the farmyard like a pony, though it is fair to say I had no control over it and was forced to go where the lamb listed. Many a tumble I took, too, as it swerved round corners, chased by the turkey-cock.

The only time I took a scunner at the herd was when I saw him sharpening his knives preparatory to killing the pig. A murderer, I thought him, and ran miles to be away from the terrible squealing. I did not come back till long after the dastardly deed had been done and the body of Grumphy washed, scraped, disembowelled and hung up in the shed so that all the blood could drain out of him.

There was great activity in the kitchen where my mother and Jessie were busy cleaning out the puddings and stuffing them with oatmeal before boiling them. They also concocted mysterious little parcels, called faggots, out of the innards:

chopped liver mixed with onions and herbs, covered with a fatty membrane for some part of the pig. Indeed, almost every part of the deceased animal was edible. Even the lugs and the trotters were singed at the fire before being cooked, and the head made into 'potted-heid'.

Later, there would be a great cutting-up and salting-down of the carcase which provided many a succulent meal for the household. And not only for us. The cottagers, the herd, the postie, and the vanman went off with parcels of spare-ribs, surely the tastiest part of the pig. Similarly, we received our share when the herd or the hinds killed their own sows. Give and take was the thing.

I soon forgave Jock for his bloody deed, especially when he presented me with the pig's bladder, dried, cleaned, and blown up like a great opaque football. The blether, he called it. He tied a long string to it so that it could float in the air, and I played with it till it burst, sparing only a few pitying thoughts for poor Grumphy. By the time the great hams were cured and ready for eating I had forgotten he ever existed.

Sometimes the hinds coming home from the fields would hoist me up and set me on the back of one of the workhorses. It was a perilous position. I felt a sense of terror mingled with excitement as I clung to Prince's rough mane as he clopped his way into the yard, jingling his harness and making straight for the horse-trough. It was touch and go whether I would land in the water head-first or if I could slither off in time to save a drooking.

Often I followed the men into the work-stable and watched them settle the horses into their stalls before feeding them. The Clydesdales seemed to be satisfied with an unchanging diet of corn, varied only occasionally with hot mashes in winter. It seemed as unpalatable to me as the cattle-cake which the stirks were given as an extra; but 'each to his ain taste' the hinds told me before locking the stable-door and going home to their own suppers.

I used to feel sorry for the horses left in the dark during the long winter nights, and wondered what they did to pass the time.

'Naethin',' said Tam, when I broached the subject to him.

I found it so difficult myself to do naethin' that I felt sure the horses must have their own ploys. Sometimes late at night I could hear them stamping their feet. Were they quarrelling, I wondered, or maybe dancing their own version of the Highland Fling?

My sister was a lady. She told me so herself, time and time again. She also told me I was the opposite and must have been left on the doorstep by a tink.

No running wild for her, no tumbling about on haystacks, no imitating the herd's broad accent. When visitors came she could always be relied on to appear neatly dressed with not even a hair-ribbon missing.

I admired her from a distance, like looking up at a star; but I knew I could never reach such heights of primness, so I gave up the struggle and continued on my rag-tag-and-bobtail path. Who wanted to be a lady, anyway? I would sooner have the herd call me 'Man-lassie'.

Elders were strange beings, never doing anything wrong and with no one to scold them, even if they did. Maybe I would learn sense, too, when I grew up, and feel as superior. But what a dull prospect it seemed.

My father was a kindly man who did not want any trouble. He would turn his head away from problems rather than face up to them. Anything for a quiet life.

Sometimes he dandled me on his knee and made his handkerchief disappear up his sleeve like a magician. Or he would sing me a song.

> 'There's one two three four five six seven eight
> funny little kids at home.

Two tom-cats and a she-cat, too,
An old poll-parrot and a cockydoodle-doo.
There's a half-bred dog with his ears cut short,
and a great big fat strong wife.
With a lot like that you can eat your hat,
If I don't lead a very merry life.

Father had a funny-bone and was an entertainer *manqué*. And yet, not all that *manqué*, for he was in great demand as a 'comic' at local concert-parties around the district. I used to hear great tales of the Darkey Troupe he had got up (it was he who was the boss of the banjo in the garret) and of the difficulties they had had in making up their faces and keeping the blacking from dripping on to their collars.

One night they had been given a great ovation – so they thought – in the town hall, and responded by bowing repeatedly to the enthusiastic audience, not realizing that the captain of the rugby club had appeared on the stage behind them, proudly displaying the trophy his team had won.

One of the songs they used to sing was a tongue-twister. Father had it off pat, and could sing it all the way through at great speed – faster and faster – without ever once slipping up.

Swim, Sam; swim, Sam; swim, Sam.
Show them you're some swimmer.
Swim like the snow-white swan, Sam,
You know how the snow-white swan swam.
Six sharp shivering sharks are going to snap your limb.
But a swim well-swum is a well-swum swim,
So, swim, Sam; swim, Sam, *swim*!

I never saw the Darkey Troupe – it had been disbanded before I came along – but later on I was sometimes taken to a draughty village hall where Father was appearing as top of the bill. The rest of the programme usually consisted of anyone who could play the fiddle, however badly, and a man or a woman singing straight songs, 'Caller Herrin!' or 'Auld Robin Gray,' with accompaniments thumped out on an untuned piano.

When Father came on the discords did not seem to matter. He always brought the house down, and though I had heard his patter often enough before, I could still laugh at his antics and call 'Encore!' with the best.

There were times when I had difficulty in recognizing him, for he always dressed up for his parts. Sometimes as a coalman with a sack slung over his back ('Coals! Coals! Coals for everybody in the toon!') or as an old wifie, wearing one of Jessie's long skirts and a straw bonnet he had found in the garret.

I can remember, too, the rehearsals that took place in the parlour at home when Father got up a play. It had to be very simple: a kitchen-comedy in broad Scots, for the caste was not accustomed to high-falutin' speech or fancy acting. But on one unfortunate occasion there was an English character in the play. I could never understand why the old man who played the part shouted 'Ba! Pasha!' at intervals, till many years later I read the script and saw the words printed as 'Bah! Pshaw!' My father never had the heart to hurt anyone's feelings by correcting their pronunciation; and in any case the audience did not seem to mind.

I was once roped in myself at a tender age to act the part of a page-boy. What play could that have been? I had nothing to do except wear a tunic over a pair of fancy breeks and bow in front of my father. When the moment came I was pushed on to the stage and stood there bewildered, forgetting to bow, till Father said something funny, not in the script. Whereupon the audience roared with laughter – why, I never knew. I just gave a quick bow and got off the makeshift stage as fast as I could, ending my career before it had begun. It was better fun sitting in the front watching the others and mouthing their words, 'Ba! Pasha!' and all.

Though Father was a comic, he was more of a public funny-man than a private one. He was a gregarious creature and liked to be in the midst of a company, setting them all laughing. But he seemed to find it embarrassing to talk face-to-face with his family, as, indeed, many parents do. If I met him out and about on the farm, it was like Jessie and the herd. We never knew what to say to each other, hardly even 'Hullo'.

I admired him greatly, and later on in life would have liked to get to know him as he really was. Not just as 'Father'. But I never did. The only letter I ever received from him was signed 'Yours truly'. Often I longed for a word of praise from him. Maybe he would have liked one from me, too; but I could never have told him how I liked him. *Love*, of course, was not a word to be bandied about. Feelings, in most Scots households, are still kept bottled up.

My father was a man of many talents. He had a great facility for all kinds of games and sports. He had been a runner and hurdler in his youth. Now and again he rode to hounds, and was an excellent shot, a first-class golfer, and a champion billiard-player. Like all Borderers he was an enthusiastic follower of rugby. The only thing he had no particular interest in was, strangely enough, farming. It was his father who had decided his career and pushed him on to the land. But he was essentially a town-laddie, brought up in Jedburgh and educated at an academy called the Nest, where he learned a smattering of this and that, including German, but nothing about farming.

Nevertheless he did his best to get to grips with his acres. It was a mixed farm, and though some of the seed fell on stony ground, his crops were not always bad nor his kine lean. Like all farmers, he had his good and bad years; and I never knew whether we were rich or poor. The main thing was, I could always mooch a penny from his pocket to spend at the sweetie-shop.

Father was popular with the men and often took his place beside them in the fields, rolling up his sleeves at haytime or harvest, and forking with the best. But he was happier when he could get away to the market or the sales and see something of the outside world. To be a farmer's boy was not enough for him. He had many an *alter ego.*

> I'm John James Ebenezer Hezekiah
> Peter Henry Zachariah,
> John James Brown.
> Don't you know me? Go on!
> Then you will very soon,
> For I'm John James Brown,
> The chocolate-coloured coon.

This was one of the Darkey Troupe songs he used to sing.

The hinds called him the boss, or the maister, and had a great respect for him without being in any way subservient. I thought my mother was very familiar when she addressed him as John.

They were a well-matched pair, for she, too, liked entertaining and being entertained. Sometimes she sang duets with him and played his accompaniments at the concerts. In her youth she had taught in a school in the town and knew nothing of country life till my father drove her home in the gig on their wedding-night. But, with Jessie's help, she soon found her feet and turned the bare farmhouse into a home. She became an excellent cook, learned how to rear chickens, and, most difficult of all, how to cope with the isolation.

I remember her as soft and fair, easier to communicate with than my father, and with an imaginative way of describing some incident so that her stories – though in a different way from Jessie's – became alive.

Once she went on an expedition to Edinburgh and came back with her head full of a play she had seen. *Mary Rose.* She went over it all, scene by scene, calling out 'Ma-ary Ro-ose!' in an eerie voice, completely carried away as if she was living the part herself.

At that time my father and mother must have been quite young, but anyone above ten seemed elderly to me. Jock-the-herd was a hundred, in my eyes, and Jessie reached away back to Biblical days. In fact, I once asked her if she knew David.

'Wha? D'ye mean Davy Scott?'

'No, the one who killed Goliath.'

'Him! He was afore ma time.'

I could not visualize Jessie as a lassie, playing with a skipping-rope. Although she did not know David, she often talked in tones of great reverence of 'the auld Queen'. Victoria the Good. She had been queen when Jessie was young, and though Victoria was long since dead and gone, I heard about her so often that I almost felt we were related. Not that I would have been fit to clean the auld Queen's shoon, as I was told many a time.

'*She* wad never hae left a dirty plate,' Jessie scolded me, looking grimly at my half-supped porridge. 'She wad think black burnin' shame o' hersel'.'

The auld Queen was perfect. Indeed, the whole world had gone to pieces – to babbyrags, Jessie said – since Victoria ceased to reign. '*She* wad hae sorted them,' she said fiercely when the newspapers reported some misdeed of the government. 'It's a wunner she's no' birlin' in her grave.'

I used to picture the auld Queen whirling round in her shroud till her crown came tumbling off her head.

For a long time I thought Queen Victoria had something to do with tea, for her picture was on the caddy which sat on the mantelpiece in the herd's hoose, a fierce-looking old lady wearing a wee lace cap. Albert was on the other side but he always had his face to the wall, for though he, too, was good, Victoria was better. Jessie handled her reverently every time she brewed the tea, and made sure the caddy was carefully dusted every day so that the auld Queen would look spick and span.

Though I found it easy enough to converse with Jessie and the herd, I found it more difficult to make contact with the hinds who all seemed like giants to me, though their names were short enough: Wull, Tam, Bob. They called me 'the wee ane' and treated me with amused tolerance, even when I asked daft questions.

'What's that you're spreading on the field, Wull?'

'Dung!'

'What's dung, Wull?'

'Och, it's just a kind o' – perfume. Can ye no' smell it?'

Sometimes they sent me running back to the house – anything to get rid of me, I expect – with a message for my father.

'Awa' an' tell the boss the binder's broken doon. Ask him to bring oot a spanner.'

'What's a spanner?'

'Hoots! just gang an' tell him.'

But by the time I had run back to the house, though I tried to keep the message in my mind, it had become so fankled that my father had to go the the field to find out for himself.

Elders and betters never made mistakes. This, I thought, was one of their most unendearing traits. To be grown-up and sensible, I considered, must be a terrible fate; never to run barefoot, never to hold imaginary conversations with a tattie-bogle or to believe that cats could speak. Old people's conversation was dull and matter-of-fact. Politics and prices seemed to be their main topics, or what the weather was likely to be tomorrow.

It was the same with the animals. The young lambs would kick up their heels and play cuddy-loup-the-dyke while their staid mothers looked on disapprovingly. The hens clucked crossly at their straying chicks, the cows turned lofty looks on their calves when they ran races, and even the cats called their kittens to heel if they showed signs of being too playful. They were all, in their own ways, saying 'Don't!'

So – it was best to have as little as possible to do with grown-ups. They were queer creatures, I thought, and it was safer to watch them from a distance.

3. The Travelling Folk

Anyone who ventured up the bumpy farm-road must inevitably be coming to visit us. Where else could they be going? There was nothing beyond but hills and more hills.

All the same, strangers did come and surprise us by chapping at the kitchen door – waifs and strays seeking food and shelter for the night. At that time there were many more tramps, tinkers, and gaun-aboot bodies on the roads; and these wanderers were never turned away from our door. My father was known to have a soft heart, and the word must have been passed round to say that free lodgings were available. Sometimes we saw mysterious marks at the road-end and wondered if this was the tramps' code.

Often they arrived at the gloaming, so weary that they were not particular where they slept; in the barn or in one of the outhouses, any place where they could lie down under cover. But one old crone, called Nellie, who always smoked a clay-pipe, had a preference for the byre as her bedroom.

'Put me aside the coos,' she pleaded. 'They mak' grand het-waitter-bottles.'

Nellie was always given permission but warned that she must not smoke because of the danger of fire; and sometimes I would be sent round to see if she was obeying instructions. Not her! I would find her sitting on the hay with her bundles around her, chatting to the cows and puffing away at her pipe.

'Ye'll no' tell your faither, wull ye?' she would say in a wheedling voice, giving me a crafty sidelong glance.

I never did, though I had a guilty feeling that if Nellie set the place ablaze it would be my fault and I would get what-for from my father whose heart was not as soft as all that.

The cows seemed pleased enough with Nellie's company, and she always gave them a fond farewell in the morning as well as a parting word of advice. 'Behave yoursel's noo! Be guid coos, an' Nellie'll be back to see ye again afore lang. Ta-ta!'

I welcomed the sight of any strange face and often acted as go-between, carrying out the tramps' tea and pieces to them when they sat on the bench near the kitchen door easing their feet in their cast-off boots. While they ate I studied their wrinkles, their matted hair, their hands ingrained with dirt, their tattered garments, and listened to their unfamiliar talk, for some of them had come from over the Border where the Geordies lived, and others from down-country where the accent was different from ours.

All of them carried untidy packs and bundles. Some trundled old prams in front of them containing all their wordly goods, consisting mainly of rags rolled up in newspapers. Yet they were always begging for more.

'Hae ye ony auld claes or a pair o' shoon? See! I've nae soles left. I'm walkin' on ma uppers.'

Some even looked longingly at the tattie-bogles who were often better-dressed. Yet they were not all as poor as they pretended. One biblical-looking couple, whom we christened

Jakob and Martha, used to drive up the road in style in a pony and trap. The skinny pony was let loose in a field where it rolled over and over, kicking up its heels, while Jakob and Martha came shauchling into the house carrying a bag clinking with golden sovereigns for my father to keep in his safe for the night.

Time and again he tried to persuade them to put their money in the bank. No! They trusted my father but would have nothing to do with banks. Yet they, too, though they were carrying hundreds of pounds around with them, would beg like paupers for a pair of shoes or an old overcoat.

Some of the tramps had goods to sell. They opened their packs on the doorstep and showed a paltry display of ribbons, boot-laces, elastic, safety-pins and cheap combs. My mother always bought something for the sake of giving them a few coppers; but they were never satisfied. Always they over-played their hands, mooching for more till our pity ran thin.

They could always conjure up a cough, real or imaginary, and put a pathetic whine into their voices when begging. Or they would send their smallest snivelling child to the door with a tear-jerking story, while the rest of them hid round the corner. Sometimes the waifs would be brought into the kitchen to get warmed in front of the fire, but they never stayed long. I remember one of them staring around like a frightened animal and crying 'Let me oot!' as if terrified he would be trapped.

The girls all seemed to be dressed up for Halloween in old shawls and trailing skirts. I used to gaze at them in envy and long to share their wraggle-taggle way of living. But it was difficult to make friends with them. I once approached a small tousle-haired bairn and said, 'Come on and play.'

Play! She shook her head and retired behind her mother's tattered skirt. The child knew how to beg but not how to play. All she wanted from me were the shoes off my feet and the ribbons off my hair, and she was welcome to them.

The gypsies were always willing to tell fortunes by way of recompense; but I was not so willing to have my hand held in theirs while they foretold fame, fortune, and a handsome husband. In any case, I was already bespoken. My intended (not that he knew it) was Jock-the-herd, who had fortune enough for me.

All the same, it was safest to keep on the right side of the Romany clan in case they ill-wished us. There were frightening tales, true or false, of crops failing, cows going dry, and hens stopping laying as the result of a gypsy curse. We were always faintly uneasy until we had seen the last of them straggling down the road.

I never remember being frightened of any of the tramps no matter how strange they looked or how eccentrically they behaved. I sat beside them on the bench, watching them re-packing their bundles and listening to their conversation. Not that it was directed to me. They were all great talkers-to-themselves and kept up long private running-commentaries which only they understood.

Jessie used to drag me away.

'You'll get beasts,' she said fiercely; and indeed I sometimes did get beasts, which resulted in terrible tussles with a small-tooth comb and in paraffin being poured over my locks.

Strangely enough, it was the most refined of all the tramps who caused us the most trouble, a true gentleman-of-the-roads, dressed in a top hat and an old waterproof tied round the waist with string. He was known as Yorkie, no doubt because he originated from Yorkshire where his father had been a parson. Yorkie, too, had been destined for the church; but he had been 'over-educated', so he told us, resulting in a weakening of the brain. He was full of high-flown talk, so disconnected that it was difficult to make head or tail of it. But Yorkie was quite content to be his own audience.

Unable to lead a settled life, he had taken to the roads with a rough-haired tyke at his heels and an old fiddle under his arm.

All the year round he roamed about the countryside, roaring out his demands for food and shelter. There was nothing subservient about him. Yorkie did not beg; he ordered.

We could hear him long before we saw him, coming shouting up the road in that eerie half-light of the gloaming. He would play a few screeches on the fiddle and then knock loudly on the kitchen door with his stick. He had originally come to the front door until firmly forbidden. If his summons was not instantly answered he came straight in, sat down and helped himself to any food he could find on the table without a by your leave. Yorkie always gave us the impression that he was a cut above us.

My father knew how to handle him, and would soothe him down if he was in a tantrum, then light a lantern and lead him off to the barn or one of the sheds. But sometimes in the dead of night we could still hear him shouting in his sleep. The only time we ever locked the doors was when Yorkie was about.

One night he came roaring up the road long after the household was in bed. My father called out of the window to him, telling him that he could go and sleep in the strawbarn. Yorkie went off, mumbling to himself, and lay down in the dark. But not for long. Soon such an uproar broke out that it wakened us all up. We could hear Yorkie yelling at the pitch of his voice, his dog yelping in a frenzy, cocks and hens cackling in alarm, and a pig screaming as if its throat was being slit.

When my father went out to investigate, he discovered that Yorkie had lain down on the straw in the barn, not knowing that an old sow had burrowed underneath. No sooner had the tramp settled himself and dropped off to sleep than the sow heaved herself up, tossed him in the air and ran grunting from the barn, looking like a white apparition.

'The place is haunted! There are devils here! I'll never come back again, never!' roared Yorkie, hurrying away down the road in the moonlight with his dog barking at his heels.

But, of course, he did come back, time and time again. Haunted or not, he made good use of the farm and its hospitality, till at length we heard he had found more permanent shelter in the churchyard.

Our most welcome visitor was the postie, a cheerful man with a bright red face and a bristling moustache. He wore a waterproof cape, carried a large canvas bag, and came at varying times of the day, depending on how long he had been detained at his previous calls. He had cycled the seven-odd miles from Jedburgh, left his bike at the herd's hoose and walked diagonally across the fields to reach our door.

The postman suffered from flat feet, and little wonder. As well as cycling on the main road he had to tramp many a mile across rough moorland, often to deliver only a postcard to some outbye shepherd's wife. Sometimes he was the only human being the cottagers saw for days on end; and it was not the mail that mattered to them as much as the verbal messages he carried. Greetings from one isolated family to another, as well as the latest clash of the countryside.

And not only verbal. The postie was obliging enough to act as message-boy if he got back to town before the shops closed for the night. He would fetch medicine from the chemist, waiting patiently till prescriptions were made up, take clogs to the cobbler, match wool, carry samples of curtain-material, even take false teeth to be mended.

The postie wrote down his transactions in a small black note-book with a stub of pencil which he licked and rubbed against his moustache to sharpen the point. Then he ticked the items off methodically once they were completed. He was never known to refuse, or to complain of the trouble it must have taken to trudge round the shops after completing such a hard day's work. Even sorting out everybody's dribs and drabs of money and giving them back the right change must have been a nuisance.

The postie himself would never take any money for his pains.

The only way to repay him was in kind. His bag was often bulging with gifts from grateful customers, and sometimes they overflowed into the inside pockets of his cape as well. He must have had many an unsteady ride home in the darkness, laden with pots of jam, home-made scones, fresh butter, eggs, and spare-ribs.

I liked the days when the postman had time to come into the kitchen for a cup of tea. He dumped his bag on the table, slung off his cape, and sank into a chair, bending down to loosen the laces in his boots. Then, having eased his feet, he gave a sigh of relief, took a long gulp of tea, and reached out to undo the straps of his postbag.

The mail was done up in little bundles tied with string. There was always *The Scotsman* for my father. Nothing, of course, for anyone as insignificant as me, except maybe at Christmas when the postbag was more than ever like Pandora's box.

'Naethin' but accoonts,' he would say apologetically to my father. He preferred handing out something cheerful, like a coloured postcard of Portobello. 'It's the minister's wife. She's enjoyin' hersel' a treat on her wee holiday.'

The postie knew everything about everybody, but we knew little about him. Where did he live? Who cooked the spare-ribs for him? Had he a wife and family to go home to, or any life of his own after plodding round the shops at night? He never talked about himself. Just licked his pencil, rubbed it against the bristles of his moustache, and asked, 'Ony messages?' before retying his laces and slinging his cape back over his shoulders.

I had a feeling he had been invented for us. He was 'our postie' and that was his only role in life.

When the turnips were ready for singling and extra hands were needed the Paddies mysteriously appeared. Goodness knows where they came from or what they did for the rest of the year. They arrived out of nowhere, rough-looking men with thick Irish brogues, knocked at the kitchen door and asked to see the boss. My father went out to speak to them, made some sort of bargain with them, and hired them on the spot if he liked the look of them.

The Paddies were paid by the piece, so much per row of turnips singled, and worked hard from early morning till darkness to earn as much money as possible while the going was good. They kept themselves to themselves, seldom mingling with the other men, and slept in one of the sheds, calling at the kitchen door for their 'meat'. Jessie handed out great pots of tea, bowls of soup, and hunks of ham, but was wary about entering into conversation with them. 'Kittle-cattle,' she called them.

On Saturdays after they had been paid the Paddies disappeared down the road and we never knew whether they would come back again. Sometimes they walked all the way to town and spent their money in an orgy of drinking, reappearing bleary-eyed and penniless on Monday morning to start all over again.

Kittle-cattle or not, the Paddies brought a bit of excitement to the place with their colourful language and their songs about Mother Machree and Dublin's Fair City.

Amongst our itinerant visitors was a strange little man who came to dig drains on the farm and set up residence in the bothy near the lambing-shed. He did for himself and left messages at the farmhouse for the goods he required, always in verse.

> Bread, if you please,
> A nice piece of cheese,
> Some raspberry jam,
> And a big hunk of ham.

I thought his poems were even better than Anon's and wondered why, with so much talent, he remained a mere drainer.

I wondered a lot of things as I watched the travelling folk coming and going. What was the world like beyond the confines of the farm? Would I ever be able to spread my wings and see for myself? The only way would be to put a pack on my back and go off, like the rest, to sell ribbons and laces.

The best way to see the world, I discovered, was to go by gig, though our main means of transport was shanks's pony. We thought nothing of walking the two miles to church and back, or trudging long distances across the hills to visit another farmstead. Or even on occasions plodding the seven-odd miles to Jedburgh, taking adventurous short-cuts by scrambling down steep screes, traversing unfamiliar woods and fields, and finally following the river Jed.

In the days before my father bought his first car (known as 'the motor') the gig was our only other means of locomotion. This, though, was not always quicker, depending on the mood of the pony, how long it took to lure her down from the hill, and how reluctant she was to be yoked into the trap. It depended, too, on how temperamentally she behaved once she finally set off, and how often we had to get down to open and shut gates across side-roads. It was best to leave a leeway of an hour or so one way or the other.

There were two gig-ponies. Flora, the white one, and Ginger, the chestnut. I liked Flora the best, perhaps because of her imperfections. Ginger was just a horse but Flora was a friend.

She had been 'in the family' for years and would turn her head at the sound of our voices. If she was in a placid mood she would come running to meet us. But she knew fine, when my father went off to fetch her with the bridle in his hand and a pocketful of corn, that she could lead him a dance; and she often did.

If she was in a capricious mood it was like a game of cat-

and-mouse. Sometimes Flora was to be found in the cow-gang cropping the clover or rolling over in the soft grass. At the sound of approaching feet she would gather herself together, jump the fence and canter off to the hill. Often the herd and his dogs had to come to the rescue and round her up; but there were times when she came meekly enough, neighing with pleasure and nudging against my father till he gave her some corn and slipped on the bridle.

The gig had been pulled out from the cart-shed and dusted down ready for the road, to the annoyance of the bantams who used it as a roosting-place, and Teenie – the lame hen – who never laid an egg anywhere else. Once she went all the way to Hawick with us before we discovered her, and flew out into the High Street to the surprise of all concerned.

The fluff and feathers were shaken off the seat-cushions, the lamps given a hasty polish, and finally Flora was backed in between the shafts, protesting as usual. But once the harness was in place and the bit between her teeth, the pony's nostrils began to quiver and she had to be restrained from taking off like a rocket before we mounted to our places.

I always had a backward view of the countryside, for the gig was like a jaunting-car with back-to-back seats, and it was only grown-ups or important folk who sat in front with the driver and had a straightforward look at the landscape.

It was strange to watch everything receding into the distance, the farmhouse growing smaller and smaller, the fields moving away backwards, and Jock-the-herd reversing out of sight. If we went quickly enough the trees seemed to be dancing a kind of waltz to the rhythm of the wheels and clip-clop of the pony's feet, whirling round and round and stretching out their branches to each other.

It had such a dizzying effect that it was best not to give way to such flights of fancy. I had to keep alert and cling on to avoid being pitched head-first into the ditch, especially when Flora swerved suddenly round a corner. Many a time I have landed sprawling on the road, with bruised knees and a frightened feeling of being left behind.

'Wait! I've fallen out!'

If my shout was not heard I had to run after the gig in the hope of catching it up on the next steep brae when the pony slowed down and the occupants got out to walk. But if the gig was spinning smoothly and swiftly along the level, it was well out of my reach in no time. I remember sitting disconsolately by the roadside, feeling abandoned by the world, till at long last my father, having discovered I was missing, turned the pony round and came back to retrieve me.

The jolting and joggling was good for the digestion, if nothing else.

'It fairly shoogles up your internals,' Jessie used to say on the few occasions when she could be persuaded to 'go for a hurl'.

We got plenty of fresh air, too, for there was no hood to cover us. We tucked an old tartan rug round our knees when the weather was chilly, and huddled under a waterproof sheet when it rained. Flora, too, had a macintosh cover, and in summer sported a straw sun-bonnet of sorts and ear-muffs to keep off the flies.

It was the pony who set the pace. My father hardly needed to do any driving for Flora knew every twist and turn of the Border byways; and on the main road to Jedburgh, when she reached one of the half-dozen drinking-troughs by the roadside, we had to await her pleasure if she was feeling thirsty. Flora knew exactly where each one was situated and would swerve to the side to drink her fill.

Sometimes she gave a hungry whinney and had to be fed from her nosebag before condescending to set off again. Or she would suddenly take a fancy to some fresh grass on the verge and stop for a nibble. When my father urged her to get a move on she turned a reproachful look at him. 'What's the hurry?' she seemed to be saying. 'I'll get a move on when I'm ready.'

But if Flora was in a frisky mood and there was a level stretch of road ahead she would take to her heels and speed like the wind. I felt like a bird flying backwards through the air. If my hat blew off I just let it go. Goodbye, hat! Unless by chance it landed on a stucking-post and we could pick it up on the way back. My mother, sitting forward, wore a long veil which she swathed over her hat and tied firmly under her chin.

When the pony was in an easy-osy mood there was ample opportunity to see the scenery and have a word with anyone we met on the way. Our friend the postie, the roadman, the gamekeeper, or the minister. Even Yorkie, the tramp.

If anyone wanted a lift and there was room in the back I had to squeeze to the side to accommodate them. In my day I have shared the back seat with many an odd customer. One was an Ingan Johnny whose bicycle had broken down. He sat holding the bicycle on his knee, spoke in a strange tongue and, naturally enough, smelt strongly of onions. He presented me with a long string of them as a parting gift, slinging them round my neck like beads.

If we came face-to-face with another equipage on a narrow road there was a great deal of jockeying to the side before we could pass without the danger of the wheels becoming entangled. Meantime, the horses rubbed noses and my parents had a chat with the occupants of the other carriage. If it was a gypsy caravan, Flora would bare her teeth and toss her head at the piebald pony till both of them reared up and we almost toppled over.

On some side-roads leading to hill farms there were as many as half a dozen gates across the road which we had to open and shut. No one ever volunteered for the job. I always hoped it was not my turn but it often was.

When I was given the order I reluctantly jumped down, clambered up the gate and had a great struggle with the sneck. Sometimes it was tied with binder-twine, and often in knots which had to be unravelled before I could swing the gate open. When the gig was driven through, the gate had to be shut again and the string retied, for even other folk's yetts must never be left open.

How I loathed those gates! If there was another within sight, it was not worth the bother of getting back into the gig. I just walked on always hoping that this time the operation would be simpler. I got to know the good ones and the bad ones, and wished Flora would jump over them, gig and all.

On a steep hill the pony would sometimes go on strike and come to a complete standstill. We had to get down and walk on in the hope that Flora would follow.

'Tak' nae notice an' she'll come,' Jessie would say. 'Fashious cratur!'

It was not so much the scenery that attracted Jessie's attention when she was riding in the gig as the washings hanging out.

'That's a guid clean wesh,' she would comment approvingly. Or she would remark on the crops and the gardens. 'See thon thristles. It's high time they were howked oot.' She kept a keen look-out, too, for any bondager she could spot working in the fields. 'Thonder's Aggie. My! she's gey stiff. She's gettin' past it.'

Travelling with Jessie opened my own eyes. She noticed so many things. Different curtains on a cottage window, a pipe-clayed doorstep, a new tattie-bogle in a field, a broken fence, a 'whummled' sheep lying on its back struggling to right itself. My father always pulled Flora to the side, got out of the gig and climbed into the field to turn the sheep right-way-up.

It was a great thrill to be promoted to a seat beside the driver and see the road stretching far in front of me. Better still to have a turn at the reins, though Flora took little heed of my driving and went where she wanted, snorting with derision if I attempted to tug her to the right when she preferred turning to the left.

If we were on our way to the big town it was strange how

Flora always settled down and stopped her capers when we approached the outskirts and saw Jedburgh Abbey in the distance. She always held up her head when we reached the High Street and stepped smartly out as if she knew people were watching. She was not so pleased to be left in a strange stable while we went to do the shopping, and always greeted us with whinneys of delight when we returned laden with parcels ready for the journey home.

Sometimes we had to light the gig-lamps and drive home in the darkness. It was eerie watching the oncoming lights and wondering if we could pass without the wheels touching. I used to stare at the sheep's eyes gleaming like little flashing beacons from the fields and try hard to keep my own eyes open, for if I drowsed off I might lose my balance and tumble out.

Often Flora drowsed, too. Her pace grew slower and slower till my father called out: 'There's the road-end! We'll soon be home.'

As we swerved into the home-straight Flora seemed to scent the corn in her own stable. She tossed her head, whisked her tail and cantered up the last lap, snorting at every step and coming to such a sudden standstill at the door that once more I was in danger of being pitched out.

If we arrived home when it was still daylight the pony could hardly wait to be freed from the shafts before taking to her heels and making straight for the cow-gang. Without waiting for the gate to be opened, she took a running-jump and leapt over. Then down she lay in the grass and rolled over in an ecstasy of freedom. The gig was pushed back into the cart-shed and left once more to the mercy of Teenie and the bantams.

How often I used to watch for a sight of the gig-lights, if I was left at home. I would stare for hours out of the dining-room window into the darkness, hoping for a first glimpse of the flickering far-away lights. I could tell by the way they were bobbing up and down if Flora was trotting and how long she would take to reach the kitchen door.

Sometimes, if we were all at home, the cry would go up: 'There's a light coming up the road,' as if it was coming up by itself. Then we would all run to the window and speculate. Was it a bicycle-light or a lantern? Could it be Jakob and Martha coming to seek shelter for the night, or maybe a neighbouring farmer paying a visit in his horse-and-trap?

There was never any curtains drawn in the house. Coming home in the darkness it was comforting to see the welcoming lamplight shining softly from the windows as if the house was alive and waiting to say, 'Come in!'

As often as not it was Jessie who acted as our Leerie and lit the lamps. It was not everybody, certainly not me, who could be trusted with the task. The wicks had to be evenly-trimmed, kept low at first, then gradually turned up, but not too quickly in case the glass globes cracked. The lamps must never be set in a draught or placed on an unsteady table where they could easily be knocked over. Above all, they must be watched carefully every now and then to make sure no accident had happened.

'Tak' a keek at the lamps,' was Jessie's constant cry; and she kept me running upstairs and down to see if all was well. If anything happened, it was my fault.

'Silly lassie! Ye've reeked the place oot!'

The lamps were in different shapes and sizes and were placed in strategic positions all over the house. Some had fat globes and some thin. One was tinted pink to give a rosier glow. There was a big reading-lamp, the little one for the landing, an even smaller one for the window-ledge at the turn of the stair, a special one for the bathroom, and bigger brighter ones for the kitchen and back-premises.

Altogether they transformed the farmhouse, softening everything and taking away its shabbiness. But there were still some pools of darkness left, and it was wisest to hurry past them when going from one place to another. The eerie shadows thrown up on the walls and ceilings could sometimes look like prehistoric monsters.

If lighting the lamps was an art, cleaning and filling them was a major operation. This ritual took place relentlessly every morning when they were all set out on the kitchen table. They looked a formidable lot which would have made even Aladdin's heart sink. Alas! no genii appeared no matter how hard we rubbed them.

Jessie rolled up her sleeves ready for action and made me follow suit, if I was in one of my helpful moods, with many a warning to, 'Ca' canny wi' the globes.'

The great thing was to breathe on them in the right places and to have enough clean dusters handy. But it was a tricky job especially with the narrower funnels, and many a scolding – and skelping – I have had in my day when, in spite of all my care, the worst happened, resulting in broken glass, and like as not, a cut finger.

We kept spare globes in the house but never enough. It was a tragedy if we ran out of them during the dark winter nights when we were snowed-in and could not get replacements. Worse still if we ran short of paraffin; then there was nothing for it but to resort to candlelight.

Not that I minded. I liked the candles better. For one thing, they were easier to light, and though they gave a different dimmer glow, they had their own charm. I loved lying in bed watching the fantastic shadows flickering across the ceiling. Cinderella's coach on its way to the ball. The horses and hounds in full cry. A witch flying on her broomstick. It was like being at 'the pictures'. The pattern shifted and changed till someone in authority came and snuffed out the candle, taking away the matches in case I should be tempted to relight it.

Apart from indoor lighting, there were the lanterns used by the men outside. The hinds carried them from their cottages to the work-stable on dark mornings; and at nights, looking from my window, I could follow the herd's progress as he went through the fields during lambing-time. The lantern-light wavered up and down like a will-o'-the-wisp with every step he took. I could tell when he was climbing a dyke or if he had laid down the lantern to attend to a new-born lamb.

Jessie, too, took a lantern with her when she went to the byre to milk the cows in the dark days of winter. Many a time I used to carry it for her and set it down in the right position so that she could see to do the milking.

In the strange half-light the byre took on an unreal atmosphere, and sometimes I dozed off on my stool with the cats sitting at my feet. In my dreams I could hear the heavy breathing of the cows, the swish of their tails, the milk streaming steadily into the pail, and Jessie's voice coming and going as she told me one of her stories.

'A'weel, ance upon a time there was a wee coo wi' a crooked horn . . .'

What a transformation when we finally installed our own 'electric' into the farmhouse and steading. The whole place came alive and we saw into dark corners where no light had penetrated before. But it was a long time before Jessie could be induced to discard the lamps. She did not take kindly to the new harsh illumination, no matter how handy it might be.

'It's no' natural,' she declared. 'Forbye, I've a feelin' it'll blaw up ony meenit.'

Whenever she turned on a switch, which she did very gingerly, she gave a shudder as if waiting for the explosion, and was never happier than when our installation failed as it did only too often. Out came the lamps once more, and Jessie was triumphant.

'See!' she said, turning up the wicks, slowly and carefully, 'ye can aye lippen on a lamp.'

I thought the full moon gave the finest light of all. Not only that, it was the best barometer. Jessie and the hinds could tell, just by looking at it, what the weather was likely to be next day. If there was a fuzzy halo round it – a brough – Jessie would say: 'I see there's a bruff roond the mune. That means snaw the morn.'

And sure enough the moon was never wrong.

4. Willingly to School

At the ripe old age of four and a half I set off to become a mixed infant at the village school two hilly miles away.

'Ye'll be nae miss,' said Jessie heartlessly; but I knew by the way she buttoned me into my new coat and tied the ribbons firmly at the end of my pigtails that she might miss me just a little bit. Not that I was gone for ever. I would be back later on in the day with the new look taken off my coat and my hair-ribbons lost and gone for ever.

I walked there and back except on the first day. As a special treat and in order to break me in gently I was driven there in style, sitting forward in the gig beside my father. My school-bag contained a new jotter and pencil, and, more important, my dinner-piece. There were no school-meals, not even a kettle to boil on the open fire in the classroom, so I always took a medicine-bottle full of milk. *One spoonful twice daily. Shake well.*

It was a one-teacher school. Edgerston School it was called, after the little community that sprawled around Edgerston House, which really was a Big Hoose, hidden away in the woods. Here the laird who owned the estate lived, when he was not away in London looking after his business interests. He was greater than God, we thought, though on the few occasions when we met him he spoke with such an upper-class English accent that we could scarcely understand a word he said.

The school was presided over by an omnipotent being, only a little lower than God, who lived in the schoolhouse next door and was known as the master before his face and Auld Baldy-Heid behind his back. Not that he was all that bald or all that old; but he had a heid all right, and certainly knew how to knock the learning into ours.

He did it the hard way by taking out the leather strap – the hangman's whip – first thing in the morning and warning us we would get what-for if we did not behave ourselves. I got what-for many a time, not so much for bad behaviour as for being late in the morning.

It was easy enough for Auld Baldy-Heid. He had only to open his garden gate and walk a few steps to the school. But I had to set off hours before he rang the bell. In winter I left home in black darkness and often the light was fading again before I returned home in the late afternoon. I felt like the wee moudiwart in Jessie's story, never seeing the daylight.

It was difficult to time the journey with so many diversions on the way. Even before I had walked a few yards down the road a dozen different things might have happened. Often I had to turn back and chase home a stray animal who had wandered after me. A pet lamb, a puppy, a calf, the lame kitten, a bantam-cock, even the pig; all were guilty of following at my heels.

At the cottages Mrs Thing – Tam's wife whose name I never knew – was usually out pegging up the washing. Sheets, aprons, goonies, and her man's long woollen drawers. Another Mrs Thing who lived next door – Wull's wife – was vigorously shaking her rag rug. I seldom saw her except in a cloud of dust. They both stopped and looked at me, since anything was better than nothing, but they seldom said more than: 'Ye'd better hurry, lassie, or ye'll get the tawse.'

I put on a spurt but there was no knowing how soon another delaying incident would happen. I would hear the clip-clop of a Clydesdale behind me, and one of the hinds would hoist me up and give me a ride on a workhorse on its way to the smiddy to be shod. If I stopped to watch the operation time trickled away and I would have earned the master's wrath when I finally reached the school.

Sometimes a sheep would run out of a field and the herd would shout to me over the dyke: 'Man-lassie, see if ye can weir in thon yowe,' an operation which could easily take another half-hour.

When I finally left the farm road-end I had a frightening feeling of being cut off from everything familiar. That is, until I reached the lodge-gates and saw Mary-Anne who lived there like someone in a fairy-tale. Her cottage looked like a little gingerbread house with diamond-shaped windows made of spun sugar. Goody Two-Shoes or Little Red Riding Hood might have felt at home in it.

Mary-Anne opened and shut the gates when the laird's carriage drove through, and spent most of the day speaking to her hens. She was always out feeding them when I passed, holding the corn in her apron. She had names for every one of them as if they were real people. Maggie, Mary, Mrs Broon, Jemima, and Wee Rascal who had a bad habit of laying away.

Mary-Anne spoke to me, too, as if I was a hen, but she fed me on something better than corn. Sometimes she gave me a jammy-piece or a home-made rock-bun which kept me going till I turned into the big road and the diversions multiplied.

This was the main road from Edinburgh to Newcastle, which

had once been the old coach-road. I had to keep well into the side for anything might be passing – a horse-and-cart, a motor-car, a lorry, a road-roller, even a gypsy caravan. By now I had reached the half-way mark. Camptown.

In spite of its grand name, Camptown was hardly even a village though doubtless it had been a Roman camp in bygone days. Now it was only a handful of houses, one of them being the local policeman's.

The bobby seemed to spend most of his time digging in the garden (looking for clues, I imagined) but now and again he donned his uniform and went cycling round the countryside to rendezvous with a policeman from another district. What did they discuss so solemnly as they stood leaning on their bicycles at the cross-roads? There was a great dearth of crime in the district. Seldom even a chimney went on fire. It was rumoured that one of the sheds in the bobby's backyard was 'the gaol', but if so I never heard of anyone being shut in it.

The most important place in the little row of cottages was the shop which was a combined general store and post office. A Jenny A'Things. It looked the same as the rest, with peony-roses and candytuft in the little garden in front, except that it had a few sweetie-bottles in the window and a bell that tinkled when the door was pushed open.

The shop was run by a plump comfortable-looking woman, like a pouter-pigeon, called Bella. She came 'ben the hoose' from the kitchen in her carpet-slippers when she heard the bell, and went round behind the counter to serve her customers.

It was not by any means every day that I was one of them; but now and again I was given some money to buy a jotter or a rubber and told to keep the change which seldom amounted to more than a penny. But a halfpenny could buy riches in Bella's, and could even be divided into two lots at a farthing each.

The difficulty was choosing between present joys and lasting pleasures. A bar of chocolate-cream was gone in a jiffy but hard toffee could be sucked for hours. Bella made it herself and broke it into pieces with a little hammer before putting it into a three-cornered paper poke which she twisted with a few deft flicks of her fingers.

Bella also sold postal-orders, pins, needles, pirns, mustard and boot-polish, amongst other things; but it was her sweeties that interested me most. Sherbet-bags, pandrops, black balls, sugar-ally, liquorice-allsorts, and dolly-mixtures. What a wealth to choose from!

There was a strange word in faded lettering outside the door. CONFENCTIONARY. I never knew what it meant or that it was wrongly spelt. I just thought it must be Bella's name. Bella Confectionery.

Another of the cottages was my half-way house where I called in every morning to see one of my grannies. My other granny lived in a bigger house in Jedburgh, but she was always in bed and I saw her only rarely on my visits to town, propped up on her pillows and wearing a mutch on her head.

She made me repeat the catechism as I stood by her bedside. 'Man's chief end is to glorify God and enjoy Him for ever.' As a reward, she would fumble beneath the bedclothes and present me with a coin. Never a silver one, though she was said to be 'rich'. A penny or a halfpenny was enough for gabbling the creed.

My other granny was no more lavish – she had little enough money to dole out – but at least she always let me have a dip into the sweetie-tin. It stood on the mantelpiece beside the china ornaments, with a picture of a shaggy dog on the lid. The tin contained an assortment of boilings, but there was no picking and choosing. I had to put my hand in, pull out the first I touched, always hoping that two might have stuck together, and then shut down the shaggy dog lid.

Granny's joints were stiff with rheumatism, so she often had an odd job waiting for me to do. A pail of water to empty, some sticks to bring in, or the top of the wardrobe to dust. Sometimes I had to thread a needle for her, for she was always losing her spectacles, and often I carried messages for her in my school-bag. Eggs, butter, ham, or scones from the farm.

I could have stayed happily with her all day and enjoyed myself fine, pottering about, if she had not looked at the wag-at-the-wa' and warned me that it was high time I was on my way.

When I left Camptown I was in foreign territory with a long stretch of empty road in front of me before I reached the most frightening part of the journey. The Dark Woods. This was a steep incline so thickly wooded on either side that the branches met across the road, letting only a little light filter through even in the sunny days of summer.

No one ever dawdled through the Dark Woods. There were too many eerie sounds to be heard on each side, and sometimes even worse, an ominous silence. I had heard tales, too, of ghosts lurking behind the trees, and was always afraid I might meet Yorkie there.

Once (but how would anybody ever believe me?) I did meet something strange and terrifying on that dark road. A dancing bear led on a long chain by a rough-looking swarthy-faced man. I stared in surprise, and shrank into the roadside to let them pass. The man said something to me in a guttural voice and the bear reared itself up and pranced about on its hindlegs before padding away after its master.

I never said a word about it; it was too strange and unlikely a thing to mention. But later the word went round that a dancing bear had arrived in Jedburgh.

'I've seen it!' I told Jessie excitedly; but she shook her head at me. It was something I was making up. If I had seen it why had I not told anybody before? It was too difficult to explain to grown-ups.

On windy days the wind soughed and sighed through the Dark Woods. Twigs snapped suddenly, mysterious creaks and crackles came from behind trees, scurrying feet could be heard as rabbits bolted into their holes or a weasel darted across the road, baring its teeth. A hundred unfriendly creatures lurked in the depths of the woods. Even the birds seemed to be screaming abuse and cawing threats.

It was a relief to emerge into bright daylight and see the Promised Land in the distance. Edgerston; the manse, the church, and the school. But there was still a long trudge ahead and many more obstacles on the way. Sometimes I met in with the gamekeeper, a great bearded man who looked like Moses in my book of bible stories, except that he did not carry a gun below his oxter or keep a ferret inside his game-bag.

The gamey was a great philosopher and talked to me as if I was a sensible human being, not just a silly lassie. He was greatly interested in the heavens and what lay up there. Not just God, but the people who lived on the planets and would maybe come down some day to visit us. I nodded my head wisely and said 'Uh-huh!' and as a reward he sometimes let me have a keek at the ferret.

Now and then I got a ride in Wat-the-Baker's cart but that did not speed up the journey for there were so many stoppings and startings while Wat delivered pan-loaves, gingerbreads and cookie-buns at the cottage doors. He gave me the reins to hold while he did his transactions, counting out the coins and tying them up in a little leather pouch. He was no better at arithmetic than I was, and we sometimes spent ages puzzling out the difference between fivepence-three-farthings and a shilling. As a reward he gave me stale cookies to eat or a meat pie that had crumbled to pieces.

One of my regulars was Auld Chuckie-Stanes, the roadman. Maybe he had another name but if so I never knew it. Often he would be sitting on a heap of stones by the roadside chipping away at them with his hammer. When he had amassed a big enough pile he shovelled the chips into holes in the road; and his great moment came when the big road-roller arrived with its tar-boiler and went puffing and snorting backwards and forwards to roll the stones firmly into place.

I loved the smell of the tar and the way it clung to the soles of my buttoned boots as I went stickily through it, instead of having the gumption to walk round and avoid it. I left marks all the way to school, like Robinson Crusoe's Friday did on the sand.

Auld Chuckie-Stanes called me the wee scholar and was always anxious to hear my lessons, particularly my poetry. I felt foolish standing before him on one leg staring at the sky for inspiration and reciting, 'I have a little shadow that goes in and out with me.' Worse still were the death-and-glory verses we were forced to gabble at school. 'Not a drum was heard, not a funeral note.' At the tender age of five I had to stand up and declaim, 'Shoot if you must this old grey head, but spare your country's flag, she said.'

Auld Chuckie-Stanes thought little of my repertoire and taught me much livelier verses.

Rainy rainy rattlestanes,
Dinna rain on me.
Rain on Johnny Groat's hoose
Far ayont the sea.

Perhaps the truth was he liked to recite himself, and would lay aside his little hammer while he gave me verse after verse about the Laird o' Cockpen who was prood and great, and about the King who sat in Dunfermline toon drinking the bluid-red wine.

I liked 'Wee Willie Winkie' best.

Wee Willie Winkie rins through the toon,
Upstairs an' doonstairs in his nichtgoon.
Tirlin' at the window,
Cryin' at the lock:
'Are a' the bairnies in their beds?
It's noo ten o'clock.'

It sang in my head to such an extent that I sometimes repeated it by mistake at school when I ought to have been burying Sir John Moore at Corunna.

The greatest thrill was to get a ride in a real gypsy caravan, covered with green canvas and drawn by a prancing pony. Usually it went swaying past me, but now and again it slowed down and I would be pulled into the back where I sat with my legs dangling out beside a squad of dark-skinned children.

The pots, pans, and pails rattled as we jogged along, and the gypsy man and his wife, sitting in front, spoke to each other in a tongue I could not understand. The children sitting beside me pulled off my hair-ribbons, fingered the contents of my school-bag and confiscated my dinner-piece. Sometimes they gave me a few clothes-pegs as a fair exchange.

As we neared the school-gate I was hopeful that the gypsy man might whip up the pony and steal off with me over the hills and far away. What an adventure that would be! But he never did. I was dumped, ribbonless, on the road, and away they went without a backward glance, leaving me to face the master's wrath.

It was a bonus if I reached the school before the bell stopped ringing, but it seldom happened. My heart gave a stound of relief if I saw some other late-comers scurrying into the playground, and could dodge in behind them. Maybe a shepherd-laddie who had walked long miles across the hills, or one who had cycled across the Border from England. But it was not easy to escape Auld Baldy-Heid's watchful eye.

'What's your excuse?' he would thunder at me when I slunk into the classroom, tousled and breathless.

'Please, sir, I haven't got one, sir.'

No use telling him about the pet lamb or the baker's horse or any of the other diversions on the way. There was only one fact that counted. I had failed to turn up in time to call out 'Present, sir!' when he was marking the register.

Some of the other stragglers were glibber with their excuses. True ones, too.

'Please, sir, I was helping with the lambing.'

'My mother's expecting, sir.'

'Please, sir, I broke out in spots.'

'Please, sir, I had to wait till ma granny mended ma breeks.'

True or false, no matter! We were all given a taste of the hangman's whip and took our punishment stoically enough, tugging down our jersey sleeves as far as they could go, to take the brunt of the blow. It was all part of the process of being educated.

But for a peerie-top like me the worst part of being at school was sitting still, without being able to get up and jump round the room when I felt restless. On the first day I had taken a rubber ball with me. When I brought it out of my school-bag the master said darkly, 'What are you going to do with that?'

'Stot it!' said I, surprised at such a daft question, and began stotting it there and then on my desk. But I was soon shown the error of my ways and gradually my wings were clipped, like everyone else's.

It was worse in many ways than being in gaol, but it had its compensations. Suddenly the world began to grow bigger and I discovered the satisfying joys of learning.

Soon after going to school I found my first friend. Two friends, in fact; and had my first encounter with death. Real death, not just Grumphy the pig.

The first of my friends was a big dark-haired girl called Kate. She had something of the look of Jessie about her, fierce and strong, with a grip like a vice when she caught hold of me.

To begin with she was my enemy. We had nothing in common except that we were forced to sit side-by-side and share the same inkwell. She was a foreigner who came cycling over the Carter Bar every day, and how could I forget that her ancestors had fought so bitterly with mine?

For a long time we kept up the old feud, taunting each other when the Battles of Bannockburn or Flodden were mentioned in a history-lesson.

'Sassenach!' I used to hiss at her.

'Scot!' she spat back, making it sound like a bad word.

At last our own battle came to a head one day in the playground. All over a pencil. Kate discovered that mine had *Made in England* printed on it.

'See!' she said triumphantly. 'You Scots can't even make your own pencils.'

'It's a rotten one!' I said, and flung it at her in a temper.

One moment we were fighting with words, the next with fists. It was another Flodden for me. I lost the battle and won my first black eye.

It was a beauty and lasted for weeks. The strange thing was, having got rid of our spleen, Kate and I became firm friends. At first I had an uneasy feeling that I was being a traitor, fraternizing with the enemy. But after a while I forgot Kate was English. She was just a lassie like myself.

Being so much bigger and stronger, she became my protector. She would push anybody out of the way with a blow that sent them spinning, re-plait my pigtails when they came adrift, tie my laces, rub out smudges on my jotter, and whisper the answers when the master asked awkward questions about arithmetic.

At the midday break we sat on the playground wall overlooking the master's garden and exchanged our dinner-pieces. Her medicine-bottle contained home-made lemonade, far more refreshing than the milk in mine. Even her bread-and-cheese tasted different and her gingerbread was dark and chewy, with a crunchy crust on top almost like Bella Confectionery's toffee. Funnily enough she preferred my barley-scones and the shortbread I was sometimes given for afters.

It was a long time, though, before I ventured over into enemy territory to visit her, but when I did I discovered other edible delights. Singin'-hinnies hot from the girdle and oozing with butter; ham cut as thick as steak and fried with pancakes; tasty faggots, and home-made bread spread with honey.

I was surprised to find that she lived in a house more or less like mine and that the English were quite civilized. Not a war-cry was heard nor a battle-axe seen; and I escaped unscathed to my own side of the Border without a drop of blood having been spilled. I began to wonder if the old stories had been true.

In wintry weather the Carter Bar was often impassable and Kate would be missing from the school, snow-bound on the other side. Sometimes she came over on the snow-plough, and one day when she was storm-stayed, and could not get back again, she came home with me for the night.

We did our home-lessons together, made toffee, and played snakes-and-ladders in the lamplight. Meantime the old book about the bad Border reivers was lying unheeded on the table. Neither of us bothered to look at it; it did not seem to matter any more. The only battles we fought were friendly ones, and we felt it a pity that our ancestors had not solved their quarrels over a game of tiddlywinks.

Before long I became bi-lingual in a kind of way, trying my best to imitate Kate's Geordie accent. She called me 'hinny' and taught me songs about Blaydon Races and the 'Fishy in the Little Dishy'. In return I introduced her to 'Rainy Rainy Rattle-stanes' and the 'Laird o' Cockpen'. But we kept off the Border ballads, just in case; it was safer not to stir up the old embers.

Kate taught me many things, amongst them how to 'go a bike', though hers was too big for me and I could not reach the seat. But I persevered till I could pedal away in a standing position, and Kate patiently picked me up every time I fell off. It did not do the bicycle much good, but I was as proud as punch at having achieved a new skill.

There was a communal boneshaker at home but it was a man's bike, and I kept hinting that it would be great if I had one of my own; but my pleas fell on deaf ears. What was wrong, Jessie said, with shanks's pownie?

Kate sometimes came a cropper herself and arrived at the school with bruised knees and torn stockings. Often I helped her to straighten the handle-bars and to light the little lamp when she had to cycle home in the darkness. It seemed a long lonely way for one so young, but Kate was not afraid of anything, bogle or human being, and, like Jessie, taught me a great deal about how to be self-reliant.

So now I had a friend. It never occurred to me that I could have two. I imagined everybody had only one, like one head. What would I do with another? But one day a new family came to live in the one big house in Camptown, the factor's house for the laird's estate. They, too, were foreigners, having come from a far-off country called Wales; and I wondered what colour they would be and if they would speak words we could understand.

They were just human beings. The youngest of the family was a small girl called Gwen, as frail and pale as a lily. She waited at her gate for me each morning and we walked up the road together to the school. It was she who made the first approach.

'Will you be my friend?' she asked me straight out one day when we were going through the Dark Woods.

I stopped and stared at her in embarrassment. It was like getting a sudden proposal of marriage. I never thought folk talked like that, putting their feelings into words. But the little Welsh girl had no such reticence.

'I like you. I want you to be my friend,' she insisted, clutching at my arm.

'Away!' I said, shaking her off. 'I've got one already.'

But she had put the idea into my head, and soon I had the same protective feeling towards her as Kate had for me. Indeed, if the truth must be told, I grew far fonder of Gwen than of

Kate, and was desolate on the days when she was not waiting for me at the gate. Sometimes I would see her white face at the window, and she would wave her thin little hand at me like a lady in a story-book.

It was a short friendship. Gwen was delicate and often absent from school. Many a day I saw the doctor's grand car with the chauffeur draw up at the gate, and heard whispers that she had a strange ailment called consumption, which caused her to flare and flicker like a candle. Before long her light went out. She dwined away, as Jessie put it.

Sometimes her mother invited me in to tea. She, too, was gentle and languid-looking. Even the food she provided was delicate compared with the hearty farmhouse fare: dainty sandwiches, fairy-cakes, and paper-thin biscuits. Gwen nibbled at them like a little mouse, while her mother looked on anxiously, feeling her daughter's fevered brow and urging her to take another sip of milk. Sometimes she looked at me as if comparing me with the invalid, and I felt ashamed of my appetite.

When winter came Gwen grew quieter and paler and began to cough a great deal. Sometimes she would cling to me on the road and gasp to get her breath back. I had no idea what was happening, but I shortened my steps to fit hers and did not try to hurry her.

At school she never joined in the rough-and-tumble games of the playground but stood shivering in the porch, her hands icy cold. Sometimes I would rub them for her, and try to shield her from rampaging boys bombarding us with snow-balls. I longed to inject some life into her limp body and some rich red blood into her veins, but did not know how to do it.

Then for days and days she was missing. I stood at the gate looking hopefully up at her bedroom window; but I saw her only once more. wrapped in a white shawl, feebly waving to me.

Was it the next day that the blinds were drawn? It was the doctor's chauffeur who told me, 'The lassie's deid,' and I went on my solitary way to school, dragging my feet and wondering if the lump in my throat would ever go away.

When the master read out the register and came to Gwen's name I said out loud, 'She's dead.'

There was a horrified silence in the classroom, and then the master came over to ask about it in a gentler voice than usual, before scoring her name off the book. But I just shook my head and continued to say, 'She's dead.'

For a time I was a kind of heroine, being the first to break the news. We had a half-holiday on the day of the funeral, but there was nothing to rejoice about. I picked hundreds of snowdrops and made a little cross for Gwen's grave and have hated the sight of the flowers ever since.

Gwen's mother gave me one of her dolls, dressed in Welsh costume, as a keepsake; but I did not play with it. I put it away in a drawer and forgot about it, but I never forgot Gwen.

There were other more robust bairns whose steps sometimes fell in with mine on the way to school. Boys in clumping boots and thick rumpled stockings; girls wearing hand-me-doon coats often too big or too small for them. The boys were destined to be herds or hinds and the girls servant-lasses. Few of them wanted higher education or indeed any education at all. It was a waste of time when they could be out in the fields doing practical things.

What on earth did we talk about? We were no great conversationalists, yet we always seemed to be saying something. Quarrelling mainly, hitting out at each other with our school-bags or engaging in long pointless arguments.

'I did not!'

'You did sot!'

'Did not!'

'Did sot!'

Sometimes we jumped in and out of the ditches or strayed over fences and played hide-and-seek, forgetting the existence of the school-bell. Or we kicked a stone up the road, passing it from one to another with our feet to keep it on the go. Occasionally a real quarrel would break out, ending in fisticuffs, tears, and torn jerseys; but we never kept it up for long. Our common enemy was Auld Baldy-Heid.

School-bairns, or indeed bairns of any kind, are great boasters, claiming feats of daring beyond the bounds of possibility. We tried to impress each other with improbable tales of having fought dragons, wrestled with wild beasts and chased away ghosts. Strange how quickly our bravery vanished the moment we were faced with the master's tawse!

One laddie called Bob could beat us all at bragging. He claimed that he could fly.

'Go on then,' I urged him one day. 'Show us.'

It was not as easy as that, he told us. He would have to start from a high place and jump off. 'All right,' I dared him. 'Climb up a tree and start from there.'

One day in the Dark Woods he did it. Bob's take-off was impressive; so was his downfall. When he fell flat on his face at our feet we feared he had killed himself and that we – or I, more likely – would be punished for it; but he was only stunned. When he got up and recovered enough breath to speak, he muttered, 'I forgot ma wings.' All the same, he was less boastful for a day or two.

There were times when I had the unenviable task of taking a new pupil, one of the hinds' bairns, to school for the first time, until he found his own feet. The one who gave me the most trouble was Wee Wullie. I thought him a nuisance, and so he was; a snotty-nosed, snivelling child who ran away across the fields if I took my eye off him. I had to chase after him and round him up like a collie-dog while he whimpered, 'I dinna want to be learnt.'

We were all learnt whether we wanted or not, by the time

the master was done with us. Goodness knows how he managed to juggle with such a mixed batch of pupils, all at different ages and stages and all crammed into the one small classroom. But he did it, his one aim being that we should all pass the Qualifying, which would take us on to the Grammar School in Jedburgh, if we were so inclined. And still he found time to put his feet on his desk and read *The Scotsman* at some point during the day, keeping the hangman's whip in evidence and giving us baleful glances over the paper now and again.

I used to sit and stare at him, wondering, as I often did about grown-ups, if he had ever been young and daft; but I could never visualize him in short trousers playing cuddy-loup-the-dyke.

From the pupils' point of view, the one-teacher one-classroom school had its advantages. Thirty or more children were all crammed in together; and though we were split, more or less, into age-groups, we could not fail to become involved in the other lessons going on around us.

Those who were still at the-cat-sat-on-the-mat stage could pick up some miscellaneous information from the top classes. Long before I had mastered the four-times table I knew about the Wars of the Roses and the source of the Nile. On the other hand it was maddening when we reached the top class to hear the infants gabbling 'Ring-ting! I wish I were a primrose', while we were trying to get to grips with vulgar-fractions.

Sometimes we found ourselves mixed up with the wrong class, answering questions that were not directed at us. It was a hitty-missy way of learning, yet we all managed to scrape through the exams and put up a good enough show when that dreadful ogre, the inspector, came to put us through our paces. For days beforehand the master frightened the life out of us with dire threats of what would happen if we failed to behave perfectly in the great man's presence. Our pockets were searched for sweets, catapults, mice, bools, and other extraneous items; and we were warned that we would get made into mincemeat if we as much as whispered during the inspector's visit.

The truth was, he was coming as much to assess the teacher as to inspect the pupils' work. It was surprising to see Auld Baldy-Heid looking apprehensively out of the window, straightening his tie, tidying his desk, and hiding *The Scotsman* out of sight, as if he feared he might be punished himself. How we would have enjoyed that, if only it had happened!

We were drilled to spring to our feet the moment the inspector appeared and greet him with 'Good morning, sir,' in unison. I once got the strap for putting up my hand and asking, 'Please, sir, what'll happen if he comes in the afternoon?'

When he did arrive he was as mild as milk. A jokey wee man with a twinkle in his eyes, who took a cursory look at our jotters, asked a few easy questions and told us we were doing fine. Fancy! not even a cross word. Somehow we felt cheated when he went away with a cheerful wave of his hand and not a drop of blood spilt.

The master was so relieved that he lit his pipe, sat down with his feet on the desk and had a good read of the paper, leaving us to our own devices.

But Auld Baldy-Heid was not often in such an amiable mood. His temper would suddenly burst into flame, and we were seldom left sitting in the same place for long, for he had a habit of bawling: 'Go to the bottom of the class, you donkey!' No easy job, since we had to shuffle past each other at the narrow desks and were never too sure which was the top and which the bottom.

But we had our compensations. Being allowed to clean the blackboard was a great reward, the peak of every child's ambition. How powerful we felt, rubbing out sums and spelling. Sometimes, in a fit of bravado, we would draw a chalky face on the clean board, an unflattering resemblance of the master. Or even compose verses which we thought witty beyond words.

Lang legs, splay feet,
He aye mak's the bairns greet.

Another gem which used to convulse us with giggles was far cleverer than any in the poetry-book.

The master's a brute,
With his baldy heid.
Bang! bang! bang!
Shoot him deid!

How we hated him! Yet deep down how we loved him in spite of his angry outbursts. He knew fine how to get round us. He had only to put away the strap, give us one of his rare smiles and say: 'What about a story?'

'Oh yes, sir; please, sir!'

Infants and older pupils alike listened avidly to the master's stories, for he had a rare talent for telling a tale. He could transport us far from the dingy schoolroom with stirring stories of the clans, or legends about ugly ducklings and toy soldiers. Sometimes he gave us a bible lesson, telling us about Jonah and the whale or Daniel in the lions' den.

We could see it all happening as the master marched up and down in front of us, waving his arms about and acting out the parts. It was like a one-man show at the theatre, and we sat entranced, hanging on every word.

Then suddenly he would drop us back to earth with a bump. Grabbing the chalk he turned to the blackboard and began to write out some sums; and life became real and earnest once more.

Now and then, to complete our all-round education, he would give us a singing-lesson, using a long cane to point out the doh-ray-me's on the blackboard; but more often he used the pointer to rap us over the head when we strayed off the tune. It was no use protesting, 'Please, sir, it wasn't me, sir.' If we were taking communal lessons we had to settle for communal punishment.

I could never get the hang of the doh-ray-me's.

'Just sing *la*,' the master roared at me, rapping my head with the pointer.

We all la-la'd our way through simple tunes: 'My Bonnie Lies Over The Ocean' and 'Clementine', with the boys groaning and grunting a few paces behind. As there was no school piano, Auld Baldy-Heid gave us a note to start us off, but it was often so high or so low that we ground to a standstill half-way through 'O My Darling.'

Sometimes he made us sing a dreary ditty called 'O Who Will O'er the Downs So Free?' It was enlivened only by the phrase 'To win a blooming bride', which we took to be a bit of bad language, and giggled behind our hands every time we sang it.

What we dreaded most of all were the times when he divided us into groups and made us sing a Round, setting us off at different times as if we were running a handicap race. 'Come, follow' was his favourite, but not mine. It usually ended in an inextricable muddle, like a tangled piece of knitting.

'Idiots!' roared Auld Baldy-Heid. 'You're all as dumb as dykes.'

He was not so dumb himself. Occasionally he segregated the sexes and took the boys off to his garden for a 'digging lesson' while his wife came in to take control of the girls and try to teach us sewing. She never succeeded in my case. My fingers were soon covered with blood where I had pricked myself, and how I longed to change places with the boys!

When we were let loose at the midday break we rushed out into the open air like bumbees from a byke, and tore about from one side of the playground to the other, jumping and shouting to give vent to our pent-up spirits. We swallowed our pieces as quickly as possible and then got on with our games. The boys wrestled and punched each other; the girls skipped in a line with a long rope and sometimes were allowed to join the boys for a game of kick-the-can or cuddy-loup-the-dyke. There were no holds barred because we were female. We had to take any dunts or bumps that were going.

Though we had an excess of exercise in our long walks to and from the school and in the rough-and-tumble games of the playground, the school curriculum decreed that we should have drill once a week. This was the only lesson not taken by the master himself. Instead, a fiery little man, known as the drilly, came cycling into the playground once a week and frightened the wits out of us with his sharp commands. I remember his blue uniform, his bicycle-clips, the spiky ends of his waxed moustache, and most of all his sergeant-major voice as he rapped out his orders.

'Jump to it, you idiots!'

The drilly reduced us all to jelly till we had no idea which was our right foot and which our left. We had to wheel and turn, double up, touch our toes, form into straight lines and run from one side of the playground to the other. The stragglers, or those of us who turned left instead of right, were given the full whiplash of his tongue.

We were all dolts, disgraces, and 'rubbish'; and the more he chastised us the more rubbishy we became. Many of the girls, and even some of the boys, were reduced to tears, and I longed to be brave enough to stand up to him and shout 'Shut up'! just to see what would happen. But we were all speechless with terror.

By the time the drilly cycled away in disgust with dire threats of what he would do to us next week, none of us had a scrap of confidence left. We would sooner have faced the master's tawse any day. Indeed, Auld Baldy-Heid seemed mild in comparison.

One kind word from the master meant more to us than any

amount of praise from our parents. I can still recall the thrill of pride I felt when he marked one of my essays 'Not bad.' The fact that he added 'Spelling atrocious' did not detract from my triumph. The word atrocious meant nothing to me.

Jammed together as we were, we all copied from our neighbours' jotters and helped each other with our sums, which was not always an advantage, for if one went wrong so did the lot. Similarly if we stuck when we were saying poetry there was always someone ready to prompt us in a stage-whisper which, though well-meant, often led us astray on the wrong verse.

We were always looking for diversions of any kind to break the monotony; even a mouse let loose from someone's pocket, or Bob (the braggart) firing off his water-pistol. He sat behind me and pestered the life out of me by pulling my pigtails, dipping them in his inkwell, and stuffing strange objects down the back of my neck. I used to wriggle round and swipe at him with my ruler, often, unluckily, at the moment when the teacher looked up and spotted me.

'Come out, you!' he would thunder; and what else could I do but go out and take my punishment?

We never told on each other. It was only clypes, or telltales, who did that. What would be the point? We were all in the war together. A far worse fate than getting strapped was to be told to stand out. This meant standing staring at the blank wall in a corner of the classroom in full view of everyone. There was no dunce's cap, but we felt the indignity just the same.

It was a great break when a visitor came, maybe the minister, or the laird from the Big Hoose who wandered in wearing a long cloak round his shoulders. He said a few unintelligible words to us, and once – how we loved him for it! – suggested a half-holiday which the master was forced to grant.

On one never-to-be-forgotten occasion another visitor came to the school, a strange little man who was staying with his friend, the laird, at Edgerston House. The purpose of his visit was to present prizes. For the one and only time in my life I was to be the recipient of the first prize. No wonder I was excited.

The visitor was no ordinary man. He was a famous author, so the master told us, who had written a play called *Peter Pan*. My first author and my first prize! But when he arrived I thought he looked a very odd little man in crumpled clothes and with a faraway look in his eyes. I would sooner have met Mr Anon whose works I knew better. The nearest theatre was over fifty miles away, so what chance had I of seeing *Peter Pan*?

All the same, I would have been bursting with pride if only the prize was being awarded for something to do with brains. The truth was, it was for the best-dyed egg. Even so, it would have been a triumph but for one shameful fact. I had not dyed the egg myself.

It was Jessie who had done it for me. It was she who had thought of covering the egg with a piece of lace so that it would emerge with an all-over design. It was Jessie who had put an onion in the water to give it its delicate colouring (only she called it an ingan), and it was Jessie who, by rights, ought to be receiving the prize.

I stood trembling in front of the famous man, hanging my head in shame and wondering how I could confess my sins. Sir James was very complimentary. He had never seen such a beautiful egg. If only hens could lay them like that every day, wouldn't it be wonderful? He would have a boiled egg for his breakfast every morning. What a clever little girl I was, and what pleasure he had in presenting me with the first prize which I richly deserved.

Every word he said cut me to the quick and made my sins seem more scarlet. More so when I saw the prize. It was a book of bible stories with a picture of the Good Samaritan on the cover. I clutched it under my arm and was sure that I would be struck dead.

I ran all the way home with a stitch in my side to present

the book to Jessie, its rightful owner. But she just took one look at it and said, 'Hoots, wumman, keep it. It'll lairn ye a lesson.'

And so it did; at least I determined to dye my own eggs in future.

5. Snow-siege

'I can smell snaw,' Jessie would say with a shiver, when the weather became icy cold. 'We're in for't!'

It was fun at first when the snow began to fall, great fat flakes floating from the sky like soft feathers. They settled gently on the hedges and trees, quietly piling one on top of the other till the whole farm was transformed into a dazzling white wilderness.

Sometimes the storm came on silently in the dead of night, taking us by surprise. When we woke in the morning we knew by the ominous hush that something had happened. Every sound was muffled as though the world had fallen asleep; and when we looked out of the window we could see nothing but great wreaths of snow. Everything looked fresh and new; as pure as the driven snow.

At other times it started with a blizzard. The wind wailed and howled as it blew the icy flakes horizontally against the window-panes. They froze where they landed, blotting out the light; and we knew that the storm was here to stay.

At first, while it was still possible to get out of doors, I was in my element. No going to school; every day a holiday with the snow for my plaything. Plenty of sledging and snowballing; the thrill of seeing everything take on a sudden soft beauty. Everywhere one looked there was a lovely sight to see. Even the cart-shed became a fairy-tale castle and the tattiebogles looked like snowmen.

There was the excitement, too, of feeling marooned. It was an adventure, like living in a story-book.

But gradually, as the farm-road became blocked and the snow relentlessly hemmed us in, I began to hate the sight of the great white wreaths that loomed over us, growing higher and wider every day. They took on monstrous shapes, like grotesque Polar beasts threatening to creep closer and swallow us up. What if we were lost for ever under a suffocating snow-blanket?

For weeks on end there was no sign of the postie, the vanman, or any human being from the outside world. No hope of even venturing outside the door. Often the hinds had to dig away the drifts before we could push it open. They made long tunnels to the steading and the byre, but it was a never-ending task, for the snow soon filled them up again. Even when it stopped falling it had frozen so hard that we were sealed in, and there was nothing for us to do but bide our time and wait for the thaw.

The worst moment came when the telephone-wires broke under the weight of snow and our last link with the outside world was gone. We could get no calls either out or in through Bella at the post office. How we longed for the shrill summons and to hear anyone, even just Bella herself, saying hullo.

The telephone was no great loss to Jessie, who hated the sight and sound of the instrument. If she was working nearby when the bell rang she gave the telephone a baleful look and ignored its summons as long as possible. At last she would snatch up the receiver and shout: 'What is't?'; then she would call out to my mother or father: 'Ye're wanted on the line,' and slam down the receiver, cutting off the call.

Even at the best of times it was not easy putting through a call. It was as well to have a comfortable seat to sit in, a book to read, or a duster in the hand to polish anything within sight, for there was often a long delay before Bella replied. Then my mother, or whoever was making the call, had to listen to the reason. Often I stood nearby and could hear her breathless voice.

'I was roond the back hingin' oot the weshin'. Ma mooth was fou' o' claes-pegs.'

Sometimes it was full of treacle-toffee. 'I was bilin' a new batch ben the hoose.'

Or: 'I was thrawin' up a scone.' Bella never baked; she threw. 'I micht thraw up a gingerbreid later on, seein' the oven's het. Are ye wantin' a number?'

Often my mother had forgotten the number because of the long delay. Or Bella would interrupt with: 'Haud on! I'll need to let the cat oot. I'll be back in a jiffy.'

The number was not so important to Bella as any news she could pass on to us or glean about what was going on upbye at the farm. How were the hens laying, had the cow calved, and when was the pig to be killed? When my mother finally got a word in edgeways and asked for a local number Bella would say, 'Och! ye needn't bother to ring them. They're oot. Awa' to Edinburgh for the day. Was't onything special?'

There were no secrets on the telephone with Bella acting as go-between; and maybe it was just as well that she knew everyone's business, for she could pass on messages from one household to another and warn us if an unexpected visitor was on his way to pay us a call.

She would ring my mother and tell her, 'That's the minister. He's been in buyin' a postal order. He's on his road up to see ye, so ye'd better pit on the kettle an' thraw up a dropscone.'

It was difficult to have any private conversations for Bella had a habit of chipping in. 'Na, na! ye're wrang! It was his wife's mother that went to Canada, no' his sister-in-law. I ken for a fact.'

And if Bella Confectionery kent for a fact, it was a fact.

No one resented these three-cornered conversations. It was understood that Bella would be listening, ready to break in with her comments. But sometimes she would bring a session to a sudden close by saying, 'Here! ye'll need to hurry up. I've got the tatties to peel.'

If a call came for us from across the Border Bella used to put on her 'fine' voice. 'Excuse me! There's a long-distance on the line. A gaintleman wishes to speak to you from Newcesstle.' She would then revert to her normal tongue and whisper, 'I think it's thon fella that sells sheep-dip. Watch him; he's an awfu' blether. Hold on, please. Ay'm putting you through.' If the man went on too long she would just cut him off in the middle of a sentence and say, 'Ay! that's enough o' him!'

All the same, Bella was our life-line, and we missed her cheerful gossip when the telephone went dead during a snowstorm. It was the most welcome sound in the world when the bell shrilled out at the end of the siege and we heard her saying, 'That's you back on the line again. Are ye a' weel? The cat's had kittlin's an' Mrs Scott's expectin'. I ken for a fact. Will ye be wantin' a number?'

While the storm lasted there were long weeks during which we heard no sound from the outside world. Wars might be raging, thrones may have fallen, friends in neighbouring farms could be lying dangerously ill. We were left in limbo knowing nothing that went on beyond the confines of the snow-bound house. Keeping ourselves alive, feeding the beasts, and trying to stay warm, were our main concerns.

There was little fear of starving, for we kept squirrel-hoards of meal and flour in the bins. There were hams hanging from the kitchen ceiling and dozens of preserved eggs laid down in vats. An entire cupboard was stocked with home-made jam: black-currant, red-currant, plum, raspberry, gooseberry, apple-jelly, and a few pots of strawberry for special occasions. But as the weeks dragged by the meals became more monotonous, and we longed for fresh food. We soon ran short of vegetables, for the turnip and potato-pits were lost under the the snow. An orange would have been a treat, or a kipper; even a baker's bun.

It was a minor tragedy if we ran short of sugar, tea, or salt, or found that our store of candles had run out. We hunted here and there for oddments and sometimes made exciting discoveries by coming across a forgotten bar of chocolate or a tin of syrup hidden in the press.

As for falling ill: 'You'd better not!' I was warned, and I did my best to oblige. Chilblains and other trivial discomforts had to be borne without a murmur. If I took a fever it just had to run its course.

The thing to do was to be as active as possible, not only to keep the circulation going but to save us from sitting about feeling sorry for ourselves. When the pipes froze and there was no running water in the house I wrapped myself up like a woollen bundle, put on my father's big boots and staggered out to collect pailfuls of snow to boil in the kettle. Every time I opened the kitchen door the bitter-cold wind nearly bowled me over and blew in a flurry of flakes which melted into rivulets on the stone flags. If Jessie was with us she was kept busy mopping up the mess with an old broom. 'Talk aboot snaw bein' clean!' she would complain. 'Ye can keep it.'

Indeed we had to keep it. As time went by I prayed every night for it to go away, but it was still there in the morning fixed more firmly than ever, as if it was there for a lifetime. How would the flowers ever grow again, and where were all the wee creepy-cráwlies? There was no sign of life anywhere.

One year we lost the coal-house. It was an old shed, situated across the road from the kitchen door, which held our store of black diamonds, fetched by the hinds in their carts from the depot in Jedburgh. 'Going for the coals' was a day's work for them. Seven miles to town with their empty carts and seven miles back with their full loads. But once they had shovelled out the contents and stacked it up in the coal-house we felt secure in the prospect of cosy fires for many weeks to come.

Now the snow had obliterated every trace of the shed. The men tried to tunnel their way towards it, but they were always off-side and never succeeded in reaching it. Luckily there were plenty of logs and kindling in the stick-house adjoining the kitchen. Everyone lent a hand at sawing, chopping, and carrying in the fuel to keep the fires going; but it was a never-ending task for the great kitchen fire was like a hungry monster greedily gobbling everything it was offered.

Though we kept as many fires going as we could it was difficult to stay warm, in spite of 'clooty sausages' laid across the foot of the doors to keep out the draughts and stone pigs which we took to bed with us. Sometimes we reinforced them with bricks heated in the oven and wrapped in flannel; but even so we were always shivering.

Great icicles hung like stalactites from all the windows and roofs. How we longed to see them dripping and melting, but they grew bigger every day, and the windows were so frosted over that we could scarcely see out. The lamps had to be lit earlier each day, though we used fewer in order to save paraffin and often had to feel our way about the house in the darkness.

Though I had never heard of the word claustrophobia I knew what it meant during a long snow-siege. Everyone seemed to be living on top of each other and it was difficult to find sufficient outlets for high, or low spirits. Trivial quarrels sprang up. We were all heartily sick of the sight of each other and more particularly of the sight of the snow. It had seemed fairlylike at first, every tree a Christmas tree hanging with glittering crystals, the whole farm softened and blurred into beauty. But now the snow was an enemy. 'Go away! Go away!' I used to shout at it and longed for a magic wand to wave.

Trying to find the hens so that we could feed them was one of our problems. They had retired to their hen-houses at the oncome of the storm and stopped laying as if in protest. But where were the hen-houses? They were dotted all over the farm and there was no hope of reaching them. Yet somehow the Wyandottes and Minorcas and Rhode Island Reds managed to survive, emerging eventually thinner than usual and ready to peck up anything within sight.

The cattle and horses had been brought in from the hill and the fields, and shut up in their winter quarters in the sheds in the steading; and the herd had gathered as many of his flock as he could into the lambing-shed. This was a kraal-like building which Jock had built himself and roofed over with straw. Nearby was the bothy where he and the hired lambing-man had their headquarters during the lambing season.

I would have liked to live in the bothy myself away from everybody and sleep in the truckle-bed with its straw palliasse. There was an open fire where the herd heated milk for the lambs and sometimes fried ham or cooked porridge for himself. The bothy had a thatched roof, a small window like a watching eye, and a story-book air about it as if Wee Willie Winkle might live there.

On days when we were not snow-bound I sometimes went there and sat with Jock while he made a new crook, watching every move as he patiently planed the wood and polished the head.

'I'd never get by withoot a crook,' he used to tell me. 'Man-lassie! it's like ma third hand.'

True enough, Jock used his crooks in a dozen different ways: to lever himself over a dyke, to cleek a lamb round the neck (sometimes to cleek me, too, if I fell into a ditch), to poke down into the snow in search of buried sheep, to dowse the lambs at dipping-time. It was not only a third, but a fourth hand to him.

I was convinced that Jock was the cleverest man in the world. The things he knew! Often I watched him coaxing a ewe to take on a motherless lamb after her own had died. Sometimes she butted the lamb out of the way – and butted the herd, too – but he did not give in. He went quietly away, skinned off the complete covering from the dead lamb and slung it over the orphan's back. This time when he carried the motherless bairn and set it down beside the ewe, she did not reject it. She sniffed at it, recognising the smell of her own lamb, and before long it was snuggling against her, sucking contentedly.

It was hard going for the herd during a storm. He had literally to fight his way through the snow to save as many of his flock as possible. Sometimes he had to dig them out of the drifts, and it amazed me to find how they could keep alive for days, even weeks, in such conditions and without any food. Sheep, it seemed, were not as silly as they looked. Certainly they had enough sense to preserve themselves.

Sometimes Jock came into the kitchen to fetch more milk and stood in the lamplight with the snow dripping off him and little icicles hanging from his eyebrows. The collies would lie down beside me on the rug, put their heads on their paws, and instantly fall asleep.

It was not often that Jessie spoke to her brother, but sometimes she would say: 'Sit doon, man, an' drink a cup o' tea.' But Jock never did. Maybe he would drink the tea, but he would not sit down.

'It I sit, I'll stert gantin',' he declared, 'an' fa' asleep, like the dogs.' Poor things! their dreams were short. 'Up, Jed! Come on, Jess! Ootbye!' And away they went into the cold, leaving pools of water on the floor where the snow had melted. Exhausted or not, they never disobeyed their master's commands.

It was difficult to remember which day of the week it was. Indeed, it mattered little; they were all the same. Too much the same. The one thing we were all waiting for was the thaw.

The men tried to open a pathway down the road by digging their way through the drifts, but it was a Herculanean task. Then at last they succeeded in dragging out the old snow-plough from the cart-shed and yoking in the Clydesdales.

They made many false starts. The horses floundered up to their bellies in the snow, slipping and sliding on the icy surface. Sometimes they could only struggle on for a few yards before they came to a standstill and the men were forced to unyoke them again.

Day after day they tried, making a little more progress each time till at length – oh! happy day – they got as far as the cottages and disappeared from sight.

Their object was to reach the farm road-end in the hope that the main road had been opened up by the big County Council snow-plough and they might catch the vanman or even get as far as Bella's shop for supplies.

By now the larder was growing emptier. We had eaten our way through the hams, and had a surfeit of barley scones and porridge. My mother concocted various soups and puddings as best she could, but we hankered after variety. What I longed for most were some sweets or even a stick of sugar-ally.

We watched and waited eagerly for the men's return. They had taken huge sacks with them to contain any scran they could forage, and it was a crushing disappointment if they came back empty-handed and exhausted, shaking their heads to let us know their mission had failed. But they would try again tomorrow.

When at last they succeeded it was better than Christmas. The men were all smiles as they lugged in the bulging sacks and hoisted them on to the kitchen table while we gathered round, eagerly watching to see what would emerge. Loaves of bread, sausages, newspapers, letters, tobacco, sweets, candles, matches, tea, sugar. Every single item was welcome.

Most welcome of all was any scrap of local news the men had managed to glean. Fancy! they had met not only Bella Confectionery, but Mary-Anne, Wat-the-Baker, the gamey, and the postie. Such richness! They had heard that the Carter Bar was still blocked, that the Scotts, like us, were snow-bound, that the minister was down with 'flu, that some ruler in a foreign country had been deposed; but that did not interest us as much as the greatest news of all. The thaw was on its way.

What a difference the prospect of freedom made to our spirits! A weight seemed to be lifted off us and we began to laugh and sing and talk about all the things we would do when we were released. Imagine riding once more in the gig with Flora trotting along the open road! Even the thought of going back to school filled me with elation.

This feeling of euphoria did not last. Strangely enough, it was the last lap that was the worst. Tempers that were frayed before became even more ragged as the reaction set in, and we seemed to be even more on top of each other.

Every day we waited impatiently for the promised thaw but it seemed reluctant to come. When it did it was even more uncomfortable than the storm. Nothing on earth can be colder and more miserable than a 'cold thaw', with everything looking bleak and the snow drip-drip-dripping as it slowly melts away.

Jessie had to hound me out of the house. 'Awa' ootbye an' get some colour into your cheeks. Ye're a peelly-wally object.'

Though I had been gasping for fresh air, the discomfort of slopping about in the slush was so great that I clung, shivering, to the fireside. The snow began to look old and dirty. Soon it ran like rivers, oozing under the kitchen door, into the hall, and all over the place. Water seemed to cascade everywhere, from burst pipes, from melting icicles, from rooftops when the snow came thudding down like an avalanche.

I had to be careful not to get buried under it for it could have felled me to the ground. There were times when I longed for it to freeze again so that everything could be neat and clean. But gradually I could see patches of black earth and sense the first faint signs of spring. The cocks and hens emerged from the hen-houses to begin their clucking and pecking, and soon the whole farm stirred to life once more.

Looking back, I wonder how we survived the long spell indoors without the diversion of television or radio. But we had a great compensation in what Jessie called the 'grammy-phone'.

It was a friendly old machine with an immense fluted horn. I used to stick my head inside it trying to get closer to Melba or Caruso. Sometimes I stuffed my doll in there, too, or used the horn as a secret hiding-place for other treasures. My elders could always tell from the muffled sounds if that bairn had been at it again.

The records had been played so often that I knew every tune inside-out and was word-perfect with every song. Not that there were many, and few of them without a flaw. Most of them were scarred and scratched but I knew the exact spot at which the needle would stick and sat on the table beside the machine ready to pick up the arm and lift it over the obstacle. Otherwise there would be a dreadful din when Harry Lauder repeated himself over and over in the midst of 'Stop Your Ticklin', Jock' till even the cat went and hid under the table.

I liked a good-going band with a rousing tune and would often replay the best bits, shifting the needle back to the cheery place. Playing the gramophone was anything but a passive performance. It entailed a great deal of hard labour but it was worth the effort. To me it was a magic music-box.

First, the unwieldy object had to be lifted on to the table, a task far beyond my capacity. I always had to badger a grown-up into lending a helping hand. Sometimes Jessie obliged but not without a protest.

'Can ye no' let's have some peace an' quiet?'

All the same she was not averse to music while she worked and even joined in now and again when 'the man on the grammyphone' was singing a song.

When it was safely set on the table I hunted through the small pile of records till I found a favourite, then set it on the turn-table and inserted a new needle if I could find one in the wee tin box with a picture of a dog on the lid, but usually they were old and rusty. Sometimes I had to recall Jessie to help with the cranking of the handle and often the record would run down half-way through with a disembodied voice groaning to a standstill.

It was fun to have such power over the musicians. I could stop them and start them, I could make them go faster or slower. Poor things! they were sadly overworked. Little wonder their voices sounded so wheezy as if they had sung themselves hoarse, for I gave them little rest and could never get over the wonder of watching the records spinning round and round.

Even before I could read the names on the labels I could tell by the scratches on the surface which was 'The Skye Boat Song' or 'The Blue Danube'. Later on in life I was surprised to hear a record playing all the way through without ever sticking. Even now when I hear an orchestra performing one of the familiar pieces I wait for the musicians to falter at the scratchy bit, and am faintly disappointed when they sail on without having to be helped over the hurdle.

I had not my father's facility but I tried to make music myself, of a kind, on the old upright piano in the parlour-drawing-room. It was a miracle that it remained upright considering the amount of punishment it had to take and the fact that it had to be thumped so hard to get any sound out of it at all. I liked its honky-tonk tinkle when the yellowed keys were struck, though there were some that remained silent no matter how hard they were hit.

Later on it was replaced by the good piano, a shining instrument with a fine tone and without a scratch on it. But I liked the old one best with its pink satin front and its ornate candlesticks which could be swung from the side. It had character if nothing else. Sometimes I twirled round and round on the piano-stool before dizzily trying to vamp out 'The Rosebud Waltz' or 'Come O'er the Stream, Charlie.'

When the spirit moved her, Miss Todd, the music teacher, came cycling up the bumpy farm-road on her wobbly bicycle to give me a lesson of sorts. If I saw her in time I ran away and hid up a tree or under the reaper in the cart-shed. But sometimes I was discovered and dragged, protesting, into her presence where I had to submit to being put through my paces with *Hemy's Tutor for the Pianoforte* propped up in front of me.

Sitting in the rocking-chair drinking tea and eating home-made cake, she would say, 'Right, dear, we'll start with the scales.'

I was fed up with scales but I played them as softly as I could so that the wrong notes would sound less jarring. Soon, if I was lucky, I would hear the tea-cup being laid down and a gentle snore coming from the direction of the rocking-chair. I could prop up *Little Women* in place of the hated *Tutor* and let my fingers stray where they pleased while I had a good read.

If she was in a wideawake mood I would be forced to go through the whole rickmatick from crotchets to semi-quavers ending with 'The Bluebells of Scotland' (two-four time, count four quavers in a bar). With variations.

I could never see the point of variations. Having played the thing in one way why go through the torture of adding twiddly-bits just to make it different? It was difficult enough to keep two hands going at the one time. My left, alas! seldom knew what my right was doing.

I thumped my way through 'Le Carnival de Venise' and 'Rousseau's Dream', which must have sounded more like a nightmare to poor Miss Todd; but 'The Harmonious Blacksmith' was the greatest misnomer of the lot. I much preferred making up my own tunes and not bothering about semibreves. They were all varied versions, but improved, I thought, of 'Scots Wha Hae' or 'Pop Goes the Weasel'.

'You're getting on, dear,' lied Miss Todd, putting on her hat, 'but you'll need to stick in. Remember those scales.'

'Oh yes, I will,' I promised, and forgot both Miss Todd and the scales the moment she went wobbling away down the road on her bicycle.

Now and then a seedy-looking gent, almost as ancient as the piano itself, came out from the town to tune it. He shuffled into the room with his tuning-fork in his hand, shook his head when he saw the piano and said, 'Past hope!'

All the same he had a kind of love-hate for the old instrument and was as proud as punch when he had patched it up and unstuck the keys. He always sat down when he was finished to try it out, playing a flamboyant piece all arpeggios and crossed hands. I thought him better than Paderewski on the gramophone and wondered why *he* had not made a record.

It was fun to watch how he took the piano to pieces. Off came the back, sides, and front. Then he turned up his nose and sent me scurrying for dusters. No wonder, considering the amount of fluff inside, and not only fluff. Goodness knows how so many extraneous objects found their way into the inner recesses, but they did.

Once the tuner came across a family of mice nesting in a corner and we had a high old time chasing them out of the house before the kitchen cat could get at them. There was no doubt that 'The Bluebells of Scotland' sounded better without them.

The old piano was kept busy when visitors came to spend the night. It was an understood thing that they would all help to entertain each other. Everyone was prepared to do a turn and indeed would have been offended if not asked to perform.

I kept well out of sight, usually under the sofa, in case I was called on to do my piece, but the visitors showed no signs of reluctance. The trouble often was to get them to stop.

There was not much variety in their repertoire. I knew for certain that the minister would start with 'When We Go Down the Vale, Lad' sung in a very low key especially if the piano-tuner had not visited us lately. He kept his eyes closed while he sang and swayed from side to side as if he was in a trance. His encore was invariably 'Juanita' which he rendered so soulfully that it brought tears to his own eyes, closed or not.

It was a relief to be cheered up by my father with one of his comic songs. 'When Father Papered the Parlour' and 'Paddy McGinty's Goat' were my favourites. Sometimes he sang 'The Galloping Major' using an old kitchen chair as his charger.

My mother played the accompaniments and she, too, sometimes sang a solo, though her songs were all tear-jerkers. I remember a touching little ditty called, believe it or not, 'Close the Shutters, Willy's Dead' which made me crawl further under the sofa. Another had an even more pathetic refrain: 'Turn your face to the wall, Daddy, Mother's no longer here.' It brought a lump to my throat every time I heard it.

Luckily it was not long before someone tuned up the fiddle and the cheerful strains of 'My Love She's but a Lassie Yet' helped to banish my gloom. And often the evening ended in a kitchen dance in which I could join if I had not been chased off to bed. The table was pushed to the side, the hearthrug rolled back and the cats and dogs shooed out of the way.

Sometimes I just sat in a corner watching and pretending I was not there, but on occasions I was brought in to make up a set if they ran short of someone for the Circassian Circle or the Eightsome Reel. Sometimes I was invited to dance a polka and had difficulty in keeping my feet out of the way of my partner's boots as he hopped like a carthorse round the kitchen.

It was strange to watch the grown-ups enjoying themselves with such abandon. The dances were like games and the dancers like children. They swung each other off their feet at the Lancers and went chasing up and down the middle at Drops o' Brandy. Their cheeks grew flushed and their eyes bright. Imagine the minister, so pompous in the pulpit, discarding his jacket and shouting 'Hooch!' like an overgrown schoolboy! And staid Mrs Scott kilting up her skirts and showing her garters. Black elastic.

It somehow gave me hope to realize that fun was not finished when folk grew old. Old! Doubtless some of the company had not yet reached their thirties. Normally their conversation was as dull as ditch-water. Crops, the price of lambs, recipes, the government, and endless talk about the weather. Never ideas-talk or fantasy-talk, the kind I liked best. 'Imagine what it would be like to have wings.' Or, 'What would you do with three magic wishes?' Grown-ups were too realistic to indulge in such foolish bairn-talk.

Usually, that is! Now they were chattering like children digging each other in the ribs and laughing till the tears ran down their cheeks. My own eyes grew heavy with sleep and I was hustled off to bed with the strains of fiddle-music growing fainter in my ears.

The sad thing was, it did not last. Next morning my elders had reverted to normal, going about their dull duties with set lips, looking a little tired and crosser than usual. If I tried to cheer them up by playing 'Polly-Wolly-Doodle' on the gramophone they would say sharply, 'Shut off that noise!' What had been fun and frolic the night before was now frowned upon. I would never, I thought, be able to understand old folk, never!

I liked to hear the bothy-ballads which the hinds sometimes sang in the stable while they were grooming their horses. Cornkisters they were called. Farmworkers used to sit on the old corn-'kists', dunting their feet against the wooden sides to beat out an accompaniment to their songs. They were rumbustious, rollicking songs with a story in them which went on for verse after verse, all about kitchie-lasses, tattie-howking and 'The Muckin' o' Geordie's Byre.' The choruses were full of fol-d-rols and tooral-oorals, in which anyone could join, even the horses jangling their harness.

The best musical sounds could be heard in the open air from the whaups, the blackies, and the shilfies. I liked to listen to the cuckoo calling 'at once far off and near'. Sometimes I lay in the long grass in the cow-gang watching a skylark hovering overhead, singing its heart out. What was it trying to say? 'Aren't we lucky to be alive?'

My most vivid musical memory is of my brother practising the fiddle after I had gone to bed. He was persistent if nothing else. I used to stuff my head under the pillow to muffle the screeches of catgut as he went over the same piece again and again, going back to pick up the wrong notes like dropped stitches.

It was the beginning, I feel sure, of my lifelong insomnia. Or maybe my sleeplessness started with that frightening prayer I was forced to say before going to bed every night.

Now I lay me down to sleep,
I pray the Lord my soul to keep.
If I should die before I wake
I pray the Lord my soul to take.

I once asked Jessie if the Lord really would take my soul.

'Ay, nae doot!' she said, firmly tucking me in, 'if ye dinna gang to sleep quick.'

But how could I go to sleep quick with 'Handel's Largo', slightly off-key, resounding in my ears?

6. Queen of the Castle

Even when I was a toddler I felt, as I do now, the urgent need to retire into my shell, to have long silences, to watch people, maybe, from a distance but not to speak to them, to think my own thoughts, above all not to do what *They* want.

It is a form of self-indulgence that was easy enough to put into practice on the farm. I just walked out of the door, ignored all enquiries as to where I was going and made my way up to the hill.

There I took up temporary residence in the ruined Border keep, with no one to disturb me except the whaups, a rabbit bolting out of the bracken, or a sheep wandering in to crop the grass on the castle floor.

The grim grey fortress was not a cosy place in which to play houses especially if the wind was howling round the draughty pile, but at least it was far enough away from *Them*. I could ignore the clanging of the dinner-bell, which I could only hear anyway if the wind was in the right direction, tolled from the farmhouse for the purpose of bringing me to heel.

I scaled the crumbling walls dislodging another old stone here and there and sat looking out across no-man's-land to the Border. Roxburghshire on my side, Northumberland on the other where the enemy used to gather their forces to invade us and where my friend Kate now lived.

Everything was peaceful. No warlike cries, no clash of weapons, no furtive figures creeping across the frontier. Only the postie on his bicycle or the baker with his horse-and-cart. All the same I kept a catapult ready just in case. *Wha daur meddle wi' me?*

Here I was queen. No one could order me about. A couple of crows had built untidy nests in one of the crannies but I did not mind them squatting in my keep. It was human beings I wanted to avoid. Jock-the-herd was the only visitor I ever made welcome.

Household chores in the castle were easily done. They consisted of picking up tumbled stones from the floor and tidying away fallen leaves. No rubbing and scrubbing, no polishing and dusting. This was a far more sensible way of living than within the confines of a house which ate up time and energy with its constant demands for cleanliness. Who needed ornaments? The Cheviot hills were a better sight than a mantelpiece full of china whigmaleeries.

When I was hungry I ate raw turnips, crab-apples or any berries I could find. Sugar-ally was my favourite beverage when I could get it. A liquorice-stick shaken up in a lemonade-bottle filled with water from the burn. It never slaked my thirst but it had a nice tangy taste and left me with a blue-black moustache.

'Man-lassie! ye'll puzzen yoursel',' the herd warned me when he wandered into my precincts, but he was not averse to taking a swig himself, wiping away the froth from his face with the back of his hand.

Jock warned me, too, if the bull was on the hill and likely to roam in my direction.

'Watch oot! He's no' to be trusted, the ugly brute!'

True, the bull was no beauty with a ring through his nose and a vicious glint in his eye, but I thought it a pity that nobody had a kind word for him. Poor thing, he was just a beast. Maybe he only wanted to play.

I changed my mind one day when I had ignored the herd's warning and the 'ugly brute' came charging at me. I was gathering an armful of dried bracken and branches of whin-bushes in the hope of lighting a blaze in the great fireplace big enough to roast an ox.

When I heard the bull bellowing behind me I dropped my bundle, took to my heels and scaled up the castle wall at the double. I had to sit there for hours, marooned, while the bull pawed the ground and roared up at me. Perhaps he was only making friendly noises. 'Come down and play.' But I felt it safer to stay where I was till Jock and his dogs came to rescue me.

'Man-lassie! I tell't ye. Wull ye never lairn?'

It was disheartening to find how often grown-ups were right and how they relished pointing out my mistakes. 'See how clever we are,' they seemed to be saying. 'We know best. We never do anything wrong.' How much better I would have liked them if they did!

The most unwelcome guests who came prowling round my castle were the archaeologists. The diggers, I called them. They were an earnest group of men and women who came from goodness-knows-where, carrying picks, shovels, spades, and little hammers.

I had no idea what they were looking for but whatever it was they never found me. I hid up the great chimney and stayed there as still as a statue while they poked around the place as if it belonged to them. Sometimes they gathered in an excited huddle and I concluded they must have unearthed some ancient relic. More often it was only a biscuit-tin or one of my discarded sugar-ally bottles.

I had a hidden hoard myself but I was not going to let on to the diggers. In the course of my residence in the keep I had discovered many old bones, stones, weapons, and cooking-utensils which I kept in a hidey-hole up on the look-out tower near one of the crow's nests. It was my own private museum. For all I know it is there to this day.

I hated when the hunt came galloping across the hillside in full cry giving chase to a frightened fox, though it was a splendid sight. It was exciting to hear the huntsman's horn and to see the pink coats, but the blood-curdling baying of the dogs filled my heart with horror. If the huntsman had lost the trail and stopped to ask me the way I would have pointed in the wrong direction, though the hounds would not have been so easily foiled.

'Blood!' they seemed to be saying. 'We want blood!' With their noses to the ground they could pick up the scent and ruthlessly follow their prey to the end, though, thank goodness, I was never in at the kill. We had a fox head hanging on the wall near the front door. He seemed to grin down on everyone who came in, smiling even in death.

It was wonderful playing houses in the keep when the weather was sunny. Not so pleasant if a sudden storm sprang up. I had an old waterproof sheet under which I could shelter from the rain, for the roof – what was left of it – leaked so badly that it was almost wetter inside than out.

When the wind howled round the crumbling ruin there was an added danger. Sometimes a rattle of loose stones blew down on my head and I had to dodge out of the way to avoid being hit, not that I always succeeded, and had plenty of bumps and bruises to show for it but it was all part of the fun.

What must it have been like, I wondered, in the days when the keep was occupied as a fortress? I tried to picture it with its roof on and great logs crackling up the chimney, with always someone watching from the look-out tower? Would there be children there, like me, playing houses?

Near at hand there was a purling burn, the small Jed, where I sometimes went to wade when the weather was hot. I had to slither down a craggy bank to reach it, past a mysterious cave where the reivers used to hide their loot in bygone days. I seldom ventured in for it was full of eerie rustles. A badger might came darting out of the darkness or a large bird fly in my face. Creepy-crawlies of all descriptions made their homes there, and there was no knowing who else. A bogle maybe or a strange monster with two heads.

The Jed was a fascinating winding burn, like the one in J. B. Selkirk's poem.

> Ah, Tam! gie me a Border burn
> That canna rin withoot a turn,
> An' wi' its bonnie babble fills
> The glens amang oor native hills.
> How men that ance have kent aboot it
> Can live their efter-lives withoot it
> I canna tell, for day an' nicht
> It comes unca'd-for to my sicht.

True enough, it is the river Jed that I can see with my inward eye, especially on sleepless nights when my mind roams back over half-forgotten childhood scenes.

In every season of the year there was something different to see on its banks. In spring and summer a profusion of ferns and wildflowers grew there: bluebells, primroses, marsh-marigolds like little yellow butter-balls, and sturdy reeds which I pulled up and plaited into pigtails after eating the juiciest parts of the stems. If I hunted long enough I could find small wild strawberries which tasted sharp and delicious.

In autumn the russet-red and golden leaves of the old trees, relics of the original Jedforest, made a splash of brilliant colour against the sky. Later, when they blew off and lay like a thick carpet, I liked to rustle through them almost up to the knees in bright leaves. Even in winter the bare branches looked elegant, stretching graceful arms from their gnarled trunks. There was always something worth looking at, at any time.

Colourful birds, too, to be seen at the waterside. Kingfishers with brilliant plumage skimming down from the sky, water-wagtails hopping from stone to stone, a long-legged heron standing pensively in midstream. They all seemed to live intense self-contained lives, not grouping together like humans but pursuing their own private ploys. I wondered if the different species could understand each other's language and if they ever greeted each other in passing.

In stormy weather the water came tumbling down from the hills in a hurry, drowning the buttercups on the bank and carrying some strange objects before it. Sometimes an old bedstead came floating by or a dead sheep. Tin cans, empty bottles, broken umbrellas, straw hats, bicycle-tyres and old boots all came whirling by as if playing follow-my-leader. Some of them stuck going round the bend and I could either rescue them if they were worth retrieving or give them a push to send them on their way. It reminded me of a song my father used to sing.

> The burn was big wi' spate,
> An' there cam' tummlin' doon
> Tapsulteerie the half o' a gate,
> An auld fish hake, an' a great muckle skate,
> An' a lum hat wantin' the croon.

Now and then I found something useful: an old tennis-ball, a mouth-organ, a tin soldier, or a cracked teapot which came in handy when playing houses. I was always hopeful that I might find real treasure, perhaps a ruby ring, but the nearest I came to it was when I fished out a sliver bracelet and found it was made of wire.

There were two ways of getting across the Jed. Three in

winter when the river was frozen and one could just walk across the ice. One was by stepping-stone, but the stones were so unsteady and set at such awkward angles that I often over-balanced and tumbled into the water.

The other was even more adventurous and had that spark of danger that appealed to me so that I had to goad myself on before I dared attempt it. At one point a decrepit wooden gate hung across the water. The water-gate, we called it. It had been put there to prevent cattle from wandering down the river, and was suspended from a stout spar, like a great log of wood. The thing to do was to climb up on top of the gate and sidle across while clinging hand-over-hand to the overhead spar.

The old gate made creaking noises and swayed backwards and forwards at each of my sideways steps. Often I got stuck in the middle too terrified to make another move especially if the burn was in spate. I had to hound myself on inch by inch till I reached the other side.

This was theoretically a short-cut to the little village of Camptown, though in reality it would have been quicker to go round by the road, though not half the adventure. Once across, I could scramble up another steep bank and arrive, breathless and bedraggled, at the back of my granny's house. I would visit her, do some odd jobs, have a dip into the sweet-tin, and, if I had been sent on a message, go to Bella Confectionery's to make my purchases.

The return journey was the most difficult if I had two or three packages to carry. Perhaps sugar, salt, or tea. The trick was to toss them one by one across the Jed at its narrowest point, always hoping the bags would not burst, before attempting to cross myself. Alas! a bag often did burst, and once a tin of mustard fell short and went floating away, like the lum hat, in the company of a bottomless pail and an old Wellington boot.

I would get what-for when I reached home, but this time

I knew I would deserve it. I did not always understand the reasons why grown-ups meted out punishment, though I was always aware of the power they had to rule my life, and longed for the day when I could make my own decisions.

Often I sensed that their psychology was wrong. Why, for instance, could they not just let me sit still and think, if I wanted to, instead of rousing me out of my reverie. 'Come on! Don't sit mumping there. Can't you go and *do* something?'

Even at an early age children need to withdraw within themselves without constantly being harassed with questions. 'What are you doing? Where have you been? Why are you sitting still?'

It seems difficult when one is young to please one's elders. Either we are too noisy or too quiet. What are we to do? Perhaps this is when we first start learning to deceive, to put on masks and become not ourselves but what our elders expect us to be: perfect replicas of our fathers or mothers.

I was lucky in that my parents had others to think about and I could often escape their notice. I was good at the game, pretending not to hear, or vanishing from sight when I thought they were about to pounce on me.

Above all, I could retreat to my crumbling castle. Then suddenly I would have enough of the long loneliness. When the sun began to fade and strange shadows crept across the hillside I would shiver and think of the pleasures of human companionship. All that I had tried to avoid before. I felt a sense of emptiness, more than mere hunger, and ran away from the keep with never a backward glance, straining my eyes for a sight of the lamplight shining from the kitchen window.

Maybe I would get a slap from Jessie when I went in but I would even enjoy that. There would be a dinner-y smell from the pots and pans on the fire and all the noise and bustle of the household going on around me. I would no longer be a lone bairn but part of a family.

This, at that moment, was what I wanted most.

How can we hope to recapture that magic moment, the split-second almost, when we made the greatest discovery of our young lives?

We could read!

It came to me like a bolt from the blue. One moment I was painfully trying with prodding finger to decipher the a's and b's in my lesson-book. The next moment the revelation happened. I could form the letters into words.

They were inane enough words. 'The cat is fat. The dog can run. The cow says "Moo".' But at least I was reading. The door was opened wide; where might it lead to?

Having learned a new skill I could never get enough of it. From then on I became, and have remained, an obsessive gobbler-up of books. The sight of printed words, of hand-writing even, had always fascinated me as a child. Now that I could make some sense out of the symbols I wanted to rush forward and devour everything that had ever been written. Never mind the long words. I could skip over them and still get some of the meaning. Even the staid *Scotsman* was fodder for me. If I could find nothing better I would try to read the Fat-Stock Prices or the Births, Marriages and Deaths. Anything as long as it was words.

I soon tired of Henny-Penny and the insipid creatures in the school reading-book. We seldom had new ones. To save expense school books were handed down like old clothes from one member of the family to another, till they became tattier and tattier, with torn pages and everyone's scribbles in the margins.

The stories in the reading-book were far too feeble to satisfy my thirst. I wanted real books with real stories, but alas! there was no school library. How I envy the school-children of today with their bright classrooms and the wealth of books at their command. A new one to read every day of their lives, if they like!

At the village school there was only one shelf which contained the entire library, such as it was. Ten dusty volumes of *Tales of the Borders*. To the master's sarcastic amusement I borrowed them one by one and galloped through them, not really understanding the contents. They were all much of a muchness. Bloodthirsty tales of dreadful deeds at dead of night, of headless horsemen, dismembered bodies, and ghostly warriors. They gave me little more than mental indigestion, but at least I learned some new words if not how to pronounce them. Fidelity, for instance, which for long enough I thought of as fiddle-ty.

There were books at home but not enough. I raced through everything in the bookcase, understanding little of *A Journey to the Amazon* and less of *The Life of Wellington*. I read my brother's *Robin Hood*, my sister's *School Friend* and my own *Chatterbox* over and over again. Re-reading was, and still is, one of my favourite occupations like getting to know an old friend even better. Sometimes I would read a book right through to the end and then start straight off again at the beginning, always finding something new that I had missed before.

The few children's books in the house, belonging to a previous generation, were all very sad and holy, with titles like *Jessica's First Prayer*. I often wished I could find one about a bad child like myself, but the heroines were all too good to live and, indeed, most of them died young.

Reading and guilt were mixed up in my mind. I still have the feeling that a grown-up will come along and snatch the book out of my hand. Jessie, particularly, made me feel I was committing a crime.

'Tak' your heid oot that book an' do something useful,' she would say.

Reading was bad for the eyes, bad for the health, bad for the mind. 'Filling your head with nonsense,' according to my elders. Especially when they discovered me reading the servant-lasses' novelettes: cheap paper-covered trash with pictures – innocent enough – on the outside. I did not think much of them myself, they were just something to read, but they had too much love in them. I was all for handsome princes marrying beautiful princesses, but the novelettes were on a lower level with too much sloppy talk in them.

Doing something useful meant knitting or sewing. I was never any good at hemming and back-stitching. The only garment I ever finished was a camisole that would have fitted a giantess, dotted with drops of blood from my fingers. Knitting was more to my liking, especially when I could combine it with reading. I soon learned the trick of plaining and purling with a book propped up on the arm of an easy-chair. In that way I could continue to fill my head with nonsense while satisfying the grown-ups that I was not wasting my time. *The Wide Wide World* and turning the heel of a sock always go together in my mind.

I dropped the odd tear along with the odd stitch for I liked reading hardship stories – as I believe most young people do – where the emotions of fear or pity could be stretched to the full. *The Little Match-Girl* always brought a lump to my throat though I knew it was only a story. Later, I wallowed in *Hard Times*, longing to help Dickens' characters over their difficulties (though somehow I could never swallow Little Nell), and if I could have re-written the books, I would have given everyone a happy ending.

What power the writers had! They could kill off a character at the stroke of a pen, or cure someone lying sick of a dangerous illness. They could carry the reader over the seas – even under the water, in the case of Jules Verne – and make him laugh or cry. I began to long for the same power; not only to read books but to write them.

There was no planned reading for me in my young days. Every Christmas I was given an Annual, take it or leave it. The school stories were remote from anything I had experienced, with their dormitories, tuck-boxes, hockey-matches, and gym-tunics. None of the characters seemed to come to life or to speak like a real human being.

I preferred the stories in the Bible. I could believe in Daniel in the Lions' Den and Joseph and his Brethren; but even at an early age I puzzled about Jesus. Where had he been during all the missing years? Why had he not begun his ministry earlier and had more time on earth to teach and heal? The Bible bewildered me in many ways, yet it was a fascinating book to read no matter how bamboozled I was by its strange language.

Nothing could surpass the thrill of opening a new book I had not read before. This happened on rare occasions, mainly when there was a sale somewhere in the district. A roup. My parents were faithful attenders of such affairs, where farm-implements and household goods were being sold off, and invariably bought something to bring home: a kitchen chair, a picture, a clock, or a jelly-pan. Better still, a bundle of books. 'Miscellaneous volumes: one-and-sixpence.'

Sometimes they had to be purchased in a lot, along with cracked ornaments, an old kettle, even a wooden cradle; and if they had been nuggets of pure gold I would not have welcomed them half as eagerly.

Black Beauty came out of the cradle and so did *Easy Geometry*, which I thought was a very dry read and not a bit easy at all, but I had to take the good with the bad. Often, alas! I was left high and dry in the middle of a sentence when I discovered that pages were missing. I was full grown before I knew that Robinson Crusoe had been rescued from the desert island, and Oliver Twist's early life was a mystery to me for years.

From reading to writing was the next natural step though spelling was still a hurdle. At school the master had a passion for parsing which took all the fun out of reading and could kill a sentence stone dead. But at least he started us off on 'imaginative writing' though his own imagination fell flat when it came to inventing subjects for our essays. If only he had let us choose our own! His were deadly dull.

'Scotland's Heritage' – whatever that meant – was one of his stand-bys; and 'A Day at the Seaside', which was also beyond our ken since none of us had ever been there. Or, 'My Favourite Hobby'.

We all chewed despairingly at our pencils and keeked at each other's jotters to see if there was anything worth copying. One shepherd-boy, after pondering over the subject for ages, wrote laboriously, 'I have not got a hoby.' End of essay!

I set down my thoughts as well as I could, making up hobbies for the sake of filling a few lines. They were so improbable that Auld Badly-Heid glowered at me after reading my efforts and barked out, 'Rubbish!' Collecting skeletons, converting salt into gold by means of magic, and flying round the world on invisible wings were hardly hobbies he could swallow.

'Rubbish!' he kept repeating. But sometimes – a fate worse than death – he would call me out and make me stand up in front of the class to read out the rubbish, with everyone sniggering at me and the boys making me their target for inky pellets. I was never sure whether the master meant it as a compliment to me or an Awful Warning to the rest of the pupils, but I considered it nothing more than a penance.

At that period in my life I had two fixed ambitions. One was to keep a sweet-shop, like Bella Confectionery's, without any customers. What bliss it would be to help myself from every bottle and jar, to weigh out caramels and fill three-cornered pokes with toffee, knowing that I could eat my way through the lot without paying for them.

The other was to be let loose to browse in an enormous room filled from floor to ceiling with books, without anyone there to tell me to go and do something useful. Perhaps I was visualizing a place I had never yet seen but where in later years I would spend many a happy hour. A public library. Even today I tremble with excitement every time I enter the portals of one of these book-palaces. And, going into anyone's house, I never notice the carpets or the furnishings. Only the contents of the bookcases.

We had, of course, a real author in the Borders. Sir Walter Scott. But he was dead long ago.

'Ay! he was a great man, Wattie,' the master used to tell us, as if he had known him personally. Rabbie, too, had been a grand fellow, though some of his poetry was best not repeated. It was safer to stick to Anon, who was purer.

The great revelation of reading meant so much to me that I wanted to pass it on to everyone else, as if I alone had made the magical discovery. I even tried to smit Jock-the-herd with my enthusiasm.

'Do you never read?' I asked him one day when he was leaning against a dyke staring at the sheep and preparing to smoke his pipe. This was no straightforward operation. The pipe had to be scraped out first with a knife, then the herd took a tin box from his pocket and began the careful process of filling the bowl, pressing down the tobacco with his thumb, before starting another search through his pockets for a box of matches. It took two or three attempts, more on a windy day, before the tobacco began to glow. Once it was going to his satisfaction Jock covered the bowl with a small metal lid with air-holes in it, and at last the deed was done.

'Read!' he said, puffing out a great gust of smoke. 'I tak' a look at the papers noo an' then.'

'But would you not like to read a book?' I persisted. The papers had nothing in them but bad news and politics.

'A book? Man-lassie, what wad I want wi' a book?

I tried to tempt him with *What Katy Did* but he was not on for it. 'If it had something to dae wi' sheep-dip, I micht gie it a try. But I'm no' fond o' stories.'

Jessie on the other hand liked what she called a good book. A sentimental story with a happy ending. Especially one written by Annie S. Swan who supplied wholesome serials for the *People's Friend.* But Jessie would only indulge in reading after she had completed every useful task. If she had finished the darning and mending she would pick up her story and settle down to read a few pages, tut-tutting now and again if she disapproved of any of the characters.

Sometimes she discussed the stories with me, as if all the people in them were alive.

'Fancy Mary Graham no' seein' through thon chap! I never liked the soond o' him frae the beginnin.' I kent he was efter her siller. She'll be better-aff in the hinner-end wi' her cousin John. Though, mind ye, I'm no' keen on cousins gettin' mairret. . . .'

Jessie would listen to me, too, often at milking-time while I gave her a precis of what I was reading. I remember giving her chapter and verse about *Uncle Tom's Cabin* and trying to arouse her compassion over the injusticies to the poor slaves. Neither of us had ever seen a coloured person in our lives. 'Though I've a guid idea,' Jessie told me, 'for I ance saw the Darkey-Troupe, but they were only blackened for the nicht.'

I often wondered how words got on to the printed page. I knew they had originally come out of someone's head, Annie S. Swan's or Mr Charles Dickens', but that was as far as I could visualize the process. In my own writings I copied the style of whatever book I was reading at the time. *Lorna Doone, East Lynne*, or a pathetic story about a Victorian child who was always ailing and who addressed her parent as 'Darling Papa'. I even made up Hiawatha-like poetry about nothing in particular which went rambling on without ever coming to a full-stop.

> See the shepherd, noble shepherd,
> With his dogs called Jed and Jess. . . .

My literary talents were sometimes put to the test when we played a communal game of Consequences round the dining-room table on a winter evening when company was present.

The others could always tell which were my contributions because of the bad spelling and the fact that I had not the gumption to disguise my handwriting.

Once, however, I was surprised to receive a word of commendation from the minister when we each tried to compose a verse in praise of the Borders. My father, I remember, wrote a funny one, but mine was dead serious.

> The Borders is a bonnie place,
> I wish that you could see it.
> England and Scotland look on its face,
> For ever blessèd be it.

'Not bad,' said the minister, patting me on the head, 'for a wee lassie.'

'She'll likely have copied it from somewhere,' said my mother, cutting me to the quick.

It was soon after this, I think, that I decided to run away from home. Nobody understood me – the age-old plaint – but I would make them sorry.

It was a pity it was not snowing at the time for my head was full of *Lucy Gray*, and I pictured my distraught parents following my footsteps through the snow and finding my frozen body. What remorse they would feel, and how I would gloat, gazing down on them from heaven!

But it was only raining. I set off in the direction of the Heathery Hill. I had never been beyond it. Indeed, there was nothing beyond except another hill and then another, all part of the Cheviot range. Not even a rainbow in the sky to follow.

It was a rough trudge and the backs of my legs soon began to ache. Before long I had an empty feeling in my stomach for I had not thought of bringing anything with me to eat. Gradually I began to long for the comforts of home and to forget why I was running away.

I sat down on the wet heather to consider my position. There were two alternatives. To run away, or to return home.

I looked back at the faraway farmhouse with the smoke curling up from the chimneys, and then at the bleak hills ahead. There was little doubt which was the more attractive.

It was the thought of a book that turned the tables. I was in the midst of reading *David Copperfield* at the time and could visualize it lying on the kitchen dresser where I had left it. It would be a pity not to finish the story, sitting comfortably on the rug before the fire.

No one had noticed I was missing. When I crept in, wet and weary, everyone was bustling about in the usual manner. *David Copperfield* was waiting for me on the dresser, and my mother was dishing up succulent kippers from the frying-pan.

'Take off your wet coat and sit in to your supper,' she said, giving me a passing smile.

How good and kind she was, I thought, changing my mind in midstream as I so often did. What on earth had made me want to run away? Never had a kipper tasted better nor my family seemed more lovable. How lucky I was to have such a good home and such an interesting book to read!

7. Suffer the Little Children

I used to stare at it every Sunday in the church. The stained-glass window opposite our pew. It was all dark reds and purples, making up a composite picture of the Good Shepherd in a long white robe, like granny's goonie, carrying a woolly lamb under his oxter. In his hand he held a long crook, like Jock-the-herd's, and at his feet sat some children looking up at him. They, too, were dressed in nightgowns.

The words underneath were difficult to read, but at last I deciphered them. *Suffer the little children.*

Who was doing the suffering, I wondered? The Shepherd or the children? Maybe the lamb? Sometimes the sun came shining through the window, brightening up the colours on the glass and transforming the Good Shepherd into a glorious angel all glowing with light. It was a great contrast to the stark kirk with its hard seats and its air of Sabbath gloom. I knew well enough who was suffering in our pew!

There was no hope of staying away unless one was seriously ill. From his vantage-point in the pulpit the minister noticed everything and counted all the heads, almost like marking the register. Even when he was praying he could look through his fingers and keep an eye on us.

Every Sunday rain or shine I had to walk the same two miles that I trudged to school during the week. But how diffcrent it was on Sundays. For one thing I was dressed in my best. I thought it strange that Jesus always wore plain garments, yet we had to tosh ourselves up when we went to worship him. In my case it was my good coat, buttoned boots, hat with elastic under the chin, muff hanging round my neck, hair tightly plaited, all adding to the general feeling of restraint. For another, the rest of the family was with me, the grown-ups keeping a stern eye in my direction and calling me to heel now and again, like a disobedient puppy.

No rushing from one side of the road to the other. No jumping in and out of the ditch. It had to be a straightforward walk with no deviations. Especially on the main road whcn wc met in with other church-goers who engaged my parents in conversation, all matter-of-fact and dull.

Sometimes they looked at me and said, 'My! isn't she growing?' as if I was a plant in a pot.

I used to scowl back at them and think of all the things I would have liked to say. 'My! aren't you getting fat? That hat doesn't suit you.'

Even when I met in with other children we never dared kick stones or indulge in any of our everyday ploys. The boys looked uncomfortable in their tight breeks and the girls self-conscious in their Sunday hats with gloves on their hands. Suffer the little children.

The solemn sound of the kirk bell always made my heart sink to my buttoned boots. So did the sight of the churhyard with its moss-covered stones, some leaning sideways. There were always a few rooks cawing a dismal dirge from the nearby trees. (Where were the cheerful birds who chirped at me on week-days?) And at the door stood the elder in his decent black suit, guarding the plate and looking as solemn as if this was the Day of Judgement.

It might be the gamekeeper or a neighbouring farmer, but they could have been made of stone. No friendly chat, only a brief nod as I extracted my penny from my muff and placed it in the plate. Then in I went to the encircling gloom.

We all marched with measured tread to our pew, took our places and bowed our heads for a moment of silent prayer. I never knew what to pray for except that I wished it was all over. Usually I peered through my fingers to see who was already there. The Good Shepherd, of course, and Jessie, Joo-anne and Jock-the-herd who sat across from us, all three bolt upright with set expressions on their faces. The Sabbath look.

It was only when he was in church that I could see Jock was as bald as a billiard-ball. For the rest of the week his fore-and-aft bonnet was never off his head, but on Sundays he wore a bowler which he was forced to take off before entering the sacred portals. As he sat down in his pew after the exertion of walking, the steam rose up in a little wisp from the top of his bald pate, like a volcano about to erupt. I watched it, fascinated, till it died away.

There was plenty to watch as the congregation came trickling in, some with shoes that squeaked with every step they took. I knew everybody's Sunday hats and coats. Bella Confectionery had a velvet hat with artificial cherries that looked good enough to eat. Mrs Scott wore a fur tippet round her neck, like a little weasel with its tail clasped in its mouth. My mother wore a veil with little dots on it, and sometimes a feather boa: and the minister's wife always turned up her costume-jacket to keep it from creasing against the back of the pew.

Some of the men carried lum hats as a kind of status symbol, and walking-sticks or rolled umbrellas which they left in the stand at the end of their pews. They all wore tight collars and kept on their overcoats for the kirk was cold as well as gloomy. But we were not here for comfort, but to consider our sins.

There was an air of expectancy when we heard the side-door leading up to the laird's Gallery being opened. If the laird himself was in residence at the Big Hoose he sometimes brought his guests to worship in their special eyrie above our heads, even though they might be of different denominations. I remember how surprised I was when I saw one of them going down on his knees to pray. But he was a Pisky.

Pisky, Pisky, A-men!
Doon on your knees an' up again.

We were Presbies and much more rigid.

Presby, Presby, dinna bend!
Always sit on your hinnerend.

The laird's party always entered last, like royalty; and when gentry was present the collection went up by leaps and bounds. Sometimes even a golden sovereign would be found in the plate. Piskies paid a lot for their religion.

It was not the done thing to look up at them but how could we help it? When we heard the rustling and the footsteps we tried not to turn our heads, but in the end everybody did. Often I saw Sir James Barrie perched up there like a little gnome, and Lady Somebody swathed in furs with a fascinating mauve-coloured toque on her head. They were all blue-blooded. Even some related to royalty. Breathing the same air as us!

After ringing the church bell, Wattie the beadle went round to the vestry and came marching in to the body of the kirk, bearing the big bible. He mounted the pulpit stairs, set the book in its place, then descended the steps and disappeared through the side-door leading to the vestry. After a decent interval he came back again with the minister behind him dressed in his long robes and with his hands clasped piously in front of him. Wattie waited till His Reverence was safely ensconced in the pulpit, then hurried up the little stairs and shut him in. It was a ritual that never varied Sunday after Sunday. I wished that either he or the minister would tumble down the stairs once in a while, just to create a diversion. Or that the minister would shut in Wattie by mistake.

The only variation was when the minister had to read out the announcement of a forthcoming wedding. Calling the banns. It was no surprise; everyone already knew about it, but it was exciting to hear it confirmed from the pulpit.

'There is a purpose of marriage between George Rutherford, bachelor, and Mary Briggs, spinster of this parish.'

The spinster sat in her pew with bowed head as if ashamed of herself, and the bachelor turned bright pink when his name was mentioned.

Miss Todd played the American organ with great gusto, pedalling away for dear life as if she was riding her bicycle. Some of the hymns were good-going shout-y ones like 'Onward Christian Soldiers' and 'Shall We Gather at the River?'; but the psalms and paraphrases were dreary and went on for-ever-and-ever. It was difficult enough looking them up with their confusing Roman numerals; and I could make little sense of the phrasing of some of the verses.

> That there is not a God the fool
> Doth in his heart conclude.

Even with all my lessons in parsing it was not easy to extract the meaning from such ramblings.

Iniquities I must confess
Prevail against me do;
But as for our trans-gress-ions
Them purge away shalt thou.

The psalmists seemed to take it for granted that we were all wicked and full of trans-gress-ions. Only God was good.

Goodness knows what Jock-the-herd made of the psalms, but he mouthed the words like everyone else. Except Joo-anne who, being hard of hearing, just stared into space and kept her lips resolutely closed. My father was the best singer in our pew, though sometimes he did not bother about the words and just sang 'la-la'.

Miss Todd set the pace, trying to keep the congregation from droning and dragging. Now and again she pulled out stops with strange words like *Vox Humana*, or pushed them in, and pedalled faster to get up more steam. But if we were walking through death's dark vale she would quieten us down to a sad whisper. The last verse was usually the loudest and most cheerful, promising us a place near the golden throne beside all the bright and glorious spirits clad in white array, and ending with a triumphant 'A-A-A-A-MEN!'

During the Long Prayer the minister gave God his orders, after first thanking him for our daily bread and other bounteous gifts.

'Help the sick, O Lord. Comfort the bereaved. Look after the poor. Bless our sovereign King and all the royal family. Give wisdom to those in authority over us. And finally, have mercy on us, thy humble servants.'

I wondered if God was sorting it all out and writing it down in a golden jotter, and if he would manage to get through it all. It would take him ages. And what about all the other prayers that were winging their way to heaven at the same time? How could he listen to the lot and do what every preacher told him? But, of course, God was omnipotent and it would be no bother to him to do a hundred things at once.

It was more difficult for me to turn up the right chapter in the Bible when the minister gave out the readings. Revelations was easy enough being right at the end, and Genesis being right at the beginning; but Ezra or Malachi were nuisances. Sometimes I was still wetting my finger and rustling through the pages when the minister said 'Amen' and shut the big bible. Often I just pretended I was at the right place and let the great mouthfuls of words wash over me.

It was a strange language but I liked listening to it. 'Verily, verily, saith the Lord'. The *Blesseds*, too, had a fascination for me, but I did not really listen intently enough to sort out the meaning, except when it was a parable which told a story. Though sometimes I tried to guess which sentence the minister would single out for his text. It would be somewhere in the two readings, from the old Testament or the New, and he would go over it again and again during the course of his long sermon.

It might be 'Blessed are the meek', or 'Six days shalt thou labour', or something about the Children of Israel. Never anything about the Children of Edgerston. It would have been nice, I thought, if he had spoken about something local for a change. But, of course, we were not in the bible.

The only time the minister mixed the secular with the sacred was when he stood up with a little bit of paper in his hand and said, 'I have the following Intimations;' but often they, too, were about church affairs.

'A retiring-collection will be taken for the Schemes of the Church' or 'Will the office-bearers stay behind after the service for a short meeting in the vestry?' But occasionally it was something special, like the announcement of a Sunday-School picnic or a Sale-of-Work. 'All contributions welcomed by the stall-holders.'

When he gave out the text there was a great rustling and coughing as everyone settled down, with looks of resignation on their faces, to thole the long discourse as best they could.

This was the moment when I longed to get up and bolt out of the door, but we were all prisoners, trapped in the House of God.

Some stared fixedly at the preacher and even cupped their ears not to miss a single word. Others slunk further back in their seats and unashamedly went to sleep. Jessie, upright as ever, never batted an eyelid, but sometimes she gave a jolt and I knew fine she was sleeping with her eyes wide open. But if Jock-the-herd slumped by her side she was always quick to rouse him with a sharp dig in the ribs.

At the start of the sermon there was much furtive passing of sweets along the pew. I was allowed one pandrop which I could either suck to make it last or scrunch and get rid of in one quick swallow. After that there was nothing left to hope for, unless the Maiden Ladies who sat behind me gave me a gentle tap and passed over an extra-strong in a gloved hand. This was a flat brown sweet so nippy that it brought tears to my eyes, but it kept me warm, if nothing else.

Jock once took out his pipe by mistake and was about to strike a match when he realized the error of his ways, but it was not often we had such a diversion.

Like everything else about the service, the sermon followed a rigid pattern so that there was never any surprise in it. The minister always divided it into heads: Firstly, Secondly, Thirdly, and Finally (Oh! how I longed for Finally)! He began quietly, then gradually worked himself up till he reached a crescendo, flailing his arms about and declaiming passionately about heaven and hell.

At times he seemed in a perfect fury of rage, very unlike the genial man who danced the polka in our kitchen when he visited us; and I was reminded of a story my father told me about the little boy's first visit to church. He watched in awe as the preacher thumped the bible, roaring like a bull at the congregation. Then he cooried closer to his father for protection and whispered: 'Faither! what'll we dae if he gets oot?'

It was strange to hear the minister addressing us all as 'My brethen'. Including Mary-Anne, and even me. Why not 'sistern'? I wondered. Usually I never listened at all except to keep a check on the heads, in the hope that he was nearing the end. I just stared at the Good Shepherd and thought my own thoughts, trying not to catch the eye of any of my school-friends who were inclinded, through sheer boredom, to make funny faces at me.

Bob (the braggart) had a habit of holding his breath for as long as he could and then expelling it in a great gusty sigh. I used to watch him getting redder and redder in the face and wondered if he would explode. It must have been a penance for such a stirring laddie to sit still for so long without even a catapult to play with.

Yet, though I never understood the sermon and considered it a wearisome endurance test, I felt there was something satisfying about the enduring words that went echoing round the church. Words I would never forget. Lo! I am with you always.

But the word I liked to hear best was Amen at the end of the sermon. There was a great rustle of relief when the minister finally uttered it and sat down with his face buried in his hands, before getting up to announce the last paraphrase. We sang it with great abandon, happy in the knowledge that release was at hand, and could hardly wait for the benediction before hurrying out into the open air. If God was watching he must have thought us very anxious to escape from his presence.

Never had fresh air seemed fresher than when we emerged from the kirk. I used to gulp it down in mouthfuls as if I was drinking wine.

We stood back respectfully at the door till the laird and his party took their departure. Sometimes he shook hands with my parents and introduced the Honourable Somebody to them before driving away in his large motor with the chauffeur at the wheel.

Even then the young folk could not run about or jump as we longed to do after sitting still for so long. We still had to hang about in a decorous manner in the background while the grown-ups indulged in their after-service talk.

This 'kirkyaird clash' was part of the Sabbath ritual. Now that God had been duly praised and the Children of Israel were safely across the Red Sea, biblical matters would never be mentioned again till next Sunday. The congregation came down to earth and discussed crops, the price of lambs, or any local gossip that was going. It was the one time in the week when they all got together and could exchange news and views.

Even Jock-the-herd, with his bowler shoved to the back of his head, leaned on his walking-stick and had a crack with some neighbouring shepherds. They all seemed different in their Sunday clothes and without their dogs at their heels. They never lingered long, not having much small-talk, besides being anxious to get back to their flock and into their old clothes.

Jessie never stopped behind but marched stiffly on ahead with Joo-anne at her side, her object being, as she once confessed to me, to get home as soon as possible so that she could take off her Sunday stays.

Though the women had more to say to each other than the men, they were the ones who broke up the kirkyaird clash and moved off first, thinking of the potatoes that were to boil for the dinner and the rice-puddings to heat in the oven. The men could follow at leisure, timing their arrival home when the meal was ready to be dished up.

The last to join us was the minister himself, transformed once more into an ordinary man. We walked as far as the manse gate with him, though I kept my distance just in case he banished me to hell. It was strange after all he had said in the pulpit to hear him talking about his cabbages and leeks with never a mention of 'Verily, verily.' Did he, too, lay aside religion with his dog-collar?

I tried to keep the text in my head till we reached Granny's half-way house, for she was sure to ask me if I had listened. I had to look it up for her in her own bible which was as fascinating as the one I found in the garret, with treasures hidden between the pages. Pressed flowers, scraps of baby-hair, faded photographs, and recipes for Christmas puddings. Granny would lay down her spectacles to mark the place and read the chapter to herself after we had gone. I was allowed a dip into the sweetie-tin and we would sit and chat with her for a while before walking the last lap home.

It was a relief to get rid of my Sunday clothes, but there were still some restraints. No rushing about or playing noisy games, no thumping on the piano, no quarrelling. 'Remember it's Sunday.' Everything was muted and low key. Even the cocks and hens seemed subdued and the bubblyjock went and brooded by himself in the cart-shed.

In the afternoon we went for a walk which I hated, for it was not a brisk walk but a quiet dawdle round the headrigs. This was a ritual on many farms, for Sunday was the only day when the farmer and his family could stroll together to take a look at the progress of the crops. Sometimes my father would stop to pick off an ear of corn and rub it between his fingers, or pull up a potato and examine the roots, while I kicked my heels in the background and longed to escape to my keep.

Sometimes I did escape. If I saw the herd making his way towards the lambing-shed, I fell behind and dodged over the dyke to join him. It was comforting to see Jock back in his everyday duds. But he still looked subdued, and in deference to the day never whistled through his fingers. The Lord, it seemed, did not like sudden noises on the Sabbath.

Last thing at night we sometimes had hymns round the

piano, with my mother playing 'Jesus Loves Me' and 'By Cool Siloam's Shady Rill', but they always made me feel faintly uneasy. I would sooner have had 'Stop Your Ticklin', Jock', and went yawning to bed looking forward to the normality of Monday.

All the same, looking back I can see the value of those long and seemingly dreary Sundays, not only because we had time to think of higher things in the kirk but also time to stand back and look at ourselves. Many a decision was made in the calm of Sundays. Small ones, maybe; even, in my mother's case, to put up fresh curtains next day, or, in my father's, to start cutting the hay in the morning. I made plenty myself, but seldom put them into practice. I would be good, like Queen Victoria; I would never lose another hair-ribbon; I would start writing a book about real people. My father and mother perhaps. But were they not too ordinary to write about?

It never occurred to me that grown-ups – parents especially – had private lives of their own. They were just there as focal-points for me. That was their function in life. To be parents.

My father, I knew, had to work on the farm in his guise as the boss and that he was out and about a great deal. I did not expect him to take much notice of me, but nevertheless I thought of him as 'Father' and nothing else.

I used to boast about him at school. The songs he could sing, the musical instruments he could play, the funny stories he told, the skill he had at games. Once, when he was passing that way, he appeared at the door to fetch me home in the gig. The master let me off without a murmur and came out to laugh and chat with my father, even helping me up into my seat. Never a word about: 'Hold out your hand!'

We said nothing on the way home. My father just whistled to himself and said, 'Get on, lass!' to Flora now and again. But I felt proud to be sitting there beside him and wished that I looked older and less tousled; then I might have called him

John, as my mother did, and discussed something sensible.

Normally, however, I saw less of him than of my mother. If she was missing when I came home from school I felt a sense of grievance. Where was she? Why had she not let me know that she would be away? When would she come back? Even though she never made much of me nor I of her, I liked to know she was there. She had no right to desert me without a word.

It had never seemed possible to me that my elders had once been young. So I was amazed beyond measure one day when my mother announced that she was having a school-friend to tea. I half-expected her to be wearing a gym-tunic and carrying a school-bag on her back. But she turned out to be as old and sedate as my mother herself. Except that when the two of them started talking they grew flushed in the face and giggled like young girls. 'Do you remember?' they kept saying to each other as if playing bat-and-ball, and went off into fits of laughter as they recalled some half-forgotten episode. What fun they seemed to have had away back in their young days!

Now and then they stifled their laughter, lowered their voices, and took a quick look at me. At last my mother said impatiently, 'Can you not go away and do something?' And though I felt aggrieved at first, I suddenly realized what a nuisance it must be to have inquisitive children straining their ears to overhear conversation not intended for them.

Then one day the pattern of life changed. I had assumed that it was set for ever, but now it would never be the same again.

Father drove away in the gig and came back with a stranger, a tight-lipped efficient woman who looked at me with cold eyes and said 'Shush!' every time I encountered her. She was a monthly nurse sent by the doctor. It had all to do with a baby which he was to bring in his black bag. For some reason my mother had to go to bed and stay there for a week or two while the nurse ruled the roost, demanding boiling kettles, hot milk, and little trays. She rubbed Jessie up the wrong way.

'Her! She's mair bother than a hunner bairns. Set her up!'

The doctor brought only one bairn. A wee boy as small as a doll, with a tuft of red hair, who squealed and squirmed as if he was unhappy with his new life and wanted back where he had come from. I thought he was not worth all the bother but my mother seemed pleased enough with him. Indeed, he took up all her attention and I was pushed further into the background while the nurse rustled up and down stairs, shushing me at every step.

At long last she departed. 'Guid riddance!' said Jessie when she drove away down the road in the gig, and I felt the same sense of relief that Jessie did when she took off her restricting Sunday stays.

Life more or less shook back into normal, except that I was no longer the youngest of the family and it was obviously the new baby who mattered most. Not that I could see anything special about him. He did nothing but sleep and cry.

Then one day 'the wee man' got all dressed up in his christening-robes – they had been mine, too – and the minister came and sprinkled water on his head from the silver rose-bowl. After that the excitement died down; but I felt myself more than ever an in-between.

I spent more and more time in solitary-confinement in the garret, or running about outside at the heels of the herd. Sometimes I 'helped' the hinds at haytime or harvest, riding home in the empty bogey at the darkening with my hair full of hay-seeds and my hands stinging with thistles. Jessie used to extract them with a large darning-needle. Thristles, she called them.

But it was at the sheep-shearing – the clipping – that I really came into my own. Even Jock thought so. 'Man-lassie, we'd never get on withoot ye,' he declared, and I believed him.

It was an understood thing that I could take French leave from school and next day just tell the teacher: 'Please sir, I was at the clipping.' It was a legitimate excuse for a farm-bairn, and better to tell the truth than conjure up 'a wee touch o' scarlet-fever' as one laddie did. And got skelped for his pains.

There was a great hustling and bustling in the kitchen beforehand as preparations were made to feed all the extra mouths. A number of neighbouring shepherds, some with Geordie accents from across the Border, always rallied round to help, and Jock would later repay them by going off with his shears to do a day's clipping in return.

Great roasts of mutton were sizzling in the oven. The biggest pots and pans were filled with potatoes, turnips, and cabbage; there were apple-pies for afters and scones and cheese to fill up the corners. Half-way through the morning my father brought out drinks for the thirsty clippers, and in the afternoon they gulped down cups of tea and ate soda-scones spread with rasp or blackcurrant jam.

It amazed me to see the amount of food the shepherds could consume at one sitting and to hear their unashamed belches as they patted their stomachs at the end of a meal. They sat in to the table in their shirt-sleeves while Jessie and my mother waited on them, and accepted everything that was set before them, never refusing second helpings.

At the end of the long hard day their backs must have been almost breaking after bending over the sheep for such a long time, and their wrists must have ached from wielding the shears. Yet they showed no signs of flagging, and set off cheerfully to trudge the long miles home. I never recollect hearing any of them grumbling about their lot. Only about the government when they discussed politics. 'A lot o' eediots.'

Our own herd was 'heid bummer.' For days he had been gathering his flock together, sorting them out, and shutting them into pens near the clipping-shed. The lambs, poor things, were bewildered and set up a dismal dirge when separated from their mothers. But: 'Hoots! ye'll a' get thegither later on,' Jock assured them as he cleeked a straggler round the neck with his crook.

A long trestle-table had been set up inside the shed at which Jessie, in yet another of her roles, presided. Her job was to roll up the newly-clipped fleeces into neat bundles, which she did with a few deft twists and turns. At the end of the day a big fleecy mountain had been built up in a corner of the shed to be sold later to the wool-merchant. But not before I had climbed it and tumbled about in its soft billowy depths.

Jessie's job was important but nothing compared with mine, for without my efforts I was convinced all the sheep would have been lost.

8. Tar-baby

The herd had lit an open-air gypsy fire outside the shed beside which I hovered expectantly. Over it he had hung a little tar-pot into which I dipped the branding-iron stamped with my father's initials. Any sheep that strayed from the farm could be recognized by the initials and sent safely home. All because of me!

I stood there waiting for the call of 'Buist!' which was the shepherds' way of letting me know that they had finished fleecing the sheep and that it was now ready for branding. The moment I heard it I dipped the branding-iron into the pot and carried it carefully to the caller, waiting till he twirled it round to get rid of the excess tar and imprinted the initials on the snow-white back of the shorn sheep.

All day long I trotted backwards and forwards answering the call till my bare legs were streaked with tar and 'Buist!' echoed in my dreams that night, mingled with the click-clack of the shears, the bleating of the frightened sheep, and the sudden bursts of talk and laughter from the men.

If only I had been a musician I could have composed a concerto out of the day's sounds, all mingled together into a continuous chorus. The Sheep-shearing Symphony. But at least I noted everything and tucked the information away at the back of my mind. Perhaps I could compose a word-picture of it some day if I ever learned how to become a writer.

It was fascinating to watch how the herds caught the sheep round the neck before turning them on to their hunkers and clipping the fleeces off in one complete whole, like peeling an apple without breaking the skin. Sometimes they stopped to sharpen their shears, to ease their backs or to light their pipes. There was a great deal of chaffing and now and then a loud burst of laughter or a snatch of song. Jessie was the target for their badinage but she gave back as good as she got while still continuing at her task. Nothing could put her 'aff the stot'.

Listening to the men's heavy-handed compliments ('Ay, Jessie, ye'd mak' a guid airmfu' ') I wondered if anyone had ever been sweet on her. She was handsome enough, a lot finer-looking than some of the herds' wives. So why had she never become a wife and had bairns of her own?

Suddenly I realized how little I knew of her inner life. Or anyone's for that matter. Borderers seldom bared their souls. Jessie's especially was as closely clamped as if she was always wearing her Sunday stays. But surely she had a secret Me, the same as I had. What did she think about when she was out in the fields doing her solitary tasks? I would have liked to listen in on her private wavelength. My own thoughts never stopped, but they were all a rag-bag of rubbish which needed sorting out. Though I had little time for private conversation with myself during the clipping with so many calls of 'Buist!' directed at me.

I was surprised to find that Jock-the-herd, usually so taciturn, had a hidden sense of humour which sometimes came to the fore when he and his cronies foregathered. Obviously he needed the right spark to set him off.

'Come on, Jock,'. they would urge him. 'Gie us a guid bar.' (A bar, I discovered, was a pawky joke.)

The herd would shake his head and protest, 'I dinna ken ony.' But presently his shoulders would begin to shake with silent laughter. 'Come on, man, get it oot,' the others would encourage him. And at length Jock would launch forth into one of his bars.

'A'weel, ye see, it was like this . . .'

It was difficult for me to pick up the thread of the story with so many distracting sounds all around. The dogs barked, the sheep kept up a ceaseless plaint, and the sharp shears made staccato snips as they steadily clipped away the wool. But it did not matter. What I was waiting for was the moment when the other herds would throw back their heads and explode into great roars of laughter. There was nothing half-hearted about them. If they were going to laugh they did it all-out.

'Man Jock, that was a grand bar,' they said approvingly, and thumped him on the back, after which he relapsed into his customary silence and it took a great deal of coaxing before he could be induced to say another word.

I could sense the feeling of cameraderie amongst the men, though now and again the old rivalry reared up, more in fun than in earnest. The Scots herds would have a sly dig at the Geordies, who were able enough to defend themselves in any verbal battle. It was comical to hear them trying to mimic each others' accents and attempting to sing each others' songs.

They showed due respect to my father, the Boss, when he came out to speak to them and bring them their drinks, but there was no touching of forelocks. We were 'a' Jock Tamson's bairns'.

Their attitude to me, as I see it now, was one of amused tolerance. I had not yet learned how to counter their bantering compliments. Indeed, I believed every single word they said, so that by the end of the day my head was in danger of being turned. Unaccustomed to flattery, it was a heady experience to be told I was a wee champion, the best 'Buister' in the Borders.

It took days for me to come back to earth and to erase the tar from my legs. And every time I saw one of the shorn sheep in the fields with the initials clearly stamped on its back I felt a stab of pride. *I* was responsible for that.

But I had to take a back seat at the lamb sales.

Again, it was Jock-the-herd who was in charge. For days beforehand he had been busy with the lambs, 'dickeying them up', even to the extent of powdering their noses as if they were Beauty Queens. It was important that they should look their best and fetch a good price, not only because it was vital for my father's pocket but also as a matter of pride to Jock himself.

In the early days Jock walked all the way to Hawick where the sales were held, driving the lambs in front of him and taking his time so that they would arrive looking fresh. It was a two-day journey. At night he put up at a half-way farm where the lambs were let loose in a field, and Jock kipped down in a bothy. These were the only nights, I imagine, that he had ever spent away from home.

There are still many side-roads in the Borders, drove-roads which the shepherds used when walking their flocks to market. Later, they were whisked to Hawick in great motor-trucks, arriving according to Jock, 'A' shoogled up'. He declared that the old way was better for the beasts who reached their destination looking 'mair like theirsel's'.

Jock preferred everything to be natural. Food, for instance. He would never eat a banana. 'If the Lord had intended me to eat bananas he wad hae grown them in the Borders.'

He used to tell me of the plain fare on which many hill shepherds existed, living alone in isolated cots and doing for themselves. They used to cook a great potful of porridge, enough to last a week. While it was still hot, they poured it into an empty drawer where it solidified. Every day they hacked off a lump and carried it with them to the hirsel.

I shuddered at the thought of it but Jock said, 'Hoots! it did them nae hairrm. I've kent drainers tak' a pickle oatmeal in their pooches an' when they were hungry they just cleaned their spades, sprinkled the meal on't, added a wee tait saut an' mixed it wi' waitter frae the burn.'

The habit of spreading both butter and jam on bread or scones had not yet reached our side if the Border, though I was introduced to it on my occasional visits over the Carter Bar.

'Nane o' your heathenish customs here,' Jessie reprimanded me when I tried to follow suit. 'It's ane or the t'ither. Ye'll ruin your stamoch.'

Jock's stomach survived his visits to the sales, though he came back both mentally and physically exhausted.

'Sic a dirdum!' he would say to me, leaning against a dyke. 'Folk! They mak' mair din than sheep. Ye can keep toons!' But if the price had been good he was justifiably proud. 'Ay! we bate Stotfield an' the Tofts. No' bad.' It was a feather in his cap as well as good money for my father.

On the few occasions when I was allowed to accompany my parents, driving all the way to Hawick in the gig, sometimes with Ginger between the shafts, sometimes with Flora, it was like going into another planet. No wonder Jock was bewildered with all that was going on. At the sale-ring, the noise was deafening. Sheep bleating, dogs barking, men shouting, the auctioneer keeping up a constant flow of talk, not one word of which I could understand. At the end of the transaction the farmers gave luck-pennies to the buyers and shook them warmly by the hand. It was sad to think of the sheep going off with strangers to be packed into railway-trucks and taken away to farms 'down England'.

The great moment came when Jock weired in our own sheep and kept them going round the ring to show off their paces. I felt the tension mounting in my father as he listened to the auctioneer and watched the bidders. If it had been shepherds who were being sold instead of sheep, I would have bid for Jock. He was the best-looking of the lot, in my opinion, with his bright red face and straggly whiskers. He must have been nearing sixty, but never mind! he was my ideal of manhood.

When the last sheaves of corn were gathered in many farms in the neighbourhood held harvest-homes which they called kirns (not to be confused with the kirns in which they churned their butter). These jollifications were held in empty granaries, swept out and garnished with greenery for the occasion. A kirn was a free-for-all with everyone on the farm and their invited friends making merry. There was singing, dancing, plenty of food, drink, and 'guid bars'; and no one thought of going home till daylight.

I have a hazy recollection of attending my first kirn at a neighbouring farm, of the cocks and hens flying up into the rafters, of someone sprinkling soap-flakes on the floor to make it slippery enough for dancing, of Wat-the-Fiddler and a wee man with a melodion sitting up on a dais, of having to waltz with an enormous farmer unsteady on his pins, of falling asleep during a long Bothy Ballad and wakening next morning in my own bed, not sure if it had all been a dream.

Looking back, I often wonder if any of it was real. Not just the kirn. It is all so far away and long ago, how can the edges help being blurred like a faded photograph? And by now I have become so accustomed to conjuring up story-book characters out of my head that there are times when I doubt if Jock-the-herd ever existed outside my imagination. I have no photograph of him, but I can see him in my mind's eye as plain as porridge; and his drystane dykes are still standing on that windswept Border farm.

The creepie-stool on which I sat in the byre is tangible enough. I still have it in my possession, and the velvet pin-cushion with rusted needles sticking into it, which Jessie once gave me at Christmas. But the memories are less easy to grasp. Sometimes they fade away, overset by the more immediate happenings of here and now. Yet it only takes a small thing to bring them back. A whiff of tar and I can hear the clash of the clippers' shears and the call of 'Buist! Buist!'

If it was all a dream it was a very vivid one.

9. Jethart's Here!

The Golden Road to Samarkand could not have been more fascinating to me than the winding way that led to Jedburgh. The big town.

To me it was like getting a glimpse of the Promised Land; and the promise I made to myself was that as soon as I grew up and escaped from the mesh of childhood I would go and live there. Or, at least, to some big city where I could see something besides scenery. People in all their variety.

In those days I did not believe that there could be a town bigger than Jedburgh. I imagined it must be the capital of Scotland if not the world, with its High Street and Cannongate, its Abbey and Town Hall, its market-place and its shops. Not just one, like Bella Confectionery's, but dozens of different ones. Bakers, butchers, toyshops, newsagents, shoe-shops, sweet-shops, clothes-shops, even an Italian café which sold mouth-melting ice-cream.

It was the human beings, of course, who mattered most. I can just remember seeing Bobby the Bellman, the town-crier who lived in a mysterious place under the town-clock, emerging to cry the news, if there was anything urgent to announce.

He was a wizened little man, like a wrinkled apple, and the bell seemed too heavy for him to lug round the streets. He stopped at intervals to ring it before launching into his spiel.

'The water-rr will be turr-rrned off at four-rr o'clock for two hourrrrrrr-rrrs. You have been warr-rrr-rrned!'

His memory was not of the best. Sometimes he had his announcements written down on a piece of paper which he consulted every now and again while fending off a straggle of youngsters following at his heels. Their main objective was to snatch away the paper and put him off the stot. As Bobby grew more and more enraged and swiped out at his tormentors with his bell, his messages became more and more mixed up, till in the end he was almost crying with vexation.

When the pictures came to Jedburgh once a week it was Bobby the Bellman who went round the town calling out the title of the film to be shown. By the time he had traversed the length of the High Street 'the fill-um to be shown on Sat-urr-day' had changed its name several times, but at least Bobby always managed to convey the meaning, if not the correct title.

'It's something aboot an earrth-quake,' he would yell. 'Starr-ting at six o'clock sharr-rrp.'

The farmers had a special day when they gathered together in little groups in the market-place while their wives went round the shops. The shopkeepers welcomed the country folk, though money seldom changed hands. The grocer, the butcher and the shoemaker all knew that farmers had no regular income and were often short of ready money, so they allowed us to run up accounts and rendered their bills once a year, usually after the lamb-sales or the harvest. The bankers, too, were sympathetic to their country customers, knowing their fluctuating finances, and leniently lent them enough funds to pay their workers and tide them over the lean times.

My father, who was my banker, could always be coaxed to produce some coins from the depths of his pocket before going off to join his cronies at the market-place. With sometimes as much as threepence at my command the whole of Jedburgh was mine; but it was not the buying that mattered so much as the staring-in at all the treasures in the shop-windows.

The old name for the royal burgh and county town of Roxburghshire was Jeddart, or Jethart. 'Jethart's here!' had been the battle-cry of the men of Jedforest when they marched against their English foes. And in a history-lesson Auld Baldy-Heid had told us about Jeddart Justice. This, he explained, was the method used in Jedburgh in the old days, when a prisoner was hanged first and tried afterwards. Though this rough form of justice had happened so long ago, I was always a trifle apprehensive lest it might still apply, and took good care not to break the law, just in case.

I always spent some of my wealth on the local sweetmeats. Jethart Snails. All Border towns have their own specialities. Hawick Balls, Galashiels Soor-Plooms, Berwick Cockles. But Jethart Snails were the best!

I used to wonder why they were made in the form of snails. The reason, I was told, dated back to the time of the Napoleonic Wars, when a French prisoner was deported to Jedburgh and lodged with a family who sold toffee made in their back premises. It was the Frenchman who showed them how to twist the toffee into the shape of a delicacy from his native country; and so Jethart Snails were born, and are still being made today by the descendants of the same family. And I am still eating them!

Jedburgh, I also learned, had another link with France, this time through Mary, Queen of Scots. She had a fortress in Jedburgh – Queen Mary's House, now a museum – and it was here that she lay ill after visiting her lover Bothwell at the Hermitage, riding over moor and mire to visit him. In after years she said sadly, 'Would that I had died in fair Jedworth.'

But she did not die. It was her French chef who helped her back to health. In order to tempt her flagging appetite he concocted a dish made out of oranges or quinces, which the Queen found so palatable that it became a regular feature of her diet. It was given the name, so the story goes, of Marie-malade.

On my own more humble visits to Jedburgh my mother occasionally took me into a shop to buy a practical garment. A new coat perhaps. I was never given the chance to choose, otherwise it would have been a bright blue or a cheerful red, instead of a serviceable brown as it usually was. The main thing was that it should have a hem deep enough to let down, so there was little chance of getting rid of it for long enough.

Sometimes, too, I accompanied my mother when she went into the draper's to purchase curtain-material. She sat on a little chair by the counter while the draper, dressed in a black tail-coat and striped trousers as if he was going to a wedding, danced about from shelf to shelf, bringing bales of cloth to show her. She fingered the material, made her calculations, and he measured off the yards with his folding ruler before snipping away the stuff with a pair of sharp scissors.

After parcelling it up to be called for later, for my mother never carried any 'messages', he twirled the ends of his waxed moustaches and peered at me over the counter. I knew what was coming. Always some facetious remark, never anything sensible.

'So what mischief have you been up to lately? My! isn't she a swell in her Sunday hat! How would you like me to cut off your pigtails?' (Taking a lunge at me with his scissors.) 'Snip-snap!'

I was used to this kind of talk from my elders though I sometimes longed for them to take me seriously once in a while. Or that I could speak back and ask the draper the same kind of silly question. 'How would you like me to snip off your moustache? Snip-snap!'

I always tried to manoeuvre my mother into the newsagent's in the hope that she might buy me something to read, but usually there was nothing much on the counter except the *Jedburgh Gazette*, yesterday's *Scotsman*, or the *Christian Herald*; and if it was near Christmas I would get a preview of the new annual Santa would bring me. Little did I know there was a public library up the Castlegate or I would have made a bee-line for it, and never even bothered about the shops.

The baker's held a strange fascination for the farmers' wives, all such excellent cooks and bakers themselves. It was the difference, I suppose, that attracted them. They bought what they called fancy-bread (as opposed to plain bread), cookies, currant buns, parkins, iced cakes; and after a visit to town every frying-pan was sizzling with something tasty for supper which they had bought at the butcher's and fishmonger's. Sausages, kippers, or finnan-haddies.

The wives enjoyed encountering each other in the High Street, stopping to exchange news and swithering at the shop-windows before going in to try on a black straw or a brown velour hat. But buying a new costume was their biggest item. This was a ritual that required great thought and care, since such garments were made of everlasting material and could not be lightly discarded. Buttons were sewn on firmly, skirts were stoutly lined, hems could be turned up or let down, jackets had a timeless cut about them so that they could be worn for years no matter what the current fashion might be.

If it was to be a ready-made, it was easy enough to choose from the small selection available: the heather-mixture, the navy, the brown or the black. One farmer's wife who went all the way to Edinburgh to buy a costume was so perplexed when she saw the rows of garments on display that she returned empty-handed.

'I just could not make up my mind,' she declared. 'I was fair bamboozled. There were far too many to choose from.'

A tailor-made was a different matter, involving a long time spent in choosing the cloth, in getting measured and finally fitted. The result was a garment that was likely to last a lifetime, with each stitch firmly inserted and every pocket lined. I remember hearing someone bemoan to my mother, 'I wish to goodness my costume would wear out. I'm sick of the sight of it!'

Many things in the town surprised me; for example, that every door was shut and that each had a letter-box. Fancy! the people would never see their postie or invite him in for a cup of tea. The windows, too, were closed and curtained, with sometimes an aspidistra on display in a brass pot or a bunch of artificial flowers. They looked pretty enough but I would sooner had had some real bluebells.

Town-folk, I found, looked on us as a different breed, a little lower and less knowledgable than themselves. We were 'in from the country', not exactly savages, but people who lived strange lives at the back of beyond amongst the wild beasts.

'I couldn't stand it!' shuddered the woman in the baker's shop. 'All that dung!'

Yet they liked the pats of home-made butter and the fresh eggs brought in by the primitive country-dwellers, and were always remarking on our helathy looks.

The Jethart folk themselves seemed primitive enough when they indulged in a strange game on Handba' Day. This ritual was held every year to celebrate the coming of Candlemas. Any stranger passing through the town must have wondered if a battle had broken out, for all hell was let loose and it was a case of 'de'il tak' the hinmaist'.

What was it all about? The stories varied; but I was led to believc that the ball which was being kicked and flung around the streets represented an Englishman's head. Yet this was no longer a battle against the old enemy but between those born above the market-place and those born below. The Uppies versus the Doonies. The whole thing savoured of the Big Endians against the Little Endians. but the Jethart folk took it seriously enough and a blow-by-blow account was printed in the *Gazette* with as big headlines as if it had been the world war.

To my sorrow I was never allowed to join in, for the contestants were ruthless tacklers and a small child might get seriously hurt in the scrum. Nor were there any rules or referee. So I only saw it from a distance; and once I watched the combatants surge towards the river Jed and continue their struggle in the water, with the local swans joining in the fight, pecking out at Uppies and Doonies alike.

On normal days there was still plenty to see. Sometimes I went and gazed through the gates of the Grammar School. A forbidding building where in due course I would go to receive my Higher Education, if I managed to pass the Qualifying. It was an exciting as well as a frightening prospect. I tried to picture what it would be like to have so many classrooms and so many teachers. One for each subject, even French and Latin, instead of just Auld Baldy-Heid for everything.

Imagine coming to the big town every day! How would I get here? On horseback or on a bicycle? I had heard a rumour that they might run a school-bus if sufficient pupils from the country could be gathered together. But that was all away in the dim furture. Sufficient unto the day.

The Town Hall was the biggest building I had ever seen.

Something like Buckingham Palace, I imagined. I can remember the first time I was taken there as a special treat to see the moving pictures. This was magic indeed. It was enough to be in the Town Hall itself without the added delight of seeing a story unfolding on the flickering screen.

Sometimes there was a long hiatus when the picture broke down. The piano played louder and the children in the gallery stamped their feet and whistled through their fingers until Charlie Chaplin or Pola Negri reappeared to act out their dramas.

I hardly breathed or even sucked a snail, carried away by the entrancement of it all. The lovely ladies, the desperate men, the last-minute rescues, the loving embraces at the end. When it was over it took me a long time to come back to reality. All the way home in the gig I sat silent, thinking back over the story, wondering where the people on the screen were now and if they were living happily ever after. It was a great consolation to know that right triumphed in the end. I hoped it would be the same in real life.

If we stayed late enough in town I could watch the leerie going round the streets carrying his long pole. At his magic touch the lights sprang on one by one, transforming the grey Cannongate into a story-book street. The figures coming and going were not real people. They were characters like those in the film; and when they turned in through an open door they were not just going home to their suppers. They had gone in to rescue a lady in distress and to enact the next scene in some exciting drama.

People in towns must lead heightened lives, I thought, with such a variety of things happening all around them. How I envied them! It was not till we were bumping up the farm-road that the umbilical chord was broken and I began to look forward instead of back. Then the envy began to leave me.

Maybe it was the town-folk who were missing something in not having such cool clear air to breathe. They could not hear the hoolets hooting from the high tree or eat spare-rib for supper. Perhaps they were sitting hemmed in, in their tight little houses, longing for wider spaces and envying us who had come in from the country.

The far off hills are always greener.

10. A Day to Remember

I was not really aware of my surroundings until some far-away friends came to visit us and opened my eyes. They had come from the great city of London which seemed as remote as the moon to me and twice as romantic. So what could they find to interest them in a windswept farm with nothing to see but fields spread with dung?

Everything! Especially Auntie Gertie who went into ecstasies every time she saw a drystone dyke. It was the first time I had heard the word *picturesque* which she used to describe every single thing she saw. Even Jock-the-herd.

'Oh! look at the shepherd whistling to his dogs. Isn't he picturesque?'

Uncle Bob and Auntie Gertie were not real relations. Uncle Bob had been a childhood companion of my father's, and had taken the big step of going off to London to seek his fortune. He had found a job if not a fortune and made a 'mixed marriage'. His wife was a neat little Englishwoman with a faintly Cockney accent which I found fascinating though not always understandable.

Auntie Gertie was a new species for me to study. Jessie called her 'a dressy little body', for she was like a dainty wee parcel all beribboned and tied up with bows. She wore little boots with high heels, frilly blouses, and a belt that clasped round her neat waist with a sliver buckle. Her hair was done up in hundreds of curls, and she had more rings, brooches and bracelets than I had ever seen before.

I just wanted to look at her and hear her speaking about London. Did she know the Royal Family and what went on in Piccadilly Circus? Were there really clowns there and performing elephants? Surely there were more picturesque things to see in the big city than on our farm.

But Auntie Gertie did not think so. She went into raptures over everything: the calves – 'such sweet little darlings' – the clockers sitting on their eggs, and Jessie milking the cows. Strangely enough, she and Jessie got on a treat though neither understood a word the other said. Jessie even overlooked the fact that Auntie Gertie was foreign. 'Puir wee body! she canna help bein' English. But it's a peety she canna speak plain.'

It was funny to hear Jessie trying to teach the language to Auntie Gertie. 'Bubblyjock!' she would say in a loud voice, pointing out the turkey-cock. Then, even louder: '*Bubbly-jock!*' She had no intention of learning anything from Auntie Gertie. Let the English keep their own language to themselves.

Auntie Gertie enjoyed the wholesome farm fare and did such justice to it that before she left the silver buckle would not meet round her waist. 'Puir stervin' sowl!' said Jessie, as if nobody ever ate any meals in London.

Uncle Bob was no stranger to the Borders. He had seen everything before and was much more interested in recalling bygone days when he and my father had been involved in schoolboy escapades. They guffawed with laughter as they relived the daft days of their childhood in Jedburgh. Sometimes I sat as still as a stone overhearing their tales of the time they stole the town-crier's bell, of how they painted a pig and sent it grumphing down the High Street, and of the day they climbed the clock-tower to try to alter the time. They were still boys at heart, I could see. What a pity they had had to grow up.

Sometimes I was squeezed into the gig beside them when they were taken for a drive around the countryside. The familiar places looked different seen through the visitors' eyes. What a lot I had missed before.

A kaleidoscope of pictures whirls through my mind of that illuminating visit. Because Auntie Gertie had an insatiable curiosity about everything I learnt more about Jedburgh than I had ever known before; that Bonnie Prince Charlie had once found refuge there; that Dorothy and William Wordsworth had lodged in Abbey Close; that Sir Walter Scott had visited them and read to them his new poem, *The Lay of the Last Minstrel*; that at Twonfoot Brig there was a pool in which the old women, suspected of witchcraft, were drowned.

One day we went to see the Eildon hills close at hand, passing by the village of Ancrum coyly hiding up a side-road, and came to Lilliard's Edge where, as Auld Baldy-Heid had taught me, the battle of Ancrum Moor was fought in 1545.

We stopped there to ponder over the sad fate of Fair Maid Lilliard who gave her name to the spot where she fell in battle attempting to revenge her lover's death. Auntie Gertie had tears in her eyes as she learnt off by heart the Fair Maid's touching epitaph engraved on the tombstone.

Fair Maid Lilliard lies under this stane,
Little was her stature but muckle was her fame;
Upon the English loons she laid mony thumps,
An' when her legs were cuttit aff, she fought upon her stumps.

On another day Flora trotted us all the way to Kirk Yetholm

where the gypsies lived. My father and mother often told the story of how, in their courting days, they had gone there together to attend the crowning of the last gypsy king, Charles Faa, whose name is said to have been handed down through a long line of kings from the Pharaohs of Egypt.

Crowds came from all parts of the Borders to see the spectacle. The royal procession arrived for the ceremony by means of a 'cuddies' quick-step' in a chariot drawn by six donkeys; and the king was solemnly crowned by the archbishop (in everyday life the local blacksmith) with a brass crown studded with imitation jewels. The band played 'Wha'll be King but Chairlie?' before the cuddies conveyed the monarch and his queen back to the tumbledown cottage which was their royal residence. It had been a great occasion, with bonfires and jollifications lasting far into the night.

On our visit we did not see His Majesty who was doubtless away round the countryside hawking pots and pans, but we did see his palace and some dark-skinned bairns who may, indeed, have been members of the Royal Family. Auntie Gertie was enthralled with it all, and squeezed so much pleasure out of everything that we all enjoyed it twice as much.

'Oh! look at that!' she was constantly exclaiming. Maybe it was just a fluffy chicken or a whin bush covered with bloom. Nothing special. But because of her enthusiasm I decided, even after she and Uncle Bob had gone, to keep my eyes open and look more closely at my surroundings. Not only places, but people.

The Mrs Things at the cottages, for example, the one perpetually shaking her rag rug and the other hanging out her washing. Maybe I could start a conversation with them instead of just saying 'Hullo' and passing by.

About what?

'It-it's a nice day,' I ventured, making a bold beginning.

Mrs Thing with the rug gave me a suspicious look through a cloud of dust, and the other took a clothes-peg out of her mouth to say, 'What's nice aboot it? Ye'd better hurry or ye'll be late for the schule.'

So I hurried by without continuing the conversation. But I had taken a good look at them for the first time; and what did I see? Faded blouses, long black skirts, stout brats tied firmly round their waists, red hands roughened and wrinkled through constant immersion in cold water, round fresh faces showing little expression except resignation. Or perhaps contentment?

Looking back, I wonder what the hinds' wives got out of their restricted lives, stuck in the wilds miles from anywhere. What if the women, living cheek by jowl with each other in adjoining cottages, hated the sight of each other? They had no one else to talk to while the men were working in the fields and never went anywhere except to church or maybe once in a long while to the local flower show.

True, it took them all day to get through their repetetive household tasks with no mod cons to lighten their loads. The women were forever carrying pails of water, feeding their hens and pig, black-leading the grate, rubbing and scrubbing, baking and cooking, mending and patching, pipe-claying their doorsteps or cleaning their windows. In their spare moments they knitted socks and jerseys for the men or long black stockings for themselves. Rarely did they take time to sit down and have a read at the paper or a look at the *People's Friend*.

Making meals, however simple, must have kept them occupied for hours. They baked floury scones, cooked rabbit-pie, and made great clooty-dumplings filled with currants. They got their milk and butter from the farmhouse, grew their own vegetables, and relied on the vanman or Wat-the-baker – when they could get up the road – for the rest. They saved up enough eggs to exchange for syrup and sugar in order to eke out the few pennies in their purses, and managed their frugal affairs without ever getting into debt.

On Saturday evenings the men sometimes dressed themselves

up and went cycling away to the town. Did the wives complain, I wondered, at being left behind? Or did they just cast on another sock? All of them must have had inner lives and secret longings. Surely it was not enough for them to be mere household drudges.

Certainly they could sparkle on occasions. One of my earliest recollections is of attending a wedding in one of the cottages. Whose wedding? All I can recall is a great feast set out on the table, of toasting the bride in ginger-wine, of the minister being solemn to begin with and them making comical remarks as everyone mellowed, of going to the door to watch the men taking part in the old custom of 'running the braes'. They set off at a brisk pace to race the measured distance and arrived back, breathless and panting, with the winner claiming a clumsy kiss from the bride who then presented him with his prize: a white silk handkerchief.

After that the jollification began in real earnest, though I saw little of it for my eyes would not remain open. But before I drifted off to sleep I heard the fiddle-music and saw Mrs Rag Rug kilting up her skirts to dance a schottische. She was wearing a lilac dress with sprigged flowers on it and a ribbon in her hair. Her cheeks were flushed and she was laughing like a girl. The other Mrs Thing was bouncing round the crowded room with the bridegroom, hooching in time to the music. She, too, had changed her personality with her clothes, and was all dimples and lace, with a gold pendant round her neck and shoes with pointed toes on her feet.

It was all so unlikely that maybe I dreamt it. Yet I am sure I heard the bridegroom stumbling his way through a speech, thanking my father who had doubtless supplied the wherewithal for the spree, and saying he was too full for words. My father sang 'The Lum Hat', and could it have been the minister who danced the sword dance with the poker and tongs laid out on the floor?

In my half-dreams I heard someone singing;

> Bessie Bell and Mary Gray
> They were twa bonnie lasses;
> They biggit a bower on yon burn-brae,
> And theekit it ower wi' rashes.

I wished the hinds' wives would wear their finery every day and dance instead of shaking their rugs. Why must there be such long gaps between high days and holidays?

But perhaps anticipation was best. It was nice to have something to look forward to. The flower show, for example. It happened only once a year, like Christmas, but we thought about it for weeks beforehand. It was so important that I could not understand why it was not on the calendar, like Ascension Day and all the rest.

'What aboot havin' a shot yoursel'?' Jessie urged me.

'Me? What could I enter for?'

There would be sports after the show and maybe I could enter for the sack race, but the show itself was for grown-ups who could grow the biggest cauliflower, make the clearest apple-jelly, or bake the best gingerbread.

We looked through the list of events, and true enough there were two things I could have a shot at. The best collection of wildflowers, and the best collection of wild fruits.

'An' what aboot this?' said Jessie, peering at the printed list. In the baking section there was an item which stated baldly: scones for spinsters.

'What's a spinster, Jessie?'

'Howts! you're ane! I'll pit on the girdle an' ye can hae a shot.'

My scones for spinsters ended in the pigs'-pail. Burnt on one side and doughy on the other, they were not fit for human consumption. So I turned my attention to the other items, and went racing all over the farm to collect as many varieties of wildflowers and fruit as I could find. I filled a jelly-jar with ragged robin, cats'-tails, silvery-shakers, star-of-bethlehem and all the rest, even ears of corn and barley-whiskers. I was not sure which were weeds and which flowers, but never mind, they made a brave show, though they began to wilt far too soon.

The thing to do with the wild fruit was to get an old tin tray, line the bottom with moss and make a pattern by embedding on it little heaps of hips, haws, rowans, barberries, brambles, acorns, scrogs and geans. It looked very colourful when it was finished. The trouble was, by the time it had been conveyed to the school (which, cleared of the desks, did double duty as the local hall) the contents were all shoogled out of place. No matter how carefully I tried to steady the tray as we rumbled down the bumpy farm-road in the gig, everything was a mixty-maxty mess in no time; and though I did a hasty tidying-up job I knew I would never win a coveted red ticket – and I was right.

It was surprising how eager the entrants were to win first prizes and how fierce the rivalry was between those showing their chrysanthemums, dropscones or hand-knitted socks. The prizes themselves were paltry enough. First prize 2s. 6d., it said in the catalogue. It was the red ticket that counted. Highly commended was no use. The judges who had been round the display earlier, tasting and examining, slunk away during the afternoon as if they feared being lynched. They could hear too many unflattering comments for their liking.

'Thon man's blind! Fancy pittin' a first on that cabbage. I wadna gie it to the coo.'

'Her! What does she ken aboot judgin' baking? Have ye ever tasted her ain sponges? Ye can hardly chowe them.'

'Three firsts for Mrs Scott! It's easy seen she's in wi' the judges.'

My father hated the occasions when he was called upon to be a Daniel and would have given everybody red tickets if he could. But he, too, was as pleased as punch if his own sweet-peas won first prize when someone else was judging them.

It was suffocating inside the schoolroom, with the heat of the people and the mingled scents of the goods on display, the heady fragrance of the flowers, the sickly smell of the jams and cakes. If the windows were opened bees came buzzing in to sample the rasp jam and honey; and a felling of claustrophobia overcame me as I tried to push my way out against the crowd.

The first time I saw anyone faint was at the flower show. It was the minister's wife and I have reason to remember it since she fell against me and knocked me to the ground; but no one, of course, took any heed of me or my bruised leg. They were too busy carrying her outside and propping her up against the playground wall. It was the speak of the countryside for days, though she recovered quickly enough and even took part in the three-legged race later on.

The sports were held in a field nearby on an uneven track full of divots and thistles. There were other hazards, too, between the starting and finishing-posts, for though the cows and sheep had been ejected for the day they had left their marks behind, and we had to be careful not to slither into a cow-plat in the course of a race.

I liked the silly races best, the obstacle race, the egg-and-spoon race, the sack-race, and best of all the thread-and-needle race. It was fun to watch the men standing at one end of the field holding needles at the ready while the women ran towards them with long threads in their hands. The women pranced about in a frenzy of impatience while the men tried to insert the elusive threads through the eyes of the needles with their clumsy fingers.

'Hurry up, Wull!' 'Get a move on, Tam!' urged the women, helplessly watching their partners fumbling with the threads and dropping the needles, while we all stood by kinking with laughter. A cheer rose up when some of them successfully completed the job, handed the threaded needles to the women who then raced helter-skelter towards the winning-post.

It was all very childish but: 'It fairly tak's ye oot yoursel',' said Auld Chuckie-Stanes, the roadman, when he came a cropper during the sack-race. That was the thing, to be taken out of oneself so that the humdrum pattern of everyday life was changed.

There were races for all ages and stages from small fry like myself to grown women. It was great to see Bella Confectionery running like a hen hotly pursued by Mary-Anne and Mrs Scott; but Jessie never took part in the races. 'Ye get mair oot o' watchin' ither folk makin' eediots o' themsel's,' she declared.

The men's handicap was the most hotly-contested, with everyone laying odds on the minister who was given a start half-way up the track, while the more able-bodied runners were left nearer the starting-post. Ready! Steady! Go! and they were off, with the onlookers yelling encouragement and the minister being overtaken when he stopped to retrieve his spectacles.

A great tea-urn was brought out to the field and refreshments were dispensed. There was fizzy lemonade for the young ones, and we ate all the gingerbreads and dropscones that had been on display at the show, whether they had won prizes or not. It was as good a way as any of getting rid of them.

The final event was the tug-of-war. The men took off their jackets, snapped their galluses and flexed their muscles before digging their heels into the ground to get a firm foothold. Then they spat on their hands and grasped the rope while the minister stood in the middle to start them off and see justice done. There were great groanings and gruntings as each side tried to stand its ground. In the end we all joined in, tagging on at one end or the other and landing in a heap on the ground when the rope gave way. It did not much matter who had won as long as we had all enjoyed ourselves.

At the end there was a sweetie-scramble for the children, with coloured jujubes and pandrops hailing down on our heads like manna from heaven. We dived to the ground to retrieve them, bumping our heads together and risking getting our hands trodden on in our eagerness to collect as many as possible. We stuffed them into our mouths, filled our pockets, and clutched them in our grubby hands, searching amongst the divots in case any had gone unnoticed.

It was a great day, one long to be remembered. But even then the gaiety was not over. For the grown-ups, at least; for now the schoolroom was cleared of its trestle-tables and wilting flowers, the floor was swept and sprinkled over with soap-flakes and a Grand Dance was held. Gents 1s. 6d.; Ladies 1s.

Being neither one nor the other but only a spinster of too tender years for such orgies, I was whisked away home; but in later years I made my debut at one of these country dances and can still recall the thrill of anticipation I felt when I sat on a long wooden bench beside the women, looking across at the men and wondering if I would be 'lifted'. It never mattered to me whether my partner was a ploughman with horny hands or a young blood from over the Border. The main thing was the joy of dancing, and not to be left sitting like a lone wall-flower.

The music was provided by Wat-the-fiddler and a wee man with a melodeon who played on till the sweat poured off their brows. Every dance was so strenuous that before long the men discarded their jackets and collars, and the dust rose up from the floor and danced, too, in the air.

We always began with the Grand March, walking solemnly round the room arm-in-arm with our partners. Then followed the Circassian Circle, Petronella, Roxburgh Castle, Drops o' Brandy, and all the rest, with an occasional schottische or polka in between, or a round-about waltz to the tune of 'Come O'er the Stream, Charlie'.

There was never much conversation, for we had to reserve our breath. Nor did the men bother to escort their partners back to their places at the end of a dance but abandoned them in the middle of the room the moment the music stopped, before going back to sit on their own benches.

Half-way through, the great urn was brought into use once more and cups of tea handed round to slake parched throats. Sometimes a volunteer would do a turn or we would all join in singing a bothy ballad. Then on with the dance till the lamps flickered low, the fiddle-strings broke, and the dawn chorus could be heard outside.

For weeks afterwards everybody spoke of the day of the Show, savouring it in every detail. It was not just put aside and forgotten, like the events in more crowded lives. Looking back and recapping was often the richest part of the fun.

Looking forward? There were long gaps between happenings. The only other social event I attended in the schoolroom was a whist drive where I won a string of onions as the booby prize. I had only played snap before and was not too sure which cards were clubs and which spades; but they were short of someone to make up a table, and I was better than nothing.

I was terrified most of the time, for there were some who took it in deadly earnest as if they were playing for their lives. Others chattered all the way through the game, not caring whether they trumped their partner's aces. I felt proud if I held some kings and queens in my hand especially if they were 'trumph'.

'What's trumphs?' the players wanted to know at the start of a new game; and the master who was acting as M.C. called out: 'Hearts!' or 'Diamonds!'. He rang a little bell when we had to change places, but there were always some still swithering over their cards before making the next move, as if they were poring over a draught-board.

Renaging – a strange word – was a deadly sin. I had to follow suit no matter how triumphantly I could have taken a trick by ignoring the rubbishy cards lurking in my hand. 'Can you not trumph it?' my partner would ask anxiously, and give a groan when I reluctantly produced my rubbish instead.

At some tables violent arguments broke out about who had played which cards, and sometimes the M.C. had to be called in as referee. His brow darkened, and I felt that at any moment he might bring out the tawse and wallop the lot of us.

The only time I had a good hand and took the most tricks was when he had called out: 'Misere!', but fortunately I was playing with Jock-the-herd at the time and all he said was, 'Man-lassie, ye couldna help it. Ye had the hale Royal Faimly in your fist.'

Next day the schoolroom was back to normal, with the blackboard filled with vulgar fractions and Auld Baldy-Heid shouting: 'Sit up and look lively or you'll get what-for.'

Once in a while the minister organized a social evening. A kirk soiree. This was a kind of congregational-meeting with some entertainment thrown in as light relief. It was strange to hear laughter, chatter, and hand-clapping in such solemn surroundings, with the Reverend in a jovial mood, telling funny stories instead of reading from Deuteronomy.

We had heard all his jokes before but they were none the worse for being repeated, and we dutifully went into fits of laughter as if they were all new to us. One I can remember still. for he retold it so often and with such gusto that I could have prompted him if he stuck, but he never did.

It was the story of a preacher who found himself face-to-face with a raging lion in the jungle. I could picture the raging lion all right, but I used to wonder what on earth the preacher was doing in the jungle.

'I'm going to eat you,' said the lion. 'Prepare yourself for death.'

What was the preacher to do? There was no hope for him. Except prayer. So he knelt down, put his hands piously before his eyes and prayed more earnestly than he had ever done before. Suddenly he keeked through his fingers and to his surprise and delight saw that the lion was kneeling, too, with his paws in front of his eyes.

The preacher looked up to heaven and said, 'Isn't it wonderful to think that my words can soften a wild beast's heart?' Whereupon the lion dropped his paws and roared: 'Haud your wheesht! I'm saying grace before meat.'

The highlight of the evening was bursting the pokes. We were all presented with paper-bags containing our feed, and a great feed it was, too; solid-looking meat-pies or bridies, hunks of cake or substantial buns with coconut-icing on top. Sometimes the contents of the pokes varied, and we compared them with those of our neighbours, occasionally swapping a cream cookie for a doughnut. But the great thing was to empty the bag as quickly as we could, blow it up and then burst it with the biggest bang possible.

We were also given handfuls of conversation-lozenges. In the dim light we peered at the heart-shaped sweetmeats to see what messages were written on them before passing them to someone of our choice. I remember handing: 'Will you be mine?' to the herd, and was a trifle dampened when he passed back: 'Not tonight', but I sucked it just the same. After that we settled down amongst the debris of crumpled paper-bags to enjoy the rest of the evening's entertainment.

The minister had imported some of his friends from neighbouring parishes who fancied themselves as singers or raconteurs. I remember a large lady and a small man standing up side-by-side to sing a duet, self-consciously avoiding each other's gaze as they launched into the song. It was a tear-jerker called *The Crookit Bawbee*, a touching tale of a love-token, a long separation and a reunion. Even though I knew the wee man would end up hand-in-hand with the big lady, they sang with such pathos and stirred my emotions to such an extent that I could scarcely swallow my lozenge.

I remember, too, the wife of one of the visiting ministers standing up to sing 'Won't You Buy My Pretty Flowers? with a bunch of artificial anemones clutched in her hand; after which her husband told a funny story – which he assured us was true, but I had my doubts – about one of his elders, a very shy man, who tried to avoid sick-visiting in case he was forced to 'put up a prayer'. The day came, however, when Mrs Brown, in his district, fell ill and he was sent off to do his duty, with instructions that he must pray at her bedside if she asked him to. He went off looking very down-in-the-mouth, but when he returned he was all smiles.

'How did you get on?' the minister asked him.

'Fine, meenister, fine! She was deid afore I got there.'

At the end of the proceedings we had to subdue our mirth and stand up to sing the Doxology. After which the minister blessed us, and we went home in the moonlight sucking the last of our lozenges.

11. Grasping the Nettle Firmly

Time did not seem to matter when I was a bairn. A day stretched into infinity and I never bothered about dividing it up into hours and minutes. The only watch I possessed was a toy one which came out of a Christmas cracker, but it did not go. So I just used to blow on a feathery clock and pretend I could tell the time that way.

There was a sundial in the garden but it was all covered over with moss, and we had a temperamental old grandfather clock in the hall which used to chime thirteen to the dozen, though never at the right hour. But if we were really stuck we could always ring up Bella at the post office. Not that she always knew.

'What are ye wantin' the time for?' she would shout down the receiver. 'I dinna even ken what day it is. But if ye haud on a meenit I'll gang ben the hoose an' tak' a keek at the wag-at-the-wa'.'

The trouble with Bella was she could never remember whether her wag-at-the-wa' was ten minutes slow or twenty minutes fast. 'It's roondaboot half past ten,' she would announce, 'but it micht be nearer eleeven o'clock, though I couldna sweir on't.'

Jock-the-herd had an enormous fob-watch which he kept shut up like a prisoner in his pooch, but it was a day's work to get it out, open it up, shake it to see if it was still ticking, and then peer at it closely enough to look at the time. Even then he had to do his calculations, for Jock, too, kept his watch fast. Or was it slow? In the end it was easier looking up into the sky and just guessing.

Jessie was the best at telling the time. She could feel it in her bones, she said. 'It's toonty past,' she would tell me; but toonty past what? 'Time ye were awa' to the schule.'

Sometimes we listened in to Big Ben all the way from London. He never made a mistake and chimed the wrong number. I used to picture him, a great fat man, sitting on top of the Houses of Parliament, hammering out the hours while I counted them off on my fingers.

The frightening thing was to wake in the middle of the night not knowing what time it was, alone in the world with not even a mouse stirring. The old hoolet outside sometimes broke the stillness with an ominous hoot, as if warning me that the Day of Judgement was at hand.

'Hoot-hoot! They're coming to get you. Hoot-hoot!'

Strange thoughts went whirling through my head about fundamental things which did not seem to matter in the bright daylight. Was God really up there watching over me? What if I died suddenly? Would Gwen, my friend, be there to welcome me or would she have forgotten all about me?

It would be terrible if I went to hell instead, into the burning fire. I thought over my sins, which were many, and determined to lead a purer life if I survived till the morning. My heart thudded when the wardrobe creaked as if it was alive and stretching its muscles. Something jumped on to my bed. It was only the white kitten. She lay on top of me purring as if she had an engine running inside her. Her presence was comforting, but the black thoughts still remained. There were a hundred questions I had never been able to ask anyone, but I would try in the morning. Maybe Jessie would tell me.

But, of course, it was all different in the daylight; and I was reminded of one of my father's stories about the minister who asked a small boy if he prayed night and morning.

'A'weel, I whiles pit up a prayer at nicht,' was the reply, 'but ony smert callant can tak' care o' himsel' through the day.'

All the same, I stuck to my purpose and tried to get Jessie to answer one of my questions.

'Jessie, where are we going to when we die?'

She did not hear me at first for she was stripping off the brown cow and the milk was rattling against the sides of the pail. But I persisted and repeated the question in an urgent voice.

Jessie gave me a hard look as if she was about to tell me to hold my tongue, but she must have realized from my expression that I was in deadly earnest for she gave me a serious answer.

'Naebody kens, lassie. We've just got to hope.'

It was a great thing, hope. My hope was that I might grow up to be good, not exactly a saint good enough to end up on a stained-glass window, but someone who might be a shining example to others. It was hardly likely at the rate I was going and with my lack of rummlegumption. But at least there was one person who thought I was perfect and in whose eyes I could do no wrong. Wee Maggie.

She was one of the hind's bairns, a toddler who used to haunt me like a shadow, hovering at the door, waiting to see if I would come out and play with her. She spoke with a lisp and trotted after me like a pet lamb, content if I threw her the odd word. She was a nuisance at times, but it was a heady feeling for me to have such a devoted slave, agreeing with everything I suggested, from turning somersaults to jumping across the burn.

'Oh yeth! Anything you thay!'

Wee Maggie was too young to go to school, so I sometimes showed off my superior knowledge to impress her, and tried to teach her to read or told her stories. She liked the stories all right but she was not so keen on the lessons. Sitting on a hay-rick I would go over the alphabet with her.

'Are you listening, Maggie?'

'Yeth!'

'Well, what comes after D?'

'I couldn't thay. Tell me a thtory.'

I found myself behaving like Auld Baldy-Heid and scolding her till her lip began to quiver. Great tears would well up in her eyes and drip down her cheeks like raindrops. Then I would feel ashamed of myself and hunt in my pockets for a consolation.

'Would you like a caramel, Maggie?'

'Oh yeth, pleathe!'

The tears dried like magic to be replaced by beaming smiles. It took very little to make Maggie happy, but I could never leave well alone. I was always trying to improve her.

'Would you not like to learn to count?'

'Y-yeth!'

'Well, come on then. I'll teach you.' Clever me!

Poor Wee Maggie had to puzzle her brains over the two-times table, getting as far as: 'Ten two'th are twenty' before I gave her any peace. She only did it to please me and had forfotten it the next day, but it gave me a great sense of power.

Then suddenly I realized I was as bad as the grown-ups, demanding instant obedience. 'Go and fetch that ball!' 'Don't fidgit!' 'Stop biting your nails!' In fact, I was becoming a bully.

In a fit of remorse I went to the other extreme and grovelled before Wee Maggie, running and fetching things for her, giving her my hair-robbons, asking her advice.

'You choose, Maggie. What would you like to play at? Hide-and-seek?'

'Yeth!'

'Or would you rather play with the ball?'

'Yeth!'

She was eating a jammy-piece at the time and her cheeks were splattered with red-currant jelly. I had to stop myself from saying sharply, 'Wipe your face!'. Instead, I asked her, 'Which would you like best?'

'Anything you thay!'

It was obvious Wee Maggie was made to be a doormat and enjoyed being bossed. But I had to keep a strict rein on myself. What if I turned out to be a monster, like the Drilly, drunk with power?

'Watch it, you!' I kept warning myself.

I watched the animals, too, to see how they behaved and if they bossed each other; but with them it seemed to be a case of live and let live. Except, of course, for the bubblyjock who had all the worst characteristics of the Drilly, and more.

It was Jessie who suggested the right way of dealing with the bully one day when he came charging after me, trying as usual to peck at my bare legs.

'Stand up to him, wumman.'

'Oh, I couldn't, Jessie. I'm feart!'

'Awa'! He's feart for you.'

Jessie was always right but I found this too difficult to believe. The bubblyjock feart!

'He's just a beast,' scoffed Jessie. 'Turn roond an' gie him a gliff.'

The very idea! It was like facing up to the Charge of the Light Brigade. But if I was feart Jessie wasn't.

'Haud on an' I'll show ye.'

When the bubblyjock came running at us on his muckle splay feet she whipped off her apron and waved it in front of his face, shouting, 'Boo! Get awa', ye ugly brute!'

The bubblyjock stopped in his tracks and gave Jessie an astonished look. Then all the fluff seemed to go out of his feathers. The next moment he turned tail like a coward and ran away to hide under the reaper in the cartshed.

'See, lassie! Ye should aye gie a firm grip to a nettle.'

But it was a different matter trying it myself. I did not mind nettles, but the bubblyjock still terrified me even though I had witnessed his downfall. He soon recovered his equilibrium, waited till Jessie was out of sight, and renewed his attacks on me, while I tried to raise enough courage to fight back.

At last I did it. Trembling with terror, I braced myself and turned on him. I had no apron to wave but I shouted 'Boo!' in as brave a voice as I could muster.

Once more it worked like magic. The bubblyjock looked even more frightened than I was, and went scuttling away backwards gobbling his head off as if I was about to murder him.

After that I had the upper hand. Though he still tried to chase me, I always turned and chased him instead. It was a great step forward in my life. I felt I could face up to anything, though I still had not the courage to say 'Boo!' to the Drilly.

I wanted big things to happen so that I could try out my new-found bravery. If I had been living in the old days I could have brandished my battle-axe in the face of the enemy and fought, like Fair Maid Lilliard, on my stumps. It was a pity I was never tested or they might have put up a monument to me. I even made up my own epitaph.

> The one who lies inside this grave
> Was very small but very brave;
> She saved her country from the foe
> But what she did I do not know.

The last line was a bit feeble, I felt, but at least it rhymed.

The trouble was there was no foe to fight. One could not live on the heights all the time, and maybe it was not the big things that demanded the most courage, but doing the every-day dull things. Just keeping going; my trudging to school every day, the herd battling against the elements without a grumble, Jessie up to her elbows in soapsuds doing the weekly washing.

Sometimes I helped her, though in the end she declared I was more of a hindrance, getting so wet in the process that she often said, 'Ye're mair drookit than the claes. I'll need to wring ye oot when I'm feenished.'

But at least she admitted I was a help in keeping the boiler going. The washhouse was a draughty old building situated in the steading, open to the world so that ducks, dogs, cats, calves and other beasts came wandering in. The boiler was heated with firewood and was, according to Jessie, 'As fashious as a twa-leggit cuddy'. Either it would roar away like an inferno, if the wind was in the right direction, blowing great gusts of smoke into our faces and making our eyes smart, or it would take the sulks and have to be relit over and over again.

It ate up sticks so that I was kept on the trot fetching and carrying, while Jessie got busy with the scrubbing-board. Sometimes she used a long wooden poss to pound out the dirt; and once to my joy when she was doing the blankets she took off her clogs and stockings and got into the tub herself. I jumped in beside her, clutched her round the waist, and we pranced about on our bare feet as if doing the Highland Fling. It was a great feeling, the hot soapy water on my legs and the squelchy blankets beneath my toes.

Not such fun when it came to rinsing them and wringing them out. They were too thick for the wringer, so Jessie commandeered the current servant-lassie or the herd if he happened to be passing.

'Here! haud on to that end an' gie a twist.'

When the great wash-basket was full of clean clothes, I helped Jessie to carry it round to the back-garden where she hung the washing-line between two apple-trees. After pegging the clothes on the line she propped it up with long forked sticks and stood back to contemplate the sheets and pillow-cases blowing in the breeze.

'No' bad,' she would say with a certain amount of satisfaction; 'but ye'll need to keep an eye on the rain.'

That was my job, to keep an eye on the rain. At the first drop I raced round to the washhouse where Jessie was cleaning out the boiler and announced, 'It's spitting!'

Jessie never said bad words. She just tightened her lips and braced herself for the worst, which meant going through the tedious process of taking all the clothes down again, and later on, if the sun shone, pegging them back on the line.

When they were dry enough she spent hours ironing, pressing, and goffering them with the old box-iron before hanging the clean clothes on the winter-dyke to air. Sometimes she put her hand to her back and said, 'Eh whowh!', but she never said, 'I'm fed up!' as I did when I got tired of a job.

She would never be a heroine in the history-books, famed for her courage, but I felt that if anybody deserved an epitaph it was Jessie.

12. Growing Pains

My mother was a witch.

She often said so herself, in so many words.

'I am a witch.'

Not the kind who flew through the air on a broomstick or cavorted around with her coven. But she had flashes.

'I'd better do a baking,' she would say suddenly. 'I have a feeling the minister's coming to tea.'

And he came.

'See,' she would say, when he opened the garden gate. 'I am a witch.'

I often wished she would look into the future and tell me, in moments of indecision, what was the right road to take. But in did not work that way. I soon discovered that the most difficult thing in life was making up one's own mind. Even choosing between an apple or an orange could be a great problem, or having a whole penny to spend on sweets at Bella's shop. Having made the vital decision, it was always the other thing I wanted most. If only an inner voice could have advised me!

One year my mother had a flash just before Christmas.

'We're in for a snowstorm,' she announced in her guise as a witch.

No one believed her, since the big snows seldom came till after the turn of the year. But she was right. The storm came on suddenly and unexpectedly with none of the usual preliminary warnings. It started with a sinister silence followed by a flutter of snowflakes and an icy wind which later blew the snow into wreaths as high as mountains. We knew the pattern. Soon we would be enclosed in a white cocoon with no hope of anyone getting near us. So what about Santa Claus, in whom I still firmly believed? If the postie and the vanman could not reach our door, how would Santa find his way through such a storm?

I asked Jock-the-herd when he came stamping into the kitchen with his boots caked with snow.

'Och! he'll come,' Jock assured me, 'if ye shout up the lum. Santy'll no' let ye doon.'

So I shouted up the chimney. 'Santa! would you please bring me a book, and a dolly, and some sweeties.?'

I heard a noise at the chimney-top as if Santa was saying, 'Ay! I'm listening,' but maybe it was just the wind.

On Christmas Eve, before going to bed with my stone hot-water-bottle, I hung up my stocking and left some sustenance for Santa to revive him after his long journey. A glass of milk and a slice of gingerbread. I had meant to stay awake to greet him, but my eyes closed and I knew no more till morning when – oh joy! – I discovered that he had come. Not a drop of milk left in the glass, not a crumb of gingerbread. And he had answered all my requests.

He had brought me a book. Not the usual *Chatterbox* but an old volume of *Lamb's Tales* with a new cover on it. There was a dolly, too, made of rags and wearing a Red Riding Hood cloak over a dress of the same pattern as my old summer frock. He had not forgotten the sweets, though strangely enough they tasted just like Jessie's treacle-toffee. As an extra he had filled my stocking with crab-apples, a few nuts, and a stick of sugar-ally.

I could hardly wait to tell Jock-the-herd.

'Santa's been!' I shouted when he came in with an armful of sticks to keep the kitchen fire going, and proudly showed him my treasures.

'Man-lassie, I tell't ye', said he, looking pleased for my sake.

Then I asked him, 'Did he come to you, too, Jock?'

The herd looked a trifle uneasy. 'Santy? Och ay! I daursay he did.'

'What did he bring you?'

Jock waited till he was almost out of the kitchen door before telling me. 'A pair o' lang drawers.'

I thought it a strange present for Santa to bring and wondered if Jock had shouted up the lum for that. Later, I gave him some of my toffee as a consolation. As for Red Riding Hood she was my constant companion for many a long day. Though she was only made of rags I liked her better than any fancy doll who could walk, talk, and close her eyes. Indeed, Red Riding Hood's eyes were only buttons which fell out every now and again. Her arms, too, had to be sewn back on at intervals; but what I liked best about her was that she understood me and approved of everything I did. She shared all my thoughts and many of my gaol-sentences. With the older ones back home for the Christmas holidays and the new baby ruling the roost, I was thankful to have somebody of my own, even if it was only a rag doll.

I cannot remember that we celebrated Christmas in any special way with a party, except that we had a plum-pudding and ate the bubblyjock. The trouble about decorating the house was finding the holly. There was plenty of it around, great prickly trees grew in the wood nearby, but the scarlet berries ripened too soon, and those not pecked by the birds had withered long before Christmas. It was Jessie who had the bright idea about how to preserve it.

'Bury it ablow the grund,' she suggested, 'in an auld biscuit-tin.'

We bought our biscuits, like everything else, in bulk; and always had plenty of big tins at our disposal. So every year we gathered sprigs of holly laden with red berries, put them into the biscuit-tins and gave them a decent burial.

The problem was finding them again. We even set up little wooden crosses to mark the spots, but routing pigs soon knocked them down, and, of course, in a snowstorm there was no hope of retrieving the buried treasure. So, as often as not, we had no holly.

Hogmanay was a more special occasion, though we had no one to first-foot except the cottagers. Every year my father gave them the same presents: boxes of shortbread, a black bun, and a side of mutton. Sometimes they came and sang bothy-ballads to us in the parlour, or joined in a kitchen dançe, ending with linked arms and everyone singing 'A Guid New Year To Ane An' A'.

Then suddenly the date changed. There were brand-new calendars to hang up. I had a feeling that I was beginning a fresh life and all my old sins would be forgiven.

One day my mother, gazing into her cup, said, 'There's a stranger floating in my tea. I wonder who it can be?'

All day long I watched and waited for the stranger. Could it be an Ingan Johnny or a French polisher or a wandering packman? It would not be the minister, for he was no stranger. I hoped it was not to be the Man from the Reformatory. For long enough he was my childhood bogey. I had no idea who he was except that my elder brother and sister were constantly threatening me with him. 'If you don't behave yourself the Man from the Reformatory will come and take you away.' I used to run and hide up a tree or in the stair-cupboard amongst the brooms any time an unknown man came near the house.

Nothing happened. For once the family witch had failed. I had almost forgotten about the stranger and was out in the stackyard skipping with an old length or rope when I saw him coming limping up the field. He was wearing a pink coat which grew pinker every moment from the drops of blood that were dripping on to it from a gash in his forehead. At his heels trotted a shamefaced horse.

I stared at him in horror, not knowing what to do or say. But he did. Indeed he seemed quite cheerful in spite of the blood on his brow and the bruises on his leg.

'Took a tumble at the hunt,' he told me. 'Do you think I could go somewhere, little girl, and get patched up?'

No one had called me little girl before or appealed for my help in such an emergency. I forgot my shyness. 'Come on,' I said and held out my hand.

Jessie was horrified when I led him straight into the kitchen instead of going round to the front door, and gave me a second scolding later on.

'Have ye nae rummlegumption? Fancy bringing the likes o' him into the kitchen!'

'It was neȧrer,' I protested; but evidently etiquette mattered more.

'Ye're a glaiket gowk!' Jessie told me. 'He micht be a lord.'

Whoever he was, my parents took charge of him, and after he had rested and been refreshed 'ben the hoose', he took his leave with a bandage on his forehead. But he insisted on saying goodbye to the little girl and thrust a silver coin into my hand. After that I kept looking in my own tea-cup for strangers, but I never saw any.

One day, however, I did have a flash myself. It was the day we broke up for the school-holidays. There was a relaxed atmosphere in the classroom. Auld Baldy-Heid had become quite human and was asking us all where we were going for our holidays. There were not many answers, for few of the country bairns went on holiday. They just ran wild, as I did, until it was time to go back to school again.

Only one or two put up their hands.

'Please sir, I'm going to stay with M'Auntie in Hawick.'

'I'm away to Kelso, sir.'

Kate, my friend from over the Border, said smugly, 'Please sir, I'm going to Newcastle.' Lucky thing!

Suddenly, without thinking, I shot up my own hand.

'I'm going to the seaside,' I heard myself announce.

'The seaside!' said the master in an interested voice. 'Where?'

'Please sir, I don't know, sir,' I said and subsided in my seat. Fancy telling a black lie like that!

The enormity of my sin weighed heavily on my shoulders all the way home. I had scarcely got into the kitchen before Jessie said, 'Ye'd better try on your new plimsols.'

'Plimsols?' I said in surprise. 'What for?'

'Ye're gaun your holidays to the seaside.'

It was a miracle, of course, like the ones in the Bible. If I had turned water into wine I could not have been more astonished. It was the opposite of be sure your sins will find you out.

The seaside to which we were going had the unpromising name of Spittal. It was near Berwick-on-Tweed and I was not sure whether it was in England or Scotland; but it did not matter as long as the sea was there.

We went in a train, a great snorting monster that belched out mouthfuls of smoke and sparks like a dragon, and rushed through dark tunnels with terrifying shrieks. The unfamiliar landscape kept running away backwards before I had time to examine it properly. I wanted to see everything more closely, even the tattie-bogles in the fields.

Then suddenly we were there. Spittal! I could see a cluster of red-roofed houses, a church spire, some coal-pits, but no sea. Our lodgings were too far away from the front, but it was there all right, and at last, in my new plimsols, I was taken down to the shore to see it.

I could not believe my eyes; there was too much of it. I had pictured the sea as a biggish pond which one could walk round or sail on in little boats. But this was beyond my imagination. The endlessness of it, stretching away beyond the horizon, confounded me. It was like eternity, which the minister talked about on Sundays. I wondered if it would spill over and drown the whole world.

It took a long time to get over my first fright or to venture as far as the water's edge. When I took off my plimsols and felt the sand falling away under my bare feet I felt sure it was going to suck me in. The waves folding and unfolding mesmerized me, and for long enough I resisted letting the salt water swirl over my toes.

But in time familiarity bred contempt. Soon I was wading up to the knees, and then, in breeks and vest – for I had no bathing-suit – I began bobbing up and down in the water and even let the waves splash over my head. It was a wonderful sensation; and I felt I could write a better essay now on 'A Day at the Seaside'.

The whole holiday was like a dream. I forgot that I ever had a past existence on the farm, though I did send a postcard to Jessie and the herd, saying, 'The sea is awful nice.' The days were filled to overflowing. Long hours spent digging castles in the sand, splashing in and out of the sea, eating unfamiliar food in our lodgings, rowing in a small oary-boat, or taking trips across to Berwick.

Here was an even bigger town then Jedburgh, with ramparts, an open-air market, and hundreds of people milling about the streets. There was so much to see that in one week I felt I had lived a lifetime of new experiences and was a woman of the world by the time I went home. Superior even to the herd.

On the last day my mother became a witch again and had another flash. We were all sitting on the sand staring at the sea as if trying to imprint it for ever on our memories. I had gathered a motley collection of 'things' to take home with me: shells, pebbles, slippery seaweed, and a defunct jelly-fish which was already beginning to smell.

'I have a feeling,' began my mother, but she was not sure what kind of feeling it was, except that she thought we were going to meet someone we knew. Here! as far away from home as foreign parts.

I wandered off to have a last paddle in the sea, then suddenly stood stock-still with surprise when I saw a familiar figure wading in the water with his trouser-legs rolled up to his knees. Auld Baldy-Heid!

'It's him!' I cried, running back to tell my parents, scattering shells and seaweed in all directions.

They called out to him, pleased to see a familiar face, and he came over to join us. But it spoiled my last day. I kept well in the background just in case he had his tawse in his pocket. Though he was in a jokey mood, I could not feel at ease in his presence. Surely there were plenty of other seasides where he could have gone for his holiday.

Then suddenly we were back home. I felt older and wiser having travelled so far and seen so much. What a lot I had to tell Jessie. I had brought a minding for her and for the herd. A stick of rock for Jock and a packet of tortoiseshell hairpins for Jessie.

'Ye've got mair siller than sense,' she sniffed; but she stuck one of the hairpins in her bun and seemed quite pleased with the result. As for Jock, he took a bite of rock and grunted, 'Man-lassie, I've fairly missed ye.'

Then, like everything else, the holiday faded away into the past. One could not look backwards for ever. The present moment was the only thing that mattered.

And the future?

I had a feeling things were going to happen. My father was behaving in a mysterious manner as if he had something up his sleeve.

My father would try anything once.

He liked gadgets and gimmicks, and would have been the first man on the Moon if he had known how to get there. He had the first wireless-set in the district. Now he had the first motor-car. A Tin Lizzie.

> Rattle his bones over the stones,
> He's only a pauper whom nobody owns.

The rough farm-road was pitted with holes, bumps, and ridges, unsuited for motor-vechicles. Flora and Ginger were accustomed to picking their way round the pitfalls, but the motor went barging on like a bucking broncho till it invariably stuck at the steepest turn and began to run backward. My father shouted 'Whoa!' as if he was still driving the pony and started shoogling about in his seat and tugging frantically at the brake. Seldom if ever did we have a straightforward run; but getting the motor was a wonderful adventure which opened wide windows on our restricted world.

Getting the wireless had been amazing enough. It was a monstrous machine almost the size of a wardrobe, full of wires and batteries (so why was it called wireless?) and far more temperamental than the old gramophone. When it worked at all we could hear mysterious crackles and the Savoy Orpheans pounding away in the background. The aerial, which was suspended on a high tree, frequently blew down and lay in a tangle on the ground; but now and again we could hear voices greeting us from as far away as London. It was miraculous. Jessie walked past the machine at a safe distance, fearing it might blow up at any moment, and indeed it sometimes began to smoke as if about to explode.

The men were invited in on special occasions, to hear the King speaking or to 'listen' to the two minutes' silence at the Cenotaph, but they did not really believe in it. 'Thon's no' natural,' said the herd and went stumping away, shaking his head,

Little did I think the day would come when I would be speaking on the monstrous machine myself. It was amazing enough to hear a voice over the crackles saying, 'This is London calling.'

The motor was a hundred times more temperamental. *Fashious*, Jessie called it. It had to be cranked up with a starting-handle before it showed any signs of life. Then suddenly it would begin to shiver and shake as if struck by the ague. It coughed and spluttered, sparks began to fly, and my father leapt into the driving-seat and fiddled with the gears. There was no driving test. He just took the motor into a field and went round and round until he got the hang of it. But he never quite mastered its mysteries, and even in later years when he bought bigger and better cars he was more at home with horse-flesh than with horse-power.

Though it widened our horizons in so many ways it was a long time before we lost our fear of the motor.

'Pomp the horn!' my mother would cry when we emerged into the main road or came near a corner. Even though we were travelling at a snail's pace there was always a sense of danger. Father knew nothing of the inner workings of the engine, and when we stuck, he used to get out, open the bonnet and fiddle away at the 'internals', with a perplexed expression on his face.

We never went on an expedition without having some mishap. We ran short of petrol, water, oil; we had frequent punctures; the horn would start blowing and refuse to stop; we would land in the ditch or get stuck in a snowdrift. I can remember sitting wearily by the wayside with bolts and nuts scattered around me, handing a spanner to my father while he tried to change a wheel. Often and often we had to push Lizzie home. How thankful I was when Father brought out the gig instead. At least with Flora we always got there and back again.

If we ventured off the beaten track we were sure to get lost, for my father had no sense of direction. If there was a wrong turning he took it. Often we ended in a farmsteading stuck in the mud at such an awkward angle that we could not reverse out of it. Once we almost landed in a duck-pond and had to leave the car and trudge home. My mother maintained that she never knew what walking was till we got the motor.

Yet on the occasions when Lizzie was running smoothly we found that the world had grown bigger and that we could reach places that had only been names before. Kelso! Galashiels! Kirk Yetholm where the gypsies lived! Otterburn over the Border!

But it was not only the world that was growing bigger. I, too, was shooting up.

It was a slow and painful process. Compared with animals, humans took a long time to mature. After many months the new baby in our house could not even toddle, yet I had watched a calf struggle to his feet seconds after he was born. Lambs began to run races when they were a few days old, and chickens fended for themselves as soon as they were out of the shell. We were the only ones who were backward.

It seemed to me that I had been in the world for centuries before I found myself amongst the big ones in the school, superior to the Infants, and with my hems let down; though still, alas! a peerie-top lacking in plain commonsense.

I could run faster, jump higher, reach up to top shelves, and do more things for myself without asking for help. My elders noticed it. 'Isn't she getting big?' they said, and kept asking me, 'What are you going to be?' as if I could suddenly turn into a caterpillar or a turnip.

The only thing I wanted to be was independent so that I need not beg pennies from my father but earn them for myself. In what way? I could single turnips like the Paddies, become a bondager, maybe, or a kitchie-las I could play the piano in a thumpy sort of way and turn the heel of sock with my eyes shut, but where would that get me? I had no other accomplishments except a facility for writing down the rubbish that was in my head. But would anyone ever want to buy it?

One of the texts on the wall-callendar – *A Thought for Every Day* – said: 'If at first you don't succeed, try, try and try again.' So I set to and filled all the odd spaces in an old jotter with stories about beasts, bogles, bubblyjocks, black lambs, cows with crumpled horns and pigs with curly tails. If I put people in the stories, a hero and a heroine, they were always Jock and Jessie in different guises.

So now when anyone asked me what I was going to be I knew the answer. 'A writer!'

'What?' they said in amazement. 'You've got a lot to learn first.'

Oh yes! and I am still learning.

I went and asked Jessie what she would like to be if she could choose. She was kirning at the time, turning the handle of the churn slowly and rhythmically, listening now and again to hear if the butter had come. Then I would get a drink of frothy soor-dook with its sharp refreshing tang.

'Me?' she said, giving me one of her straight looks. 'Just masel'.'

'But, Jessie, would you not like to be somebody different? The queen maybe or – let's think – a fairy godmother?'

'Dinna be daft!'

Jessie put her ear to the churn and then went on turning the handle; but suddenly she surprised my by saying in a confidential voice, 'I tell ye what I've aye wanted.'

'Go on, Jessie, tell me!'

Imagine her having secret longings! I vowed I would make them come true, whatever they were. 'What is it?'

'A nice nose.'

I looked at Jessie's hooked nose and said, 'But I like it the way it is.'

'Huh! it's no' on your face,' said Jessie grimly, and withdrew into her shell once more. A dull thud-thud from inside the churn warned her that the butter had come and she had no more time to indulge in silly flights of fancy.

I was disappointed that I could not grant her wish, but at least her confession revealed something I had never suspected. Even Jessie had a pride in her appearance, and it was high time I followed her example. I did not care a button what I looked like, up till now, and only hoped nobody was noticing me. Otherwise they would be sure to remark on my wrinkled stockings, tousled hair, lost ribbons or torn jersey. Clothes were nothing but a nuisance, and I envied the beasts who never bothered about them.

But all of a sudden they assumed a greater importance and I was forced, whether I liked it or not, to take stock of myself. I was to make a new beginning and must be kitted out from stem to stern. From Liberty bodice outwards. All because I had passed the Qualifying.

I have no recollection of sitting the exam itself. I only remember the moment when Auld Baldy-Heid came across to my desk and patted me on the head. At first I thought he was going to hit me and prepared to dodge the blow, but instead he said, 'Good for you! You've passed!'

I felt my face flush scarlet, more from embarrassment than pride. But it was not long before the master brought me down to earth. 'Mind! you'll need to watch your p's and q's at the Grammar School. You'll be up against some stiff competition there, so you'll have to pull yourself together.'

Pulling myself together meant restrictions of all kinds. Not just Liberty bodices. There would be new rules and new laws in the big school, new teachers, new lesson-books, new subjects. Latin, for example. What on earth would I make of that? I could not even speak English properly. The town teachers, I was warned, would be bamboozled if I came away with some of Jessie's or the herd's expressions. I must learn to get rid of my country accent, and stop running wild.

The nearer I came to leaving the familiar little village school the fonder I became of it and the more reluctant to say goodbye even to Auld Baldy-Heid. On the last day I felt a sudden surge of warmth towards him and wished I could put it into words. But what could I say? 'Dear Master, I love you.' He would have dropped dead and so would I.

At the end he shook hands with me. His grip was so tight that I would have winced if I had not lost all power of feeling. He might have squashed my bones to pulp without my noticing. All I could manage to say was 'ta-ta' which surely was the height of inadequacy.

I had to say ta-ta, too, to my school-friends. Kate from over the Border was to go to Newcastle for her Higher Education and would disappear from my ken, though we wrote stilted letters to each other from time to time. 'How are you getting on? I am getting on fine.'

I walked down the road with Bob (the braggart) who showed no signs of sorrow at my departure. 'Stuck-up thing!' he shouted and tried to trip me into the ditch. 'Away you go to your grand school.'

So I went on alone.

It was strange to be passing Auld Chuckie-Stanes for the last time. Never again would I stop and say my poetry to him. No more shivering with dread in the Dark Woods, or riding in Wat-the-Baker's cart. I would have to purchase my pencils and jotters in a strange shop in town instead of in Bella Confectionery's.

Everything was changing. But Jessie was still the same. She had the right answer for everything.

'How'll I get on?' I asked her, bewildered at the thought of the unknown future.

'Fine!' she said. 'The back's aye made for the burden.'

ANOTHER BREATH OF BORDER AIR

LAVINIA DERWENT

Another Breath of Border Air

Illustrated by Elizabeth Haines

To Jessie – once more

Contents

1. Childhood in the Cheviots

When I was a child I could go abroad without a passport every single day if I liked. Across the Cheviot hills, over the Border and into that other country called England. Where the heathens lived, according to Jessie.

Jessie was my best friend. The others were mainly four-footed or feathered. Some were even wooden, like the tattie-bogles dotted around the fields to scare the crows, though I doubt if they ever did, for I often saw birds perching on the scarecrows' heads or pecking in their pockets for crumbs of comfort.

They gave me comfort, too, for they had time to stand still and listen, without assuming that grown-up air of always knowing best. The beasts, too, would lend an ear when I talked to them. Even Grumphy the pig turned his head and put on an interested expression when I had some news to impart.

'I was top of the class today and never got the strap once. Fancy that!'

Fancy that, indeed. Even if he only gave me a grunt in reply it was something.

Jessie would listen if she had time, but unlike the scarecrows she seldom stood still. If I wanted her attention I had to run after her from back kitchen to byre, or out into the fields if she was spreading dung or stooking corn. Jessie had a dual role, working in the house on some days and in the fields on others. But always working, never sitting still.

The men who worked on the farm were called hinds and the women bondagers. It was the height of my ambition to become a bondager when I grew up, but Jessie doubted if I had enough sense. Rummlegumption, she called it.

It was a world of its own, far from the main road and isolated from neighbours and passers-by. Everything revolved round the farmhouse where I lived. The Big Hoose, Jessie called it. She lived in a little house across the fields with her brother the shepherd and her sister Joo-anne who was a stay-at-home, except at busy times when she came out and worked as a bondager.

The hinds and their wives lived in the cottages down the road which I passed every morning on my way to school, and though the occupants of the herd's house never changed, the cottages sometimes had different curtains on the windows and new people at term time. But not often, for my father kept his workers year after year. It was an exciting event if a new hind and his family arrived. A chance to see some fresh faces, maybe some bairns to share my games.

I was an in-between, the third member of a growing family, less than the dust in the eyes of an elder brother and sister who were away getting their higher education. There was a young baby in the house taking up much of my mother's attention, so I had to make a life of my own. And I always had Jessie, strong and steady, the same yesterday, today, and for ever.

Out and about was the best place to be, with endless pleasures to pursue on the farm – even just swinging on a gate, though this was strictly forbidden. Gates were not toys. They were there for a practical purpose, to keep animals in the fields, and must never be left open.

'Shut that yett!' Jock-the-herd would shout at me. 'Man-lassie, are ye donnert?'

Being donnert meant having no common sense. No rummlegumption. We had a language of our own in the Borders, full of expressive words which I learnt from Jessie and the shepherd. I knew that if they called me a sumph it meant that I was stupid; but if they told me on rare occasions that I had smeddum, it was meant as a compliment. I had guts! But more often I was a sumph and swung on the gates whether it was forbidden or not.

It was a great feeling, sailing backwards and forwards, faster and faster, like flying through the air, until, of course, the inevitable happened. There came an ominous creak as one of the spars gave way, and then I was in real trouble. Jock would have to come with hammer and nails to patch up the damage, but, give him his due, though he told me my character, he never seemed to begrudge the time and trouble.

'Maybe ye'll lairn,' he would say hopefully. I did try, though not with much success. It would be wonderful to be grown-up and perfect. Or would it? Did Jessie never long to swing on a gate or turn somersaults? What a lot of fun I would miss when I was old and full of sense.

If I wanted to get away from everyone I took to my heels and went off to foreign parts. The best way was a short cut across the fields and braes instead of following the winding main road up to the Carter Bar. The coach road it was called in the days when the horse-driven mail-coaches came rattling over the twisting route from Newcastle to Edinburgh.

There, at the summit, I really was in the Borderland, one foot in one country and one in another, though I could see no sudden change in the landscape. An English tree looked much the same as a Scottish one; Redesdale rabbits ran about on four legs, and there was heather growing on foreign soil.

The cows on the other side chewed thistles just as ours did, and a lark flew carelessly in the communal sky. The people, too, looked like ordinary human beings.

Only their tongues were different. They were Geordies and called me hinny instead of man-lassie as our shepherd did, but I could never see anything heathen about them. They were just people whose ancestors, true enough, had fought with ours in the old reiving days. But that was long ago and best forgotten.

The hills all had names. On the Northumberland side were Carterfell, Catcleuch Shin, Peel Fell, Hartshorn Pyke and many more, though I just lumped them all together as the Cheviots. I knew the Roxburghshire ones better, on our side: the Eildons, Ruberslaw, Minto Crags, the Dunion. But what did names matter? We had two of our own on the farm, which we just called the hill and the heathery hill and thought none the less of them.

I was convinced the Cheviots were in the Bible. Or, at least, in the psalm we sang at the kirk. 'I to the hills will lift mine eyes.' I often lifted mine to look at them and found them full of surprises, different every day. Sometimes with clouds scudding across their peaks, sometimes lost in a mist like a lady hiding behind her veil. At times they were far out of reach. On other days they seemed to have crept so close I could almost put out my hand and touch them.

> When Ruberslaw puts on his cowl,
> The Dunion on his hood,
> Then a' the wives o' Teviotdale
> Ken there will be a flood.

Jessie was an even better barometer. She could tell by the feeling in her bones when it was going to rain. No use washing blankets or starting the spring-cleaning if her big toe was 'stoonding'. There was sure to be a downpour.

Jessie never let on whether she liked me or not. It was different with her brother. I was sure of Jock-the-herd, but

I suppose he had nothing better to compare me with than one of his yowes. With Jessie around there was no chance of getting above myself. There was little I had to boast about, anyway, except that I had passed my Qualifying at the country school and was about to go to the Grammar School in Jedburgh, some eight miles away, to learn all sorts of strange subjects, including French.

'French!' scoffed Jessie. 'Ye'd mair need to lairn gumption.'

But that was not in the curriculum. Any I learned I got from Jessie herself. To this day I stop and think, 'Would *she* approve?', and if I still persist in disobeying my invisible mentor I have a feeling that she will 'give me my licks'.

I was well used to licks, especially from the teacher's tawse. Auld Baldy-Heid, the master at the village school, did not spare the rod. Once the leather strap was in his hand – the hangman's whip, we called it – he laid it on hard and fast, to boys and girls alike. We took it stoically enough and thought none the less of him. Indeed, deep down we had a great affection for the schoolmaster. One word of praise from him could send our spirits sky-high, and though his rage at times was fierce, he never actually carried out his constant threat to skin the lot of us alive.

Although I had now escaped from his clutches, Auld Baldy-Heid would always be the master to me, not just an ordinary man who sometimes came to visit my parents at the farmhouse. On such occasions I was on tenterhooks. 'Like a hen on a het girdle,' Jessie said. But how could I sit calmly beside him at the tea-table and pass the butter without trembling with terror? At any moment he might ask me to parse something or put his hand in his pocket and bring out the dreaded tawse.

If I was warned in time that he was coming I ran away and hid up a tree, or went off to my private haven, the broken-down Border Keep on the hill. This meant foregoing the special spread that had been laid on for his benefit, the sponge-cake oozing with fresh cream, the iced cake, the shortbread, the pancakes, and the variety of small scones, brown, plain and curranty. Not even the best strawberry jam would entice me. I could always eat scrogs – the wild crab-apples – or just starve. Better than being skinned alive.

Food, in any case, was not my priority. I preferred 'rubbish' – sweets, condensed milk, a sugar-piece, or any odds and ends I could cull from the hedgerows. Meals with a beginning, middle and end were a nuisance. It was a waste of time sitting in to the table and solemnly going through each course.

Yet, looking back, everything seemed to taste better in the old days. Floury potatoes, a feast in themselves, clooty-dumplings filled with juicy currants, roly-poly puddings, treacly gingerbread, barley-fadges, tasty ham from our own pig, occasional treats of succulent sausages bought from the butcher or kippers caught in far-off Loch Fyne.

Perhaps it was the long slow cooking over an open fire that gave the stews and stovies their extra flavour. Certainly we were never asked whether we liked anything or not. It was just served up to us, take it or leave it.

Town folk considered it a treat to drink warm frothy milk straight from the cow, but I preferred it after it had cooled in the dairy. The milk-hoose, we called the little room off the back-kitchen. Better still I liked the sharp taste of soor-dook, the buttermilk which was left after the churning. Beistie-pudding, made with beistie-milk, the first milking of a cow after she had calved, was thought to be the greatest delicacy. But not by me. I hated the sight and taste of it so much that I always tipped it into the pigs' pail rather than eat it.

'Mony a stervin' heathen wad be gled o't,' said Jessie; but I would sooner have starved.

I had been a passive observer often enough in the byre, where I sat on a small stool with a row of cats beside me waiting to be fed, but now Jessie decided it was time to teach me the art of milking for myself.

'It'll come in handier than French. Watch, lassie.'

I watched, but I would sooner have listened. Jessie had a great fund of stories, and though I had heard them over and over again I could never get enough of them. They were all about animals. Wee moudiwart, the mole, who lived under the ground, or the pig with the curly tail. Jessie had a great gift for words and told the stories so expressively in her rich dialect that I could see the furry creatures crawling under their earth-heaps or hear the curly-tailed pig crying for his mother when he was lost.

'Tell me a story, Jessie.'

'No, I'll no'. No' till ye've lairnt to milk.'

'A riddle, then. Please, Jessie.'

If I pleaded long enough she might give in. I knew all her riddles and their answers off by heart but I still liked to hear her recite them for she put on a different sing-song voice. The cats sat up on their tails and the cows turned their heads to watch her through their great solemn eyes when she began.

'Bonnie Kitty Brannie, she stands at the wa',
Gie her little, gie her muckle, she licks up a'.
Gie her stanes, she'll eat them – but waitter, she'll dee.
Can ye think o' an answer an' tell it to me?'

'Yes, I can, Jessie. It's a fire.'

'Ay, so it is, lassie;' but when I asked for another Jessie was not to be coaxed. 'Watch the milkin',' she said firmly. 'See hoo I strip the coo.'

Stripping was done gently but firmly at the end so that not a drop was wasted. I sat on my stool obediently watching, while the cats mieowed hungrily beside me and the bubbly-jock keeked in at the open door. The milk made a pleasant sound as it splashed into the pail. It looked easy enough, I thought.

During that first lesson we had company in the byre. A tramp woman who had been sheltering there for the night sat on the straw in a corner, itching to smoke her clay pipe but not daring to light it, for Jessie had given her a sharp warning about the danger of setting the place ablaze. She kept mumbling to herself and fingering a hidden pocket in the folds of her tattered skirt. If I had been alone with her, she could have smoked to her heart's content. But, then, I had no sense.

'Ye can begin wi' Bessie,' said Jessie, getting up from her stool. 'She's a quiet beast.'

Bessie, the brown cow, was not all that quiet. At the first go she gave me a skelp on the ear with her tail which sent me flying from the stool and brought stinging tears to my eyes.

'See!' said Jessie. 'It's no' that easy. There's a knack in't.'

So there was; one that took me ages to master. Bessie was none too pleased with my bungling attempts, nor was Jessie when the cow kicked over the pail and the milk went running in little rivulets across the byre floor with the cats lapping it up in hot pursuit.

The old crone drew out her empty pipe and sucked it for consolation like a baby with a dummy while Jessie gave me my character. The cats cowered, licking their milky mouths, and even the bubblyjock turned tail and fled. But there was no escape for me. I would not have my sorrows to seek, she warned me, unless I stuck in and made a better job of it.

So I did. Perseverance pays. After many a hard battle I mastered the art, even of stripping, and was prouder than having passed the Qualifying when Jessie gave me a pat on the back to show her approval.

'There noo, lassie! Ye can milk a coo, so ye're ready for onything. Ye'll never look back.'

But I do look back, often and often, and wish I could still be there in the byre with the cows whisking their tails and Jessie telling me one of her stories.

'A'weel, ance upon a time there was a wee weasel ca'd Wullie. . . .'

2. Freedom on the Farm

I learned a lot more during that long summer as I ran barefoot all over the farm, making the most of my freedom before plunging into the big world of the Grammar School.

Sometimes I spent the entire day in the old Border Keep, the ruined castle on the hill, queen of all I surveyed. I had no spy-glasses but there was plenty to observe with my own eyes, even just the sky itself which was always full of surprises. There were times when it seemed – like the hills – far out of reach, so high up that there was nothing there. On other days it was just above my head, with dark clouds bumping into each other as they scudded by. In sunny weather they were white and woolly, like newly clipped fleeces, or faintly tinged with pink from the rays of the sun. Heaven was up there amongst the clouds but I could never see it or hear any of the angels sing.

If I was lucky I would see a rainbow. Where was the pot of gold? I ran down the hill to the burn – the small Jed – to look for it, but tantalizingly it had changed its position.

Always the rainbow's ending was out of reach and there was no treasure to find, except an old boot bobbing about in the water or maybe a tattered umbrella.

From the look-out tower in the keep I could watch the comings and goings on the main road, not that there were many: the minister emerging from the manse gate with his little dog at his heels, the postie on his bicycle, the baker's horse and cart. Sometimes a more colourful sight, a gypsy caravan swaying on its way over the Border. Or perhaps 'the man with the stallion' walking the road on one of his mysterious missions. From time to time he came to our farm with his great prancing beast, and strange things took place round in the steading, but I was never allowed to be an onlooker.

Nearer at hand there was another road, moss-grown and rutted. The back road which was the driveway leading to Edgerston House where the laird lived. It was used by vans delivering goods to the Big House, and sometimes I saw a chauffeur-driven car gliding by with the laird himself sitting in the back.

He never noticed me, of course, though sometimes the chauffeur gave me a sideways smile. The laird was a higher being, akin to the Almighty, except that he did not give his all to the poor but gathered gear from his business enterprises in London where he spent most of his time. Yet he was kind enough to his estate-workers and sometimes, like God, he, too, could work miracles. When he visited the village school he made Auld Baldy-Heid give us a holiday.

Now that I think of it the laird had a look of the Good Shepherd about him when he arrived at the school with a cloak draped over his shoulders and a long stick in his hand like Jock's crook. We all sat up straight and hoped he would not speak to us for we could never understand a word he said. He spoke English, we presumed, but not plain enough for us to comprehend, and we were never sure whether to say 'Eh?' or 'Beg pardon' when he asked us a question.

Doubtless he was equally bamboozled by our replies. I remember one day he paused at Big Bob's desk. The laddie was chewing his pencil at the time and trying his best to look invisible.

'And what are you doing, boy?' asked the laird in his clipped tongue.

Big Bob looked up at him like a startled rabbit.

'Eh? Beg pardon'

The laird repeated his question a little louder and a little faster. 'I said what are you doing, boy?'

Big Bob got the message at last and answered literally, 'I'm chowin' ma pencil.'

'Oh,' said the laird, looking puzzled. 'Well, carry on, boy.'

So Big Bob took him at his word and carried on chewing his pencil.

The only time the laird stopped at my desk he asked the customary daft question older people so often put to children.

'And what are you going to be when you grow up, little girl?'

My answer was brief and to the point. 'Big.' I added 'sir' when I saw Auld Baldy-Heid glowering at me, but I was not being cheeky, just truthful like Big Bob.

Strangely enough we had no difficulty in understanding the laird when he announced, 'I have asked the teacher to give you a half-holiday and he has agreed. Does that suit you, children?'

'Yessir!'

We cheered him to the echo and he went away with his cloak flapping behind him, feeling no doubt that he had done his duty nobly. And so he had. We were out of the classroom like bumbees from a byke before the master could change his mind.

Having a half-holiday did not mean getting home any earlier. Often the opposite. With all the time in the world at our disposal there were a hundred pleasant ploys we could pursue. We could indulge in a rowdy game of kick-the-can in the playground before dawdling down the road, hitting out at each other with our schoolbags or climbing fences to play hide-and-seek in the woods.

I cannot recall feeling tired or hungry in those far-off days. Or even wet, though surely it must have poured with rain many a time. Not that a drenching would have dampened our spirits. If we were engrossed in some pursuit we just went on and on, with no grown-up to stop our fun.

Often it would be dark by the time I arrived home, with holes in my stockings, my hair in a tangle, and the buttons torn off my coat.

'Sic a slaister ye're in,' Jessie would say severely. (A slaister meant a mess.) 'What kept ye so late?'

'I got a half-holiday,' I told her, and that was explanation enough.

But now that I had left the village school I had whole holidays every day and never any problem about how to fill the long hours. Sometimes I went and lay in the meadow – the cow-gang – rich with gowans, grasses and myriads of wild flowers all mingled together. They had a heady perfume which attracted the bees and butterflies, and I lay in a drowsy haze of scent and sound, feeling slightly tipsy. The cows nibbled at my bare toes and Flora, the white pony, came cantering from the other end of the field to crop the grass near by. I felt as if I belonged to the earth and was part of everything that grew around me.

When I heard the shepherd shouting to Jed and Jess I came to life. According to Jessie I was a peerie-top and liked to be on the go. And it was not all play, for I took my turn at helping in the fields, fancying myself as a fully-fledged bondager. Without me the hay would never have got cut or the corn stooked. It was a puzzle how they managed when I was away at the school.

Mine, in truth, were the most menial tasks, fetching and

carrying for the hinds or holding the horses' heads, if I could reach up to them. I was not at ease with the Clydesdales when they showed their strong teeth. Were they smiling at me or sneering? Sometimes they reached down with a jangle of harness and tore out great mouthfuls of grass from the ground. They would eat anything, even a piece of sticky toffee if I offered it to them on my palm, but I was always afraid they might swallow my hand as well.

Turning the hay was a simple enough task except that the giant forks used by the farm-workers were too cumbersome for me to manipulate. So I did the job with my hands, which were soon stinging with thistles. Thristles, Jessie called them. She would gouge them out of my thumbs with a darning-needle, putting on her spectacles for the purpose. Communal glasses they were, for I sometimes saw her sister, Joo-anne, wearing them as she sat by the fire in the herd's house, turning the heel of a sock; and I think Jock wore them too when he was looking up Deuteronomy in the kirk.

The men never seemed to get thristles, nor Jessie. Perhaps she wore leather gloves, though I doubt it. Her hands were as hard as iron except on washing-days, when her fingers were covered with soft ridges after rubbing the clothes for so long on the scrubbing-board. On Sundays she certainly wore gloves when she went to church, and blew into them when she took them off and laid them neatly on the ledge in her pew.

When the hay had been raked into little ricks and left long enough to winnow, the great day came when it was ready to be carted in from the fields and built into haystacks.

Weather was the important factor, and it was my father, the Boss, who decided when the operation should begin. I often wondered if he had a direct line with God, for he looked skywards so often before passing on word to the workers. Father was never an orderer, only a suggester, and the hinds seemed to respect him all the more for this seeming lack of authority.

'The weather looks right. Maybe we should make a start.'

It was all hands to work. The herd came in from the hirsel, Jessie abandoned her household tasks, and Joo-anne joined us, wearing her big bondager's hat. The men dragged out the wooden bogey from the cartshed and yoked in one of the horses, while the cocks and hens who had been using it as a roosting-place flew off with indignant protests, leaving a trail of fluff and feathers behind.

As soon as Tam shouted 'Gee-up!' and the bogey began to move, I jumped on for my first ride out to the hayfield.

> Rattle his bones over the stones,
> He's only a pauper whom nobody owns.

One of the men used to quote this to me. Tam or Wull. True enough the bogey was an uncomfortable mode of transport. It creaked and shook as it rumbled on its way, and I was always in danger of sliding off, especially when it stuck going through a gate.

'We'll need to get that yett aff,' the men would shout, then Jock-the-herd would have to come to the rescue to take it off its hinges. Nothing ever stumped him, making or mending. He always had nails in his pocket and a ready hand with a hammer.

The bogey came and went with its load, swaying into the stackyard where the neat pyramids of hay began to mount up into a small forest, later to be thatched and held in place with straw ropes. There was an art in building the haystacks from the base upwards, not too tightly packed for fear they would steam and go on fire. No amateur was allowed to do the job, though that was the height of my ambition, to prance about on the stack, fashioning it into the right shape.

It took an expert like Jessie, helped sometimes by the

Boss himself. They stood there at the receiving end, gathering the great forkfuls of hay into their arms and placing them in positions which looked higgledy-piggledy at first glance but which always miraculously ended in the right pattern.

The higher the stacks grew the harder it was for the men to fork up the hay from the bogey. Often the sweat broke on their brows, and they must have been thankful to rest their aching arms when I was sent running to the farmhouse to bring out the tea.

I liked when they let me climb the ladder propped against the haystack so that I could hand the tea and scones to Jessie and my father. The men had a quick draw at their pipes, then they were up and at it again, making the most of daylight and good weather while it lasted.

It was often pitch dark before they brought in the last load, and not a grumble from any of them about overtime. If the going was good it never occurred to any of us to stop. Often I was half asleep and the owls were hooting before I took my last bumpy ride on the bogey. My hair was full of hayseeds, and my legs covered with scratches. And even though I was only one of the lower orders, I had a feeling of achievement every time I went into the yard and saw the sturdy stacks standing there. I had helped in some small degree to build them.

There was even more hustle and bustle at harvest-time. I liked watching the whirring flails of the reaper going round and round, cutting the corn till there was only one small patch left in the middle of the field, the last refuge for the wild creatures who had been lurking amongst the corn. Rabbits, hares, mice, hedgehogs and lame birds had retreated out of the way of the relentless reaper and were now huddled together, strange bedfellows, awaiting their fate.

> Wee sleekit, cow'rin tim'rous beastie,
> O what a panic's in thy breistie!

Their fate was sealed when the herd whistled up his dogs and the hinds advanced on the corn patch shouting and brandishing sticks. I turned my head away from the slaughter and was always glad when a scurrying rabbit darted through the men's legs and went bobtailing away to safety.

That night everyone went home with a share of the spoil, and, in spite of my squeamishness, I enjoyed the rabbit pie or hare soup as well as any. Somehow, now that the beasties had lost their identity I could only spare them a passing pitying thought while relishing their savoury taste.

Though we used Shanks' pony a great deal in the country, we never just went for a walk. There was always a purpose behind it.

I walked the two miles to school, of course, and two miles back, then sometimes at night I was sent to shut in the hens. This meant another long trudge to distant parts of the farm where the henhouses were dotted around. And, since hens were not early-bedders, it meant going in that eerie half-darkness of the gloaming when there were strange rustlings to be heard and bogles seemed to be lurking behind every tree.

Fashious creatures, Jessie called the hens, and so they were. The last thing they wanted was to be shut in for the night. Yet I had to make sure that every one of them entered the wee trapdoor, for there were foxes prowling around and I would get what for if any of the Black Minorcas or Rhode Island Reds were missing in the morning.

The hens tried every trick to elude me. I pleaded, threatened, and chased after them in a desperate game of hide-and-seek. They seemed to be laughing up their feathers at me, but at length I always captured the lot. What a relief when every trapdoor was finally shut and my task was over.

Not quite over, for I had been told by Jessie, 'Never come hame empty-handed. Aye pick up a wheen sticks to bring back.'

So I used to gather odds and ends of firewood as I wended my way home. Some were large branches so unwieldy that I had to drag them behind me and often dropped more than I picked up, especially when I had to open gates or climb fences. But I always came home with something even if it was only a handful of fir cones. They gave out a fine fragrance when flung on the fire. I liked to hear them sizzling and watch their changing colours.

I never met a bogle on those evening walks, but sometimes I came face to face with the herd who was much more comforting and helped me over dykes with my burdens. He also offered me some sound advice.

'Man-lassie, can ye no' cairry the sticks ablow your oxter?' Under my arm, he meant.

The trouble was, my oxter was not as strong as Jock's. Try as I would, I always left a trail behind me and was for ever having to turn on my tracks to pick up the fallen.

Sometimes, in the dim light, I picked up more than I expected. One night I took hold of a prickly hedgehog by mistake thinking he was a lump of wood. On another occasion it was a small black kitten who had come creeping after me in the darkness. No wonder I was always glad when I could see the glow of the lamplit kitchen window.

I remember one murky night I saw something white moving towards me. A ghost. What else? Too petrified to turn and flee, I stood stock still letting my load of sticks fall to the ground. The next moment the ghost spoke to me in Jessie's familiar voice.

'Where the dickens hae ye been, lassie?' she said, advancing towards me wearing a long white apron over her black skirt. 'I thought ye'd gane an' got lost. An' you empty-handed, tae! I've tell't ye afore, ye should never come hame withoot something under your oxter.'

3. The Back of Beyond

As well as owning our own farm, Overton Bush, my father rented another in the Oxnam district some six or seven miles away in the wilds. A hill farm called Swinside Town-head. From a duke, no less. The Duke of Roxburghe who lived in an enormous mansion like Buckingham Palace: Floors Castle at Kelso.

I never set eyes on the duke who was an even higher personage than the laird, but once a year my father and the other tenants were bidden to a gathering at Kelso where they lunched with His Grace and ceremoniously handed over their rents.

In real money, I think; for I can remember Father with a bag of golden sovereigns which he kept locked in his safe. They were not my kind of money, of course, like the homely halfpennies I spent at Bella Confectionery's shop, but it would have been fun, I felt, to play with such clean clinking coins.

I used to picture the duke sitting before a great heap of

shining sovereigns, like the king in his counting-house, letting them run through his fingers and gathering up more as each farmer came forward and showered down his offering.

When Father came home he always had great tales to tell, for he was a fine raconteur, of what the duke had said and done, but I was disappointed to hear that His Grace behaved like an ordinary mortal, eating steak-pie with the rest, and that the knives and forks were not of solid gold.

The hill farm, Swinside Townhead, seemed to be run by remote control. Except that once a week Father yoked Flora or Ginger into the gig and drove away to see what was what. My mother often accompanied him, and on rarer occasions I was allowed to go, sitting back-to-back with my parents and always in danger of tumbling out into the ditch.

At our farm road-end, instead of turning left as I did when going to school, Father tugged the pony's head to the right and the gig wheels went spinning away into less familiar territory towards Oxnam. Ousenam was the old word for it, and the river was called Ousenam Water. We were great ones in the Borders for double-naming. Swinside Townhead, to which we were aiming, was often called Soonside Toonheid. Little wonder we puzzled the foreigners from the other side.

They had been here, the Sassenachs, in the old feuding days, creeping across to pillage our farms while we were creeping in the opposite direction to steal their cattle; and they had left many a mark behind them. One of the farms we passed by was called Bloodylaws. 'For three days,' said an old account of the massacre, 'it had been running with blood.' I always expected Ousenam Water to look like the Red Sea, but it went purling on its way as pure as our own small burn at home.

There was not much traffic on the side roads apart from the odd tinker or mugger driving their lean half-starved horses. I was never sure which were muggers and which tinkers. The muggers had originally made earthenware mugs and hawked them round the countryside, but now both tinks and muggers appeared to specialize in pots and pails, and in mooching what they could get at each cottage door.

They had the reputation of being tarry-fingered and were different from the gypsies, less romantic, more scruffy, with tangled hair and wild looks in their eyes. They did not wheedle, they demanded, pushing their way into houses and helping themselves to any scraps they could find lying about. Yet they were skilled workmen when it came to soldering pots and pans, sharpening scissors or mending broken implements. For all that, they were not welcome guests. They were God's creatures, of course, but according to Jessie, 'He must hae made them on ane o' His aff-days.'

When we came near to Swinside there always seemed to be a look-out laddie at the turn of the road who ran helter-skelter into the farmhouse to give the warning that the Boss had arrived. The grieve who acted as factor in my father's absence lived there with his family, and always seemed to be leaning on something. Against the door, on a spade or a chair, never actually doing anything except chewing his droopy moustache.

Everything about the grieve was droopy. His trousers, his buttonless shirt, his braces which he held on to and twanged now and again, his left eye which looked in a different direction from his right. And his wife, the Missis.

The Missis was a dim, colourless, apologetic creature. Indeed she had a great deal to be apologetic about. Even I could sense the general air of discomfort and see how fushionless she was, with her down-at-heel slippers, her skirt fastened with a safety-pin and her lank locks coming adrift from their hairpins. The draughty kitchen was always in a state of chaos – dirty dishes on the table, ashes strewn in the fireplace, unwashed clothes scattered untidily on the chairs, cocks and hens wandering in through the open door. There was always a bairn, who would have been the better of a handkie, tugging at his mother's torn skirt.

While my father and the grieve went off to look around the farm, the Missis put on the kettle and dusted a chair for my mother to sit on. Then she started her apologizing.

'We're a bit behind hand this morning. The bairn was teething in the night.' Or the cow was calving. Or Himself, her husband, had been working late. A likely story!

I never waited for the tea out of the cracked cups served with slices of dubious seed-cake, but went off on my own up to the cottages where the Swinside hinds lived. They were all strangers to me, for unlike those on our own farm they seldom stayed more than a year. At term time my father was for ever having to hire new ones. They liked the place, and the Boss all right, but maybe it was the grieve who was the problem. My mother often urged Father to give the man the sack, but the Boss was too soft-hearted. 'Where could he go with all those bairns? Nobody would hire him.' So the farm suffered.

My objective during those visits was the Back of Beyond, past the cottage gardens on the brow of the hill where the wind whipped the washing on the clothes lines and bent the stunted gooseberry bushes to the ground. There was one gean tree – a wild cherry – which seldom bore fruit. The delicate blossom no sooner appeared than it was blown away; and so was I if I did not plant my feet firmly enough on the ground.

It was a strange feeling leaning against the wind, walking and yet standing still. Past the cottages there was nothing but a bumpy road leading away to the hills. The Back of Beyond. It was a breathless sight in more ways than one, this unfamiliar view of the Cheviots, fold upon fold all merging into each other. Even the birds that winged overhead seemed wilder, giving out strange calls as they skimmed off into the unknown.

There were farmsteads out there even more isolated than our own. I remember driving with my parents to visit the folk living in a house lurking near a wood at the foothills. I had to jump down from the back of the gig to open the rickety gates across the road, and wait to shut them again when the pony had cantered through. It was a tiresome task, getting off and on, and manipulating the awkward fastenings. Some were tied with binder-twine, others had home-made hooks that took me all my time to unlatch; and though we were sure of a warm welcome and a splendid tea when we arrived, I wondered if it was worth it. There was always the journey back and those awful gates to face. There was the dread, too, when it grew dark that the gig would drive away without me and I would be left in the wilds to perish, like Lucy Gray.

Even in daylight I did not linger long in the Back of Beyond, long enough, though, for the scene to be firmly implanted in my mind, so that today I have only to close my eyes and I can see that bleak landscape and hear the whaups calling in the blustery sky.

I had to keep on the alert for I was never sure when my parents would be ready to drive back home. Sometimes I saw Father and the grieve wandering round the fields or talking to the hinds. When they made their way towards the farmhouse I ran back to the kitchen where the Missis was still whining as she packed some eggs into a battered basket. We had plenty of eggs at Overton Bush but these were to sell to the vanman when he called at our door, as a nest-egg for my mother's private purse. But not before they had been cleaned and sorted out. The grieve's wife apologized for the shells being dirty and some of the eggs cracked. She had had no time to get them ready. There had been the calves to feed and the cows to milk, and she had had to send for the doctor last night for wee Mary who had come out in a rash. Ringworm. Caught from the pig. The bairn *would* wander into the stye. Then there had been the chimney smoking and the roof leaking.

I never listened, the story was too familiar. It was a relief to get away with the entire family waving us off and Himself leaning against the garden gate, his eyes looking in opposite directions. I could hear my father and mother discussing the unsatisfactory situation as I sat with my back to them in the gig, guarding the eggs.

They never brought me into the conversation. What would I know about anything? I could not even be trusted to look after the eggs properly, for on one dreadful occasion Ginger stumbled going downhill, jolting me out of the gig, and the basket came flying after me. I did try to catch it before it came crashing down beside me on the road, but it was no use. The next moment I was surrounded by egg-yolks and broken shells, and somehow it was all my fault. Solitary confinement in the garret would be my punishment when I got home.

Though I enjoyed my drives in the gig I longed for transport of my own. There was always a niggle of worry in my mind. How was I going to travel every day to the big school in Jedburgh when the time came? My elder brother had ridden there and back on Flora, but I could not see myself staying in the saddle long enough, far less getting on the pony's back in the first place, even with the aid of the mounting-stone at the kitchen door. The loupin'-on stane, Jessie called it. And who would hoist me up for the return journey?

The solution to my mind, was a bicycle. I had always hankered after one, and for years had pleaded with my parents, and with Santa Claus, to bring me one, but they were all deaf to my pleas. So I had to content myself with a broken-down machine which had long lain in the scrap-heap. The baneshaker, the herd called it, and he was not wrong.

I was no mechanic myself, but when I begged Jock to

help me, he put it into some sort of shape. At least he straightened the handlebars, tied them up with string and fixed the loose pedals. There were still some spokes missing, the tyres were punctured and the brakes unreliable. But the bell was perfect.

The biggest drawback to the baneshaker was its sex. It was a man's bicycle with a high spar which I could never manage to negotiate, so I had to ride sideways with one leg under the spar, a perilous way to pedal and no mean feat, now that I come to look back on it. In later years, when I came to grips with a real bicycle, I had a long tussle before I could ride it in a straightforward manner.

'Man-lassie, that contraption'll be the daith o' ye,' the herd used to warn me, and sure enough the baneshaker did its best. Many a time I went crashing into a wall or landed in the ditch with the baneshaker on top of me, but its erratic behaviour was all part of the fun.

I did not venture far, of course, but only around the farmyard, ringing the bell to scatter the livestock out of the way and occasionally coming to grief if the sow suddenly crossed my path. I realized I could never get as far as the Grammar School on such a broken-down charger. Once and once only I ventured out on to the main road. It was nearly the end of me as well as the bicycle.

I had been told to go to Bella's shop at Camptown about a mile away to get some bath-brick which the servant-girl used when scouring knives. In a fit of bravado I decided to go on the bicycle, but only as far as the road-end.

I set off riding sideways as usual. It was a rough journey down the bumpy road and I took many a toss. Once I fell into a clump of nettles and had to rub docken leaves on my hands and legs to take away the sting. No sooner was I remounted than I was off again, into a whin bush this time, but I was used to such mishaps and so was the bike. I had meant to leave it propped against a tree at the foot of the road, but as I was nearing the road-end the brakes refused to work. It was downhill and I was gathering speed all the time, so there was nothing for it but to turn left and continue my wobbly ride on the main road.

It was the first time I had ridden on such a smooth surface, and I had no idea the baneshaker could go at such a speed. I clung on, trying my best to keep a straight furrow and praying that no one would stray across my path. There were no cocks, pigs or bubblyjocks here. Worse, there were motor cars and lorries swerving past and a tinker's cart in front.

I rang my bell in desperation but the tink did not hear me. By now the baneshaker was out of control and all I could do was close my eyes when it ran slap-bang into the back of the cart. For a moment I saw stars, and the next thing I knew I was lying on the roadside with the tinker's pony cropping the grass beside me.

It was the end of the baneshaker for a time. The tink tried to make a bargain with me. He could use the remains of the bike as scrap if I liked to swap it for one of his pots or kettles. But, bleeding nose and all, I stuck to my guns and refused. When he had gone, I hid the broken bicycle in the ditch and struggled on to Bella Confectionery's to buy the bath-brick.

'Ye're a sorry sicht,' she told me, and lent me a red-and-white spotted handkerchief to stem the blood. She also gave me a piece of her home-made toffee which helped to soothe my wounded spirits.

Later, I persuaded Jock-the-herd to rescue the baneshaker's remains. He carried it home over his shoulder, protesting, 'Man-lassie, I doot it's had it this time.' But, 'Oh no,' I protested, 'the bell still rings.'

Once more he patched it up and I was able to pedal round the farmyard again. It was my plaything for years, and finally ended up on the rockery with all kinds of greenery growing over it. Perhaps it is there yet, and if so the bell will still be working.

It would be about this time that I saw my first aeroplane. It was when I was alone in the keep on the hill. A sudden shower had come on and I was sheltering in the great stone fireplace when I heard the throbbing in the sky as if a hundred motor cars were riding overhead. At first I thought it was the end of the world. The sky would split and a host of angels, or maybe devils, would come down and fetch me away.

I remember cowering down and trying to pray, but all I could think of was one of my father's comic songs. 'There was a wee cooper wha' lived in Fife. Nickety, nackety, noo-noo-noo!' So I settled for that instead.

It had no effect on the monster in the sky. The throbbing grew louder and louder till the giant seemed to be hovering immediately above my head. I looked up in terror through the open chimney-place, and there it was, a great mechanical bird, flying away through the mist in the direction of the Carter Bar. Mystified, I went out into the rain and watched it till it vanished over the Border. Then there was nothing. I waited for ages to see if it would come back, but it never did.

4. Gilding the Lily

It is an old Scottish characteristic that we see the faults in other people and never notice our own. When the minister preached on Sunday from the text, 'Judge not that ye be not judged,' I had a feeling he was aiming at me. I was for ever trying to put folk right, but seldom succeeding.

The servant-lasses, for example. We had a succession of these gawky creatures whom Jessie tried to lick into shape as if breaking in wild animals, but they never came up to her high standards. Poor things, they must have had a hard time, sent to work the moment they left school, longing to go out and play instead of washing up endless dishes, scrubbing the kitchen floor and blacking the fireplace.

Some stayed in, others tramped across the hills from neighbouring farms where their fathers were hinds or shepherds, and trudged back again at night when their work was done. I remember their hands, red and rough, sometimes covered with hacks and chilblains in winter. One I used to see blubbering into the kitchen sink. My heart bleeds for her; too late.

Liz-Ann is the one I remember best. She had been one of the big girls at school when I was an infant. Not very bright, according to the master, but he said the same about us all. Certainly she got the strap more often than the rest of us and used to sit on her hands afterwards, staring blankly at the blackboard.

Mental arithmetic was her downfall. Mine, too. How could one keep all those figures in the head and add them up, especially if one of the big boys was trying to put us 'off the stot' by tugging at our hair or thrusting inky blotting-paper down the backs of our necks? Poor Liz-Ann got lost right from the start. Her answer was always, 'I dinna ken.' Even with a pencil and jotter she never got as far as fractions.

Her efforts at writing essays were even more disastrous. The cruel thing, far more wounding than the strap, was that Auld Baldy-Heid sometimes read them out for all the class to giggle over. The spelling, too, must have been terrible, but we never saw that, only heard the master's sarcastic tones as he read out Liz-Ann's latest gem.

'Listen to this,' he would begin in a gloating voice. ' "My holiday. I have not had no holiday. Was once at m'Auntie's in Hawick. Just for the day. Nice. Seen shops, got a new ribbing for my hair, blue. M'Auntie's got a bad leg." ' And so on.

Maybe it was funny, but I used to glower at Auld Baldy-Heid, hating him as he read the smudged writing, and pitying poor Liz-Ann with her reddened shamed face. Judge not that ye be not judged.

When she turned up in our kitchen I determined to be nice to her and shield her, if I could, from Jessie's wrath, but soon I was seeing her faults myself. Everything Liz-Ann touched seemed to come away in her hand. She burnt the potatoes, knocked over pans, broke bowls, dropped bags of meal on the floor and fell over the cat. She was such a clumsy clattering creature that Jessie christened her the Cairthorse.

She lived in, and sometimes I had to share her bed if visitors were staying the night. Her room was small with a skylight, and no space for a human being to turn round in, far less a carthorse. I was surprised to see how Liz-Ann climbed into bed in her long goonie, lay down and went instantly to sleep, as if she had died. I never did. I had to stay awake for ages, sorting out all the things in my head and thinking over everything that had happened that day.

It seemed that I had no sooner fallen asleep than the alarum rang with a harsh ugly sound. It roused me immediately, but not the Cairthorse who only grunted and dived deeper under the bedclothes. By this time I was hanging half out of the bed, for it was narrow enough to begin with and Liz-Ann seemed to have expanded in all directions during the night. Often I had to shake the poor creature awake, and she rose in a heap, her face crumpled and her eyes still half-shut.

She lit the candle and dressed like a whirlwind in the freezing darkness of the dawn, pulling on one unshapely garment after another, and finally tying herself into an enveloping apron.

I felt it unfair that I should lie on, in the warm nest she had left, while she trailed away downstairs to her tasks, and had half-hearted thoughts of getting up to lend her a hand, but I never did. Instead, I fell into a blissful sleep in the great hollow left by Liz-Ann, with the patchwork quilt all to myself, and did not wake till the sun came streaming in through the skylight window.

Goodness knows how many dreary jobs the Cairthorse had done by the time I went down into the kitchen, ready for my breakfast. She had lit the fire, swept the floor, stirred the porridge, carried in sticks, scrubbed the table, peeled the potatoes. And doubtless broken the teapot.

What did Liz-Ann do in her spare time? I remember her

sitting dejectedly at the kitchen table, leaning on her elbows and staring into space, or turning over the pages of the sheep-dip catalogue. Sometimes I tried to cheer her up by playing the wheezy gramophone and getting her to hop round the kitchen with me, but she could never keep in time to the tune and only tramped on my toes. In her stocking-soles, fortunately, not in her clogs.

Now and again she came out to play hide-and-seek, but even at that the Cairthorse had no skill. I could crouch behind the water barrel, keep as still as a mouse, and never be seen. Not Liz-Ann, who blundered about like a bullock and always gave herself away by her heavy breathing.

On her day off she went clumping away home and had little to say when she came back with a bundle of clean clothing under her arm, tied in brown paper.

'How did you get on, Liz-Ann?'

'Fine.'

One day I discovered that the Cairthorse was not as dumb as she looked. She had a secret. I found out about it when she was struggling to write a letter at the kitchen table, and making heavy weather of it, sighing, sucking her pencil and staring at the ceiling for inspiration.

She tried to shield it from me, then in despair she asked, 'How d'ye spell crossroads?'

'Crossroads?' said I, not very sure myself. 'Who are you writing to?'

Liz-Ann turned as red as raspberry jam and looked over her shoulder to see that no one was listening. Then, with a faint touch of pride in her voice, she confessed. 'I'm writin' to ma lad.'

'Mercy me!'

I stared at her, dumbfounded. I knew it was every servant-girl's ambition to 'get a lad' and eventually a wedding-ring. It was their only escape from service, though it seemed to me they were only exchanging one set of shackles for another. But it had never occurred to me that the ungainly Cairthorse could ever attract a follower. Yet here she was sweating over a letter to her lad.

His name, she told me, was George (though I saw she had spelt it Gorge, which was near enough, I suppose). A herd-laddie, he lived somewhere in the region of the Back of Beyond and sometimes met Liz-Ann on her day off. That was as far as it had gone, but it was enough to put a sparkle in her eye when she spoke his name. He was a lad, and the Cairthorse was not going to let him slip through her fingers, clumsy though they were.

In the end she handed over the letter to me and I finished it off as well as I could. If Auld Baldy-Heid had seen it, with its crossings-out and misspellings, he would certainly have given Liz-Ann the strap, and me, too; but at least it was short and to the point.

The burden of it was 'Dear Gorge, will meet you at the crossroads on Sunday at six. Yours truly, Liz-Ann.'

'Would you not like to put with love, Liz-Ann?' I suggested.

'Oh no! What wad he think?'

I never met Gorge, but I saw him once wheeling his bicycle near the crossroads, with Liz-Ann striding along a few paces behind him, like a shaggy sheep-dog. He was only a wee fellow with tousled hair and tackety boots, but he was better then nothing. I often wonder if Liz-Ann married him and had lots of little carthorses. Perhaps she and Gorge spent their honeymoon at M'Auntie's in Hawick.

I remember that in anticipation of the wedding (if there was to be one) I made an attempt to save up to buy something for her bottom drawer. At that time I kept my riches in a china pig on a shelf in the kitchen. A thrifty, Jessie called it. It reminded me of the ditty she sometimes sang in the byre when milking the cows, about Coltart who made a special kind of candy, flavoured with aniseed, and travelled in the Borders selling it.

Allabally, Allabally bee,
Sittin' on your mammie's knee,
Greetin' for another bawbee
To buy some Coltart's candy.

Mither, gie's ma thrifty doon
Coltart's comin' to the toon,
Wi' a feather in his croon,
To sell some Coltart's candy.

There was never much money in my thrifty so I used to put in a few buttons and safety-pins to make it rattle a bit more. I found a small key and popped that in as well, never thinking it had a vital use.

The day came, of course, when everyone was hunting high and low for it.

'Ye've no' swallowed it?' asked Jessie, looking at me suspiciously. 'The key to your faither's hat box. He's gaun to a funeral an' he canna get oot his lum hat.'

'What's it like?' I asked guiltily.

'The lum hat? Toots! ye ken fine what a lum hat looks like. It's got a high heid. . . .'

'No, no. The key. Was it a wee small one?'

'Ay, it was a wee sma' ane,' said Jessie, grabbing me by the scruff of the neck. 'Whaur is't?'

'It's in the pig,' I had to confess.

'Ye're a daft eediot,' said Jessie angrily. 'Come on, get it oot.'

The trouble with the thrifty was, though it was easy enough putting things it, it was not so easy getting them out. It took the entire family working with bread-knives and scissors to disgorge its contents. A farthing here, a half-penny there, a button, a back-stud, a darning-needle. Finally the missing key, but by that time my father had been forced to go hatless to the funeral.

'Noo, see here,' said Jessie, beginning to read me one of

her lessons, 'there's naething to gang into that thrifty but siller. D'ye hear me? Naething.'

Suitably chastened, I put back the few coins and replaced the pig on the shelf. I used to rattle it now and again in the hope that its contents had multiplied by magic, but they never did. Sometimes the herd or the postie, or even an Ingan Johnny who came in for a cup of tea, added the odd halfpenny, but my savings seldom grew beyond sixpence, so there was little hope of buying anything for Liz-Ann's 'doon-sittin' ', apart from maybe a duster. Then one day the cat knocked the thrifty off the shelf and smashed it to smithereens. So that was the end of the pig.

In my efforts to be helpful to the Cairthorse I suggested she should curl her hair with the tongs to improve its lankness. The 'tings', Jessie called them. But Liz-Ann made a mess of that, too, by burning her brow and looking a worse sight than ever.

Who was I to speak? My hair was always 'toozy', and the only treatment it received was getting the ends singed once a week. A perfect pest. It was Jessie who did the deed, and I was always in terror lest she set my whole head on fire.

'An' so I wull, if ye dinna sit still.'

Singeing the hair was supposed to make it grow thicker. 'Though your heid's thick enough already, an' no' muckle intil't.'

Jock-the-herd was as bald as a billiard ball, not that he was often seen without a hat, except in the kirk. He seemed so self-conscious about his bare head that he kept taking out a large handkerchief and rubbing it over his pate, till Jessie dug him in the ribs and gave him one of her glowers.

I once asked her, 'Did you never singe Jock's hair?'

'No, I never. It's only lasses.'

So I tried it on a doll with a mop of bright flossy hair (but that was before I passed my Qualifying and learnt a modicum of sense). The results were disastrous. Flames shot all over the poor creature's head, her waxen face began to melt, and Jessie had to plunge her hastily into a pail of water. She was never the same again.

Though the herd would never have dreamt of beautifying himself, he sometimes tried to improve the looks of his flock before taking them to the sales. 'Toshing them up', he called it. He even dabbed a kind of powder on their faces and clipped away bits of wool here and there to make their fleeces look neater. The hinds, too, were for ever toshing up their horses, combing their manes, brushing their tails, and polishing their harness.

Jessie did not believe in gilding the lily. 'A guid scrub wi' soap an' waitter' was as far as she would go. I sometimes tried putting self-raising flour on my freckled nose, following the herd's example with the sheep, but she soon rubbed it off. 'Floor'll no' cover your sins. An' what's wrang wi' a wheen fernytickles, onyway?'

I remember once giving her a bottle of cheap scent at Christmas. She sniffed at it and made a wry face – it was certainly very strong – before putting back the cork and saying, 'Mercy me! it wad knock ye doon.'

I found the bottle days after in the duster drawer, and for ages the dusters smelt so strongly of perfume that they had to be washed in the boiler and hung on the line to get rid of Ashes of Violet. The next time I bought Jessie a present it was a bar of carbolic soap, and she was better pleased with that.

It was hardly worth my while doing good deeds or trying to improve folk, so often my plans went wrong. Yet I felt I ought to do something about the strange woman whose cottage door I used to pass every day on the way to the village school. She had a name, I suppose, but I just thought of her as Mrs Pot Plant, for she seemed to spend most of her time taking care of a sickly-looking aspidistra.

It was like a spoiled bairn; indeed, I often wondered if Mrs Pot Plant would have made such a fuss of the aspidistra if she had not been childless. She was always bringing it to the door for a breath of air, or polishing its pot. And her spirits rose and fell depending on how the plant was looking. She used to talk about it as if it was human. I would not have been surprised if she had given it a name, Wullie or Geordie.

I tried to slink past her door, for I always felt embarrassed when she brought me into the conversation. I was fond enough of plants but not to that extent.

'D'ye no' think he's lookin' doon-in-the-mooth this mornin'?' she would ask me anxiously.

'No, no; he's fine,' I would say, just to cheer her up.

But if I was not feeling fine myself, if I had the sneezes or the sniffles, Mrs Pot Plant would not let me come within coughing-distance of her precious pet.

'Watch oot,' she would warn me, 'ye micht smit him.'

Sometimes I overheard her talking encouragingly to the aspidistra. 'Come on, noo, cheer up. See! I'll set ye on the windy-sill an' ye'll get a sook o' fresh air. D'ye fancy a wee drink o' cauld tea?'

She had tried everything, she told me. Setting the plant near the fire to keep him warm, putting him through in the best room away from draughts, propping up his leaves with sticks, and giving him strange concoctions to drink in the hope that they would act as tonics. But still the aspidistra drooped and dwindled as if he was in the last stages of consumption.

Then one day a terrible tragedy happened. The pet lamb had followed me right down the road, and I was trying to shoo him away back home when he suddenly swerved and made a dive at the aspidistra which was sitting dejectedly outside the door. For once Mrs Pot Plant was not on guard to see the disaster, which was just as well, for my blood ran cold when I saw the lamb knocking over the pot, smashing it to pieces and scattering the soil in all directions.

As for the aspidistra, he lay dying on the doorstep, but I was too cowardly to wait for the requiem. I took to my heels and ran for my life; and for days afterwards I did a detour to avoid meeting the bereaved woman.

Then one day I forgot and came down the road past her cottage as usual. To my surprise Mrs Pot Plant greeted me as bright as a bee.

'See!' she said triumphantly. 'See what's happened to him.'

She pointed proudly to the aspidistra sitting in a new pot on the window-sill, looking sturdier than I had ever seen him before, with glossy leaves and his head held high.

'He's come on a treat since his accident. I thought he was a goner, but he's never looked back. D'ye no' think he's improved?'

'Oh y-yes! Yes, he has,' I agreed, and went hastily on my way, not sure whether I could take the praise or the blame. All the same, I thought it safer in future to keep detouring past her door.

5. Away to Edinburgh

It was Jessie who broke the astounding news to me. She always knew everything before I did.

'I hear ye'll be seein' Auld Reekie the morn.'

'Auld Reekie! Who's he?'

'He's no' a he. He's a place. Auld Reekie's the nickname for Edinburgh. Ye ken that, shairly. Ye're to gang there for the day. Wi' them.'

Them being my father and mother.

I would have turned a cartwheel on the spot at the thought of such an exciting adventure if I had not been feeding a calf at the time. No easy matter. The creature was half-drowning in the pail I was holding up to his head. Now and again he would extract himself and look up at me with limpid eyes before slobbering at my fingers. It was a messy performance, with the milk dribbling from the calf's mouth and running up my sleeve.

'Sook, sook', Jessie urged him. 'Mind your manners. Sook, sook.'

As soon as I could, I laid down the pail and jumped into the air like a daft thing. Fancy me going to Edinburgh, the capital of Scotland! It was the height of bliss to go to Jedburgh once in a while and see half a dozen folk in the High Street. What would it be like in Princes Street with real crowds, not to mention tramcars?

It was no wonder I could not settle to anything for the rest of that day, but wandered about like a knotless thread, visualizing the joys to come. The castle, the One o'Clock Gun, Holyrood House, Sir Walter Scott's Monument, Edinburgh Rock.

That night my mother laid out my best clothes and said, 'You'd better get to bed early. We'll have to be up at the crack.'

I hardly slept a wink, I was away in Auld Reekie all night. The crack came at the darkest hour before the dawn, and I rose bleary-eyed, feeling I was in a dream world, eating my breakfast by lamplight with my Sunday hat on my head.

The cocks were crowing and the hinds plodding up the road on their way to work when we passed them in the gig on the way down. Flora was as frisky as a flea at that hour in the morning and whisked us in to Jedburgh in record time, stopping only once at a drinking-trough by the wayside. We drove down the High Street, past the Grammar School where I was soon to be a pupil, and into the station yard where the pony was unyoked and led away to be stabled.

The train stood waiting for us, getting up steam for the journey ahead, huffing and puffing like a giant smoking a great pipe. I sat on the faded red cushions in the old three-a-side carriage and stared at the long mirror opposite. Crude coloured pictures hung above it, depicting bracing North Berwick, beautiful Inverness, and lovely Largs, all of which one could visit by train, but not on this single line.

The station-master looked in at the window to have a word with my parents and passed the usual silly remark about me, 'My! isn't she shooting up!' as if I was a beanstalk.

Then he blew his whistle, waved his flag, and we were off.

The engine let out a great mouthful of steam as we went chugging along by the riverside, with red-hot sparks flying through the air like small stars. We ran through fields, past woods and cottages. A woman hanging out her washing waved and I waved back, thinking, 'Poor soul! what a dull life she leads compared with me. Away to Edinburgh in a train!' Then, as it gathered speed, the wheels changed their tune and the scenery rushed past at such a rate it was all merged into one.

All of a sudden there was a fearsome shriek as the engine tore into a tunnel, leaving us in blank darkness. Bracing North Berwick, beautiful Inverness and lovely Largs all were blacked out. I held my breath, wondering if we would ever emerge at the other end. It seemed ages before I could see daylight ahead.

Somewhere along the line we got out, crossed over a bridge and stood on a platform awaiting the big train that would whirl us to the Waverley station. There were others sitting three-a-side when we got it, and I was separated from my parents, sitting between a man reading his paper and a woman with the hiccups.

The newspaper restricted my view, expecially when the man held it at arm's length and shook it out before rustling over another page. Every now and then the woman hiccupped when I least expected it, almost bouncing me off my seat. If Jessie had been here she would certainly have shoved a cold key down the sufferer's back and said, 'Haud your braith, wumman.'

I could have stayed happily in the Waverley station all day when we reached it, there was so much to see; but I was forced to follow my parents up the windy steps and out into the street. Princes Street. No longer just a name. A reality at last.

I had never seen a crowd before except a flock of sheep. They all had the same faces, though Jock-the-herd could tell the difference, but here there was no mistaking the individual identity of every single person hurrying along the pavements in their hundreds. How on earth – or in heaven – had God managed to make them all so different, without ever repeating the pattern? Each face was distinctive; not a shape, size or contour the same. The only thing they had in common was the careless way they strayed across the street in the teeth of the traffic. Jock would have had a hard job rounding them up with Jed and Jess.

The thing that surprised me most as we set off along Princes Street was that we met the minister. Imagine seeing a kent face in that alien throng! There he was, coming towards us, raising his hat and looking as astonished as we were. He stopped and conversed with my parents while I got bumped in different directions by the passers-by. Then we went our separate ways; but we talked about it for days afterwards.

'Fancy meeting *him*! In Edinburgh, of all places.' As if we had been to the ends of the earth.

I would have been content to stand and stare at the passing scene. Especially at a small girl jumping on to a tramcar with a schoolbag on her back. How I envied her and wished there were tramlines all the way from our farm to Jedburgh. It would be better than going to school by baneshaker.

'Come on; you'll get lost.'

My parents kept tugging me along with them. I had a feeling, as I often did, that I was being a nuisance and that they would have got on better without me. I tried hard not to lag behind, but how could I help gawping with so many unusual sights to see? A coal-black man, surely the King of the Coconut Islands, striding along the street in a white nightgown. A lordly-looking lady with a monocle, dressed in knee-britches and sporting a feather, like Coltart's, in her hat. A woman swathed in furs and carrying a trembling poodle in her arms. A Russian princess? Nothing like these could be seen around the farmyard at home. Every strange face was untapped territory, like a new book to be read.

We stopped and looked at the windows of a large shop called Jenner's. The dummy ladies gazed vacantly back at us, smiling their sweet set smiles. They wore elegant garments with price-tags on them. Pink flounced nightgowns, evening-dresses glittering with sequins, fur-lined velvet capes. Even the little girls with their golden ringlets were dressed in silks and laces, not a hair out of place, not a wrinkle in their stockings. If only I could look like that!

We went inside. The door was held open for us by a man in splendid uniform with a row of medals on his chest. Another grand gentleman dressed in tail-coats came forward and bowed to my mother as if she were a duchess. I felt she ought to have curtseyed back.

'What would you like to see, madam?'

'Gloves,' said mother firmly.

I felt proud of her as she sat at the counter on a little gilt chair, throwing back her veil and trying on one pair after another. Father wandered away to look at lum hats, and I had a feeling we would never see him again, but he came back after a while, carrying a mysterious parcel, and paid for my mother's purchases.

The prim sales-lady rolled up the money and screwed it into a wooden container, like a round cricket-ball, before sending it on its journey along an overhead railway. I watched, fascinated, till it disappeared from sight and waited till it came rolling back with the change. I wished Bella Confectionery at the village shop would deal with my halfpennies in the same way.

Afterwards we entered a lift which shot upwards, stopping at each floor to let the people in and out, with a great clanging of gates. 'Boots!' shouted the man in charge. 'Perambulators! Carpets! Curtains!' What fun to ride up and down with him all day.

I was kitted out with a sensible navy-blue coat for school – no silks and laces for me – and new shoes, to be posted on later. 'Overton Bush,' instructed my mother. 'Near Camptown, Jedburgh, Roxburghshire.' It seemed a world away and I felt almost homesick at the sound of it.

We went up the Bridges to have lunch in another big store where there was a restaurant. A three-piece orchestra, better than our gramophone at home, played sweet music above the clatter of cutlery. I admired the way the deft waitresses in their frilly white aprons and caps carried their laden trays without even dropping a saucer. The Cairthorse, I felt sure, would have smashed the whole lot in no time.

I did not eat much, I was too busy watching the people. My parents, too, gazed around and made comments.

'I wonder who she is?' mused my mother, seeing a well-dressed lady at another table. 'She looks somebody. That's a smart hat.'

'I've got a better one here,' said Father, patting the parcel at his feet.

'What? Did you buy yourself a new tile?'

'No, it's for you.'

'Oh, John!' protested my mother; but I could tell how pleased she was by the pinkness in her cheeks. The strange thing was, Father could always buy her a hat that suited her. The right shape, the right size, with a little bit of dash about it. Whenever he went to the big town without her, he never came back without one, and never once had a failure. What did he say to the sales-lady? Did he try on the hat himself? I often wondered, but he never let on.

'What colour?' asked Mother, trying not to sound too eager. 'Blue?'

'Wait and see.'

It was brown with a little frill of pheasant feathers round it, but I did not discover that till next day when I saw it on her dressing-table at home. Meanwhile there were better things to do than look at hats. When we emerged into the street the One o'Clock Gun went off with such a sudden explosion that I nearly jumped out of my skin.

Edinburgh folk had funny ways of telling the time. We went to look at the Floral Clock in Princes Street gardens, ticking slowly round under its weight of blossoms. There was little chance to examine anything closely, for we were always on the move, bound for a place called Corstorphine where the zoo was, and before that to make a duty-call on the Misses Somebody who lived near the Meadows.

The Meadows were not meadows like ours at home, with cattle and sheep grazing on them. The grass was trodden into the ground and a few people wandered around, walking their dogs. Perhaps they had a feeling they were 'in the country', even though they could hear the din of the traffic nearby.

The old ladies we were to visit lived in a crescent. It was a new name to me and I wondered if it might be some strange kind of dwelling, like an igloo, maybe, or a mud hut, but it turned out to be a flat in a curved row of houses. Very ordinary except for the magic gate.

We went there in a bus. I could have ridden in it all day round Edinburgh, catching glimpses of Sir Walter on his monument, of tramcars swaying past, and watching the conductor ringing his bell to let the people on and off. It surprised me to see a man sitting across the passage from me, reading a book. With all that stirring life going on around him! Much though I loved reading, I would not have missed a moment of it.

When we reached the locked gate in the crescent Father peered at the names, then pressed a bell to let the Misses Somebody know we had arrived. Presently the gate swung open as if an unseen hand had unlatched it, and we went in, up steep stone stairs, past other flats till we reached the right door where an elderly servant was waiting for us.

Miss Jeannie and Miss Kate were distantly related to my father, second cousins, I think. I could scarcely see them in their darkened drawing-room. Heavy lace curtains dimmed the daylight, and even the old-fashioned furniture seemed sunk in gloom. A depressed-looking canary hung in a cage near the window, hiding its head, poor thing, under its feathers.

Miss Jeannie rose to greet us, creaking as she moved, but Miss Kate sat still with her feet on a footstool and an ebony stick by her side. She had a little black beard which attracted my attention. I kept staring at it till my mother nudged me and told me to go and sit on a small chair near the canary.

We had been invited for a cup of tea and that is literally what we got. It was served with great ceremony in such delicate cups that I was petrified lest I dropped mine and was disgraced for ever. The servant brought in the tray, spread a fine lace cloth on a small table, and Miss Jeannie took charge of the silver teapot. There were little tongs for the sugar-lumps and a strainer through which she poured the tea, puckering up her lips and taking care not to spill a single drop.

Grown-up conversation went on, mainly about the health of the old ladies, but I did not listen. I was trying to read the titles of the books locked in the glass-fronted bookcase. They looked as if they had never been read. Sets of the Waverley novels in dark red bindings, the *History of the World*, encyclopedias, sermons and dull-looking volumes of Shakespeare's works.

Suddenly my eyes lit on a shabbier book with a more familiar title, *Little Women*. I longed to unlock the bookcase and let it out, and looked across at the old ladies, wondering if they had ever shed tears over Beth, or laughed at Jo's exploits. But it seemed unlikely that they could ever have given way to such foolishness.

When it was time to go, Miss Kate beckoned me to her beaded footstool, fumbled in a pouch hidden amongst the folds of her skirt, and brought out a silver shilling.

'There! Take care how you spend it.'

'Oh yes, I will! Thanks!'

Miss Jeannie patted me on the head and said I was very

like somebody, but she could not remember who. I hoped it was someone nice.

Then the servant showed us out, and we went down the stone stairs, back through the magic gate. The visit was over, and I took a great gulp of Edinburgh air, thankful to be free.

I did not like the zoo. Father and mother seemed to expect me to enjoy seeing so many strange beasts and birds, but all I wanted was to open their cages and set them free. I would sooner have had one of our own Clydesdales than the great lumbering elephant with its swaying trunk. I refused to ride on its back, and took a scunner at the gorillas grinning at me through their bars. I wanted to get back to the shops to spend the silver shilling.

We went back in a tramcar and had a proper tea in a Princes Street tea-room, looking out towards the castle. The waitress brought a three-tiered dish with scones on the top, pancakes and currant bread in the middle, and little iced cakes on the bottom. One worked one's way down from plain to fancy. It was like a dream, looking up at the battlements and eating pink icing at the same time.

After such an early morning start I was beginning to feel drowsy, and for the rest of the day I went about in a daze, not sure that I was really awake. Everything seemed to have grown bigger, noisier and more confusing: the clang of the tramcars, the roar of the traffic, the tramping of feet. I seemed far away from reality and began to long for a sight of the quiet hills at the Back of Beyond.

On the way back to the Waverley station we went into a shop to buy some Edinburgh Rock. Which colour to choose? White, gingery brown, pale pink? Around the shelves there were hundreds of bottles of strange sweet-meats never seen in Bella's shop. It would have been great to stay there and sample the lot.

In the train I held the little box of rock in its tartan wrappings on my knee, and tried to resist the temptation to open it. I wanted to save some for Jessie, the herd, and Liz-Ann. Now and again my fingers fumbled with the paper, then the train gave a jerk and slid out of the station. Before long the rhythm of the wheels acted as a soporific, and I fell asleep sitting bolt upright.

I awoke in a fright to find myself in pitch darkness. Had I died and gone to the Bad Place? There was a flash of fire, a flurry of sparks, and suddenly the train rushed out of a tunnel. For the rest of the journey I stayed wide awake, watching the lit windows and wondering what the folk were doing inside their houses. Eating their suppers, maybe, or reading the paper before going to bed.

At long last I was back in my accustomed seat in the gig, with Flora kicking up her heels as she cantered home. It seemed years since we had made the reverse journey in the early morning, and I felt I had lived through a lifetime of experiences since then.

It was so late that we met no one on the way. There was nothing to be seen except the sheep's eyes shining from the fields. The night air was keen, as sharp as soor dook. It kept me from nodding off and falling out.

Then suddenly the pony turned in at our road-end and my heart gave a little leap. We were back on our own home ground. It had been exciting seeing all the glories of the great city, but it was nice to know the shabby old farmhouse awaited us. Maybe I would get tired of Princes Street, never of our own homestead.

6. Into the Unknown

I thought I knew everything till I went to the Grammar School and learnt that I knew nothing.

Had I not passed my Qualifying? I could milk a cow, stook corn, feed calves, turn the heel of a sock, read anything from the *Scotsman* to the *Pilgrim's Progress.* I knew a stirk from a stot, a yowe from a gimmer, and had even been to Edinburgh for the day.

But I had never heard of algebra or science. Or of those strange marks called circumflexes over unpronounceable French words. Indeed, the first word I learned was a Latin one. Ignoramus. It described me, according to my new teachers, and was only a different way of telling me I had no rummlegumption.

It was frightening on that first morning going down the rough farm road knowing I was not on my way to join my former classmates. For the first time in my life I felt homesick, not so much for home as for a sight of my familiar desk at the old school. Even old Baldy-Heid in a rage would have been a pleasanter prospect than the unknown terrors awaiting me in the town.

The cottage wives turned the screw as I walked past, self-conscious in my new togs: navy-blue gym-tunic, white blouse, navy-blue coat, new shoes that hurt after running barefoot all summer. I was even wearing a pair of gloves.

'Look at her!' said Mrs Thingummy – I could never remember the names of the hinds' wives – shaking her rag rug and barely visible behind a cloud of dust. Where did it come from every day? 'A' dressed up! She'll soon get the stuffin' taken oot her.'

'So she wull,' agreed the other Mrs Thingummy, dolefully. I never saw *her* shaking a rug. She was more often hanging out her man's long drawers and flannel shirts on the line. 'She little kens what she's in for, puir cratur'.'

Thus encouraged, I went off to my execution with lagging steps, but brightened up when I saw Jock-the-herd leaning over a dyke.

'Man-lassie,' he shouted, taking no notice of my new outfit, 'see that black-faced yowe? Could ye weir her in through the yett?'

'Yes, I could, Jock.'

For a few blissful moments, during which I lost a hair-ribbon and one of my gloves, I forgot my impending doom. If only I could have changed places with the collies and spent the rest of the day rounding up sheep! But the school bus was to come for me at the road-end, and I had been warned not to be late, especially on my first day.

No need, after all, to travel by pony or by bicycle. It was a relief to me when I heard about the bus which was to collect me and several other scholars at road-ends on the way in to Jedburgh. I waited for it outside Mary-Anne's lodge-house at the corner while she fed her hens and talked to them, as Mrs Pot Plant did to her aspidistra. Maggie, Mrs Broon, Jemima, Wee Rascal, and the rest. She had a name for the cockerel, too. His Nibs.

Mary-Anne was like a wee wizened apple, all wrinkled and with only one tooth. The pockets of her apron were always full of corn or new-laid eggs.

'Maggie's aff her meat,' she told me, looking disconsolately at one of her drooping hens. 'She's feelin' a bit upsy-doonsy. Nae appetite. What aboot a jeelly-piece?'

If Maggie had no appetite, mine was sharp enough in the early morning to do justice to the slice of pan-loaf spread with rasp jam when Mary-Anne brought it out to me. I never ate much at meal-times but was always ready for 'shivery-bites' in between.

As I was licking the jam off my fingers, Big Bob, the braggart at the village school, came along, kicking a stone in front of him. I would have given anything to fall into step beside him, even though he stuck out his tongue at me and jeered, 'Silly thing! Dressed up like mince an' tatties.'

It was a lonely feeling standing there by the roadside wondering if I would ever be picked up. But presently a small bus came rattling to a standstill beside me, and a stout red-faced driver leaned out. 'Hop in, wee ane,' said he, hauling me up the steep step as if I was a sack of potatoes, and slamming the door behind me.

I was off into the unknown.

But the great thing was, I had found a new friend. Black Sandy. I never found out how the driver came by his name. Certainly not by the colour of his hair, what was left of it, for it was as carrotty as mine. Perhaps he had been christened Sandy Black and someone had reversed it. Black Sandy he remained to me, and to the others whom he picked up on the winding road into Jedburgh.

All the way in he whistled like a linty and sang at the pitch of his voice. 'The Muckin' o', Geordie's Byre', 'The Bonnie Lass o' Fyvie,' 'Paddy McGinty's Goat'. When he ran short of songs, he had a shot at hymns. 'By Cool Siloam's Shady Rill', 'Onward Christian Soldiers', 'Abide With Me'.

He would shout, too, at the bus as if it was a horse. 'Whoa there! Steedy! Gee-up, auld cuddy!' He was great.

The best thing about Black Sandy was his sense of justice. He did not mind how much din we made in the bus, and we made plenty for we were a boisterous lot, but if I was getting the worst of it, he would roar over his shoulder, 'Leave the wee ane alane, or I'll clout ye on the lug.'

It worked both ways. I always stood up for the portly driver when the others became cheeky and shouted abuse at him.

> Black Sandy,
> His legs are bandy.

'No, they're not,' I would protest, and put up my fists, ready for battle.

Black Sandy himself did not seem to mind the insults.

> Sticks an' stanes'll break ma banes
> But words'll never hurt me.

He could have hurt any of us with one sweep from his powerful arms, but it never came to that. His threats were enough.

On that first day I rattled about in the empty bus like a loose pea in a pod before Black Sandy drew up at the roadside to collect his next passenger. His stops and starts were so jerky that I was often black and blue by the end of the journey; but he always got us there even in the iciest days of winter when he had to put chains on the wheels and we were often ordered to get out and push.

There were about a dozen of us in the bus by the time we passed the old Capon Tree, the last giant of Jedforest, and came within sight of the ruined abbey. After rattling down the High Street, Black Sandy drew up at the school gates. 'Whoa, auld cuddy! Oot, everybody!' he shouted. I had reached the point of no return.

I began my Higher Education with a blot. Worse, I

dropped a ruler with such a clatter it attracted the attention of my first new teacher and foiled my main object, which was to keep quiet and not be noticed.

'Fumble-fingers!' she said, pointing me out to the rest of the class. 'You, the gingery one.'

I had often been called Carrot-heid at the village school. Now I was Ginger. Not that names mattered. It took me weeks to get the hang of what the teachers were called. There were so many of them, and we were constantly coming and going from one classroom to another. No sooner, it seemed, had we got settled to one lesson, than a bell would ring. All change! We had to pick up books and pencils, troop off to another room and turn our minds to an entirely different subject, taught by yet another strange teacher. I was bamboozled for weeks before I settled into the routine.

The first teacher was an indomitable character called Miss Crichton, who came from the North-East and taught us French in an Aberdeen accent. Later on, when a real Frenchman came to visit the school, I thought he could not speak the language for toffee. His accent was so different from ours.

On that first morning I never got further than *la* and *le*. It seemed daft to me that a table should be feminine and a ceiling masculine, but if Miss Crichton said so it must be true, for she spoke with such authority and emphasized every word by blowing her nose. She was troubled, poor soul, with persistent catarrh and was for ever drying her handkies on the radiator. But for all that she was a born teacher and dinned the learning into us with many a rap over the head with a long pointer.

All that day I went in a daze from history to English, algebra to science, with my mind becoming more and more muddled. I longed to be back in Auld Baldy-Heid's domain, where I could sit in peace doodling on my jotter while he taught the little ones their poetry.

I have a little shadow that goes in and out with me,
And what can be the use of it is more than I can see.

It seemed a lifetime before we were let out into the vast playground for a break. There were no communal games of kick-the-can or hide-and-seek. The laddies went their own ways, playing with a real football, while the lasses leant limply against a wall, or played a half-hearted game of rounders.

They looked upon me, rightly enough, as 'in from the country'. No doubt they thought I lived in a byre or a hen-house. Indeed, I felt like a shaggy sheep-dog beside them, and kept my distance, humbly grateful if they allowed me to retrieve a ball that had fallen at my feet.

Then one of them called: 'Hi, Ginger! Catch!' I was in!

Many of the pupils went home for their midday meals, but those from a distance ate their pieces in the playground, and could buy a steaming-hot bowl of soup for a penny from a vast cauldron in one of the sheds. It was boiled up and ladled out by a wee woman who called us all You.

'Come on, You! Haud oot your bowel!'

The soup was thick and tasty, full of fresh vegetables. A meal in itself. But if we preferred 'rubbish', as I often did, we could go out into the street and look for the nearest sweet-shop. Or buy an ice-cream slider at the Tally's shop up near the market-place.

It was a long time before I was bold enough to leave the safe precincts of the playground and venture out into the town on my own. A fearsome man called the Janny guarded the gates and ruthlessly locked them the moment the school bell summoned us back for the afternoon session.

What if one got left outside? No use looking imploringly through the bars, or trying to climb over. The gates were too high, and the janitor deaf to all pleas. Timing, therefore, was of first importance, and I had no watch. The town clock was up in the market-place, but could one be certain that it was always at the right time?

After a while I overcame my anxieties and took my first tentative steps to freedom. Thereafter a whole new world was opened to me as I explored the streets, closes, and back alleyways. I could never get over the excitement of being let loose in a town, of watching people, seeing the shops, hearing other sounds than the crowing of cocks and bleating of sheep, of finding treasure-trove every time I turned a corner.

The house, for example, where Bonnie Prince Charlie sought refuge during the Forty-Five. I stood gawping at it, picturing him riding into the town at the head of his band of wild Highlanders, looking for recruits. If I had been there at the time I would have joined him in a jiffy.

The town was full of history, better than the dull contents of the lesson-books in the Grammar School. Sometimes I stood on the ramparts and gazed sadly at the ruined abbey, thinking of the skirmishes which took place when the old enemy came over the Border to ransack the place. Or I looked up at a little window in Queen Mary's House, half-expecting to see a sad sweet face looking out and a lily-white hand waving to me.

Down at the Townfoot Brig I could lean over and look at the ducking-place where suspected witches were tested in the old days. If they sank they were innocent. If they floated they were guilty and burned alive. There was no hope for them either way, poor things.

One day in my wanderings round the town I found the house at Abbey Close where Wordsworth of the dancing daffodils, and his sister Dorothy, had lodged.

As I was staring at it a little man in a long ragged coat came and stood beside me. A wandering tramp, maybe, for his pouches seemed to contain all his worldly possessions. He talked half to himself, half to me, in an English accent.

One of the auld enemy clan. But I could forgive him that, since he was so full of information.

'Did you know that Sir Walter Scott visited the Wordsworths when they stayed here? No? Well, he did. And, what's more, he read his new poem to them. *The Lay of the Last Minstrel*. In this very house.

'The way was long, the wind was cold,
The minstrel was infirm and old. . . .'

He went on, stanza after stanza. Then he took off his bonnet. At first I thought it was a gallant gesture in honour of Sir Walter, but when he held it out to me I saw that he wanted recompense and had to fumble in my pocket for my penny. There was no ice-cream or sweets for me that day, but it was well worth the sacrifice. I felt that I was personally acquainted with Sir Walter and the Wordsworths for ever after.

Later on I learned that Robert Burns had also come to Jedburgh with his head full of poetry, and true to form had wandered by the banks of the Jed with a bonnie lassie. I considered it remiss of Shakespeare not to have visited the town, and thought he might have written even better plays if he had come.

As always, though, it was people rather than places that mattered most. I loved the Cross, the hub of the universe, where multitudes it seemed to me foregathered on market-day. I might see my father there surrounded by his cronies, all laughing uproariously at some of his quips. Father's funny stories were the talk of the countryside. It was not so much the stories themselves as the way he told them. I knew them all word for word but I could have listened to him for ever.

I did not go near him, of course. The market-place was not for females; but if he caught sight of me standing on the pavement he would come across, thrust his hand into his pocket and bring forth some coppers to spend.

'There, lass!'

That was all he said before rejoining his fellow farmers at the Cross. But it left a warm glow at my heart, and it was not only because of the pennies.

It was a bonus if I met my mother in the High Street, dressed in her fur coat and wearing the hat Father had bought her in Edinburgh. I felt proud to be walking by her side, especially if one of the town scholars saw us together. Maybe I was only a tousled tyke from the country, but my mother looked a lady. I felt my stock rising if she walked me down as far as the school gates. Even the Janny touched his cap to her.

But these were rare occasions. Mostly I was on my own, content to roam from the Castlegate to the Bow, from Duck Row to the Friars (I got to know all the names eventually) but always rushing back to the market-place so that I could keep an eye on the town clock.

All this was far in the future. On that first day I was too bemused to stray out of step. I kept in line with the others, following them like a sheep from one classroom to another. By the time the final bell rang I could not believe it was only that same morning I had walked down the farm road and helped Jock with his stray yowe.

Black Sandy was waiting with his bus at the school gate. 'Hop in, wee ane,' he said, giving me a mighty heave up. 'Onward Christian Soldiers!'

We were off on the road home.

I got out at the Camptown road end and walked the mile back to the farm, trying to untangle all the new experiences that were whirling through my head. What a lot I would have to tell everybody! All about *la table*, the janitor, and the science master who called me miss. 'Come on, miss. Look lively. Have you never seen a Bunsen burner before?' Indeed, I had not.

I came down to earth with a bump. It was a great blow to find the whole household was not waiting breathlessly for my return. They were all too engrossed in their own pursuits to show any interest in mine. Jessie was out milking the cows, the servant-lassie was scouring the churn and did not even look at me when I came in. My mother was ben the hoose whirring away at the sewing-machine.

'There's some supper in the oven,' she called through, and that was all.

So in the end I sat down at *la* kitchen *table* to my solitary meal, dumped in spirits but realizing that amongst all the lessons I had learned that day, the hardest was that I must continue to plough a lonely furrow.

What a lot one had to keep to oneself for the lack of a listening ear. But there was always an inner self with whom one could share experiences. So as I ate my mince and cabbage I went over it all again in my own head.

When Jessie came clattering in with the milk-pails, she asked, 'Hoo did ye get on, lassie?' But by now I wanted to keep it to myself, so I just said, 'Fine.'

7. Men and Beasts

I was now a town mouse as well as a country one, living in two dimensions, travelling to Jedburgh every day and coming back up the bumpy road to the farm every evening.

The things I knew! *Ouvrez la porte*. Isosceles triangles. The exports of Australia. The wives of Henry the Eighth.

But I was still nobody at home, glad enough to shed my town skin with my school clothes and run wild at the weekends and during the long summer evenings. This was my real world. The other was only a confused muddle of French verbs, English essays, and dead kings.

There was a creaking swing in the wood where I sometimes sat swaying to and fro. In fits of derring-do I would try to raise enough impetus to fly as high as the treetops, frightening the cushy-doos from their perches and causing the herd to shout up to me, 'Watch oot, wumman! Ye'll drap deid!' But I could usually persuade him to give me a push, and once I even inveigled him to sit on the swing himself.

'Here! no' so high!' he roared when I shoved him off with all my might. He was so much heavier than I was that he sailed away sky-high. It was strange having Jock at my mercy. I laughed while I swung him round and round till the rope was in a twist and he whirled about as helpless as a baby, while Jed and Jess sat on their tails, their tongues hanging out in amazement.

When he was back on his feet again Jock shook his fist at me, picked up his crook and said, 'Ye wee deevil, ye! I've a guid mind to cut doon that swing.' But, of course, he never did.

I still followed at his heels like an extra collie, clambering over dykes and sometimes helping to 'shed' the sheep when he was trying to count them. This meant shooing them through a narrow opening while the herd began in a sing-song voice, 'Ane-twae-three-fower.' Often he got mixed up when the sheep darted through two at a time or doubled back on their tracks. Then he would give a groan and say, 'Was that toonty-fower or toonty-five? Dammit! I'm a' mixed up.'

I liked to hear the Northumbrian shepherds counting their flock. None of your one-two-three-four. They had a kind of rigmarole which I learnt off by heart.

Een-teen-tethera-methera-pimp.
Awfus-dawfus-deefus-dumfus-dik.
Een-a-dik, teen-a-dik. . . .

On to bumpit and jiggit. A much better way of doing arithmetic than bothering about vulgar fractions.

Jock had various evil-smelling medicines with which he doctored sick animals from time to time, but there were occasions when a horse or a cow developed some serious ailment which necessitated a visit from the vet.

He was a big bluff man who came all the way from Kelso, driving a rattletrap of a motor car as if it was a charger. He had the reputation of being fond of a dram, and after ministering to the sick beast he always came into the house with my father for a secret refreshment.

I kept out of his way, for he was a jokey man, given to great gusts of laughter at my expense, and I was never sure whether his leg-pulls were real or not. If I was within reach, he would grab me by the hair, brandish a fearsome-looking instrument from his bag and roar, 'Is this the patient? Right! I'll soon cure her. Off with her top knot!' He was terrifying.

But Jock said he had a wonderful way with beasts and could make them understand what he was saying. I wondered what kind of noises he made when communicating with a cow or a Clydesdale, but I was much too frightened of him to find out. It was said, true or not, that he used to drive through gates without bothering to open them, charging at them in his rattletrap and not caring what wreckage he left behind.

We were used to having ailing animals in the kitchen. Lambs needing to be bottle-fed, a sick calf that lay on the rug beside the cat, or drooping chicks which we wrapped in flannel and popped like pies into the gently heated oven. As soon as they revived and we heard their cheep-cheeps, we took them out and let them stagger about on the floor. Before long they were pecking at crumbs or snuggling down beside Blackie, the kitchen cat, who accepted any strange bedfellows that came her way.

Blackie was different from the other cats who roamed around the farmyard, superior to them in that she had the run of the house, and above average, too, in intelligence. Her greatest feat was to open the kitchen door.

The first time it happened we were all startled out of our skins. Suddenly the door swung open, like the magic gate in Edinburgh, and in walked the cat as calm as could be. I ran out to see if anybody had helped her, but there was no one there. The door had a high sneck which had to be pressed firmly to release the catch. It took me all my time to reach up to it. So how on earth had Blackie done it?

Time and again the same thing happened. In the end I waited outside to see if I could solve the mystery. There was a high garden wall by the kitchen door, adjacent to it. Blackie sat there, sunning herself as a change from basking at the kitchen fire. Then suddenly she rose and stretched herself. She had had enough fresh air for the day. Time to go inside.

The door was firmly shut, but Blackie knew what to do. She gathered herself together, took a sideways spring, twisted herself round in mid air, and pressed her paws down on the sneck. Clever thing! But she did not succeed at the first attempt. It was a case of try-try-try again. Down she fell on to the doorstep, and back she leapt on to the wall, to go through the whole performance over and over again, maybe a dozen times, without ever wearying. Persistence paid, for the door finally swung open. Blackie arched her tail proudly and stalked in. I felt she ought to be in the history-books, like Bruce and the spider.

The outside cats were a mixed lot, supposed to wage war on the rats and mice that infested the farmyard, but always turning up in the byre at milking time. My own favourite was the small white kitten who sat next to me and mieowed up at me as if telling me all her troubles. I mieowed back at her and we got on a treat.

Every now and then one of the cats would seek a safe hiding-place where she could produce yet another brood of fluffy kittens.

'We'll need to droon them,' said Jessie, but with no great conviction She even allowed Blackie to 'kittle' in the cupboard below the stairs, and for ages afterwards we were stepping over small squeaking creatures crawling about on the kitchen floor

One of my favourite friends was a small brown bantam hen, the wee banty. She laid the smallest egg, which was lost in an ordinary egg-cup; but I had a special one, not much bigger than a thimble, just the right size to hold the brown banty's offering.

Everything about her was tiny, except her courage. She would even turn on the bubblyjock and chase after him if he was pestering me. The same with her husband, the bantam cockerel. She would rush at him with her small wings outstretched and every feather bristling with rage, chasing him round the farmyard till he cried for mercy.

It was not every day the wee banty laid an egg for my tea, but when she did, it was like playing hide-and-seek, trying to find it. She never went near the henhouse, but had secret laying-places of her own in the corner of the byre or by the side of a hayrick, sometimes even in the pigsty.

But often the banty could not keep the secret to herself. After laying an egg she would come peck-pecking at the kitchen door.

'Wha's that?' Jessie would say, listening with her head to one side. 'It canna be the postie; it's no' lood enough. It'll be that banty o' yours. Ye'd better gang an' find oot if she's laid.'

So out I would go, and the banty would strut away in front of me, clucking to herself and looking back now and again to see if I was following. She never took me to the right place, but near enough. It was all part of the game. Then when I finally found the small egg she would flap her wings as if clapping them. I could almost hear her clucking 'Well done!'

One day she went broody and vanished into the wood, where she had a hidden hoard of eggs on which she sat patiently till they hatched out. It was great to see her marching proudly back to the farmyard at the head of a procession of five tiny chicks.

'Cluck-cluck! Oh the cleverness of me!'

On the farm it was always a case of multiplying and subtracting. Life and death. Cows calved, horses foaled, new litters of piglets appeared, lambs were born. But their lives were short. Cattle and sheep were taken away to be sold, Grumphy met his sad fate, and cocks and hens had their necks drawn.

I wondered if they all went to heaven.

'Och aye! nae doot there's a special place for beasts,' Jessie assured me.

'Who looks after them?' I wanted to know.

'Moses, maybe. Or ane o' thon disciples.'

'Which one?'

'Hoots! they tak' turns. Get oot ma road.'

All the beasts on the farm seemed to have bottomless stomachs and no set meal-times. They pecked and chewed all day long. There was little else for them to do, poor things, not even a book to read. I felt especially sorry for the cows who lay amongst the buttercups and daisies for long monotonous hours, with no other diversion than swallowing their cud.

I wondered if I ought to organize some activity to take them out of themselves, games perhaps. Surely they could run races or play with a tennis-ball, tossing it to each other with their horns. But if I approached them, all they did was get up and wander away to lie down on a fresh patch of grass and continue their chewing. It seemed to fulfil all their needs, so what was the use of trying to improve their lot? At least they did not have to trouble their heads about isosceles triangles.

I never had any desire to tame a wild creature or trap a bird in a cage, nor could I understand the town-folk who kept dogs as pets, making them sit up and beg for a biscuit and taking them out on a lead. 'Good doggy! Come for walkies!' Farm animals, at least, were free.

The day I hated most was when Father held a 'shoot'. His sporting friends, dressed in knickerbockers and stout boots, would come with their guns, game-bags, and retrievers to stride over the heathery hill, with the hinds and the herd acting as beaters. All day long I heard the death-knell in the distance, the cracking of shots, the screaming of pheasants, the baying of dogs.

Meantime the house was astir with activity. Feverish preparations were being made for a great feast to greet the return of the hungry hunters. The largest ashets, platters, and soup tureens were brought out, the dining-room table spread with a white cloth, and the best cutlery laid at each place. Great roasts of mutton were sizzling in the oven, mountains of potatoes had been peeled, and a big pot of turnips was on the boil. A cauldron of soup hung on the swey over the kitchen fire.

There had been a great baking of apple pies, gooseberry tarts and puddings. And one of Mother's special trifles, laced with sherry and topped with whipped cream, was cooling in the milkhouse.

The sideboard was already laden with dishes, carving-knives, jugs of cream, sauce-boats, the cheese dish, the bread board, and sundry extras such as plates of scones and short-bread to fill up odd corners. Though how anyone could have a corner to spare after such a feed was beyond my comprehension. But killing seemed to sharpen the appetite, and the hunters were ravenous enough to eat several helpings of everything when they returned from the slaughter.

My task was to fill the cruets. A fikey job, Jessie said, and so it was. I had to clean and polish the big silvery one, wash the china set in soapy water and clear out any salt that had caked in the bottom. No matter how careful I was with the pepper I always ended up sneezing; and if I spilt any salt I always flung a pinch over my left shoulder to keep bad luck at bay.

Sometimes, too, I was set to work with a pair of wooden 'bats' to roll the butter into little round pats. And what a performance that was, dipping the bats into hot water to prevent the butter from sticking. I could never see the point of it. Butter was butter, and would the men care what shape it was?

At the darkening, when the last shot had been heard, the flurried activity in the kitchen reached a crescendo, with an opening of oven doors, a stirring of pans, a champing of potatoes. Faces became redder, and Mother hastily changed into her best blouse – lilac with lace down the front – while Jessie tied on a clean apron. The lamps were lit, the fires piled high with logs, and the shabby old house looked cosy and welcoming. But the men did not come straight in. We heard them in the out-house, laughing and talking, as they gutted the hares and rabbits, hung up the game birds and divided out the spoil.

At last they came trooping in, reeking of blood and gun-shot, and after a great cleaning up they settled round the dining-room table, my father at the head.

First things first. He always said grace. 'Bless this food and forgive us our sins. Amen.' If the minister was present he took over and addressed the Almighty at greater length.

I liked the Sheep's-Heid Grace, which I had heard from Jock-the-herd, though it was Robert Burns and not Jock who had composed it. What a busy man he must have been! He and Anon and Shakespeare seemed to have written almost everything between them.

> O Lord, when hunger pinches sore
> Do thou stand us in stead,
> And send us, from they bounteous store
> A tup or wether head.

While father sharpened the carving-knife the soup was dished up from the big tureen, and they were off. I acted as an extra serving-maid, fetching and carrying, getting my plaits pulled and having to put up with much boisterous banter. It seemed that in my youth nobody ever addressed a sensible word to me. I was only good for a joke. 'My, you'd make a tasty bite, lassie. Ask your Father to carve me a slice.'

I hated them all.

Yet, looking back I can see they were a nice jovial lot, appreciative of all the good food and full of compliments to my mother whose face grew more and more rosy as the evening wore on. In the back-kitchen the servant-girl was up to her elbows in soap suds, coping with the piles of dirty dishes, while Jessie, her lips set in a grim line, kept serving up more and more potatoes or extracting pies from the oven.

'If ye drap that tray I'll murder ye!'

When it was all over, the men sat back and lit up their pipes or cigars. Then the stories began. My father was the best, as always. I hardly listened to the others, but sat invisible, I hoped, on a footstool in the corner, watching.

Sometimes a rollicking sing-song started up. 'The Lum Hat Wantin' a Croon', 'Paddy McGinty's Goat', 'By Yon Bonnie Banks', with my mother joining in.

If they caught sight of me and tried to get me to do my piece, I fled to the kitchen and sat beside Blackie on the rug, listening to the bursts of laughter till Jessie chased me off to bed with my candle. When I closed my eyes all I could see were rows and rows of carcases hanging in the shed outside.

8. Out in the Wilds

'What's it like, then, away out in the wilds?'

I was constantly being asked this question by town-folk who had a strange idea of what country life was like. They were terrified, I discovered, of cows and thought pigs were filthy brutes. Some of my fellow-scholars had never even seen a hen in their lives.

Butter, eggs, and milk were commodities to be bought in a shop, all ready-made. How they got there was a mystery the town children never bothered to solve. They knew nothing about milking, mucking out a byre, churning butter, or hunting for new-laid eggs. Nor had they any idea what a tattie-bogle was, let alone a bubblyjock.

I was little more than a savage, living amongst the hills with not a neighbour within sight.

'What on earth do you do with yourself out there?'

It was difficult to explain. How could I convey the pleasures of swinging on a gate, watching a bird build its nest, feeding a calf, climbing the old oak tree, running barefoot in the flowery meadow, listening to the skylark singing? I could never find the right words to say. In any case, they already mocked my way of speaking, especially when I came away with some of Jessie's expressions. Words like donnert, dumfoonert, and peelly-wally they had never heard of; and shrieked with mirth when I referred to the tap of drinking-water in the playground as the sprigget.

'Listen to her! She's like a foreigner.'

I had to be careful, too, when speaking to the teachers, some of whom had sarcastic tongues, far more hurtful than the tawse.

'Explain yourself properly. You're in civilization now, not in the wilds.'

The wilds, always the wilds, and always a snigger from the rest of the class. No wonder I never put up my hand or volunteered an answer. It was best to remain invisible and dumb.

My worst moment came when the English teacher, a pale woman who wore high-necked blouses and long black skirts, made me come out in front of the class, as Auld Baldy-Heid had sometimes done, to read out my essay.

It was a compliment, I suppose, but I would sooner have been flung into the fiery furnace. I remember praying feverishly to God to strike me dead on the spot, but He took no notice.

I think I have seldom suffered more through all the trials and tribulations of life than on that day, forced to shuffle out and face my giggling classmates, conscious of all my deficiencies, in particular my country accent.

The essay was a fanciful affair entitled 'My Dream Holiday'. It had looked all right when I was writing it, apart from the odd blot, but now as I read it out it sounded rubbish. Who wanted to hear about my visit to an unknown country in the clouds – Skyland, I think it was called – and of my unlikely adventures running up rainbows and swinging on stars? I was shaking at the knees and red with shame as I finished. Luckily a bell rang – all change – and before anyone could make a comment the class had trooped off to algebra.

I was so used to being in the wrong that it never occurred to me to criticize the way the town-folk behaved. Yet I was beginning to find that living in a crowded community had its drawbacks. I had always longed to see different faces. Now I was seeing too many, so that I could not sort them out and place them in their proper categories.

In the country everyone was an individual. Mary-Anne and her hens, Auld Baldy-Heid, the minister, Bella at the shop, the folk on the farm, my granny in her cottage at Camptown. I had had a long time to study them and knew every wrinkle on their faces, every gesture they made, every peculiarity in their speech.

Now I was flung into a maelstrom of strangers. It was difficult enough to distinguish the teachers let alone the hundreds of pupils. But the one who stood out above them all was the headmaster.

He was known in the Grammar School as the rector, an irascible little man, very red in the face, like a volcano about to explode. His name was Mr Archibald, and he was known to all as Archie-Bald. Or Dafty, behind his back.

Dafty was as soft-footed as a cat and would suddenly appear in a classroom, watching and listening but seldom saying a word. This was the most terrifying thing about him. We never knew what he was thinking or when the explosion would take place. When it did, even the teachers looked faint. I preferred Auld Baldy-Heid who never reined in his rages.

The only lesson the rector took himself was Latin. It was an extra subject, and for some strange reason it had been decreed that I should take it. I was the only girl in my year who did; so on certain days I, along with five or six boys who were also forced to undergo the same form of purgatory, was sent off to Dafty's room to suffer the tortures of the damned.

Mr Archibald would be sitting at his desk, lost in thought. Away in a dwam, Jessie would have said. He took no notice of us, but fiddled about with a paper-clip, tapped his teeth with a ruler, and stared into space. Suddenly, and we never knew when to expect it, his eyes would focus on us, and the shouting-match would begin. Dafty never spoke. He roared. For such a small man he had the bellow of a bull.

'Man, you're an ass! Sit down, you donkey.'

I remember this above all his other expletives, directed at the boys and me alike. He never took the trouble to explain anything, just expected us to get to our feet in turn, read from our Latin primers, and that was that. It was like floundering through treacle. I never came anywhere near getting the hang of it and was frightened out of my wits most of the time. The dead language remained dead, as far as I was concerned.

There were long gaps during which Dafty retired into his shell and we were left to study our books on our own. Mine was tattered and torn, being a hand-me-down from my elder brother and sister who had evidently suffered the same tribulation in the past, according to the despairing scribbles on the fly-leaf.

'If all the world should be submerged, this book would still be dry.'

'Hear, hear,' I wrote after it.

The boys and I sometimes played noughts and crosses on the endpapers instead of learning *amo amas amat*. Later on in the book there was a piece about Balbus building a wall. As far as I know, he may still be building it.

'Man, you're an ass!' Archie-Bald would suddenly spring to life when we least expected it, and catch us flicking blotting-paper pellets at each other to break the monotony.

The lessons were sometimes enlivened by the janitor coming in with a complaint.

'Maister Archie-Bald, thae heathens have went an' broken another windy. It'll need to be seen to.'

It was better than Balbus and his wall.

We welcomed all interruptions, even when Miss Crichton or one of the other teachers dragged a reluctant pupil into the room for punishment, though we felt sorry enough for the sinner. The teachers had no straps of their own. The rector kept his own hangman's whip locked in his desk and acted as general executioner, a job he seemed to relish. It was much larger and nippier than Auld Baldy-Heid's tawse. Even the biggest boys would bite their lips and fight back their tears when the rector went into action.

Somehow we, the watchers, felt as shamed and guilty as the victim when a teacher brought him in and complained of his misdeeds.

'Cheeky, eh? Making trouble, eh?' roared Archie-Bald, his fiery face growing redder as he brought out the strap. 'I'll make trouble for *you*, boy! Hold out your hand.'

I was thankful not to be at the receiving end. Indeed, only once did I incur the full force of the rector's wrath when, in a fit of exasperation at my ignorance he hit me over the head with my primer. My hair was thick enough to withstand the blow, but half the pages fell out of the book. No great loss.

Still, in spite of his hot temper, Mr Archibald could be as gentle as a lamb when any sick pupil was brought to him. He kept smelling-salts and sticking-plaster in a drawer in his desk, and would apply bandages to bruised knees as soothingly as any nurse.

'There, there! You'll soon feel better.'

He was a study, this strange little man, as difficult to fathom as the Latin language itself. It would have been hard enough for any psychoanalyst to comprehend him, let alone me, though I used to sit looking at him and wondering what was going on in his head during his long withdrawn silences. Perhaps, like me, he had another self with whom he could communicate. Something seemed to give him a secret sense of satisfaction, for now and then a smile flickered across his face, but he soon wiped it off if he saw we were watching.

I liked the English lessons best of all, so long as Miss Pale-face ignored me and did not force me to read out my essays. She had a real love of poetry and used to recite it to us in a genteel voice.

> 'Over the cobbles he clattered and clanged
> In the pale moonlight.'

She introduced us to Oliver Twist. I lived every moment of his vicissitudes and was always away ahead of the chapter we were meant to be studying. I related it all to Jessie when I got home, and must have fired her with indignation, for I remember her clenching her fists and crying, 'If I could get ma hands on that Maister Bumble, I'd gie him what for.'

The people were as real to her as they were to me. How I envied Dickens's power to create such lifelike characters. Had *he* ever sat in a classroom, blotting his copybook? I could not imagine him writing such trivialities as 'My Dream Holiday'.

Maybe I, too, ought to try to write about real people. Not Archie-Bald, who was too complex a character, but perhaps I could write about Jessie or Jock-the-herd whom I understood better. But I could not see them as heroes or heroines, or fix them in any other setting than the farm. Would anyone want to hear about cows calving or Jessie tramping the blankets with her bare feet?

At the back of my mind there was always the burning desire, not only to write like Mr Dickens, but to earn enough money to be independent. Not big money, just a sufficiency of coppers to keep me going in sweeties, with maybe a little left over to buy Jessie some hairpins or Jock a twist of his black tobacco. But where could I find such wealth?

While I was still a mixed infant at the village school, I made my first fortune. Fourpence. For 'running with a telegram'.

There was little need to run, for the telegram was of small importance. I knew its contents off by heart. Bella at the post office had told me.

'Will come tomorrow if convenient. Please reply. Signed Chrissie. Stop.'

It was addressed to the minister and I knew fine who Chrissie was. His cousin who lived in a faraway place called Glasgow. Imagine her wanting to leave the fascinations of Sauchiehall Street for a visit to Edgerston Manse! Chrissie, in my opinion, was off her head.

But it was a bonus for me, one that did not often come my way, for few telegrams flew back and forth in the Borders, and when they did Bella had no other means of despatching them than by commandeering anyone who happened to be passing at the time. So I was the lucky one she spotted that morning on my way to school, and called out, 'Will ye rin to the manse wi' a tellygram?'

For fourpence, the rate for the job, I would have run over the Carter Bar. Think of all the caramels and jujubes I could buy. The manse was only a mile away from the post office and I would be passing it anyway on my road to school. So what could be easier?

I clutched the telegram in my hand and ran like the wind, as if the message was of life and death importance. The minister was in his garden, weeding the rockery, when I dashed in through the gate. He looked a trifle startled when I rushed up to him and breathlessly blurted it out.

'Will come tomorrow if convenient. Please reply. Signed Chrissie. Stop.'

He took the telegram, put on his spectacles, and had a close look at it. Then he scribbled a reply, 'Convenient' and handed it back to me.

It might have been convenient for the minister but it put

me off my stride. I had not realized it was a reply-paid telegram and that I would have to go all the way back to the post office with the answer, risking the wrath of Auld Baldy-Heid if I was late for school, as I was sure to be.

It had to be done, so there was nothing else for it but to tear away down the road again, encountering some of my fellow-scholars dawdling on their way up.

'What's wrang?' asked Big Bob, as I went dashing past him. 'Ye're gaun the opposite way.'

'I'm running with a telegram,' I announced, as if I was carrying the Olympic torch.

When I reached the post office I had to do a quick turn round. There was only time to say to Bella, 'Convenient' and ask for a pennyworth of her home-made toffee before I was back on the road again, with a stitch in my side, trying my best to beat the school bell.

But, of course, I was late and had to suffer the consequences. Still, it was worth it, with Bella's toffee to suck and three pennies left in my pocket for future pleasures. I only wished Chrissie would send telegrams more often, but I was never as lucky again.

My only other means of earning money was to cut thistles. My father said he would set me on by the piece, as he did with the Paddies when they were singling turnips. I thought he was pulling my leg, though he seemed serious enough when he handed me a vicious-looking cutter with a long handle, and advised me to use it carefully, suggesting that I make a start on the Lang Field.

Never was there a longer field or one where thistles grew more prolifically. It was like emptying the sea with a teaspoon. The thistles were so tough that they needed several swipes at them before they would budge, and though I worked with a will there seemed more of them in the field when I had finished. But I had some fine blisters on my hands and some scarlet scratches on my legs.

When I went to claim my pay I found that the Boss had

gone off to a lamb sale, taking his wealth with him.

I reminded him when he came home. Fair's fair.

'How many did you cut?' he asked me, as if calculating the rate for the job.

'Thousands .Well, hundreds.'

I was truthful, if nothing else. It was a great handicap.

'Let me see.'

My employer made a play of counting on his fingers and then produced a silver threepenny-piece from his pocket. It was as good as a sovereign to me and I accepted it gratefully. But I realized that if I was ever to make my fortune it was not likely to be in the Lang Field.

I wondered how much Dickens had earned for writing *Oliver Twist* and if he had any blisters on his fingers when he finished. I tried to invent some characters of my own but they all turned out to be animals, with alliterative names, Sandy Squirrel, Willy Weasel, Charlie Crow, Rob Rabbit. And a fish who was later on to swim into the limelight as Tammy Troot.

9. On Four Wheels

It must have been about this time that we took a big plunge and made our first excursion into foreign territory, not just over the Border as far as Otterburn, but beyond Newcastle to the seaside near Whitley Bay: the farthest distance I had ever travelled in my life, except, of course, to Skyland in my imagination.

Father – or was it Mother? – had a relative who had made a mixed marriage and now lived with his English wife at a place called Cullercoats. Sometimes they came to stay on the farm, and then I would be relegated to the servant-girl's bedroom. Now they were returning hospitality, and had invited us to come and holiday with them. Father was to drive us there in the motor car.

The Tin Lizzie was a new acquisition and my father had not yet got the hang of it. Indeed, even when he bought bigger and better cars as the years went by, he never really felt at ease with horsepower. Four-legged beasts were more in his line.

Though it was an exciting prospect, spending a whole fortnight in another country, I had little hopes of arriving there. For one thing, the Boss had no bump of direction. He would turn down any side-road he saw, landing us in dead ends. Often the motor would stick in the mud at the edge of someone's duck-pond. Then we would all have to get out and push before we could get Lizzie back on the road again.

'Ye'd be safer wi' the pownie,' said Jessie, shaking her head dolefully. 'I hae ma doots if ye'll ever mak' it.' She was not the only one.

In order to ease the burden on Lizzie we had packed all our togs into an old trunk, which the hinds had taken by cart in to Jedburgh station to be sent in advance to Cullercoats. It would be waiting for us on arrival. So we thought. In the event, it arrived the day we left, by which time we were all in borrowed raiment and I was wearing somebody's sand-shoes several sizes too big. But we were not to know that on the morning we all packed into the car and the door fell off.

We had to get Jock-the-herd in from the hill, and after a great deal of activity with hammers, screwdrivers and binder-twine, we set off back-firing down the rough farm road.

'I'll keep the kettle on the boil,' called Jessie, as she waved us off. 'Ye'll likely be back.'

But we made it. At least, as far as the main road without any major disaster.

We had our first puncture at the Carter Bar, halfway in England, halfway in Scotland, We could not have chosen a better place if it was scenery we were after.

> Where every prospect pleases,
> And only man is vile.

Looking both ways there were sights to gladden the eye. Catcleuch and Redesdale on the one side and the hills of home on the other, with yellow broom blazing indiscriminately in both countries.

Nearer at hand the picture was not so pleasant. My father was down on his knees wrenching away at the jack, with several of the car's entrails spread out on an old waterproof sheet on the ground – a sight with which I was only too well accustomed whenever we went out on a motoring expedition.

We made it in fits and starts. A puncture was not so bad. Worse trouble came when, miles from a garage, the car gave a splutter and came to a standstill for no apparent reason. Father opened the bonnet and a spout of steam came gushing out. What could be the matter?

'She needs cooling down,' said he, and sent me tramping along the road to the nearest habitation to beg for a kettle of cold water. The lot always fell on Jonah.

My elder brother and sister were with us, home for their holidays from their colleges in Edinburgh, but such menial tasks were not for them. My lady-like sister would never demean herself by begging at doors, and my brother was otherwise occupied, gazing into the mechanism of the engine as if he could cure it by the power of the eye. My mother was sitting by the roadside, patiently prepared to wait for ever, with the baby in her arms, a bouncing youngster by now.

I felt like one of the gypsies who came mooching to the farm for cast-off clothes when I rat-tat-tatted at the nearest door.

'Hullo,' said the child who opened it. Golden ringlets, large blue eyes, a doll tucked under her arm.

'Could your mother lend me some cold water?' I asked. It seemed a silly thing to say.

'Yeth,' she lisped. 'I think tho.' Then she remembered something and her blue eyes grew bigger. 'My mammy'th not in.'

'Oh!' What next?

'My daddy'th here.'

He came to the door in his shirt-sleeves and took command of the situation. Yes, he could provide the water, and brought it out to me in such a large kettle that I could not hold it even with two hands.

'I'll take it,' he said, and closed the door behind him. He went swinging along the road at a great pace, leaving me trotting breathlessly behind him, with the child at my heels, dropping her doll at intervals. By the time I stopped to pick it up and took her by the hand her father was out of sight.

'Come on, we'd better hurry,' I said, urging the child along. But her eyes filled with tears.

'I want a carry,' she wailed, so I had to pick her up, doll and all, and stagger along the road with my burden. Perhaps I would have been better off with the kettle.

When we reached the car, the deed had been done. The motor was ticking over once more, and my father was looking embarrassed, not knowing whether to compensate the man or not. But my mother solved the problem by giving him some fresh eggs which we had brought with us, and he hoisted the child on to his shoulder and went back home.

Once more we packed ourselves into the car and were off.

Beyond Otterburn we were in unknown territory.

'Watch out for signposts,' was the cry.

If there were none at a crossroads, Father with unerring judgement, took the wrong turn and went rattling up to a farm steading, adding miles to the journey. Reversing was one of his weaknesses, and we had to get out and beckon him backwards and forwards.

'A wee bit to the left. Watch out! You'll be in the ditch.'

The greatest problem was how to get through Newcastle without disaster. The town was a confusion of bridges, rivers, docks, and side-streets, many of which Father explored before finally finding the right route.

'Stop blowing the horn,' cried my mother when it

suddenly let out a raucous blast in the middle of the main street; but Father could not stop it, nor could the policeman who rushed forward as if about to arrest the lot of us. Something had seized in the mechanism, so we had to blow our way to the nearest garage, with all the people scuttling out of our path and my lady sister hiding her head in shame.

It was only one of many episodes. Father often said he could write a book, and so he could. I, for one, would have loved to read it, especially if it was written in the pawky way he told the tales of his misadventures on four wheels. It was fun at the time of retelling, not so pleasant if we were involved and had to suffer the tortures of standing shivering by the roadside in wintry weather when the car was stuck in a snowdrift.

Many a time we had to put clanking chains on the wheels, dig ourselves out with spades, and end up as often as not walking home over the slippery roads, leaving Lizzie abandoned by the wayside. I often felt I would have done better on my old baneshaker.

It was late and dark when we finally reached Cullercoats, feeling as if we had circumnavigated the globe. We could not see the sea or anything except some winking lights from the pier and the intermittent flashing of the lighthouse. It was an exciting sight, but I was too tired to take it in.

The discovery that the tin trunk had not arrived meant a hurried consultation about clothes, nightclothes particularly, though I felt that for once I could have slept standing up, and was ready to go to bed in my topcoat if necessary.

The family was to be split up. My parents and the baby were staying at the cousins' small villa. The rest of us were sleeping out at Mrs Somebody's house several streets away. I had a put-up bed in her sitting-room, so narrow and unsteady that I feared it would fold under me and deposit me on the floor. But on that first night I went instantly to sleep in the landlady's pink nightdress and wondered where I was in the morning, with chinks of light coming in through red velvet curtains.

Every morning we went back to the villa to have breakfast with our parents and every evening walked home to our sleeping-quarters. Or, more truthfully, I ran to keep with my brother and sister who crossed streets and disappeared round corners so rapidly that I feared I would get lost and have to spend the night like a ghost wandering through the strange town. Occasionally they called back to me impatiently, 'Hurry up, you! You're a nuisance!' I thought it best to keep out of their way as much as possible during the day.

I had been to the seaside before, at Spittal near Berwick-on-Tweed, and was prepared for the vast ocean but not for the mass of humanity that thronged the beach. There was scarcely a vacant space on the sand, no place where one could just sit quietly and take it all in. As I was accustomed to being on my own for long periods, the constant clamour confused me.

I heard snatches of different dialects. 'Ee! ba goom!' for the first time, as well as the Geordie accent with which I was more familiar. It was my first real taste of communal life. Even when bobbing about in the sea one seemed to be side by side with half the world.

I began to feel as if we had been there for years and could scarcely recall a former existence. I had forgotten what Jessie looked like. I sent her a picture postcard of a fat lady riding a donkey. 'I was on one yesterday', I boasted, but I did not tell her I had fallen off. 'Give my love to Jock.' Love was maybe going a bit too far. I had forgotten what he looked like, too.

I have only muddled memories of that holiday. Deckchairs, donkeys, pierrots, noisy youths playing with a beach ball, a trip to Whitley Bay in a train, and the warm-hearted family from Yorkshire who took me under their wing.

They were always eating out of paper bags and sharing the contents with anyone near by.

''Ave a doughnut, loove.'

Greta, the girl of the family, was like a wild pony. Tawny hair, long legs, and a rough-and-tumble attitude to life. She used to knock me down with an affectionate push and tussle with me on the sand till I cried for mercy. She was as ignorant of Scotland as I was of England, and once asked me if I knew Annie Laurie.

'D'you mean the song?'

'Ee no, loove. I mean her.'

She taught me about Ilkla Moor and I introduced her to the Wee Couper o' Fife. We always ended up in stitches of laughter at our attempts to master each other's language. Still, it was better than struggling with Latin. By the end of the fortnight I felt I belonged to the Kilburn family, and would gladly have gone home with them to their Dales (as indeed they suggested) had it not been for the tug of my own Cheviot hills.

The day came when we had to face the journey home. We all seemed to have expanded in every direction and to have acquired various bulky treasures to take back with us. Shells, smelly seaweed, outsize bars of bright-red rock, and a fuzzy teddy bear which the Kilburns had given me as a parting gift. I was long past the teddy stage so I gave it to the baby who flung it out of the car every time the window was open, adding to the many trials of the journey home.

The tin trunk, having just arrived, had to be taken back again. Father tied it on behind the car, and my task was to look back every now and then, like Lot's wife, to see if it was still there. 'It's loose!' I would call out.

We had so many stoppings and startings one way and another that it was dusky dark by the time we reached the wildest part of the moorland leading up to the Carter Bar, the right moment for the lights to fail.

Father did his best. Indeed, we all gave him advice. What

about pulling out that wee knob? Or turning that screw? Maybe that loose wire has something to do with it.

He tried everything, but without any result. So in the end there was nothing else for it but to park at the roadside and wait for the daylight, taking turns to act as look-out for approaching vehicles who might run into us.

We had no torch, so we struck matches when we heard a car coming, waving them in the air like will o' the wisps. The traffic was few and far between, and no one stopped to ask about our plight. Only a tramp shuffling by inquired if he could have a fill of tobacco for his empty pipe. My father gave it to him, as well as something from his pocket, and I broke off a piece of Cullercoats rock to help him on his way.

Now and again we dozed off in the back of the car or wandered about in the eerie darkness. Gradually a faint glow showed in the sky and soon the birds began to twitter their morning song. When we could see a few hundred yards ahead, Father said, 'I think I'll crank her up now. It's safe to go.'

The hinds were on their way to the work-stable when we came rattling up the home stretch. It was comforting to know that Jessie would be in the kitchen with the kettle boiling, and that we were safely back in our ain countree. Tin Lizzie would be put to rest next to the gig in the cart-shed. It was great to get rid of her.

As days went by a variety of strange equipages found their way up the farm road. The homely horse and cart was still to the fore, but some adventurous souls had branched out into motor-bicycles and sidecars. They dressed up in goggles, large leather gloves and coats, with the passenger, tucked into the sidecar, swathed in shawls and scarves. They were usually stiff with cold when they emerged, and declared that our road had 'rattled their internals' till everything was out of place.

Once in a while an enormous lorry came rolling up the road laden with sacks containing a mysterious concoction called guano. The men unloaded the sacks and later spread the contents on the fields, like a sprinkling of snow.

'What is it?' I asked them.

'Och! it's just birds' droppings,' said Tam. 'Guid for the grund.'

Certainly it looked more pleasant than the dung which the hinds usually spread on the fields, and had a less 'healthy' smell.

The largest vehicle which ever negotiated our rough road was the mill, which came out from Jedburgh once a year after harvest-time to convert the sheaves into corn. It was like a puffing Billy, all steam and loud shuddering noises. Even the proud bubblyjock went and hid to keep out of its way.

For some reason, the mill required a constant supply of water to keep it shuddering and shaking. Anyone with strong enough arms was sent with pails to the water-barrel or to the kitchen taps to slake its thirst while it was regurgitating the sheaves. I was afraid to go near it, like the bubblyjock, for it belched out so much smoke that it blinded me. And there was always the fear that it might draw me into its clutches, mistaking me for one of the sheaves.

The hinds fed its hungry maw with the ripe sheaves, while my father waited anxiously to test the quality of the corn that came trickling out. He gathered a sample of it into a little bag to be shown later to the corn-merchant. The men shovelled it into sacks and forked the chaff into a corner of the straw-barn. The kaff-hole, it was called, a dark place which I dreaded when hunting for eggs. I knew there would be some there, but there was always the danger of a rat lurking amongst the chaff or a hen flying out in my face.

On the whole I preferred the horse-driven traffic, the gigs, the baker's van, and our own carts pulled by the Clydesdales.

We had not yet come round to the idea of a tractor, though the Boss was considering it. So the hinds told me one day when I was in the work-stable at lowsing-time.

'Damned nonsense!' grumbled Wull, using the curry-comb on Prince's sleek coat. 'Your faither'll hae us fleein' aboot in airyplanes next. Gie me a horse ony time.'

'That's so,' agreed Tam, lighting his pipe. 'Horses is human, an' what's mair, *they* never break doon.'

10. Growth

By now I seemed to have lived for centuries and sometimes said to Jessie, as if I was a weary woman of the world, 'D'you remember away back in the old days when I was young . . . ?'

But I was still not too old to be shut in the household jail as a punishment, and spent many a long hour in the garret in solitary confinement.

It was a great place for contemplation, not for thinking over my sins – I was always unjustly imprisoned, in my opinion – but for dreaming up a story or wondering why I was here. Not in the garret, but in the universe. If God took care of every sparrow that flew and every blade of grass that grew, what I wondered did He make of me? He must have some plan in His head? I pictured Him sitting up there turning over the pages of a golden jotter till He came to my name. Did He shake His head and sigh, like Jessie?

'That lassie! What'll I mak' o' her? She's got nae rummlegumption.'

But, of course, God would not speak in a Border accent, would He?

There were many things to puzzle about, crime and punishment for example. It was always for doing good deeds that I was sent to jail. I was a great giver-away, especially of other folks' belongings, and when a gypsy woman came to the door one day whining that her man had 'nae soles to his shoon', what could be kinder than to give her a pair of my father's?

They were old brown ones, and I thought he would never miss them. But, of course, he did, and I had to pay the penalty.

The worst of being in prison was that my jailors never indicated the length of my sentence, and often forgot that I was still there. Setting me free depended on when it came up their backs, if they were passing by the garret door, or if they heard me calling, 'Let me out! *Ouvrez la porte!*'

I remember that particular day because it grew dark so early and there was nothing to be seen except the faintest glow from the moon shining in through the skylight window.

During daylight there was always plenty to do in the garret, old books to read, a rocking-horse to ride, the contents of a large wooden chest to explore. It was full of feather boas and other discarded finery, a great place in which to rummage when looking for garments to clothe a new tattie-bogle. It was bitterly cold in the garret so I often dressed myself up as well, in old shawls, beaded dolmans, or a moth-eaten fur cape.

On that day I felt I had been abandoned when I heard the Tin Lizzie being cranked up. Were my parents going out for the evening leaving me to my fate? By the time I had climbed on to the rickety washstand and propped up the skylight window, the car was puttering away down the road. I could see Jessie disappearing, too, into the darkness on her way home to the herd's cottage. There would be no one left in the house except the sleeping baby and a servant-lassie miles away down in the kitchen. The Cairthorse, I think it was.

I pictured her sitting drowsing by the cosy kitchen fire with her slippered feet on the fender, or maybe trying to pen a letter to her lad, Gorge. She would never be thinking of me. Nobody seemed to miss me when I was out of sight, I was so used to going my own way.

No amount of rattling at the door or calling for help would attract her attention at that distance. There was nothing for it but to wait till she came upstairs to bed. The garret, friendly enough in the daytime, was now full of frightening shadows. I could hear strange creaks and rustles, the scampering of mice on the skirting-boards, the eerie hooting of an owl from the roof. Everything took on fantastic shapes. Even the old rocking-horse seemed to be moving, and the dressmaker's dummy in the corner was swaying from side to side, as if she had come to life.

The only consolation I had was in thinking of the remorse my parents would feel when they found my corpse stiff and cold, stretched out on the garret floor.

'Dead, dead! beyond recall. . . .'

I visualized my own funeral and heard the minister in a broken voice, proclaiming my virtues. Never speak ill of the dead. All my shortcomings would be forgotten. Never had there been such a bright beautiful biddable child. What a loss to her sorrowing family, one that could never be replaced.

I looked down from Paradise on my heartbroken parents and decided to forgive them, but not for a while. Let them suffer first. Serve them right.

At last a step on the stairs. The Cairthorse lumbering on her way to bed, carrying her candle and her stone hot-water bottle. The pig.

I left the pearly gates and hurried to the garret door, calling, 'Let me *out*! Open the *door*!' No use *ouvrezing la porte* for her.

Liz-Ann almost dropped the pig, but at least she heard me and had the sense to set me free.

'Mercy goodness! I thought ye were a ghost,' said she, as white as a sheet.

'Well, I'm not,' I said crossly, and ran past her down to the kitchen to warm myself at the dying embers of the fire.

The clothes-horse was standing there – the winter-dyke – airing its load of clean washing. Jessie had been doing the ironing and goffering earlier that day, using the old box iron with its three-cornered stones which she heated in the depths of the fire till they were red hot. There was a hole in the corner of the stones through which she pushed the poker when she wanted to retrieve one. It was a perilous performance, conveying it, sizzling with heat to the iron which she held in one hand, open at the end to receive it, and a great relief when it was finally shut in. I was always terrified she might drop it on the cat.

Not Jessie. All her actions were co-ordinated, unlike the servant-girl with her fumbling fingers and two left feet. Jessie had an economy of movement and a steady pace, never dashing at things or getting into a fankle. All the fairies must have been at her christening, for she even had the gift of green fingers, and when she had nothing better to do in the house she would go out into the garden with a trowel in her hand.

'Come on, wumman,' she would say to a drooping dahlia. 'Stand up an' show some smeddum.'

Ten to one the dahlia would respond, and before long would be standing upright straightening out its petals. I felt Jessie could have given a lesson or two to Mrs Pot Plant.

Country gardens on the whole were hitty-missy affairs, not plotted and planned but left to grow wild, with nettles and weeds mixed up with the flowers. Most farmers had too much to do with sowing and growing during their working hours to bother about cultivating finicky little patches around their houses in their spare time. Why waste hours weeding a small garden when a whole field of thistles was awaiting their attention?

Often it was left to their women folk to attend to the garden but they, too, had little enough time to spend on such a task, with the result that many farmhouses had nothing to show in the way of flowers at their doors other than a few rambler roses, a sturdy bush or two, and some clumps of candytuft. Anything that grew without needing constant attention.

Not so, in our case. My father and mother were keen gardeners. In theory, that is. Mother took turns and Father was constant in his fondness of growing sweet peas. But it was a hunger or a burst.

As for gardens we had not one but four, the front garden, the side garden, the back garden, and the top garden. The top garden was the biggest of all, across the road and some distance away from the house, where there were masses of berry-bushes, rows and rows of vegetables, my father's sweet peas, and the greenhouse in which he often took refuge.

It was his hidey-hole, a place where he could escape from family bothers and retreat when he wanted to pursue some ploy of his own. Not just planting out seedlings, but practising a comic song, playing the fiddle, or puzzling over unpaid accounts. He kept an overflow of odds and ends in the greenhouse: old newspapers, unanswered letters, sheet-music, false moustaches and wigs which he used when doing a funny turn at local concerts, his old fiddle, and a little notebook in which he jotted down goodness knows what. His chaotic accounts perhaps.

'Where's the Boss? Away and fetch him.'

When I was given this order I always knew where to find him, but I hated being the one to disturb his peace. I was all for secret withdrawals myself and knew how I would resent being jerked back to reality if I was in the middle of a reverie. Sometimes I could see him through the glass panes gesturing away to an unseen audience. Or maybe he would have his spectacles on, studying a seed packet.

Would it be better to knock at the door or throw a handful of pebbles at the glass windows to warn him of my approach?

'You're wanted,' I mouthed, if he turned and saw me. But I never went in. It was his castle, and I had mine on the hill. Privacy was precious.

Father was not always in the greenhouse. Often I found him pottering amongst his precious sweet peas, training them up in the way they should go, nipping off dead buds or just standing admiring their delicate colourings. He was known in the district as an expert and always won first prize, not only at the local show but at the big one in Jedburgh, held in the town hall and with all the county competing.

Every year there was a special prize for the best decorated table. A flower-arrangement. It was the women folk who did the decorating, with the men standing by giving advice. There was as much tension in the air as if they were competing for a crown.

When the day came my mother was 'up to high Doh', having to bear such a burden of responsibility on her shoulders. Father had been in the garden at the crack of dawn, gathering his best blooms and deciding which shades would look best. A mixture of pale blues and pinks? Or dark blues and salmon? Or just pinks alone with trails of gypsophila in between?

It was a difficult decision to make. In the end he took bunches of all kinds and colours, and waited to see the effect when Mother had set to work in the town hall.

I had a humble hand in the proceedings, for it was not only the flowers that were being judged but the general layout of the table. Various appurtenances had to be brought out and cleaned, in particular the silvery epergne which we used on the dining-room table on the rare occasions when we wanted to impress visitors.

It was a perfect nuisance, in my opinion, as it was made up of complicated bits and pieces which had to be fitted together, as well as cleaned and polished. Apart from the ornamental centre-piece, there were four little gates to be set at each corner of the table, also to be filled with flowers. And though the final effect, with airy-fairy gypsophila trailing in between, was pleasing to the eye, I agreed with Jessie when she said, 'Gie me a plain vawse ony day. It's less palaver.'

Her task was to produce a sparklingly white tablecloth stiff with starch. So in the end we all felt a stab of pride when our combined efforts resulted once more in another win for Overton Bush. But it was really Father who had done the deed with his sweet peas.

I remember when Mother decided to make a rockery in the side garden, to fill up an ugly corner, and set us all to work building a base of large stones, cast-off kettles, broken tubs, handleless pails, old crockery. Anything and everything went into it. We tried to cover them all with soil, but if a downpour came, the rain washed it all away and we could see a kettle spout or an old teapot coming to the surface. It would have been less bother to build the Pyramids.

Livestock, too, would get into the garden, no matter how hard we tried to keep the gate shut. Grumphy liked nothing better than routing in the rockery, and did his best to knock the whole edifice down, cocks and hens scratched up the soil, dogs buried their bones there, and the bubblyjock pecked at the plants.

But in the end Mother succeeded. The wilderness was not entirely transformed, but at least she could see results for her labours when flowers began to flourish in between the stones and old teapots. I was never sure of their names. They were just blue flowers or pink ones. Indeed, I was not certain which were weeds, and wondered why a dandelion, for example, should rate lower than a primula. They were both flowers, were they not?

My own efforts never came to much. I had been given a small patch in the back garden around a gnarled old apple tree, which must have been blighted judging by the few wizened apples it produced. The soil seemed sour, for nothing I planted would flourish, even though I begged some guano from the hinds to sprinkle on it. But maybe it was my fault, for I always expected seeds to sprout instantly and plants to take root even when I had dug up primroses, forget-me-nots, and marshmarigolds from the banks of the burn. Poor things, they must have felt homesick, for they soon shrivelled and died. My one success was a bush of southernwood. Appleringie, Jessie called it.

Once a year the laird's garden at the Big Hoose was thrown open to the public, and we would walk sedately along the well-kept paths and admire the formal layout. It was all too precise for my liking, with every flower standing to attention and not a weed to be seen.

I preferred the higgledy-piggledy arrangement of my granny's cottage garden at Camptown, and spent many happy hours pottering about amongst her peony-roses and rasp-bushes. She did not mind the odd wild flower or bishop-weed, or even dandelion. I had more success there than in my own unproductive plot at home. The butterflies and bumblebees, too, seemed to prefer the mixed scents in Granny's garden.

One day we were ordered by the art master at the Grammar School to bring in a bunch of flowers to draw. Fancy having an art master! Auld Baldy-Heid never bothered with such a subject. The only thing I drew at the village school was a cow on the blackboard, and not a very convincing one at that. Now we had to think of backgrounds, perspectives, and still life. We had already tried out our talents on an apple, an orange, and a vase. We were now to progress to higher things. Flowers.

I wondered if I could mooch some sweet peas from my father, but, remembering I would have to draw them, I settled for something simpler, a bunch of gowans from the meadow.

I got up early to gather them in the morning dew, and they looked fresh enough when I started out, but by the time I reached the road-end they had already begun to wilt.

Black Sandy took one as he hoisted me on to the bus. 'Tooral-ooral-addy!' he roared, sticking the flower into his lapel. Then he began to sing 'Auld Lang Syne' at the pitch of his voice.

> 'We twa hae run aboot the braes
> An' pou'd the gowans fine. . . .'

When we arrived at the school gates I had only one solitary flower left intact, which I had managed to rescue from the boisterous onslaughts of my fellow-passengers. I stuck it in my pocket for safety and dreaded the moment when I would have to bring it out to show to the art master. He was a nice enough man, but his tongue was sarcastic, and I knew I would be walking right into his trap.

'What's this?' he asked, peering at my crumpled offering.

'It's a g-gowan,' I gulped.

'You mean it was a gowan,' he said, throwing it into the waste-paper basket. 'Don't you grow any decent flowers out in the wilds? Perhaps I should have asked you to bring in a pig. Here!' He thrust a rose into my hand, from a bunch which one of the town scholars had brought in. A beautiful scarlet, scented bloom. '*That's* what a flower should be like. Go ahead and draw it.'

But I didn't. I drew the gowan instead. Or, at least, I tried to. Anybody, I argued to myself, could draw an upright rose. A wilting gowan called for much more artistic skill.

It was a pity I had none. After taking one look at my offering, the art master tore it up and pitched it into the wastepaper basket to keep the gowan company.

'There's one thing you'll never be,' he told me darkly, 'and that's an artist.'

11. Visitors and Visiting

One day Bella Confectionery from the post office rang up.

'Have ye heard the latest?'

'No, not yet,' I replied, all agog.

It was not often I got the chance of answering the telephone myself, but I happened to be alone in the house at the time except for Jessie who would sooner have had all her teeth drawn than speak into 'thon noisy beast'. Mother was busy at her rockery and Father was shut up in the greenhouse. Bella was a trifle disappointed when she found she had no better ears than mine to fill, but she drew a deep breath and made the most of it.

'Wait till I tell ye! Ye ken the minister?'

'Yes, fine.'

'Well, ye'll never guess!'

'Mercy me! what's happened?' I had visions of him confiscating the contents of the kirk plate or running away with the organist.

'Fell aff his byke. Right fornent ma door.'

'Goodness gracious! Is he dead?'

'Nut at all!' This was going a little too far. 'Bumped his heid. I've just put a bandage on't. But ye should see his byke. Ruined. The baker's given him a lift hame in his cairt, but I doot if he'll manage to preach on Sunday.'

'But the baker never preaches. . . . Oh, I see, you mean the minister. Oh well, maybe we'll get a holiday,' I said hopefully.

'Nut at all! They'll likely get a locum.'

'A what?'

Bella clicked her teeth impatiently. I could tell she was not enjoying the conversation as much as she had anticipated.

'Are ye sure there's naebody else in? A'weel, ye'll pass on the news? Ta-ta, lassie.'

As it turned out, the minister was less damaged than his bicycle and was able to preach on Sunday with a black eye and a bandage on his brow. It was something to look at during the long sermon, and the drama of the affair kept Bella going for weeks.

She was our lifeline for, apart from passing on gossip, Bella acted as a warning system.

'That's the Scotts awa' by. They'll likely be on their way to veesit ye. The hale jing-bang's in the buggy. Ye'd better get the kettle on.'

Not only the kettle. Her advance warning gave us time to put on the girdle as well, to bake a batch of scones and pancakes, so that thanks to Bella we were able to feed the hungry visitors when they arrived 'unexpectedly' in the buggy.

When we were storm-stayed in winter, what we missed most during the snow-siege was Bella's chatty voice on the telephone when the line went dead. Even Jessie rejoiced at the sound of thon noisy beast when the thaw came and we heard the first ring, followed by Bella telling us, 'That's you back on the line. Are ye a' richt up there? Have ye heard the latest? Mrs Broon's chimney went on fire, Mary-Anne's got the mumps, an' the Mains's coo's calved. . . .'

It was like music to our ears.

Sometimes, in spite of Bella's vigilance and the fact that the farm led to nowhere but the great beyond, we had the odd unexpected visitor who had strayed off the beaten track. It was exciting to see an unknown carriage or car coming up the road and to speculate on who could be coming to call.

I remember a strange man arriving one day at the front door, wearing plus-fours and asking, 'Can you show me the way to the golf course?'

'The what?' I asked, stupefied.

Father and Mother were away on their weekly visit to the other farm, Swinside Townhead, and once more I was the only one at home. It would be a tale to tell them when they came back, but they would likely not believe me.

'The golf course,' repeated the man impatiently. He looked at me as if I was the village idiot. 'Don't tell me there isn't one, after I've driven all the way up this terrible road. I've seen people playing somewhere up here when I was motoring by on the main road. So I thought, seeing I had my clubs with me today, I might fit in a round or two. Where is it?'

'Oh, that!' I said, beginning to understand. 'Well, you see, it's not really a golf course. . . .'

How could I explain that Father, who had a selection of broken-down mashies and niblicks, sometimes took a few golf balls out on to the hill and swiped his way round an imaginary course? He had made little holes on the 'greens' but the balls seldom went into them, disappearing instead down rabbit-holes, never to be seen again. So many, indeed, went to ground that he used to say a rubber plantation would spring up on the hill one day in the future.

It was a hazardous course, full of ups and downs. Father had appropriate names for the different holes: The Himalayas, Crossing the Styx, The Slough of Despond, Danger Ahead. Apart from divots, bracken and rabbit-holes, there was always the problem of beasts. The sheep refused to get out of the way, and it was no use shouting 'Fore!' to the bull.

I tried to explain all this to the stranger but he still insisted that he wanted to play, and was about to get his gear out of the car when I gave him my parting shot.

'The bull's there. He's awful wild.'

That did it. Without another word he got into the car, hastily reversed it and shot away down the road.

'Guid riddance,' said Jessie who had been watching from the kitchen window. 'They'll be comin' speirin' for the circus next.' As if we had hundreds and thousands of strangers beating a path to our door.

Friendly droppers-in were always welcome, whether Bella had warned us of their approach or not, and were invited to take pot luck at the kitchen table if we were having a plain meal instead of a fancy one. But if they came by special invitation they were assured of a big spread in the dining-room with a vase of flowers gracing the centre of the table, if not the epergne. Even in autumn and winter we had rowan berries or holly, and Christmas roses as pale as porcelain. Mother had not served her apprenticeship at the flower show for nothing.

When we were invited out as a family I was warned not to eat too much or ask for a second helping, which I thought strange since Mother was always pressing second and third helpings on the folk who visited us.

'Pass in your cup for some more tea, and you'll take another slice of cake? Oh nonsense! you've eaten nothing. Try another wee bit.' But it did not seem to work the other way round.

Other folk's food, of course, always tasted better. It was the difference that did it. Even seeing it served on other dishes with unfamiliar patterns on them somehow sharpened the appetite. I wondered if castor-oil might not taste so terrible out of a crystal goblet, but I had my doubts about that.

Though we lived well enough at home it was not always easy to vary the menu. Being so far from shops we had to eat what was available. It was a treat when we could get tasty kippers, or herring fried in a covering of oatmeal; and though there was no shortage of game, I thought sausages the rarest of foods and far more succulent than grouse.

Looking back, I marvel at the variety of puddings mother and Jessie managed to concoct. Not 'sweets'. Good wholesome stick-to-the-ribs puds. Clooty dumplings, so called because they were boiled in a clout – the Scottish word for a cloth – roly-poly puddings, treacle and syrup sponges, apple dumplings, Bakewell tarts, and a variety of fruit pies. They were not just afters, they were a meal in themselves, especially when topped with plenty of fresh cream.

'Ye dinna ken what's guid for ye,' Jessie would scold if I left some on my plate. 'Och weel! it's no' lost what a freend'll get,' she said when she tipped it into the pigs' pail.

The cottage wives seldom saw the inside of a shop and had to rely on Wattie, who came once a week in his horse-driven van with a variety of goods to sell. It was scarcely a supermarket, but to country eyes it contained treasure-trove. Fresh pan loaves, meat pies, cream cookies, flour, sugar, boiled sweets, paraffin oil, bootlaces, scrubbing-brushes. There were shelves in the back which Wattie drew out to display his goods while the wives stood by with their purses in their hands and their aprons gathered up ready to receive their purchases.

Like the postie, Wattie obliged by doing messages in the town. He took clogs to the cobbler, collected sheep-dip, and sometimes brought a selection of blouses for the wives to try on. Many a Sunday hat had journeyed out the Jed in Wattie's van.

'There's a broon felt an' a black straw. Tak' your pick.'

It was little wonder we all waited so eagerly for the road to be cleared after a snowstorm. Wattie's visit was the high-light of the week.

His horse, whom Wattie just called 'Horse', must have been a very tough beast. He pulled the creaky van the long miles from town, and went all over the district, struggling up farm roads even rougher than ours to visit outlying cottagers. When he arrived at our door, Horse almost sat down with relief, sensing he could have a long rest and a nibble in his nosebag while Wattie came into the house for a cup of tea.

'Bide there an' dinna budge, Horse,' Wattie told him before coming into the kitchen and sinking down in the nearest chair. 'I'll just rest ma shanks for twa-three meenits,' said he, loosening his bootlaces.

The twa-three meenits were sometimes elongated, depending on the state of Wattie's shanks and how long it took him to drink his tea. It was no ordinary operation, for Wattie had a walrus moustache, and Jessie served him his tea in a moustache-cup. I was always fascinated by the precedure. Wattie swept up his bristles so that his lips were clear before taking a one-sided swill from the cup. Then out came his red spotted handkerchief to mop his moustache after every mouthful. It would have been easier, I thought, to trim off all that hair, but Wattie would not have been Wattie without it.

'I'll need to be on the go,' he sighed when he had tied up his bootlaces; but not before he had turned every penny he could, for Wattie was something of a Shylock, a great buyer and seller, with as many sidelines as a railway junction. He was always on the look-out for fresh eggs, butter, cheese, sacks of potatoes or garden produce which he could buy in the country and sell at a profit in the town.

He drove a hard bargain down to the smallest farthing, and noted each transaction in a bulging notebook, sucking the point of his pencil through his drooping moustache.

When settling-up time came there was a great hunting around for small change, and many a calculation had to be done while Wattie deducted the cost of cookies, loaves, syrup and Abernethy biscuits from the price he was offering for eggs and butter. He had a leather pouch jingling with coins from which he carefully extracted the odd pennies before tying it up again and replacing it in a secret pocket in the inside of his jacket. The heavier it became the broader Wattie beamed as he went back to his van.

'Come on, Horse, we'll need to be gettin' doon the road.' And that was the end of Wattie for another week.

Apart from his visit and that of the postie we had little to hope for unless the hunt rode by in full fling or a gypsy caravan came creaking up the road. But once in a while a miracle happened and a new set of human beings arrived, not just for a day but to live on the farm.

There was little chopping and changing amongst the workers, but I remember the excitement when one year a new hind and his family arrived at term-time.

Every year, long before the term, Father went through the motions of 'speaking to the men', asking them if they meant to stay on. Or, indeed, sacking them if they were unsatisfactory workers, though this seldom happened. If they indicated that they were content, all was well. If not, it behoved the Boss to stand in the market-place in Jedburgh on hiring day and find replacements from the farm-workers who gathered there in search of employment.

I was never sure how this worked or how a bargain was struck. It seemed to be done so casually, by word of mouth. No signing or sealing. Yet I never heard of anyone going back on his word.

The wives in question did not set eyes on their new home till the day of the flitting. The hind himself came in advance on his bicycle for an odd Saturday afternoon for the purpose of setting the garden. He would dig over the soil, plant potatoes and turnips, set rows of seeds, and hope that everything would be sprouting by the time he came to take possession.

On the day of the flitting there were great comings and goings, for the one cottager had to get out with all his belongings before the other could come in. Father sent men with empty carts to the farm which the new hind was leaving, while strange carts arrived at the cottage door to take away the furniture of the departing family.

All day long they carried out chairs, tables, grandfather clocks, crockery and bedding. Everyone prayed for 'a guid day for the flittin'', for it was a pitiful process trying to pack the carts in pouring rain and to fit everything under waterproof covers. Sad, too, to see the familiar nick-nacks disappearing from sight for ever: the china dogs, the aspidistra, the jelly-pan, the family Bible. But there was little time for sentimental goodbyes. The out-goers had to be smartly on their way to reach their new abode before the darkening, often passing their opposite numbers on the road.

The fires were kept going in the empty house, and Jessie saw that there was food and milk left there to await the arrival of the weary travellers. It would be late that night before they got to bed, for the carts had to be unloaded before the flitters could finally settle in. But at least there would be a kettle on the boil to welcome them.

I remember watching the carts coming rumbling up the road in the gloaming, and wondering what household treasures lay under the tarpaulin covers. There might be livestock, too, a piglet, perhaps, a few hens, or a bantam cockerel.

Jock-the-herd used to tell me of a family who flitted so regularly every year that when term day came round the bantam lay down on the rug and held up its legs to be tied; but I knew it was just one of Jock's tales.

In the morning there would be different curtains on the windows, different patterns of pipe-clay on the doorstep, and a new Mrs Thing shaking her rug. The most interesting thing for me to find out was if there were any children in the family who might play with me, or allow me to boss them, if they were small enough. I could show off my superior knowledge to impress them.

'You don't know what a triangle is? Oh well, I'll tell you.' Poor things!

As it turned out, there was a gaggle of them, all looking more or less alike. I called them Eeny, Meenie, Miny and Mo till I got their names sorted out. I liked Mo best, for she was only a toddler and thought I was perfect. There was another on the way, so the new Mrs Thing had little time to shake rag rugs or gossip on the doorstep. But she seemed contented enough, for I sometimes heard her singing as I passed by.

'O can ye sew cushions,
Can ye sew sheets,
Can ye sing Ba-loo-loo
When the bairnie greets?'

12. Trials and Tribulations

'This has been the worst day of my life,' I announced to Jessie when I reached home one snowy evening, chittering with cold and my hair frozen into icicles.

Jessie's reply was characteristic. 'Hoots, lassie, ye're no' feenished wi' life. Ye'll hae mony a worse day, if ye live lang enough.'

It was cold comfort on such a freezing day, but at the same time she was taking practical steps to thaw me out by divesting me of my outer garments, dishing up a bowl of hot soup and keeping me at a safe distance from the direct heat of the fire, 'in case ye come oot in chilblains'.

It was not only the bitter cold that had troubled me that day, though that was bad enough, eating as it did into my bones and chilling my very marrow. There were other forces working against me, as if all the gremlins in the world had taken a scunner at me. I tried to tell Jessie about it, but nothing ever sounded the same in the retelling. Either I understated the turn of events or exaggerated them. It was the same when I tried to write things down. Maybe Charles Dickens, with his sharper pen, could have made a better job of it.

It began in the raw darkness of the early morning.

> In winter I get up at night
> And dress by yellow candle-light.

I felt like a pit pony or one of the moles Jessie used to tell me about, the moudiwarts who lived underground and seldom saw the light of day. It was dark when I set off to school in the morning and pitch black by the time I reached home again. But the worst part was getting up in the icy-cold bedroom, with the windows frosted over and the hot-water bottle stone cold, knowing that I would be forced to go out into the even icier atmosphere that awaited me beyond the shelter of the farmhouse walls.

The trouble about being a scholar at the Grammar School was that, unlike Auld Baldy-Heid's institution, it never closed when there was a storm. The main road to Jedburgh was kept open by snowplough, and I was expected to struggle down to the road-end as best I could to board Black Sandy's bus, often up to the armpits in snow-wreaths.

No excuses. Archie-Bald, the rector, had a heavy hand with truants. There were deadly exams looming up, and all dolts and dunces were expected to attend every lesson, frozen stiff or not. Easy enough for him, living in a house cheek by jowl with the school. He could leave his warm fireside five minutes before the bell rang, with no pitying thought to spare for country pupils who had to get up hours before in the cold dawn.

Nothing could be bleaker than that walk over the snowy wastes in the early morning, with the chill air finding every chink in my armour. Even though I was well wrapped up, with a long woollen scarf – a gravat – tied over my head and round my neck, I was soon shivering. There was no chance of walking smartly to keep the circulation going.

Every step was hazardous, slipping and sliding without making much progress. And there was no telling whether I was on the road or the hillside, everything was so blocked up. Only the tops of some snow-laden trees helped to give me my bearings.

Time and again I fell into a snow-filled ditch and had to haul myself out. By now my fingers were so frozen that I had no feeling in them and could scarcely carry my school bag. All the time I thought of the day's lessons awaiting me and the poem I had to learn off by heart.

> I chatter, chatter as I flow
> To join the brimming river.
> For men may come and men may go
> But I go on for ever.

It did not apply to our burn at home which was lost beneath the snow, nor to the river Jed which lay silent and unchattering under the frozen ice.

At last I reached the road-end and saw the bus waiting for me. Black Sandy was out on the road, flapping his arms and stamping his feet to keep warm. Usually I was there in good time but he always gave me a few minutes' grace in snowy weather.

'Come on, wee ane. Speed up. Jings! ye look like a frosted tattie. Hop in.'

The cold had done little to curb Black Sandy's spirits. He sang louder, if anything, as we rattled in the Jed road. Rattled was the word, for Sandy had put clanking chains on his tyres, which made a raucous din every time they spun round. Even so, they did not drown his song.

> 'There ance was a very pawky duke
> Far-kent for his joukery-pawkery.
> He owned a hoose wi' a grand ootlook,
> A gairden an' a rockery.

Hech mon! The pawky duke!
Hoot ay! An' a rockery!
For a bonnet laird wi' a sma' kailyaird
Is naethin' but a mockery.'

Sandy went on for verse after verse, stopping when he had to collect another shivering young passenger by the wayside and picking up again where he had left off.

'His nose was red as ony rose,
His legs were lang an' bony. . . .'

Indeed, all our noses were redder than roses by the time we reached the town, for we had to get out so often to heave the bus forward when it skidded or stuck in a snow-drift. I was terrified the worst would happen and the school gates would be closed against us when we got there, with the fearsome Janny glowering at us through the railings. But Black Sandy did his best to make up for lost time by riding his charger at full speed when the going was good, and tooted his horn in triumph when he swung into the High Street.

We made it. The bell was giving its final clang when we shuddered to a standstill outside the gates.

'Oot ye get!' roared Black Sandy. 'Ye're just in time. Onward Christian Soldiers!'

In we trooped and the prison gates were shut behind us. I thought there was a disappointed gleam in the janitor's eye. Little did I realize I would see that gleam again later in the day when my blackest nightmare came true.

Miss Crichton's catarrh was worse that day. She spent a great deal of time blowing on her handkies and drying them off on the radiator. It seemed an unhygienic practice, but who were we to complain? Soon we were all steaming, as our wet garments began to dry off in the comparative warmth of the classroom. Before long I had a swimmy feeling in my head and a great desire to lay it down on the desk. It was difficult to concentrate on lessons, but we were forced to remain alert, for, busy though she was with her handkerchiefs, Miss Crichton was determined to put us through our paces, with the impending examinations in mind.

We all had to say '*Bonjour, mam'selle*' to her and answer her questions in French, an impossible task for me. I had not yet sorted out the males from the females, and was rapped smartly over the knuckles for referring to my book as *une livre* and to my seat as *un chaise*.

'*Tu es une* idiot,' she ranted to me in her North-East accent. '*Une* silly idiot!'

I felt sillier as the lessons went on. Strange what a word of praise can do or alternatively a word of blame. If one is designated a donkey one does one's best to bray. By the time I reached the English class, where I could usually hold my own, I could not remember without constant promptings the verses I was supposed to repeat. The poem sounded idiotic, intoned in my broad Border tongue.

'I slip, I slide, I gloom, I glance
Among my skimming swallows.
I make the netted sunbeams dance
Against my sandy shallows.'

I could not blame the other pupils for giggling behind my back. It was not done out of malice, it was just something to break the monotony. For were they not all my friends by now? This revelation had completely overwhelmed me, coming as it did out of the blue.

It had happened during the time I was forced to stay off for a whole fortnight with a 'fever', bad enough to necessitate a visit from the doctor. He came smelling of antiseptic, in his chauffeur-driven car, and after sounding me with his stethoscope, took my temperature and left instructions that I was to lie still and take light nourishment.

There had been a great to-do in anticipation of his visit,

with the bedroom fire lit for his benefit and a tray set out with the best china and a lace cloth in case he fancied a cup of tea. I felt guilty at causing such a stir and making my mother dress up in her best frock in the middle of the morning. Father, too, could not settle to anything till the great man had come and gone, for the visit always ended in the parlour with the doctor receiving some stronger refreshment than that on the tea-tray.

Lying still and taking light nourishment no doubt helped to reduce the fever though it made me feel like a trapped animal at the zoo. Jessie or the servant-girl brought the food up on a tin tray – no fancy lace cloths for me – dumped it down on the rickety bedside table and said, 'Here ye are. Eat every bite, or else!'

Thin gruel, lightly boiled eggs mushed up with bread in a cup, beef tea and tapioca pudding did little to tempt my appetite, but it was not the eating that mattered to me. I would sooner have had a gulp of fresh air, and felt sure I could have cured myself faster if I had been left up a tree rather than in a stuffy bedroom.

Lack of reading material added to the dreariness of the long days. I had devoured everything from *Oliver Twist* (twice) to the text on the wall calender and the stock market in the *Scotsman*, and was almost reduced to my Latin grammar when the Cairthorse came stumping upstairs after the postie had called.

'Here's a letter for ye.'

'Never!'

My temperature shot sky-high when I saw that it was indeed addressed to me with a Jedburgh postmark. Inside was a get well card with a picture of an elephant on it (not forgotten), signed by every single one of my classmates and with an added message: 'Come back soon, we're missing you.'

Fancy that!

I could not have been more surprised if Dafty had sent

his love to me or the great Miss Crichton herself had written, '*Je suis* absolutely lost *sans toi*.'

I could hardly wait to get back, though I felt a little embarrassed when I came face to face with them again; but I need not have bothered, for they showed no outward signs of affection. All the same, I felt it was there. They still pulled my leg mercilessly and laughed at my accent, but there was no malice in it. I was no longer just an oddity, I was one of them.

But it did not help me much with 'The Brook'. Even the mild English teacher had succumbed to Miss Crichton's temper and to her cold.

'Sid dowd, you're hopeless,' she told me between sneezes. 'You'll have to begid at the begidding and leard it all over agaid. Atishoo!'

By the time we were let out for the lunch break I felt that many a long year had passed, and the day was still far from done. Indeed, the first lesson in the afternoon was the one I feared most, Latin. Archie-Bald, in view of our general stupidity ('Man, you're an ass! Sit down, you donkey!') had let it be known that we must all be present, dead or alive, so that he could cram us for the exams. But before that there were important affairs I had to attend to in the town.

Being cut off at home from the vanman and the postie, it was left to me to do the vital shopping. For this purpose I had been given an old haversack and a long list of necessities to purchase, including a tin of treacle, bread, sausages, tobacco, the mail and newspapers, as well as many other odds and ends. I could see by the length of the list that there would be no hope of visiting the soup kitchen that day, but I could buy a bun or a bar of chocolate on the way. The main thing was to get the messages done.

Unhappily, I was no sooner out of the school gates than a blast of icy wind blew the list out of my hand, and away it sailed over the rector's house, never to be seen again.

For a brief moment I wondered where it would land. In France, or some other foreign country? And what would the natives think of such a strange missive? D-thread, saus., sug., treac., tob., and all the rest.

Then the awfulness of it struck me and I started to shiver with fear rather than cold. All the way up the High Street I tried to visualize the scrawls on the lost list. It was worse than memorizing 'The Brook'.

'Tobacco, sugar, tea, treacle, bread, sausages. I slip, I slide, I gloom, I glance. . . .'

I did what I could, going from shop to shop and swithering on each doorstep. Was it blue darning-thread or brown? Had I to get cookies at the baker's or a pan loaf? What kind of tobacco? How many sausages? Pork or beef? I went to the post office for the letters, to the newsagent for the papers, and finally to the fruit shop for some oranges. I had not had time to buy a bun, but I was past eating.

There were four or five folk in front of me in the shop and I had to stand in line, shuffling my feet and shifting my loaded haversack from one arm to the other. The town clock was nearing the dreaded hour. I prayed for it to slow down and for the folk in front of me to hurry up.

The shopkeeper was a nice enough man, but too good a listener. And the wives who were making their purchases had plenty to tell him, about their varicose veins, the price of apples, and wasn't the weather terrible?

The clock was beginning to chime by the time I took possession of the oranges. 'It must be awful bleak outbye in the storm. Are you not frozen, lass?' he asked, and handed me a banana as a bonus.

'No, I'm fine. Thanks for the banana,' I said hastily, and ran for my life, skidding down the street at top speed. But not quickly enough. The clock had stopped ringing and so had the school bell by the time I came in sight of the gates, only to hear the janitor clashing them shut. When I reached them he was walking away, leaving me gazing through the bars as if I had been shut out of Paradise, though Archie-Bald was hardly my idea of a deity.

I had no notion what to do. Stand and shiver for the rest of the day? Or shout? The janitor had no name, as far as I knew, so all I could call was, 'Janny! Janny!'

He turned round and I could see by that gleam in his eye that I had made his day though I had ruined my own.

'I'm sorry I'm late. Please let me in,' I pleaded.

'No, I'll not,' he said bluntly, and that was that.

For a moment I wondered if I might soften his heart by offering him the banana, but I knew his crust was too hard. He had turned his back on me and was walking away when I gave one last despairing call: 'Janny! Come back! Let me in!'

And then I was aware of someone standing beside me. A large gentleman with a benign look on his face and a clerical collar round his neck. 'Smith! Come back here, Smith!' he called out in a commanding voice.

The janitor turned, gave a start, and came walking back, touching his cap.

'Open the gates, Smith.'

'Yessir!'

It was a miracle, of course; the first nice thing that had happened to me that day. The gleam had gone from the janitor's eye as he turned the key to let me in, and I felt faintly sorry for him. I had spoiled his little hour of triumph.

'Thanks,' I breathed to my saviour – perhaps I should have given *him* the banana – and took to my heels, not stopping to draw breath till I reached the rector's room.

Dafty had not missed me. He was away in one of his dwams, sitting at his desk playing with a paper-clip. The boys gave me a sympathetic glance as I slunk into my seat. I shared the banana with them, a bite each. Unfortunately I was in the midst of chewing mine when Archie-Bald suddenly looked up.

'Stop chewing, girl!' he cried in an irritated growl. (At

least he had called me *girl.*) 'Get on to your feet and read page seven.'

I wondered if the day would ever end, but of course it did. After struggling through algebra ('What does x equal?') the final bell rang at last. The Janny gave me a queer look as I passed out of the gates but I got a warmer welcome from Black Sandy, though he warned me, 'Dod! I doot we'll hae oor troubles on the road oot.' And so we did, for the snow had begun to fall again and it had been dark since early afternoon.

We were in and out of the bus half a dozen times, helping to push it over icy patches, and once we skidded into a snow-filled ditch.

'Heave ho!' roared Black Sandy encouragingly. 'Scots Wha Hae!'

The worst part was my lonely walk in the darkness to reach home. What a relief to see the lights in the windows and to stumble at last into the warm kitchen.

My head was nodding over my supper as I recounted the day to Jessie. But I must have waxed eloquent enough, though I had not noticed her hanging on my words, for at the end she said, 'Mercy, lassie! ye're as guid as the *People's Friend.*'

This was praise indeed. I felt as if Dafty had given me an Excellent Plus mark. It helped to thaw me out as I went to bed clutching my stone hot-water bottle.

There was always the hope that tomorrow might be better.

13. Leisure and Pleasure

Tomorrow was a wonderful word. There was always the prospect of something exciting happening, a new beginning.

It came, and with it the thaw, which meant a return to activity on the farm and an end to listlessness. Strange how the Bible was always right. 'Seedtime and harvest'. Who would have believed, in the depths of winter, that anything could ever grow again on that dead frozen earth? Or that lifeless trees could bring forth fresh shoots? Yet before long the cycle would begin all over again: the ploughing, the sowing, the reaping, the mowing. The hidden flowers would rise like Lazarus from the dead, and the air would be full of bird song.

At the turn of the year the humans, too, began to emerge from their cocoons. All winter long the men had gone about wrapped up 'like dumplings in a cloot' with sometimes only their noses visible. Goodness knows how many layers of woolly sarks and long drawers they wore underneath their corduroys. It was sometimes difficult to tell who was who. 'Are you Wull or Tam?' They both wore khaki-coloured gravats round their necks and sometimes balaclava helmets on their heads.

The herd had a coat with sagging pockets stuffed with miscellaneous objects, medicine for the sheep, his all-purpose knife, a hammer, nails, screws, bolts, binder-twine. He kept his pipe and baccy somewhere in an inner pocket. Often I saw him crouching behind a dyke, as if he was hiding from the enemy, and knew that he was trying to shelter from the blast until he found his pipe and got it going.

During the dark days of winter when the ground lay fallow the men occupied themselves by doing odd jobs about the place, winding straw into ropes, cutting up turnips in an ancient guillotine, chopping sticks, sawing wood, mending implements, crawling about on the roofs to patch up loose slates, and looking after their horses in the work-stable.

Jock-the-herd always had his hands full, especially at lambing time; but the hinds, I felt, grew restless, longing to get back on the land and start ploughing. Sometimes I heard them singing their endless repetitious songs, the corn-kisters, so called because farm-workers had a habit of sitting on the cornkist – the wooden corn-chest in the barn – and dunting their feet against its sides in time to their fa-la-las and tooral-oorals.

One of the songs I remember was about an iron horse. What on earth could it be? An iron horse! It was a long time before I solved the mystery and discovered they were singing about a railway train.

'There were hooses in a lang straight line, a' standin' upon wheels, man,
And the chiels that fed the horse were as black's a pair o' deils, man.
And ne'er a thing they gied the brute, but only coals to eat, man.
He was the queerest beast I've seen, for he had wheels for feet, man.'

I used to wonder what the men did at night shut up in their small cottages. Sit in their stocking-soles staring into the fire?

They were not the kind to have hobbies, except the herd who spent much of his spare time whittling away at a length of wood, an embryo crook, or polishing its handle. But the hinds just sat. Sometimes they read the local paper, the *Jedburgh Gazette*, or had a look at the *People's Friend* which their wives took in weekly, but there were seldom books to be seen lying about, except the Bible and it was only for the Sabbath.

Now and again they had a game of draughts. In many cottages the dambrod – the draught-board – hung on the wall in pride of place. And I remember Tam saying to Wull, or Wull saying to Tam, after they had finished their tasks in the work-stable, 'I'm thinkin' o' takin' doon the dambrod the nicht. Are ye on for a game?' It was a challenge, like throwing down a glove.

'Richt! I'm on,' said the other, flexing his muscles as if in preparation for a boxing-match.

The game would be like a fiercely fought battle, though little was said by the contestants as they sat opposite each other poring over the board and communicating only by grunts after each move. Next day they replayed it again as they went about their work.

'Ay! I had ye cornered, Tam,' said Wull triumphantly.

'No, ye didny! I could have got oot if I'd tried.'

'Ye could not!'

'I could sot!'

'Weel, what for did ye no' try?'

'I wasny thinkin'. But I'll get ye the next time. . . .' And so it went on.

Sometimes they played dominoes in more light-hearted vein with their wives joining in. But for real jollification a kirn was the thing.

I thought it strange that a kirn, which was the name

Jessie called the churn in which we made butter, should also be the name for a harvest-home, but so it was. A kirn-supper. The first I ever attended was at a large farm in the Oxnam district, and I wonder why I came to be asked to accompany my parents to such a spree? Perhaps it was because there were some young folk in the farmer's family, for I remember dancing an energetic polka with the son of the house, a young gent of nine, destined to become a rugby player. I had bruises on my shins for weeks afterwards, not only from him but from many a tackety boot, for there were no such refinements as dancing-pumps at a good-going kirn.

We drove first to the farmhouse and were piped out to the yard and up the granary stairs where the company was assembled. The rafters had been decorated with greenery and the wooden floor swept well and sprinkled over with soapflakes to make it slippery enough for dancing. It was a strange ballroom, with the cows lowing underneath, the pigs grunting, and a hen appearing from nowhere to peck for loose grain in a corner. But to me it was like fairyland, with the lights from the lanterns swinging overhead softening the scene, the jolly music setting everyone's feet tapping and bringing a sparkle to their eyes. A complete change from anything everyday.

It was the only time I saw Jessie dancing. She was there with her sister Joo-anne and her brother Jock-the-herd. She was still upright, still in a long black skirt, black stockings, black shoes, but wearing a blouse I had never set eyes on before, black, too, but with some shiny ornaments on it and a touch of lace at the neck. What a handsome woman she looked, with her face flushed after executing a Highland Scottische with my father as her partner. He kicked up his heels and hooched with abandon, but Jessie remained dignified, with the same expression on her face as when milking the cows. She had her Sunday stays on for I heard them creaking when I encountered her in the eightsome reel. 'Roond this way, lassie,' she said severely, during the grand chain. 'Ye're gettin' a' fankled.'

I think she was enjoying herself, but she would never let on.

The music was provided by two fiddlers perched precariously on chairs set on top of a small wooden table. They played vigorously in their shirt-sleeves throughout the long dances, stamping their feet to the rhythm and resting now and then when someone was called upon to do a turn.

I was terrified I might be asked to recite, but I need not have worried. There were too many willing volunteers, especially as the night wore on and tongues were loosened after frequent refreshments. The highlight, of course, was my father singing his comic songs. I shouted, 'Encore!' as loud as the rest and laughed at his patter though I knew every word that was coming.

'Isn't he great?' I heard on all sides.

'Oh yes, isn't he?' I agreed. It was not reflected glory. I thought he *was* great.

Others got up and sang sentimental songs ('My Love She's but a Lassie Yet'), the farmer and his wife rendered a duet (The Crookit Bawbee') and the grieve recited an interminable Border ballad, swaying on his feet in the middle of the floor with his eyes firmly closed. Like the brook he went on for ever.

> 'The moon was clear, the day drew near,
> The spears in flinders flew;
> But mony a gallant Englishman
> Ere day the Scotsmen slew.'

The English teacher would have been proud of him, for he never stumbled over a word, but the company began to grow restless and clapped so loudly at the end, with relief, that he took it for an encore.

'I'll gie ye "Tam o' Shanter",' said he, opening his eyes, but luckily we were spared, for just then we were bidden to sit in at the trestle tables set along the sides of the granary, the farmer at the head of one and his wife at the other. It was time for the kirn-supper.

Before we began to eat, the Oxnam minister gave the old Covenanter's grace.

> 'Some hae meat that canna eat,
> And some wad eat that want it;
> But we hae meat, and we can eat,
> And sae the Lord be thankit.'

'A-men!' said the company, and fell to.

It was truly a groaning board, though I cannot recall any detail of the meal, except of drinking a refreshing tumblerful of home-made lemonade and of exchanging conversation-lozenges with my companions.

The young son of the house, flushed with food and long past his bedtime, as, indeed, I was, too, handed me a heart-shaped sweetmeat with 'Do you love me?' printed on it in smudged lettering. The idea! My reply was short and sharp. Fortunately I was in possession of a white lozenge with pink lettering on it. 'Not tonight'. Time and again the sweets changed hands, passing them from one to another, but in the end we ate them all, no matter how grubby they were.

It was strange seeing Jessie sitting still and being served instead of clattering back and forth dishing out potatoes and handing round plates. All the same, she kept a watchful eye on the helpers and I expected her to give them a sharp rebuke when they dropped a fork on the floor or spilt some cream on the tablecloth.

At the end tea was served from a great urn, and the farmer rose to his feet to make a speech of welcome to his friends and thanks to his workers. The unfortunate hind who was to reply had his speech written out on a piece of paper which he held in his trembling hand. He grew purple in the face, petrified with terror when the moment came, and had to be helped on to his feet by his neighbours, with encouraging calls of, 'Come on, Geordie. Do your stuff. Get it aff your chest.'

Somehow or other Geordie stumbled through his stuff and sat down to sympathetic applause, easing his braces and giving a great sigh of relief. It was obvious from the way he gulped at his glass that he was about to enjoy the evening to the full, now that his ordeal was over.

The tables were cleared, the dusty floor re-swept with great stable-brooms and sprinkled once more with soap-flakes. On with the dance. The local minister, a waggish kind of man, came and bowed before me as if I was the Queen of Sheba. 'Would you care to trip the light fantastic with me, young lady?'

I had no idea what he was talking about, but I was flattered, of course, at being called a young lady, and willingly became his partner in the Lancers, during which he whirled me off my feet as if he was an ordinary man and not a servant of God.

The dances were all energetic: Circassian Circle, Roxburgh Castle, Petronella, Triumph, Drops o' Brandy. Some were more like games than dances. It was a sight to see the droopy grieve from Swinside Townhead chasing his wife, the Missis, down the middle and up the sides, ducking and dodging, poussetting and *pas-de-bas*ing. She left a trail of hairpins wherever she went, and it was noticeable that his galluses – like the rest of the company he had long since cast his jacket – were hanging by a thread. But at least he was putting his heart and soul into the dance, which was more than he did with his jobs on the farm.

I felt a glow of pleasure when Jock-the-herd came stramping across the floor to 'lift' me for one of the waltzes the fiddlers played now and again to change the tempo and give the perspiring dancers a breather.

There was no finesse about Jock. 'Man-lassie, come on,' said he, grabbing me by the hand. None of the light fantastic for him. He was heavy on his feet. And mine! Indeed, he danced mainly on his heels, propelling me round and round, to the tune of 'Over the Sea to Skye', as if he was hauling a sack of corn.

'Ane-twa-three, turn! Ane-twa-three, turn!'

Sometimes he tried to reverse, with disastrous results. The other dancers jostled and bumped us back into place till I felt like a football. Still, it was a treat to be dancing with Jock and I would not have changed partners for Rudolph Valentino if he had suddenly appeared in the granary and knelt at my feet to beg for a waltz.

The cocks were crowing and the grey light of dawn creeping into the granary by the time the fiddlers played the last dance, a roundabout waltz called the Hoolachan in which everyone joined, changing partners as they progressed round the floor. Then we all clasped hands to sing 'Auld Lang Syne', gave three cheers for the farmer, and made our ways home, some not too steadily.

The story is told of a farmworker who had been imbibing too freely at a kirn and was making such a nuisance of himself that he was repeatedly asked to leave. In the end he had to be forcibly removed, at which point he was heard to mutter, 'A'weel, I dinna care. It's been a gey dry affair, onywey.'

Strange how everyone seemed to be crosser after an evening's jollity. Next day Jessie had an attack of her mysterious ailment called the bile, and kept her lips in a thin tight line. I knew better than to talk to her. Now and then she took sips of hot water and thumped her stomach angrily before giving a belch. Even Jock was a bit grumpy, and when I asked him how he had enjoyed the kirn mumbled something about a 'sair heid'. Even I felt dizzy through lack of sleep. It seemed one had to pay dearly for one's pleasures, but oh! they were worth it.

It was better than a tonic from the doctor to explode now and again and let feelings go free instead of always bottling them up. Borderers have a habit of fencing themselves in, encasing their minds in armour as restricting as Jessie's stays, so that no one can ever guess their innermost thoughts.

The most they will ever say to each other in meeting is, 'Nice day.'

'Ay, no' bad.'

Or, like Jessie and Jock when they met in the farmyard, pass each other with scarcely a grudging grunt of recognition.

'What do you talk about at night, Jessie?' I once asked her. 'You and Jock and Joo-anne?'

'Naethin'.'

Maybe the feeling was there, deep down. The pity was it never came to the surface.

This reticence, I felt, ruined many a relationship. Even as a bairn, I sensed it myself. There were times when I longed to run after Jessie, throw my arms round her neck, and say, 'Oh, Jessie! I love you!' But I could never bring myself to do it. What would be her reaction? 'Away, lassie! Dinna be daft.'

Or, might it have been that she, like the rest of us, was waiting for a sign of affection? And all of us afraid to take the first step.

But it would have taken a bold soul to bell a Border cat!

14 Spring-Cleaning

After the turn of the year the hinds were eager to get on with the ploughing. It seemed to give them some inward satisfaction to see the long straight furrows in the fields and to know that the familiar cycle had started once more. For weeks beforehand they had been examining the ploughs in the cart-shed, seeing that the cutting-blades were in good order, and mentally flexing their muscles for the work ahead.

Now that I was going to town each day I had gained some small degree of importance in their eyes, for not only could I do little bits of shopping for them, I was also learning to keep my eyes open so that I could pass on useful information.

'They've started ploughing at Sunlaws.' Or the Bairnkine, or one of the other farms I passed in the school bus.

'Weel then, we'll need to get on. Tell the Boss.'

But they knew, and so did the Boss, that Overton Bush was outbye and the other farms inbye. They were more sheltered, with softer soil. Why risk breaking the ploughshares on ground that was still as hard as iron? The day would come when a warmer spell of weather would make the earth yield, then out would come the Clydesdales with their great stamping feet and tossing heads. Operation ploughing would begin.

When the first bright rays of spring sunshine penetrated through the farmhouse windows, showing up all the deficiencies hidden during the dark days of winter: the dusty corners, the damp patches on the ceilings, the faded cushions, the torn wallpaper, another operation far deadlier than the ploughing was under way. The spring-cleaning. Everything in the house was upside-down – 'tapsulteerie', Jessie said – and for weeks we lived in such discomfort that Father shut himself up in the greenhouse and I escaped to the ruined castle as often as I could.

I often wondered why anyone bothered, for no one seemed to enjoy it. But it was the done thing. Perhaps nobody would have started at all if it had not been for inquisitive enquiries from neighbouring farmers' wives. 'Have you started the cleaning yet? Oh yes, we're well on. Papered the spare room yesterday. Pink roses. You should have seen the *oose* below the bed!' (*Oose* was the dusty fluff that collected below beds and in unswept corners.) 'How far on are you? Not started yet! Oh well!'

We were made to feel outcastes.

It was not just a cursory cleaning. Every single piece of furniture had to be moved from its moorings, every item of bedding, every curtain and carpet was taken outside to be given an airing. And a beating. I can still see Mother and Jessie standing one at each side of a carpet slung over the clothes-rope in the back garden, belabouring it in turn with stout sticks till their arms ached, while clouds of dust rose up into the air after every blow.

It all had to be done the hard way. What would they have made of today's labour-saving aids to instant cleaning:

electric polishers, spin-dryers, dish-washers and all the rest? Elbow-grease was their greatest asset. And Jessie and the servant-girl used plenty of that in the course of their everyday tasks, with waxcloth to be polished, grates blackleaded, fire-irons rubbed with emery paper, tables scrubbed, cutlery cleaned with bath-brick, doorsteps washed and milk-pails scoured. Little wonder their arms were so sinewy and their hands so rough.

It was not just elbow-grease that was needed at the spring-cleaning. Staying-power was the thing. Relentlessly they went on day after day, turning out one room after another, even the garret which looked strangely tidy the next time I was sent to solitary confinement, but it did not take me long to get it back into its higgledy-piggledy mess.

One of my own tasks was to take all the books out of the bookcases, bang them about to get rid of the 'stoor' and dust them down before replacing them in neat rows on the shelves. It was impossible during this process not to dip into *Black Beauty* or *Lamb's Tales*, or to have a keek inside an old primer belonging to a past generation. At the bottom of each page there was an uplifting saying. One I remember was, 'Go to the ant, thou sluggard, consider her ways, and be wise.'

It was good advice but I did not benefit from it until Jessie found me sitting on the floor surrounded by piles of undusted books and gave me a sharp reminder to look slippy.

The worst part of the cleaning, to my mind, was the tossing, turning and airing of all the mattresses from the beds. Each had to be dragged outside, beaten to death, and left propped over garden seats till it was time to haul them back into the house again. Jessie called them the *tykabeds*.

A tykabed was one of the first household necessities a young woman acquired for her 'doon-sittin'' when she was about to settle in to her new home on her marriage and which saw her through her lifetime. Some folk, according to Jessie, became so attached to their own tykabeds (in a manner of speaking) that nothing would induce them to sleep on any other.

'But what did they do if they went on their holidays?' I once asked her.

'Sent their tykabeds on in a cairt,' she declared.

I wondered what would have happened to our own mattresses if we had sent them in advance to the seaside along with the tin trunk. Indeed, at the spring-cleaning, I often wished we could send them away never to return, especially the feather-beds.

I had a kind of love-hate for the fluffy mattresses on which some of us slept. It was bliss on a cold night to sink into such a soft nest, but there was always the terror that it would engulf me while I was asleep, and often I woke up, fighting my way out for fear of being smothered. I preferred a harder resting-place, but it was all the luck of the draw. The beds and the sleepers thereon were chopped and changed depending on the exigencies of the moment.

At the cleaning the covers had to be washed, and the contents taken out to be picked over and sorted through. A fresh supply of clean feathers had been collected during the year and kept in a large white bolster-case to be added to the reconditioned feather-bed. This was a tricky performance not to be undertaken on a windy day when the feathers would fly through the air like snowflakes. I sometimes saw the hens pecking at them, blissfully unaware that they, too, would be plucked in due course.

Now and again Father emerged from the greenhouse and wandered about like a lost soul. There was no comfortable place for him to settle in the house, with carpets rolled up, chairs piled on top of tables, brooms and buckets everywhere, and nothing in its rightful place. Sometimes he was forced to lend a hand by knocking in a nail here and there, putting up a curtain-rail or whitewashing a ceiling. But he was not really a handyman. I was sure that one of the comic songs he sang had been specially written for him.

'When Father papered the parlour
You couldn't see him for paste.
Dabbing it here, dabbing it there,
Paste and paper everywhere.
Mother got stuck to the ceiling,
The kids were stuck to the floor,
You never saw a bloomin' family
So stuck up before.'

Once in a while we were forced to send for a real tradesman to do a professional job. These were big occasions in our lives, for the plumber or paper-hanger had to come all the way out from Jedburgh and stay for the entire day, sometimes even overnight, till the job was finished. I found it fascinating to watch how they set about their work with such skill, and admired the ease with which they used blowlamps, took doors off their hinges, unscrewed plugs, tore up floor-boards, or scraped paper off the walls. It seemed a miracle that they could ever put things back to rights again, but somehow they did.

Jessie was for ever telling them not to make a *slaister*, a slaister being a mess. She was in no way intimidated by workmen, no matter how professional, and soundly rated one who left his dirty finger-marks on a clean wall. 'I've a guid mind to gie ye a skelpin'.' But she always had the kettle boiling and a meal of sorts ready for them when she felt they had earned a 'sit doon' at the kitchen table.

The new wallpaper had been chosen weeks in advance, with my mother going through a sample book page by page, pondering over flowery patterns for the spare bedroom or whirly designs for the dining-room, the busier the better. Nothing plain. Lying in bed in the candlelight I fancied I could see 'things' on the walls, witches and warlocks hiding behind sprays of violets, or huntsmen chasing their prey through clumps of cornflowers.

It was a pity we never had the sewing-woman to stay. I had heard tales of Shewin' Sarah who went around the countryside with her portmanteau, staying for days at a time at various homesteads where she made curtains, mended breeks, repaired sheets and passed on tittle-tattle from one household to another. Mother and Jessie had already done the making and mending and had no need of extra help, but I would have liked to listen to Sarah's gossip and maybe get a new frock made from a different pattern.

I used to feel sorry for the 'body' when she was brought down from the garret to be used as a model. She got so many pins and needles stuck into her. But Jessie used to scoff at me and say, 'Hoots-toots! she's only a dummy. She canna feel a thing. Pass me the pirrn.'

The reels of cotton were the pirrns, the pins were the preens, and the stitches the steeks. Jessie's steeks were sewn so firmly that they were there for life, and no button ever left its mooring once she had stitched it firmly into place.

My job if I was there was to thread the needle, for though Jessie would never admit her eyes were not as sharp as mine, her own attempts often ended in failure. It was the needles that were at fault, she declared. They were making the eyes too small these days.

Many of my garments were hand-me-doons or concocted out of discarded curtains. Jessie had only one pattern, take it or leave it. No frills, fancies or finery.

'Could I not have a wee bit lace for a change?' I would sometimes plead.

'Lace!' said she, with her mouth full of preens. 'Set ye up! What are ye wantin' lace for, an' you aye climbin' trees?'

I liked the whirring sound the wheezy old sewing-machine made as the needle leapt from one stitch to another, but though Jessie pedalled away with a will she preferred sewing by hand. 'The steeks last langer.'

There was no sitting down and sewing during the spring-cleaning. We were all up and at it, stopping only for scratch meals when anyone had time to cook them. Indeed, on the day the kitchen chimney was swept we were lucky if we got a hot meal at all. Father and one of the hinds did the deed, ending up as black as darkies, with sacks of soot to be dragged outside and trails left on the kitchen floor. If ever Jessie used the word slaister it was then!

Throughout the year she sometimes set the lum alight herself, to clear away the cumulation, taking pages of the *Scotsman*, putting a match to them and thrusting them as far as she could up the chimney. I always ran out to see the sparks flying sky high and to hear the roar of the flames if the chimney really went on fire.

'It's on haud!' Jessie would cry, grabbing the shovel to catch the avalanche of red-hot soot that came tumbling down into the fireplace. All the pots and pans had been cleared out of the way and Blackie, the kitchen cat, had taken refuge under the table.

Afterwards the sticks and coals burned more brightly in the grate and the servant-lassie had less trouble lighting the fire in the morning. Liz-Ann, the Cairthorse, always had difficulty in coaxing the kindling into life. She would go down on her hunkers and try to fan the flames by blowing into the fireplace until she was red in the face. Or she would seize the bellows and blast away with all her might. Sometimes in desperation she sprinkled paraffin on the sticks, risking scorched eyebrows and worse, a ticking-off from Jessie.

Taking up the stair-carpet, beating the dust out of it, polishing the rods, and laying it back again step by step with its underfelt in place, was one of the most tedious tasks at the cleaning. Each stair had to be washed and scrubbed, and strict warnings were given that we were not to traipse up and down in dirty shoes. There seemed no place to turn for comfort. Tempers grew shorter as the house became cleaner, till everyone was squabbling. 'Catter-batterin',' Jessie called it.

It was a wonderful day when I heard her say, 'That's it

feenished,' and the last ornament was put back into place. For a time it was difficult to settle in such a spotless house. The homeliness seemed to have rubbed off with the elbow-grease. Father grumbled that he 'couldn't find a thing', but Mother was pleased with the results, worn out though she was with her efforts. I sometimes watched her standing back to admire her handiwork, with a look of satisfaction on her face. Then, trying to look guileless she would say, 'I think I'll just ring up the Scotts.'

I would hear her at the telephone saying smugly, 'The spring-cleaning? Oh yes, we're through! New curtains in the spare bedroom and we've re-papered the dining-room. You must come for your tea soon.'

It was all over for another year. But, like our sins white-washed every Sunday, the purity would not last long. We were soon back to our old topsy-turvy ways, oose below the beds, cluttered cupboards, untidy drawers, and muddles on every chair and sofa. To tell the truth, I liked it better that way.

Every year nature did its own spring-cleaning with far less fuss, as if an unseen hand had been busy with spit and polish. The primroses suddenly appeared by the burnside, the buds opened out on the trees, and there was a clean sparkle in the sky as if it, too, had been scrubbed with soapy water. The sun was still feeble and the weather a mixture of smiles and tears, but warm enough to coax the seeds to sprout and the wild flowers in the meadow to show their faces.

It was a young hopeful time, the silly season for lambs, chicks, foals and calves. Humans, too, who walked with sprightlier steps and gave way to sudden bursts of whistling. With the rising of the sap, I too, felt an urge to do something special, to fight for my country or save the Chinese from famine. (Jessie was always telling me how the starving Chinese would be glad of my discarded crusts.) But I had to content myself with helping the herd when he was mending a drystone dyke. Not that he appreciated my assistance.

'Man-lassie, get oot ma road an' I'll get on quicker.'

My attempts at beautifying the doorstep with pipe-clay were no better received. I tried to liven the look of it by putting my art lessons into practice. A flower here, a vase there, an apple, an orange (still life) all joined together with curly loops till there was not a vacant space left. It was an impressive sight, I thought, but not to Jessie.

'Wumman, hae ye nae gumption!' she raged. 'Ye'll gliff folk awa'. An' did ye no' think o' *weshin'* the doorstep first?'

The road to hell, the minister told us, is paved with good intentions. But the day came when I got the chance to prove my worth.

15. Another Blue Day

That day I had taken particular notice of the text on the wall. It was written by someone called T. Carlyle.

So here hath been dawning
Another blue Day;
Think, wilt thou let it
Slip useless away?

It was Saturday and I was free for the whole day. And there was blue in the sky. So what could I do to fill the fleeting hours with something worthwhile? I might do my homework and learn some of Dafty's Latin or Miss Crichton's French, but how would that help the starving Chinese?

'Would you like to do a good deed?' Mother asked me at breakfast, as if reading my thoughts. 'You could go round collecting.'

'Collecting what?'

'Money, of course.' She handed me a tattered notebook. 'For the Schemes of the Church.'

I had no notion what the church was scheming, but it would likely be something good, so here was my opportunity. I hastily finished my porridge and had a look inside the notebook. It was filled with smudged names and addresses of all the folk in the district who had contributed their shillings and sixpences last year. My task would be to call on each one and extract the same amount this year. Or more, if I was lucky; in which case T. Carlyle would surely be pleased with my efforts.

The only way to go my rounds was by Shanks's pony. The old boneshaker bicycle was in no fit state to carry me far, and many of my ports of call could only be reached by trudging across the braes; but who wanted to achieve martyrdom the easy way? The harder the road the higher marks I would gain from up above.

I set off like a pilgrim carrying an old handbag of my mother's in which to collect the money. There were a few false starts before I could shake off various followers who wanted to accompany me, including the banty hen, the pet lamb, and a small child who had toddled up from the cottages, hoping I would play with her.

'Hide-and-theek?' she lisped.

'No, not today. I've got things to do,' I said importantly.

'Can I no' do thingth, too?'

'No, you can't. Go away home.'

Her bottom lip began to tremble, and I hunted in Mother's handbag in the hope of finding a sweetie there, a leftover pandrop from the church, but there was only a hairpin and a stub of a pencil.

'Here, have the pencil,' I said, thrusting it at wee Maggie. It was better than nothing.

'Oh, thankth,' she said, beginning to suck it there and then. 'Will you play hide-and-theek when you come back?'

'Maybe,' I said cautiously, and hurried away on my mission.

It was flattering to feel wanted if only by wee Maggie,

but I had bigger things to do than hide behind haystacks.

My first encounter with danger came when the bull snorted after me as I was traversing the hill on my way across to a neighbouring farm called Stotfield. He pawed the ground and came close enough for me to hang Mother's handbag on his horns if I had been daft enough, but I had sufficient sense to sidle towards the dyke and scramble over like lightning, doing my stockings no good in the process. Perhaps the beast was only being friendly, but I was learning a modicum of gumption and it was better not to take risks at the start of my pilgrimage.

I had to approach my objective by a roundabout route through a dark wood filled with eerie rustlings, where beasties and bogles seemed to lurk behind every tree. It was only the thought of the halo on my head that kept me going. Onward Christian soldier.

It was a relief to emerge at the other side and see a friendly house in the distance. The dogs came out to meet me, barking and frisking. There were familiar cacklings and grunts from the farmyard, and the wife herself came to the door, welcoming the sight of any stranger, even me.

'Come in. The kettle's on the boil. What's the news?'

I tried to tell her about the Schemes of the Church, but what she wanted was local gossip, the schemes of Overton Bush, Camptown and Edgerston. While she toasted bread on a long pronged fork in front of the fire she plied me with questions. How had we got on with the spring-cleaning? Had I heard that Mary-Anne's varicose veins had broken out? Was it true that the minister's wife had been left a fortune? Fifty pounds from her auntie in Edinburgh. She was going to buy a new fur coat with it, so it was said, and a carpet for the minister's study. High time, too. Had I noticed how threadbare the old one was?

For one who lived so far off the beaten track Mrs Stotfield seemed surprisingly up to date with the news. I wondered if Shewin' Sarah had visited her lately.

She handed me a slice of pan-loaf, evenly toasted on each side, and pushed a jar of bramble jelly within reach. Then she delivered a bombshell.

'I hear your mother's expecting again.'

'What?'

I was so stunned, the very thought put me off my toast.

For a moment I wondered if Mother herself knew, then realized that, of course, she must. Living on a farm I had learned enough of the facts of life to know that babies were not found under gooseberry bushes. The news was both exciting and depressing. If Mrs Stotfield's story was true it meant I would be pushed further out of the nest and become even more of a nonentity. Yet it would bring a bit of stir about the place, with the doctor coming and going, the monthly nurse in residence and the prospect of another christening in the parlour.

Having drained me dry of news and at the same time given me plenty to think about Mrs Stotfield now began to rummage in the dresser drawer for her purse but could only raise ninepence in assorted coins, which was threepence less than last time. So I felt a poor missionary for the church as I left the house with her calling after me, 'Mind an' tell your mother I was asking for her. Maybe it'll be twins this time.'

I did better with the gamekeeper whom I met striding across the braes with a gun below his oxter, and saved myself a long trail to call at his cottage door. I always felt that the Gamey, with his white beard and wise sayings, looked like Moses in the Bible, and would not have been surprised if he kept the ten commandments in his game bag, but it was usually a live ferret or a dead pheasant.

When I told him my mission he thrust his hand in his pocket and brought out a silver shilling.

'You're only down for sixpence,' I told him truthfully, taking a look in the notebook. 'D'you want change?'

'No, the kirk could be doing with it.' He gazed up at the

sky as if it was the Promised Land. 'The ways of the Lord are wonderful to behold. Think of all the folk up there in heaven, and millions more maybe on the planets.'

But I was thinking of something more practical. 'Could you lend me a pencil, please?' I had to write his name in the notebook, and Mrs Stotfield's, too, and was regretting my generous gesture to wee Maggie. The Schemes of the Church would get all mixed up if I had to do mental arithmetic and keep a note of everybody's contributions in my head.

The Gamey hunted in his pockets and brought forth an assortment of string, wire, nails, knives and matchboxes. No pencil. 'Ah well, the Lord will provide,' he said, hoisting up his gun and going on his way.

The Lord provided at my next port of call, the cluster of cottages near the Big Hoose where the estate workers for the laird lived. It was easy going from one to the other instead of trudging miles across the hills .The gardener gave me a pencil and sharpened it into such a fine point that it broke as soon as I started to write Mrs Stotfield's name.

'Ye're pressin' ower hard, wumman,' said he, and sharpened it again. I was more careful next time and succeeded in keeping my accounts in order, even spelling the names correctly. But it was a worrying job and I felt I was not really cut out for big business.

One of my most terrifying tasks was to call at the Big Hoose. I was petrified in case I might meet the laird himself and prayed that he would be away in London. It was a deed that had to be done, for he was the biggest contributor in the book. Ten shillings. If I missed him, my takings would plummet to the depths.

I went round to the back door hoping to hand in the book to his housekeeper and perhaps get threepence from her, too, but who should advance towards me from the kitchen garden but Himself, wearing shabby old knickerbockers and carrying a spade in his hand? Fancy the laird digging! We were face to face so there was no chance of my darting away.

'Hullo,' he said, eyeing me from his great height. 'What are you doing here?'

'C-Collecting for the Schemes of the Ch-Church.'

'Oh!' I could see he had no idea what *they* were, but catching sight of the notebook in my hand he asked, 'What did I give last time?'

'Ten shillings.'

It seemed a fortune, even for such a wealthy man, but the laird did not blench. Instead, he took out a pocket book, extracted a pound note and handed it to me. 'There! Will that do?'

I was flabbergasted at receiving such a vast sum of money and carefully tucked it away in Mother's handbag beside the humbler coins. The man must be a millionaire, though at this moment with mud on his boots and his shirt-sleeves rolled up he looked almost like an ordinary human being.

He made some other remark, but in such a high-falutin' voice that I could not translate it, then held out his hand. For a moment I thought he wanted his pound back but he was only saying goodbye. It was strange shaking hands with God. Mine were grubby enough but so were his, so I parted from him feeling more or less on even terms.

I came down with a bump while traversing a wild stretch of moorland at the foothills of the Cheviots to reach my farthest away shepherd's cottage. There was no road to it, only a beaten track. Agnes, the herd's daughter, was a middle-aged severe-looking woman, seldom seen except once a week at the church. She had never been known to converse with anyone. 'Uh-huh!' was as much as she would say.

'She keeps hersel' to hersel',' Jessie used to declare; but maybe I could break through the barriers. Clever me.

I was thinking out a line of approach – perhaps it would interest her to hear that my mother was expecting – when a dreaded roar startled me. 'Hull – oo – a!' It was Yorkie, the gentleman tramp who roamed the country on both sides of the Borders and who often turned up at our farm demanding food and shelter. He was said to be a harmless lunatic, but we were all afraid of him, for there was no knowing when he might turn ugly. It all depended on the moon, according to Yorkie himself. Even in daylight I kept well out of his way, but there was no escape here on the bleak moorland with not a bush or a tree to hide behind.

He came lurching towards me with a crazed look in his eyes, brandishing his stick and talking gibberish to himself. I hastily hid the handbag behind my back, feeling I must defend the church's funds to the death. What if Yorkie got hold of the laird's pound note?

I need not have worried for he brushed past me as if I did not exist and continued to 'Hull-oo-a!' as he went on his way. It was a relief to see him stumbling into the distance, but the encounter had left me shaken, and my candle was not burning quite so brightly by the time I reached the cottage door.

It was open and all was still inside. I could hear the ticking of the wag-at-the-wa' – the clock on the wall – and the clicking of knitting-needles. Agnes was sitting at the kitchen table turning the heel of a sock. In front of her was a batch of newly baked barley scones propped up on their sides to cool. All the baking-dishes had been tidied away and everything was spotless, not a speck of dust, not a thing out of place, as if she did a perpetual spring-cleaning every day. Agnes herself was all-in-the-one-piece, as Jessie would say. Black skirt, black blouse, black apron, black hair tightly drawn back into a bun; and a black frown on her brow.

She did not look up when I gave a tentative knock at the open door and said, 'Hullo.' Unlike all the other houses I had visited there was no warm welcome here. No cry of, 'Come in. What's the news?' Agnes ignored my presence. She was knitting a sock, and that was that.

'I've come to collect for the Schemes of the Church.

You're down for ninepence.' I was not going away without it, after trudging so far across the moor.

'Uh-huh!' she acknowledged, and continued knitting till she reached the end of the row. Was her life so regulated and self-contained that she had no need of outside diversions, no desire to communicate with other human beings? Perhaps she had forgotten how to laugh and speak.

I wondered if her everyday tasks gave her all the satisfaction she needed. Cleaning the house, milking the cow, feeding the hens, making butter, washing, turning the heel of a sock. What did she say to her father, the shepherd, when he came in from the hills after his day's work? 'Uh-huh!' and set his food in front of him?

Presently she got up, went to the dresser drawer and carefully counted out ninepence from an old leather purse with a strong clasp on it. I thought I would break the silence by saying something, so I told her that Yorkie had just gone past. She took no notice. Yorkie had gone past, so what else was there to say? She handed me the money and went back to her knitting. My visit was over.

'Ta-ta,' I said half-heartedly, and went away musing on the mysteries of the world and the strangeness of other folk's lives. The laird in his Big Hoose, Mary-Anne talking to her hens, Yorkie with his head full of mad notions, Dafty at the Grammar School bursting into sudden rages, the Gamey seeing things in the sky, Black Sandy shouting, 'Gee-up!' to the school bus. All made from the same mould and yet so different.

Who was I? What was my role in life? A runner and fetcher! 'Run and fetch the Boss.' 'Run upstairs and fetch down the bedroom lamps.' 'Run and chase the pig out of the garden.'

I was suddenly mindful of an old man at the farm, the father of one of the hinds, who drank himself to death, with water. His thirst was so fierce that he could literally have drunk the burn dry.

I remember the first time he shouted to me, when he was out helping in the fields, 'Rin, lassie, an' fetch me some waitter.'

'In a tumbler?' I asked.

'No, no. A pail.'

I can see him clasping the pail with both hands and feverishly drinking from it, like a horse at the trough. But it never seemed to slake his thirst.

'Rin back an' fill it again,' he would say when he had drained the last drop. 'Ay, lassie, ye're a great rinner an' fetcher.'

It was the first funeral I had ever seen, when the old man died. From a distance I watched the sad procession of men, dressed like black crows, carrying the mysterious box out of one of the cottages and bearing it away. The man's thirst was cured at last.

Running and fetching, I supposed was better than just standing still. And it bore results. By the time I had finished my rounds and reached Granny's cottage at Camptown I was a wealthy woman. The heaviness of my handbag was proof that I had not let another blue day slip useless away. Granny gave me threepence, which was all she could afford, poor body, and let me have a dip into the sweetie-box on the mantelpiece. I did a bit of running and fetching for her, too, carrying in sticks from 'round the back', filling her kettle, and dusting the top of the wardrobe which she could never reach.

As I neared Bella Confectionery's shop the devil crept up behind me and whispered in my ear. 'Think what you could buy with all that money. Jujubes, caramels, pandrops, liquorice-allsorts. Mountains of home-made toffee. It would be easy enough to fiddle the books. The laird's contribution, for instance. You could pretend he only gave you ten shillings, the same as last year, then you would have the rest to spend. Ten shillings' worth of chocolate-drops, all to yourself!'

I could taste them in my mouth, sweet and cloying, hundreds and thousands of them.

I walked past the shop, of course, but I still felt a sinner at heart for the wicked thought had been there. The last climb up the steep farm road was the worst. My legs were aching by now and I was not as pleased with myself as I had been. But it was nice to smell kippers frying when I finally reached the farmhouse and to see my mother laying out the knives and forks on the table. I took a quick glance at her but I could not tell whether she was expecting or not. She just seemed the same.

'You're back,' she said without turning round. 'Good! You can run and shut in the hens before you have your supper.'

It was not easy being a pilgrim.

16. Uncertainties

There always seemed to be a touch of magic in the air when the first call of the cuckoo was heard near the farmhouse. There was something alluring about the sound, but try as I would I never succeeded in seeing the elusive bird. He was only a wandering voice.

'Where is't?' I would puzzle, running through the wood to the cow-gang trying in vain to locate the mocking sound, at once far off and near. It was like playing a game of hide-and-seek with an invisible companion.

The cuckoo is a bonny bird,
He sings as he flies;
He brings us good tidings;
He tells us no lies.

He drinks the cold water
To keep his voice clear,
And he'll come again
In the spring of the year.

Jessie called him the gowk. (She called me a gowk, too, but that was a different matter.) And she sometimes talked about a gowk-storm, which was a sudden tempestuous squall in the early part of the year. Where did she cull all her knowledge? From bound volumes of the *Quiver*, from the sheep-dip calendar, or the *People's Friend*? Maybe she had been born with it in her head. I felt she could have taught Auld Baldy-Heid a thing or two. And Dafty at the Grammar School as well.

But she knew nothing about French.

I was sitting idly swaying on the swing, listening to the cuckoo calling and doing my home-lessons in my head, in a sort of a way.

> '*Allons, enfants de la patrie,*
> *Le jour de gloire est arrivé. . . .*'

Miss Crichton had been trying to teach us the Marseillaise, which was like Scots Wha Hae to the Frenchies, but that was as far as I could go. What came next?

'Cuck – oo – oo – oo!'

Jessie emerged from the kitchen door with a little three-cornered shawl thrown over her shoulders, on her way home to the herd's hoose, her day's work done. I was about to shout, 'What's next, Jessie?' when I realized it was no use asking her. She thought little enough of English let alone French. Anything other than broad Border Scots was a heathen tongue.

I watched her as she walked away. There was something about Jessie's back view that brought a pang of pain to my heart. Could it be a foreboding that she was going away for ever?

All the sad thoughts of youth came tumbling into my head. The uncertainties about the future, above all the dread of death.

But Jessie was invulnerable. Wasn't she?

'Cuck – oo – oo – oo!'

The bird seemed to be jeering at me. Surely, surely nothing could happen to Jessie.

As if sensing my fear she turned round and gave me one of her direct looks.

'I'll see ye the morn's mornin', lassie.'

My heart leapt up. 'Right, Jessie,' I cried and swung myself sky high. Never mind the Marseillaise. I began to sing one of Black Sandy's songs instead.

'Come, love, come, the boat lies low,
She lies high and dry on the O-hi-o! . . .'

If I flew high enough and looked in the right direction I could catch a glimpse of the Eildon hills away in the distance. Like Jessie they never changed. And if I twirled round the other way I fancied I could see the top of Big Cheviot, equally steadfast.

I watched the hinds going down the road walking side by side in their big tackety boots, on their way home to supper. Then the herd came by carrying a lump of wood in his arms.

'What's that, Jock?'

'Wud.'

'What for?'

'Naethin'. It'll come in handy. Man-lassie, look oot or ye'll tummle.'

'No, I'll not. Swing me higher, Jock, please.'

'Nae fears. I'll awa' an' split the wud. It'll mak' guid kinlin' for the fire.'

There was something about his back view, too, as he walked away that brought back that vague feeling of uncertainty.

'Jock!' I called out urgently.

'Eh?'

'Nothing's going to change, is it?'

He half turned and stood for a moment not scoffing at me but pondering over the question.

'A'weel, the Borders'll aye be here, onywey.'

It was almost a reassurance. Enough, anyway, to dispel my fears.

'Come, love, come, won't you come along with me?
I'll take you down to Ten-nes-see.'

Next morning the worst of my forebodings were realized, though by that time I had forgotten all about them and came skipping into the kitchen as bright as a bee. Another Saturday morning with a whole blue day to myself.

'Jessie! I'm ready for my breakfast.'

She was not there.

Her sister Joo-anne, in a clean white pinny, was stirring the porridge.

I stared at her blankly. 'Where's Jessie?'

'She's d-d-d . . .' Joo-anne always spoke with a slight stammer, especially when she was excited. At first I thought she was trying to tell me Jessie was dead. 'She's d-doon.'

'Doon?'

'Wi' her st-st-stamoch.'

'Mercy me!' I stood there looking at Joo-anne and still not taking it in. 'Is she – is she awful ill?'

'Daursay no. She'll be f-fine. Get oot me r-r-road, lassie. Sit doon an' eat your br-br-breakfast.'

She was nice, was Joo-anne, but she was not Jessie. How could I swallow my porridge or do justice to the succulent ham that was frizzling in the frying-pan? I could only think of Jessie being 'doon'. All I wanted was to go to the herd's hoose and see for myself.

Never before had she given in to any illness. The rest of us came out in spots, took 'hoasts' or whooping-cough, broke our ankles, cracked our noses, or caught ringworm. Not Jessie. Illness was something to be ignored. 'Stop thinkin' aboot it an' it'll gang awa',' was her creed.

I ran all the way through the fields. If the cuckoo was calling I did not hear him. I wanted to take Jessie a present, but what? A minding of some kind. I could stop and pick a bunch of wild flowers but they would be wilted by the time I reached her cottage. Suddenly I saw something glinting on the grass, the sheen of a feather, made up of a mixture of greens and blues and deep reds, with a clean white quill at the end. Maybe Jessie would like it. I stooped to pick it up and ran on.

The door was on the latch. I lifted the sneck and walked in. Jessie was in the box bed, not lying down but sitting bolt upright in a white nightdress – her goonie – with her hair in a spirally pigtail, thumping angrily at her chest as if trying to hit the pain away.

'Oh, Jessie!' I could not think of anything else to say.

She gave me a sharp look and said crossly, 'What's up? What are ye here for?'

'I – I came to see you, Jessie.'

'A'weel, ye've seen me.' She turned her head to the wall as if to hide the pain and the fact that she had been caught off guard.

'Is it the bile, Jessie?' I knew, though she always tried to hide it, that Jessie suffered from a recurring ailment which had something to do with heartburn and wind in the stomach. 'Can I not do anything?'

She screwed up her face. 'Pit the kettle on.'

I knew what she meant, for I had seen her often enough in the kitchen at home, sipping piping-hot water which seemed to relieve the pain. So I laid down the feather on her bed, swung the kettle on the swey and waited till the water was hot enough. Then I filled a cup and handed it to her. For a time she sipped and thumped, thumped and sipped, while I waited for the explosion.

At last it came. She let out a loud long satisfying 'rift'.

'*That*'s better!' I said, as pleased as punch. 'How are you feeling now, Jessie?'

'Hoots, I'm fine.' There was more colour in her cheeks and she had stopped thumping her chest, but she was still angry at having been caught with her defences down. 'Awa' hame,' she ordered me. 'Awa' an' gie Joo-anne a hand.'

But as I made my way to the door she seemed to relent a little and said in a softer voice, 'If ye look in the dresser drawer ye'll mebbe find a sweetie.'

I went home sucking the treacle toffee, not sure whether to feel happy or sad. Jessie was not dying, but she had shaken my belief in the permanence of life. The farmhouse in front of me looked strong and solid, but would it crumble to ashes one day? How much time was left?

'Cuck – oo – oo – oo!'

The mocking bird had come back but he had no answer to give.

I was eager to go to church next day. The Sabbath. Not to hear the minister quoting, 'Verily, I say unto you,' or to listen to his long driech discourse. I wanted to have a private word with God. 'Make Jessie well. Let everything stay the same as it is. For ever and ever, Amen.'

I waited till all the folk were in, the laird and his lot rustling their way up to the gallery. Was that strange little man with him Sir J. M. Barrie? He looked like a gnome, perching in his pew and peering down at the commoners in the body of the kirk.

Everyone looked different on Sundays in their good clothes and with solemn expressions on their faces. Had they dressed up for God, I wondered, or for their fellow-worshippers? Even Big Bob's hair and been slicked down and Mrs Stotfield's costume showed signs of having been pressed with a hot iron.

I looked across at the picture of the Good Shepherd on the stained-glass window, and just then our own shepherd came in, doffing his bowler hat. This was the moment I always waited for, to see the steam rising from Jock-the-herd's bald head. Joo-anne followed him, carefully turning up the back of her costume jacket before settling in the pew.

Then – goodness gracious! – who was that upright figure

marching in to join them? Jessie herself! A shade paler than usual, her lips a little tighter, but how wonderful it was to see her. Everything was back to normal.

I wanted to call across to her, 'Jessie! It's great to see you.' But we were on our feet singing the opening paraphrase, with Miss Todd, the organist, pedalling away at full steam.

> 'Let not your hearts with anxious thoughts
> Be troubled or dismayed. . . .'

Father was singing lustily, enjoying the sound of his own voice, with Mother's sweet soprano blending in. I did my best to keep somewhere in between as unobtrusively as possible, fixing my eyes all the time on Jessie across the way.

There was something different about her head. What was it? A glint of green and blue and deep red.

Suddenly I knew, and felt richer than the laird up in the gallery.

Jessie was wearing my feather in her velour hat.

A BORDER BAIRN

LAVINIA DERWENT

A Border Bairn

Illustrated by Elizabeth Haines

In memory of Overton Bush

Contents

1. There is a Happy Land

When I was very young the past seemed a long way off. I used to talk to Jessie about the olden days. Meaning last week.

'Havers, lassie! Wait till ye're as auld as me.'

I have waited, and true enough, the past seems nearer. Like yesterday.

I can see it all as plainly as if I were there in the farmhouse kitchen in the Cheviots, sitting on the rug in the lamplight with the big black kettle spitting on the swey and the sheep-dip calendar hanging on the wall. *When Did You Last See Your Father?*

The noise I hear is the clatter of Jessie's clogs on the stone kitchen floor, the rattle of her milking-pail and the piercing whistle outside from Jock-the-herd calling his collies to heel. I smell the fragrance of appleringie growing in the front garden amongst the tangle of flowers and weeds, and feel the sting of nettles on my bare legs as I go stravaiging through the woods.

I am there and it is all happening.

Sometimes the picture blurs and in the fading light I begin to wonder. Was it really like that or am I making it up, filling in the gaps with imagination? Memory can play strange tricks. Yet the mind's eye often produces a truthful picture. I have been back to the old homestead and looked at it face-to-face. It was real enough, but no more real than when I see it from a far distance. Long sight is sometimes better than short.

Half-forgotten visions often sharpen into focus, and I am suddenly reminded of someone who dominated my young life for many a year. The strange thing was I never met him in the flesh though he lived with us and was as much part of the household as the grandfather clock in the hall. I could see the clock clearly enough but I never set eyes on the mysterious stranger who caused such havoc about the place.

I used to puzzle my head about him, wondering what he looked like and where he hid himself. In the garret, maybe, though I never saw him when I was imprisoned there for my misdeeds. In the dark press we called the glory-hole, or even under the floorboards? Sometimes I heard creakings at dead of night. Could they be caused by the invisible man's footsteps?

Jessie was the one who knew him best, and not a good word had she to say for him. According to her he was a bad rascal. 'Maister Naebody' she called him. A nasty nuisance who deserved a good skelping; and Jessie's skelps were not soon forgotten.

I had a sneaking sympathy for Mr Nobody in spite of his wicked ways, for were not his habits much the same as mine? Mr Nobody broke windows, knocked the teapot off the table, stopped the clock, spilt ink on the floor, hid keys and lost the scissors. A clumsy creature with no rummle-gumption. Jessie's word for common sense. She was full of it.

'Ye'll no' hae seen the poker onywhere?' she would say to me accusingly.

'Me? No, I've not.'

'A'weel, somebody's gane an' lost it. It'll be that Maister Naebody at his tricks again, the bad rascal.'

Jessie herself was perfect in every way. Staunch and true, as straight as a die, her word was her bond. Every job she tackled was done with the utmost thoroughness, from scrubbing the kitchen floor to extracting a skelf from a sore thumb. She could milk cows, stook corn, spread dung, patch breeks, bake scones, kirn butter; and, if the occasion arose, lay out a dead body. 'The back's aye made for the burden' was one of her sayings, and certainly hers was often overloaded.

With such an example to follow it was disappointing that I did now grow up more perfect myself, instead of copying Maister Naebody. But Jessie's goal was far beyond my reach. She saw everything in black and white; good or bad, no half measures. The good went to heaven and the bad to hell. There was no doubt in which direction I was aiming.

The minister often spoke about sins when he was preaching in the village kirk on the Sabbath day. Transgressions, he called them. What a wicked lot we were, straying from the paths of righteousness, thinking evil thoughts and doing bad deeds. We had all erred – that was another of his Sunday words – in the sight of the Lord, and broken all the commandments. The Thou Shalt Nots. Unless we repented and humbly begged for mercy we would be cast into outer darkness and end our days in the fiery furnace. All except His Reverence, of course. He was above all that and never transgressed. At least, not on Sundays.

At the Sunday School we had to learn the Shorter Catechism off by heart. Gabble-gabble-gabble. If there was a longer one, we were fortunate not to come across it. What a driech treatise it was, full of obscure ramblings.

'Man's chief end is to glorify God and enjoy Him for ever.'

'What does it mean?' I once asked Big Bob, who was sitting beside me on the hard pew, staring into space and fingering the catapult in his pocket for consolation.

'I've nae idea,' he said, looking startled. 'It's just blethers.'

It seemed impossible for a sinner like myself to pass the qualifying exam that would let me in through the pearly gates; so, as I was on the road to hell anyway, why bother to be good? I might as well tell lies, break crockery, kick the cat, plunk from the school, and enjoy my transgressions. But there was something that held me back. Could it be that strange inward thing the minister called conscience? Or maybe it was Jessie's upright example.

'Is there nothing you can't do, Jessie?' I once asked her.

'Ay,' she said with a straight face. 'I canna pit ma big tae in ma mooth.'

Even to hear her talk was a treat, she had such a rich store of expressive words. Sometimes she spoke to Blackie, the kitchen cat, sitting yawning on the rug.

'Daursay! what are ye gantin' for? Stir your stumps an' get oot ma road.'

She never had to tell me to stir my stumps for I was always on the go. On the randan, like a peerie-top, Jessie said. But I would sit still long enough on my stool in the byre if I could coax her to tell one of her stories while she was milking the kye. About a cushy-doo, maybe, or a wee centipede called Meggy-Mony-Feet.

I lived in a world of double-talk. English as it was spoken at the Grammar School and broad Border as spoken by the hinds who worked in the fields. With a sprinkling of Geordie dialect from the Sassenachs who lived beyond the Carter Bar. Bitter enemies in the days when we harried each others' nests; now friendly neighbours who came to pay peaceful visits unarmed with battleaxes. I could even master a few French phrases now that I was in the Higher Grade. The less said about Latin the better.

But amongst all the voices from the past it is Jessie's I hear most often, muffled as she dug her head into the cow's side. 'A'weel, ance upon a time there was a wee weasel ca'd Wullie Whitterick . . .'

Though the farm was so far removed from human contact it had the great charm of being surrounded on all sides by the beauties of Nature. 'The Borders is beautiful' was a common saying. Yet I once heard a cottage wife sigh in the depths of boredom: 'Eh whowh! I'm fair fed up wi' scenery. Day in, day oot. Naethin' but scenery.'

For my part I never grew tired of gazing at the Cheviots or at the triple-peaked Eildon Hills where King Arthur and his knights lay slumbering, awaiting the call that would one day release them from 'the bondage of enchantment'. It was the great Wizard, Michael Scott, who had cleft the hills in twain, merely by saying some magic words. I often wondered what they could be. We were studying Sir Walter Scott's *Lay of the Last Minstrel* at school. *He* knew the answer.

> And, Warrior, I would say to thee
> The words that cleft Eildon hills in three
> And bridled the Tweed with a curb of stone,
> But to speak them were a deadly sin,
> And for having but thought them my heart within
> A treble penance must be done.

So Sir Walter kept the secret to himself and I never found out. Otherwise I might have tried the magic on our own hill at home.

Some of Jessie's words were difficult to translate into plain English, but they were so expressive that their meaning was easily guessed. A chatterbox was a bletherskite, a tell-tale a clype, a round-shouldered person was humphy-backit, a throat was a thrapple, a turkey-cock a bubblyjock, upside-down was tapsulteerie, and dumfoonert meant astonished. It was far better fun than a dead language like Latin.

There was another language. Bad language. But strangely enough I never heard much of it around the farm. Maybe the hinds curbed their tongues in my presence, and the most I heard the herd say when aggravated by a straying sheep was: 'Damned eediot!' And on occasions he would call me a wee deevil, which I took to be a form of endearment.

In the Sunday School we sniggered at rude words in the bible. Belly, for example, and fornication, which we guessed was something dirty though we were not sure what. The minister was forever talking about hell and damnation, but he had been specially chosen by the Almighty and could say what he liked. As for hidden parts of the anatomy, we never mentioned them at all, and as far as I knew they had no names, not even Latin ones.

It was always to Jessie and the farmworkers I turned rather than to the immediate members of my family who seemed too engrossed in their own affairs to bother about mine. Perhaps I am doing them an injustice. Who was I, anyway? Only an in-between. Father and Mother were kind enough, providing me with what they considered the necessities of life. Food, clothing, a roof over my head. My elder brother and sister were naturally more important, being the first son and daughter. A fourth child was already toddling around on unsteady feet, and a fifth was expected, though as yet I could see no visible signs of it. So there was nothing special about me.

Except to myself. Young or old, we all crave recognition.

'Look at me! Listen to me! Talk to me! I am somebody! Not merely a mouth to be fed and a body to be clothed. I am not an also-ran. I am a person in my own right.'

Jessie noticed me, at least, now and again, for which I was truly grateful. So did her brother, the shepherd, who accepted me more or less as one of his flock. A yowe or a gimmer, a stirk or a stot. Or maybe just a damned eediot. 'Man-lassie', he called me.

There was always plenty for me to notice in the things around me. The self-sufficiency of Nature never failed to amaze me. There was surely a touch of Michael Scott's wizardry in the way a fragile snowdrop forced its way through the frozen ground or a crocus suddenly appeared from nowhere. I had a great curiosity to see how things grew, to listen to the earth and hear seeds bursting into life, but though I watched and listened I could never notice any movement. The flowers seemed to wait till my back was turned before thrusting their way through the ground.

It was the same with my baby brother who suddenly stood on his feet and began to stagger around by himself. The day before he had been a helpless child, unable to fend for himself and having to be carried everywhere. I, too, was shooting up like the snowdrops, though I could not feel myself growing. Yet I was constantly needing larger sizes in shoes and the hems of my frocks let down.

The first foreign visitors I ever saw were the swallows who flew all the way from Africa to nest under the eaves of our sheds. I wondered how on earth they had found their way from all that distance. Nature was full of unexplained mysteries, and who could give the answer? God, who had made all creatures great and small.

Sometimes in spring I went into the nearby wood and listened to all the sounds around me. Restless exciting sounds like those of an orchestra tuning up. The cawing of the rooks mixing with the melody of other birdsongs, the soughing of the wind, the hum of insects scurrying secretly in the undergrowth, the yelp of a fox in the distance, and Jock shouting to his sheepdogs. 'Doon, Jess! 'Way by, Jed!'

If I kept still enough I could watch the birds building their nests, astonished at their energy and ingenuity. The results were always perfect, though the raw materials at their command were so simple. Anything they could carry in their beaks was grist to them. Wisps of wool, hair, straw, mud, moss, feathers, rabbits' fur, spiders' webs. There was never anything slapdash or higgledy-piggledy about their home-made houses. Each bird was his own architect, fashioning his nest to suit his own special needs.

A wee bit biggin', neatly made
To keep ma bairnies in the shade . . .

Some of the nests were concealed in the hedges. Others under eaves, in tree trunks, rusty pails, discarded wheel-barrows, or in the bole of a tree. Pheasants and partridges were experts at camouflage, making simple bields on the ground amongst heather and bracken, carefully covering them with dead leaves or grass before flying off to forage for food.

It was a sin, I had been told, to rob a bird's nest. The mother would come flying after me and peck my eyes out.

The robin and the lintie,
The laverock and the wren,
Them that herries their nests
Will never thrive again.

It was exciting enough just to find a nest, perhaps a hedge-sparrow's, which I could watch till the fledgelings hatched out and flew away to begin another cycle of life on their own.

I began to puzzle, as young folk will, about the eternal verities of life. Everything must have been put on earth for a purpose, from the moles under the ground to the eagles in the sky. It was the same, I supposed, with human beings, though as yet I had not discovered my own purpose on earth, but there must be some reason for my existence, apart from just being a nuisance to everybody.

There were so few human beings around me that I was able to study each one individually with such intensity that I came to know every wrinkle on the hinds' faces and each bristle on their cheeks. The herd had shaggy eyebrows that shot up and down, and Father had a dimple in his chin.

My father was a good-looking man, I thought, and never handsomer than when he wore his straw hat in summer. The straw basher. He put it on at a rakish angle and looked quite the gentleman, according to Jessie. But anything he wore, even his night-shirt, seemed to suit him, giving proof to another Border saying: 'A weel-faured face sets a dishcloot.'

When I saw a strange face at the door, even if it was only a packman's, it was like having a new book to read, though such treats were few and far between. A young gallant straying from the hunt might ride by or a salesman arrive in a motor car, trying to talk the Boss into ordering some farm accessory. And once the Maiden Ladies who were real gentry, related to the laird himself at the Big Hoose, drove up in their dog-cart and deigned to come in for a cup of tea.

Luckily for us, Bella at the Post Office, acting as our go-between, had rung up to give us advance warning. The best china and the lace-edged tablecloth were set out in readiness, and a batch of pancakes and scones – daintier than usual – had been hurriedly baked.

The visit of the high-bred Maiden Ladies, with their spotted veils, their silks and frills, their gold pendants, bangles, brooches and rings – and above all their refined conversation – kept me going long after they had driven away in their buggy down the bumpy farm road, leaving a waft of eau de Cologne behind. They were made of finer stuff, yet I liked the tramps best. The criss-cross lines on their weatherbeaten faces seemed to tell more adventurous tales than those of the papier-poudréd Ladies.

The gaun-aboot bodies, as Jessie called the tramps, were

adepts at mooching, and never refused any cast-off especially if it could be worn on their extremities. Carpet slippers, wellington boots, plimsolls, clogs, leggings, spats, elastic-sided boots. Everything was welcome. They themselves never discarded any of their gear no matter how down-at-heel. Even if the soles were hanging off they clung to their old bauchles, wrapping them up in newspapers in the belief that they would come in handy some day.

'They'll kep a catch,' was their way of expressing it.

An old crone called Nellie Naebody was one of our regulars. When I asked her if she was related to the mysterious Maister Naebody who lived in our house she said, 'Ay, he's ma faither.' But she had a glint in her eye as she spoke, and I knew from Jessie that she was not quite right in the head, apart from being over-fond of the bottle. I liked to watch her puffing at her clay pipe. Being toothless, she could suck in her cheeks and contort her face as if it was made of india-rubber.

If we were left on our own Nellie would sidle closer to me so that she could whisper confidentially in my ear, as if she had an important secret to impart. Usually it was only a request for clothing.

'A pair o' drawers or an auld semmit. Onything'll do.'

If I came back with a torn blazer instead, discarded by my elder brother, or with a moth-eaten fur tippet, she accepted them gratefully and put them on there and then.

'The verra dab! Jings! this is ma lucky day. Here's a ha'penny left in the pooch.'

One day when we were sitting alone on the bench outside the kitchen door Nellie gave me a nudge and whispered: 'What aboot gettin' me a drap oot the bottle? Just a moothfou', for ma asthma.' She gave a convincing wheeze. 'Ye can easy manage it, a clever lass like you. Mum's the word.'

Flattery of any kind always went to my head, so off I set on my furtive mission, not too sure how much a wee drap was or if I could escape the watchful eyes of the rest of the household. At least I knew where my father kept his secret bottle. In the parlour cabinet.

Luckily the key was in the lock, but first I had to look for a container of some kind into which I could decant the whisky. The best I could find after a hurried search was a small cascara bottle with some of the medicine still in the bottom. There was no time to wash it out so I just left it there.

Filling the small bottle from the big one was a tricky job, requiring great concentration and a steady hand. Mine was shaky through fear of being discovered. Blackie, the kitchen cat, came through and lapped up the overflow that trickled on to the carpet, than gave a strange miaow as she licked her lips. She looked up at me with a puzzled expression as if asking for an explanation, but I had problems of my own.

At last the deed was done. I managed to dodge Jessie and bore the cascara bottle in triumph out to Nellie who was waiting impatiently for my return.

'That's the stuff!' said she, seizing the bottle and draining its contents to the last drop, medicine and all. Then she belched blissfully, wiped her mouth on her ragged sleeve and gave me a toothless grin. 'Clever lass! Ye'll get your reward in heaven.'

But not on earth. There was a great to-do when Father found out that someone had been tampering with his whisky bottle. Who was the culprit?

'Maister Naebody,' said Jessie, pursing her lips. 'The bad rascal.'

I never confessed, and felt guilty about it for a while, but at least Nellie went down the road singing.

I sometimes sang myself but only if I was out of earshot of other folk. On the hill was a safe place, in the old keep which was my favourite sanctuary, with only the whaups and the shilfies to hear. I sang anything that came into my head. Miss Thing, the music-teacher at the Grammar School, was obsessed with part-songs. 'Who is Sylvia? What is she?' We were not allowed to bawl as we had done at the village school when Auld Baldy-Heid used to teach us 'Come, follow', or 'Oh, who will o'er the downs so free?'

Miss Thing conducted us with a long cane and rapped us over the head if we strayed from the tune. We had to keep thinking about breath-control, and beats in the bar. She sorted us all out into sopranos, contraltos, tenors and basses, with some of the boys – known as the grunters – being neither one thing nor the other. I would have liked to join them, but I had been classed as a soprano and often had to push my voice up to impossible heights, always terrified I would end up in a skirl.

Out on the hill it did not matter. I could be a grunter if I liked. The main thing was to make a joyful sound. And in spite of the many sad thoughts of youth it was surprising how often happiness had a habit of breaking through. The only way of expressing it was by singing. Not about Sylvia and her swains. Rollicking songs which Father sometimes sang at local concerts. 'Paddy McGinty's Goat', 'The Bonnie Bonnie Hoose o' Airlie', and 'The Lum Hat Wantin' a Croon'.

Sometimes for a change I sang one of the children's hymns we were taught in the Sunday School about the happy land that is far away. But as I sat singing it on the crumbling castle wall, I knew that the hymn was wrong. The happy land was not far away. It was here in the Borders.

2. Milestones

The first recognition I ever received was when I had my name printed in the local paper. The *Jedburgh Gazette*, known locally as the 'Jethart Squeaker'. For winning second prize in the egg-and-spoon race at the Sunday School sports.

It would have been better if I had been first, but I was quite pleased to be mentioned at all. There was my name for all to see, alongside an item on foot-and-mouth disease and underneath a blurred photograph of the laird. He, too, had been at the sports, though not competing against me, but he did present me with my prize. A silver sixpence. The first prize, won by a lassie from over the Border, was a shilling. Such wealth.

Not that the money mattered; it was the fact that I had done something worth recording. Up till then fame had never been my spur. I had determined that if ever any of my writings were published I would sign them 'Anon', like the poet in my schoolbook. Not only so that none could shower me with fulsome flattery, but chiefly that they should not scoff.

'Fancy her writing stuff like that! Set her up!'

For, of course, no home-brewed talent could be worth anything.

'Her! *She* canna be famous. I went to the schule wi' her.'

It was always the stranger, the unknown quantity, who was worthy of praise.

But when I appeared in the Squeaker I threw all scruples to the wind.

'See, Jock, look!' I cried, running out to the shepherd with the crumpled newspaper in my hand. 'There's my name!'

'Where? Haud on till I find ma specs.'

Jock fumbled in his pooch and finally brought out the family spectacles shared in turn with his sisters Jessie and Joo-anne. 'Mexty me! so it is. Weel done, you!'

It was a great moment of triumph for me, compensating for all the hard training I had put in, running round the farmyard with a nest egg balanced on an old teaspoon. I could never find anyone to compete against me – Jessie had better things to do than run races – nor could I always lay my hands on a nest egg. So sometimes I used a real one, which made the operation a great deal trickier, often ending with the egg smashed to smithereens and Jessie raging, 'Ye're a wastrif article, so ye are. Think o' a' the stervin' Chinese.'

When Jessie called me an article I knew I had reached rock bottom. But even she was impressed when I drew her attention to the item in the paper, though she could not see it properly without her spectacles. I read it out to her – twice – in case she missed anything.

'Weel, fancy that!'

It was nothing much to say but I knew she was pleased. I was no longer just an article.

Then she astounded me with her next statement.

'It's no' the first time ye've been in the Squeaker.'

'Me?'

'Ay, you! Ye were in when ye were hatched.'

'When was I hatched?'

'Hoots! when ye were born. A'body gets into the paper when they're hatched, matched or dispatched. I've been in masel'.'

I tried to imagine Jessie hatching from an egg, cracking her way out through the shell and struggling to her feet to tie on a coarse apron. A brat, she called it. She would set about at once to stir the porridge or milk the cows. I could not visualise an interim period when she played with a skipping rope or made daisy-chains.

'When were you hatched, Jessie?'

'Mind your ain business, an' dinna let the Squeaker gang to your heid.'

But it did, of course.

I had forgotten all about Anon and my desire to hide my light under a bushel. With the inconsistency of youth I changed direction like a weathercock. My likes and dislikes were never too rigid to alter. One moment I would fancy I disliked the taste of tomatoes. The next I would see someone else eating them with such relish that I decided to follow suit. They were good; I liked tomatoes! The same with my Sunday hat. I hated the sight of it till someone praised it, after which it was seldom off my head.

I had an off-on relationship, by the same token, with the cottage wives. One day I decided never to speak to Mrs Thing again. Never-ever! She had deliberately, I felt sure, shaken her rug in my face as I passed on the way to school. So that was the end of her.

The very next day she was at her door calling out to me, 'Hi, lassie, wad ye do an obleegement for me? I'm needin' a new scrubbin'-brush. Could I bother ye to buy me ane in the toon?'

'No bother,' I agreed readily, pleased that she had credited me with enough gumption to undertake such a mission. When she handed me the money and said, 'Ye can keep the change,' her stock rose higher. She was nice, Mrs Thing.

But it was even nicer finding fame in the local paper, and not merely in the district, for the Squeaker was posted overseas to exiled Borderers hungry for home news. Cousins and uncles who had emigrated to Canada and Australia. Imagine them reading about me in the Rocky Mountains or New South Wales.

I could picture them eagerly opening the paper, scanning every item and saying when they saw my name, 'Ay! that'll be her frae Overton Bush. The Buss! A wee smout o' a lass wi' red hair. I kent her faither an' mither. Nice folk. Ye got a grand spread in their fermhoose. Sic teas! Toddie-scones an' sponge-cake. Melted in the mooth.'

The great thing about the Squeaker was that no detail was left out. Every name was mentioned, down to who brewed the tea at a whist drive, who won the booby prize and who said a few well-chosen words in the vote of thanks. 'Mr Tom Scott of the Mains made some witty remarks. (Applause).'

Never mind the outside world. The *Scotsman* could take care of revolutions, assassinations and general elections. What we wanted to read about was a roup at a neighbouring farm (a roup being a sale), that there had been an accident in the High Street (two bicycles bumped together: one wheel buckled), that the kirk soirée had been a resounding success, the laird was laid low with sciatica, a runaway bull had been rounded up at Southdean, and Mrs Rutherford's washing had been stolen from the line (vagrants suspected).

If there was a shortage of happenings the gap was sometimes filled by the insertion of a starting headline: OUTBREAK OF SMALLPOX, with a statement underneath to the effect that 'There have been no cases of smallpox in the district lately'. It was a sure way of riveting the reader's attention.

I liked the Fifty Years Ago column where I might come across a familiar name. Maybe my Granny's. 'Perfect attendance at the Sunday School.' Or an item about good Queen Victoria. 'Her Gracious Majesty has arrived safely at Balmoral. May the sun shine on Her.' Surely it would never dare to rain.

Sometimes there were touching little poems in the dispatched column. In Memoriam, written no doubt by Anon.

> A year ago on this sad day
> The Lord called Agnes Scott away.
> The pearly gates were opened wide
> And angels welcomed her inside.

More cheerful items could be found amongst the court cases. 'A labourer of no fixed abode was apprehended after attempting to climb the clock tower. He pleaded that he was short-sighted and wanted to see the time, but PC Brown believed the man had been imbibing strong drink. Thirty days.'

What a lot one could learn from the Jethart Squeaker. That there would be a retiring collection next Sunday for the schemes of the church, that there was to be a sale of damaged goods in a shop in Jedburgh (terrible bargains), that a garden fête would be opened by Lady Somebody at Edgerston House (entrance 1/-, tea thrown in), that a part-time woman was wanted in a farmhouse (must be strong, willing and a good milker), that a budgie had been lost, stolen or strayed (answers to the name of Bobby and can whistle 'Happy Birthday to You'. Reward).

Now that I had appeared in it myself I held the local paper in even higher esteem and tried to prevent Jessie from lining the dresser drawer with it.

'Stop! Wait till I've cut out the bit about me.'

'Ye're a conceited article,' she sniffed; but all the same she handed me the scissors and I kept the cutting till it became too frayed to read. By that time, in any case, I had gone on to higher things. *First* prize in the sack race. But the thrill was never the same again.

Earlier in my life, while I was still at the village school, I passed another milestone on the day I was promoted to a pen, a sure sign that I was no longer a backward infant.

Auld Baldy-Heid, the teacher, came round with a huge earthenware bottle of blue-black ink and poured some into the little inkwell on my desk. Then he presented me with a new pen and a sheet of blotting-paper, warning me at the same time not to make a mess. What he actually said was, 'You'd better not make a slaister.' A slaister being something even messier than a mess.

He might have saved his breath. In next to no time I succeeded in making the biggest slaister possible. It was quite easy. With all that ink at my disposal there were soon stains on my fingers, smudges on my face, blots on my copybook, and the pen itself was needing a new nib.

The copybook had uplifting proverbs on the top of each page in perfect calligraphy which I was supposed to copy in the same flawless style. 'Waste not want not.' 'A rolling stone gathers no moss.' 'He who hesitates is lost.' And so on. I felt there ought to have been another one, specially for me. 'Thou shalt not slaister thy copybook.'

Being newfangled at the job I was constantly dipping the pen too far into the inkwell and pressing too hard on the nib, with the result that it splayed out and spluttered ink in all directions. Without even trying I scored a bull's-eye on Big Bob who was so enraged when a blob of ink landed on his nose that he retaliated there and then by seizing my pigtails and dipping the ends in his own inkwell.

If I had been in a mess before I was in a real slaister by now.

Still, I felt quite proud of my battle-stains as I wended my way home that day. Anyone could tell just by looking at me that I was on my way up in the world. Anyone except Jock-the-herd whom I met on the farm road and who never noticed anything unless it was connected with sheep. He played into my hands by asking, 'Man-lassie, are ye needin' ony pencils sherpened?'

'No, thanks. I'm in pens now,' I said haughtily.

All the same I would miss the ministrations of my chief pencil-sharpener. For years Jock had done the deed for me with a fearsome-looking jack-knife which he took out from the depths of his pocket. It had several blades of varying sizes and was used for a multitude of purposes. Howking turnips out of the field, cutting off lengths of bindertwine, clipping tufts of wool from a sheep's back. Even, as I discovered to my horror, cutting their throats when they had to be killed. Gouging tobacco from his pipe, and, of course, sharpening my 'keelies', as he sometimes called them.

As time went by there were occasions when I wished I was back in the old days when I could rub out my pencilled mistakes. Not so easy to erase wrong answers penned in blotchy ink. Jock agreed with me. 'Man-lassie, when I was at the schule it was slate pencils. Awfu' handy. Ye could just wipe oot the mistakes wi' your sleeve.'

Never will I forget the day we were set to write an essay. My Favourite Holiday. Most of the class had never been on holiday at all, except Chrissie Scott who was always boasting about visiting M'Auntie in Hawick. All very well for her. The rest of us dipped our pens despairingly into our inkwells and dredged our brains for inspiration. Mine came when I suddenly decided the essay need not be true, and embarked on a long saga about spending a week in London. The idea! London!

What a week it was! I missed nothing. I sailed on the Thames, visited the Houses of Parliament, fed the pigeons in Trafalgar Square, and was about to have tea in Buckingham Palace when my pen ran dry. My inkwell was empty.

I put up my hand to attract the teacher's attention. On such occasions Auld Baldy-Heid, who normally had eyes in the back of his head, seemed to have lost his sight. Or, as on this particular day, had hidden himself behind the *Scotsman* and refused to emerge. The thing to do in such a situation was to snap one's fingers so that he could hear the noise and look up. But snapping my fingers was not one of my accomplishments. Try as I would I could never make even the feeblest sound, so I prevailed upon Big Bob, who could snap like a thunderclap, to do the deed for me.

'Yes?' said Auld Baldy-Heid, reluctantly looking up. I could see from his expression that he meant 'No!'

'Please s-sir, I've r-run out of ink.'

A black frown from the master. 'Again!' he said in an irritated voice. 'What do you do with it, woman? Drink it?'

'N-no, sir.'

Auld Baldy-Heid rustled his newspaper. 'You can use your pencil,' he said sharply and went back to his reading.

'Please s-sir, I've l-lost it.' Which was not quite true. I had given it away to Wee Maggie who was still working painfully at her pothooks. 'What'll I do, sir?' It would be a pity not to have tea in Buckingham Palace for want of a drop of ink.

More impatient rustlings of the *Scotsman*. Then, 'Go and help yourself,' said Auld Baldy-Heid gruffly. 'And don't . . . ' The rest of the sentence was muffled but it was not difficult to guess he was warning me not to make a slaister.

It was a moment of triumph for me, going out in front of the class to lift down the heavy jar from the shelf, the envy of all eyes, particularly Big Bob's. No one else had ever been granted such a privilege.

'See me!' I thought proudly. 'Auld Baldy-Heid trusts me. I'll make a good job of it.'

I did.

If only the jar had not been so heavy all would have gone well. It was an awkward job unscrewing the stopper and tipping the bottle at the right angle so that the ink would trickle rather than gush into the small inkwell. The overflow ran down my desk and drip-dropped on to the floor like a waterfall.

'Slaister!' hissed Big Bob, gloating at my mishap. 'You'll catch it!' At which point the worst happened. Somehow or other the heavy jar slipped through my fingers and crashed to the floor, shattering into a hundred fragments.

Before horror overtook me, I spared a sympathetic thought for one of our servant-lasses, a clumsy creature nicknamed the Carthorse, who was for ever dropping teapots and breaking jugs. 'It just fell oot ma hand,' was her constant excuse.

As I stared at the rivulets of ink running across the floor like blue-black streams, I shared some of her feelings. Blacker than the ink was Auld Baldy-Heid's frown as he flung aside his newspaper and sprang at me like a tiger on its prey.

'You stupid idiot!'

He got no further. I was saved by a knock on the school-room door, followed by the entrance of the minister arriving on one of his periodic visits to 'give us our religion'.

He saw the mess on the floor, of course. How could he help it since he stepped into one of the puddles and splashed ink on to his socks? Black, fortunately.

'Just a small accident,' said the master with a false smile on his face; but out of the corner of his mouth he hissed at me, 'You'll stay behind tonight, my lady!'

My lady knew this was equivalent to the death sentence. We were all accustomed to being punished by the strap. Short, sharp, and soon over. If it did us no good it did us no harm. Staying behind meant being left alone at the mercy of Auld Baldy-Heid who used this form of punishment only in the most stringent cases, since he was always in a hurry to get rid of the lot of us and go home to the school-house for his tea. I had no idea what form of torment he had up his sleeve. It had never happened to me before, so my imagination ran riot and I saw myself strung up from the ceiling, tortured with red-hot pokers, my head scalped and my eyes gouged out. Would I ever live to tell the tale?

When the minister gave out a hymn I found it difficult to join in the singing of 'I'm a little pilgrim' accompanied on the piano by Auld Baldy-Heid playing with one finger. Between verses I tried to mop up some of the ink with my blotting-paper and any I could borrow from my classmates. Even Big Bob was sympathetic enough to lend me his. By the time His Reverence had given us his blessing most of the mess had dried up though one blotch remained never to be erased, a permanent mark of my shame. Perhaps it is there to this day.

My visit to Buckingham Palace never took place, for as soon as the minister left Auld Baldy-Heid decided to turn his attention to sums. Mental arithmetic. Not another word about spilt ink. This was ominous in itself, and for the rest of the day the sword of Damocles dangled over my head and I wondered if I ought to make my will, not that I had anything much to leave.

Mental arithmetic was not my strong point. The master rapped out the numbers at top speed. I tried to catch them and add them up as they flew through the air. Five, seven, twelve, sixteen, twenty-two, thirty-eight . . . It was hopeless trying to reach the right answer. Fortunately I was not the only defaulter and in the end Auld Baldy-Heid gave up in exasperation.

'You're a lot of dolts. Stupid idiots! I'll write the sums on the blackboard.'

As the dreadful day went by we pursued the uneven tenor of our ways, jumping from sums to history – Bruce and the spider – and from there to poetry.

> Up from the meadows rich with corn,
> Clear on a cool September morn,
> The something spires of Brunswick stand . . .

Something was a great word if mumbled in the right way and if the teacher was not listening too intently. We could get away with murder, but not in my case with staying behind, though I kept hoping against hope that my executioner might forget. Not Auld Baldy-Heid.

When the lucky ones rushed away like convicts escaping from prison, some pausing long enough to throw me a backward glance of pity, I was left in limbo, wondering if I would ever see any of them again. Auld Baldy-Heid was rubbing out the sums from the blackboard and replacing them with a warning sentence. 'Be sure your sins will find you out.'

'Copy that in your best writing, over and over again,' he said sternly. 'I'll be back.' With that he went away round to the schoolhouse for his tea, locking the door behind him.

It was not the copying that worried me. It was the 'I'll be back'. With what weapons of torture? Thumbscrews, a sharp knife, maybe even a gun?

It was strange sitting alone in the empty classroom with no shuffling feet to be heard. No sniffles, giggles or groans. I would have welcomed even Big Bob, the bully, tugging at my hair or Wee Maggie whispering, 'Could you lend me a penthil, pleathe? I've loth mine.' I could only plough on, filling page after page of my copybook. At least I had plenty of ink.

Be sure your sins will find you out. I was certain by now.

Having served so many sentences of solitary confinement in the garret at home, I was accustomed to being imprisoned; but that was a familiar gaol with plenty of distractions. An old rocking-horse to ride, bound volumes of the *Quiver* to read, a chest full of discarded finery to rummage through, a rickety washstand to climb on when I wanted to push up the skylight window and peer down at the free world. Here I was forced to sit in one place and await my fate.

The shades of night were falling so fast that I could scarcely see my copybook. The blackboard creaked and shadowy figures lurked in every corner. By now I was writing the sentence mechanically and getting it all fankled. Be sin your sures will out you find.

It was the *Scotsman* that saved me. Auld Baldy-Heid, having forgotten all about me and my sins, remembered he had left his paper in the schoolroom and came round to fetch it. Otherwise I might have spent the entire night amidst the ghosts of past pupils.

'Mercy goodness me!' he exclaimed in a startled voice, as if he too had seen a ghost. 'Are you still here, lassie? Away home as fast as you can.'

And that was it. No red-hot pokers, no thumb-screws, not even the tawse or a tongue-lashing. It was a tame ending, but at least I had left my mark behind on the floor, and it was good practice with the pen.

3. Growing Pains

Whenever I think of the dentist it is always in French.

Not that ours was a foreigner. He came from Kelso once a week to perform his dark deeds in hired rooms overlooking Jedburgh Abbey. Many a time have I stared in despair at the ruined walls across the way while Mr Crow, foot on pedal, set his whirring drill in motion inside my mouth, Or, worse, extracted a nerve.

'There! It didn't hurt much, did it?'

True, it never hurt him.

Robert Burns knew what he was talking about when he described toothache as 'the hell o' a' diseases'. He even went the length of writing a poem about it. That was what I liked so much about him, he could write about ordinary things. Not just larks soaring in the sky.

> My curse upon your venom'd stang
> That shoots my tortur'd gums alang,

An' thro' my lug gies sic a twang
Wi' gnawing vengeance,
Tearing my nerves wi' bitter pang
Like traction engines.

I wondered if he had ever tried any of Jessie's cures. Sometimes she tied a woollen stocking round my jaw in the hope that the heat would bring relief. A spoonful of whisky held in the decayed tooth was supposed to do the trick, but the taste was terrible when the fiery liquid trickled down my throat, though Robert Burns would doubtless have enjoyed it. In my case it seemed there was no cure for the hell o' a' diseases but to make the dreaded appointment with the dentist.

He was a nice enough wee man, Mr Crow, humming ''Way down upon the Swannee River' while he mixed strange concoctions with a small spatula, prior to filling up the holes he had drilled in my teeth. Meanwhile my mouth was gagged with cottonwool which made it difficult to answer his inevitable questions.

'Getting on all right at school?'

'Glug.'

'Going on holiday?'

Shake of the head.

'Is the harvest in yet?'

Half in. How could one answer that? An eye-blink was the best I could do.

'Top of the class yet?'

Top of the class! What a hope! By now he had a half-nelson round my throat and I could neither glug nor blink. All the same, though not anywhere near the heights, I could have told him I was making some progress up the ladder of learning.

Now that I was in the Grammar School, I was a woman of the world, travelling every day to the big town by a bus which I boarded at the roadend a mile away from home.

Old enough to be entrusted with messages to do in the shops during my lunch break. I took tackety boots to be mended at the cobbler's, matched wool, bought kippers, even chose new stays for the cottage wives and long drawers for the herd.

The stir of the traffic no longer held any terrors for me. I had become accustomed to being jostled on the pavement and to hearing Bobby the Bellman shouting out his announcements. 'There will be a stoppage of watterrrr for two hourrrrs. You have been warrrrned.' But I was still a country mouse at heart and my real life was at home on the farm at nights and at the weekends. The rest was only a confused dream. Sometimes more like a nightmare.

I tried hard to get to grips with the perplexing pattern of ever-changing classes at the Grammar School, my mind darting from algebra to science, then on to French, history and Latin. Auld Baldy-Heid had knocked the essentials into me at the village school, but here the methods were very different. And so were the teachers, all with their own quirks. It would take a lifetime, I felt, to sort them out. Especially Mr Archie-Bald, the rector – Dafty, as he was known behind his back – who grew more and more remote, only occasionally coming to life in the Latin class when he lashed out at us with his tongue, threatening to roast us alive or skin the hides off us. A fate not far removed from the tortures of Latin grammar.

Part of my problem was that there was no one at home with whom I could discuss my troubles. Sometimes Mother would ask in an abstracted way: 'How did you get on today?' It was easier just to say 'Fine' than go into details about declensions I could not comprehend, or tell her that the drawing-teacher thought my perspective was up the pole, and that Mary-Ann Crichton had said I did not know an isosceles triangle from a rabbit's foot.

She was our best teacher, Miss Crichton, in spite of her

constant catarrh and her North-East twang which we sometimes found difficult to understand. French and algebra. I was learning a little about the former though my pronunciation – and Miss Crichton's – was further up the pole than my perspective. But set-squares and hypotenuses left me in limbo. I could never see the point of them. What use would they be to me in later life if I was going to follow either of my chosen professions? To be a bondager like Jessie and Joo-anne, or a writer like Anon. They got on fine without square roots.

It was Miss Crichton who first made me think of the dentist in French, and all because of one of her schemes to knock the language into our thick heads. Now that we had progressed a step or two beyond *sur la table* she decided to widen our horizons by making us take part in a simple little French play.

Simple! It was entitled *Madame Lemoine chez le dentiste* and I am never likely to forget it. Even now on sleepless nights I repeat snatches of it to my pillow, hoping it will act as a soporific, but it never does. I grow wider awake as that scene in the classroom comes back to me, so vividly that I can hear Miss Crichton's sniffles, see her hankies drying on the radiator, and cringe as she raps her cane over my knuckles.

'*Non, non! Stupide! Commencez* again.'

We had to take turns at being the hapless Madame Lemoine, which involved going out of the classroom, knocking on the door and waiting for someone to call '*Entrez!*'

Once inside, Madame L. was overcome by fright, easy enough to simulate in my case. The next step was to gaze around the dentist's waiting-room and give voice to a few disjointed observations.

'*Beaucoup de livres sur la table. Des journaux illustrés, mais je n'ai pas envie de lire.*' A few sighs and groans. She wants to escape. What is the time? '*Si seulement je savais l'heure. Mais il est à remarquer qu'il y a rarement des pendules chez le dentiste . . .'*

One dreadful day when the fates were against me there arrived at the Grammar School a real Frenchman. Tight-waisted, pink-cheeked, red-lipped, and with a natty jet-black moustache. The first pretty man I had ever seen. I could visualise him in miniature standing on the mantel-piece made of porcelain. Or perhaps two of him as book-ends.

What was this bright bird of Paradise doing in the Scottish Borders so far away from the Eiffel Tower? The hows and whys we never found out, but it appeared the main purpose of his visit was to assess our progress in his native language. Truth to tell, we thought he had made little progress himself, since his accent was not a patch on Miss Crichton's. He spoke, too, at such a speed, rolling his rs like a Geordie, that it was almost impossible to understand a word he said. But Mary-Ann Crichton was not put off. She was determined to put us through our paces and let the Frenchman see we could even *act* in his language.

We all slouched in our seats, hoping not to be called upon, while the Frenchman flashed his eyes and settled down to be entertained. What on earth could have possessed Miss Crichton to single me out to play the part of Madame Lemoine? I would willingly have changed places with a prisoner in the death-cell, but there was no escape.

'*Allez!* Out the door!' she ordered me; and away I trailed, conscious of the Frenchie's amused glance following me.

I stood shivering in the corridor for some time trying to gather up enough courage to knock. Then Miss Crichton called in a commanding voice from inside. '*Frappez!*' I took a deep breath and frapped at the door.

'*Entrez!*'

A scared voice invited me to come in. Jeannie, one of my classmates, had been chosen to be the dentist's assistant, and was trembling with stage-fright, though not half as terrified as I was now that the moment had come when I must make my dreaded entrance. I was about to turn the handle when I was aware of someone looming up behind me. Mr Archie-Bald, the rector.

Dafty had a habit of appearing like ectoplasm when least expected after stalking along passages as silent as a cat.

'You!' he roared, grabbing me by the arm. Dafty never bothered to find out anyone's name. We were all addressed as 'You' or 'Idiot'. He glared at me and demanded, 'What are you doing outside the classroom?'

'Please s-sir, *je suis* Madame Lemoine . . . '

It seemed difficult, even impossible, to tell him either in French or English why I was there. One cannot argue with God.

But now that I was there Dafty suddenly decided he had a use for me. I could hear Jeannie from inside repeating in a frightened voice: '*Entrez! Entrez!*' but there was no escaping Archie-Bald's vice-like grip. 'You'll do,' he said, shaking me loose, 'seeing you're out of the classroom already. Go and find the janitor and tell him to come to my room at once.'

'But, please s-sir, *je suis* . . . '

'At once!' roared Dafty, pointing dramatically down the corridor. 'Go!'

So I went.

There was no knowing where the Janny might be found if he chose to remain invisible. There were so many hidey-holes where he could take cover. In cupboards where he kept cleaning-materials, in store-rooms, or sheds out in the playground. He might even have plunked and gone home for all I knew. It was like playing hide and seek with a slippery eel.

All the while I could sense Miss Crichton's wrath rising to the boil and hear the smiling Frenchie making joking remarks in his strange tongue. How he would roll his eyes and his rs. As for poor Jeannie, was she still calling '*Entrez!*' in a despairing voice?

I finally found the Janny in hell, away down in the nether regions of the boiler house, sitting on a pile of coke reading an old copy of the Jethart Squeaker. He was not a bit pleased to see me.

'*Je suis* Madame . . . ' I began. 'I mean, Dafty wants you in his room. At once.'

The Janny said a bad word and threw his paper aside. 'You're naethin' but a nuisance,' he told me, which I thought was not quite fair, since I was merely a messenger from above. 'Get oot ma road.' And away he went, rumbling and grumbling, leaving me alone in hell.

I was too shaken to go back to the classroom immediately so I sat down on the coke and had a look at the Squeaker, turning the pages to see if by chance it was the one with my name in it, but it wasn't. Fifty years ago, I learned, there had been a torrential downpour of rain in Jedburgh, with the High Street awash, shoppers stranded, and a swan seen swimming in the direction of the Free Church. Fancy that!

By the time I had summoned up enough courage to go back, the class had gone off to science. As for the Frenchie, I never set eyes on him or his wee moustache again. But retribution, of course, overtook me later when Miss Crichton, snorting with rage, gave me my character in no uncertain terms. I did try to explain but it was no use. As part of my punishment she made me write out Madame Lemoine's soliloquy a dozen times or more. Little wonder it is so indelibly fixed in my memory. Yet, though I now knew the part better than any of my classmates, I was never again chosen to play Madame L.

Oh well! that, I supposed, was life.

Not real life, though. That was lived in a shabby old farmhouse in sight of the Cheviots, or out on a windy hillside in my own ruined castle, surrounded by beasts, as

Jessie called all the creatures on the farm, whether bantams or carthorses. I sometimes envied them their lot. No teachers to chivvy them, no foreign languages to learn, no lines to write. But what a lot they missed, particularly the pleasures of reading.

The great boon of going to the Grammar School was that I could now borrow books from the school library. I had long ago swallowed up every item of literature to be found at home, from *The Wide Wide World* to Spurgeon's *Sermons.* Sometimes I found a tawdry novelette discarded by one of the servant-lasses – *Love Conquers All* – and read it at a gulp. On the whole I preferred *Enquire Within Upon Everything*, even though it concentrated on how to take stains out of tablecloths.

'I've got something in the hoose ye might like,' Jessie said to me one day out of the blue.

'Oh, what is't, Jessie?'

'A book.'

'A book! Could I borrow it, please?'

'Daursay. I'll bring it the morn.'

But the morn seemed a million years away. 'Could I not come and get it tonight?' I pleaded.

Jessie hesitated as if hunting in her mind for the book. Was it maybe in the wall press or below the box bed? I had never seen any reading material in the herd's hoose other than the *People's Friend*, the Squeaker and the bible.

'Please yoursel',' said Jessie, having obviously tracked down the book in its hiding-place. 'But ye're no' to mak' a slaister on't. I'll pit a broon paper cover on its batters.'

'I'll be careful, Jessie. What's it called?”

'Wait an' see. It's a guid read.'

When I rapped on her cottage door that night Jessie did not invite me in. She had the book ready in her hand and passed it out to me with another reminder not get it into a slaister. Behind her I could see into the lamplit kitchen. A quiet scene. Jock sitting by the fire unlacing his boots and Joo-anne bolt upright on a hard chair knitting a long black stocking. A savoury smell lingered about the place. Stovies. The dishes were still on the table, and Jessie had her apron on, ready to tackle the washing-up. So she had no time for small talk with me.

'Awa' hame, lassie.'

It was tantalising not to see even the title of the book in the darkness. The moon was hidden and there was scarcely a star in the sky, so I sped homeward at a spanking pace and hardly drew breath till I tumbled down on the kitchen rug beside Blackie the cat. I opened the book at the title page, drew a deep breath and settled down for a good read.

Seldom if ever have I experienced such a blank feeling of disappointment as I did at that moment when I read the title. Only one word. *Dictionary*. I could scarcely keep back my tears and would have flung the book into the flames had I not feared Jessie's wrath. Was this her idea of a good read? Certainly it contained plenty of words, but what were words to me if not put together in the right way to form a story?

Could this be what Jessie meant? 'Get on wi't, wumman, an' write your ain stories.' Sitting sulkily beside the cat I idly turned a few pages. There was a name written on the fly-leaf. J. Taylor. Jessie? Joo-anne? Jock? A communal schoolbook, perhaps. If so, what care the three had taken of it. No smudges, scribbles, inkblots or torn pages. No despairing calls of 'Help!' as in mine. 'Auld Baldy-Heid's a monster.' 'I'm fed UP.' Every page was pristine. If any had been turned at all, it must have been with the cleanest hands.

Next morning I found it difficult to face Jessie and did not even look at her when she placed my plate of porridge beside me. But when she dumped something else on the table my whole world lit up. It was a book, covered like the dictionary in brown paper, but this was a real storybook with a title. *The Mill on the Floss*, by George Eliot.

'I gied ye the wrang ane last nicht,' said Jessie gruffly. She was not one to apologise. 'Took it oot the room press in the derk, withoot ma specs. Here ye are. It's a guid read.'

A good read!

It was a blessing it was Saturday when I was free to sit on the swing for hours engrossed in the lives of Maggie Tulliver and her brother Tom, described so vividly that I felt I knew them. They might have lived at Edgerston and gone to the village school with me. George Eliot, I felt sure, must be the most wonderful writer in the world, but I thought that of every new discovery.

All that day I was oblivious to the rest of the world; cocks and hens cackling around me, the bubblyjock pecking at my feet, pigs squealing, dogs barking, carthorses clumping in from the fields, till I was pestered by a small lisping child from one of the cottages.

'Will ye come an' play hide-an'-theek?'

'No, I'll not,' I said heartlessly and ran off to my own private refuge on the hill, where I spent the rest of the day crouching amongst the old stones in the great fireplace of the ruined castle. Reading, reading, reading.

'Man-lassie, your een'll drap oot,' said Jock-the-herd who had observed me from a distance and was now leaning on his crook to light his pipe. When I looked up at him *he* seemed someone from another world, not half as real as the characters in the book. But nothing could stop me in my headlong hurry to see what happened next. Later I would start all over again at the beginning to pick up any scraps I had missed. Like second-day soup, there was always a richer flavour in a re-read book. Though nothing, of course, could beat the thrill of first discovery, the finding in the school library of such treasures as *Black Beauty*, *Lorna Doone*, and *David Copperfield*.

It was a meagre enough library. Only a shelf or two in a classroom cupboard, supervised by Miss Paleface, the

English teacher, who made a great fetish of entering our names in a special ledger, noting the dates when we withdrew the books and when they were due to be returned. We were only allowed one a week. I wished it could have been one a day, and was always the first to queue up at the cupboard.

'You'll take care of it, won't you?' said Miss Paleface in her genteel voice. She was much too ladylike to use the word slaister but I knew what she meant and did my utmost to return the books unblemished. It was not easy, reading as I did at the kitchen table or in any hole and corner where I could find sanctuary. All too often the books were splashed with grease, gravy, porridge, or blobs of raspberry jam, and had to go through a great cleaning-up process before they were fit to return.

I can never forget the awful day when *Little Women* fell into the pigs' pail. My own fault. I had left it at the corner of the back-kitchen table where I had been sitting reading amongst the clutter of dirty dishes waiting to be washed, when the telephone rang. It gave me a great sense of importance if I was the only one at home to answer the call. True, Liz-Ann, the Carthorse, was clattering about in the kitchen but she was less likely to lift the receiver than Blackie the cat. So it was left to me.

When I heard Bella's voice from the Post Office I knew I was in for a long session. Goodbye Jo, Beth and all the rest. Real-life drama was happening in Camptown, the small village about a mile away; and though Bella was disappointed that it was only me and not Mother at the end of the line, she gave me chapter and verse, leaving no word unsaid.

'Ye'll never guess! Ye ken Mary-Ann at the lodge gates? Her an' her hens. A'weel, ane o' them's been run ower. By a coal lorry. She's awfu' upset.'

'The hen?'

'No, no; Mary-Ann. The hen's deid. It was ane o' her

favourites. Teenie. The wee speckled ane. Puir sowl! she's in a terrible state . . .'

It was ages before the saga of Teenie came to an end, by which time the dirty dishes had been washed and Liz-Ann had gone out to feed the pig. No sign of *Little Women* on the back-kitchen table.

After a distracted search I faced the Carthorse accusingly when she came trailing in.

'Where's my book?'

'Dinna ken. Never seen it.'

'You have sot!'

'Have not!'

Then the terrible truth hit me. It had tumbled into the pigs' pail and was now lost amongst the swill.

I tore round to the sty to discover Grumphy routing about in the trough in company with half a dozen squealing piglets. The sow was greedily gulping down the unsavoury mixture of left-overs that boosted her daily diet. Potato peelings, cabbage leaves, porridge, bread crusts, stale cake. And *Little Women*! Now and again Grumphy sniffed enquiringly at the book and gave an angry grunt when I snatched it up from under her nose.

It was beyond being in a slaister. I washed it, dried it in the oven, rubbed it down with scented soap and re-covered it with brown paper, but it still looked a sorry sight when I returned it in fear and trembling to Miss Paleface.

It was the pained expression on her face that hurt me most. Far worse than the ticking off I deserved.

'It was an – an Accident,' I told her. I really could not go into all the unpleasant details about the pigs' pail, and wished she would just punish me and be done with it. But instead she sighed and looked at me so reproachfully that it cut me to the quick. And then, to my horror, Archie-Bald made one of his sudden appearances.

'What,' he demanded, 'has happened to that book?

How did it get into such a dreadful mess? Tell me that.'

There was no escape. I was about to launch into a truthful explanation when to my complete amazement, Miss Paleface spoke up.

'I'm afraid it was my fault, Mr Archibald. I took it home to put a new cover on it and must have left it lying about. My puppy-dog got hold of it and began to chew it up. See what a mess he made! It was very careless of me.'

'Very careless,' agreed Dafty, glaring at her. 'Oh well, you'd better get a replacement.' With that he turned on his heel and went away.

I was too thunderstruck to say anything. I felt my face flushing with embarrassment and could not meet Miss Paleface's gaze. Fancy telling all those black lies! Even though she had done it to save my skin, somehow I never felt the same for her again.

It was the first time I had heard a grown-up tell a deliberate untruth. But it was not to be the last. I was still under the domination of my elders. But were they so infallible? I was beginning to see chinks in their armour. Even Jessie's.

4. Playing the Game

The first time I saw Father set off to go to a rugby match it surprised me that he did not take a gun under his arm. Not even a fishing-rod in his hand, a snare or a ferret in his pocket.

I was only a toddler at the time and had no idea what rugby was, except that it had something to do with sport and that was synonymous with killing. So I expected Father to come home with a brace of something feathered or furry.

'Did you not get any?' I remember asking him when he returned empty-handed.

Father shook his head sadly. 'We lost,' he sighed, and was down in the dumps for the rest of the day.

As I grew older I soon came to grips with the great Border game. It was not long before I became familiar with the fluctuating fortunes of Jedforest, Hawick, Selkirk, Kelso, Gala, Melrose, Langholm and all the rest. Rugger was the same thing but it was mostly university or college chaps who called it that. Rugby was good enough for us.

But it was a man's game, discussed in great detail where two or three were gathered together. The finer points of rucks and scrums were thought to be above the grasp of the female intellect, though some women were allowed to accompany their men to a match, for the sake of an outing, but not to make any comment or ask foolish questions.

'Oh Archie! what's that man doing?'

'Hold your tongue, woman!'

Usually they had the sense to sit mim-mouthed with only an occasional gasp when a player fell flat on his face or had his jersey torn off. Sometimes his breeks, too, at which point the others would discreetly gather round him till someone came running on to the field waving a new pair.

There was great wear and tear, not only of garments, but of arms, legs and collar-bones. It was a poor match if there were not at least one bloodied nose and a broken ankle. Few of the players who ran on to the field at the start could do more than limp off at the end, if not carried on a stretcher. But the wounds were all honourable, and every detail was reported at great length in the Jethart Squeaker. Famous Victory for Jedforest. Or, more often, A Sad Defeat.

I began to read about it myself, striving to figure out the difference between a forward and a scrum-half, why a score was called a try and why the spectators sat on something called a stand. Time and again I pestered Father to take me to a match so that I could solve some of the mysteries. His answer was always the same. 'It's not a game for lasses,' which, of course, only made it sound more desirable.

Occasionally my mother accompanied him 'just for the jaunt', but more often stopped off in the High Street to look at the shops or to visit friends; for, she confessed, if she went to the match she spent most of her time sitting with her eyes shut to avoid seeing the slaughter.

It was a great day for me when Father finally gave in and said, 'Oh well, you can come if you like, if you promise to keep quiet.'

It was mid-winter, bitterly cold, with a flurry of snow in the air, a day for the chimney-corner rather than a chilly rugby field, but nothing would dampen my enthusiasm. Certainly not Jessie's warnings that I would catch my death of cold. Excitement was as good as central-heating, but to please her I took my muff with me to keep my gloved hands warm, and a woolly gravat to wind round my neck.

'Ye'd be the better o' a het-waitter bottle,' she said as I mounted into the gig. 'I'm warnin' ye, lassie, ye'll get nae sympathy if ye come hame deid.'

It was in the days before father's first motor-car, so we drove in the open trap drawn by Flora the white pony. Always at her friskiest in nippy weather, she high-stepped her way in the Jed road like a racehorse, stopping only once for a drink at a trough. It was always Flora who set her own pace and who decided when to swerve in at the roadside to slake her thirst at one of the horse-troughs. She knew them all, and would choose her pick as the fancy took her.

I felt proud to be sitting in front like a lady beside my father instead of in my usual humbler place at the back, often in danger of being flung out if the pony pranced round a corner too quickly. There was not much conversation. I had promised to keep quiet, so I did. I was accustomed, in any case, to keeping my own counsel, and was content enough to sit still watching Flora's steady progress between the shafts. Father held the reins lightly in his hands. He had a whip stuck at the side of the gig but he never used it. 'Steady, lass,' he would say now and again, but that was the only guidance Flora needed. Sometimes he whistled through his teeth or sang a snatch of one of his comic songs.

> Farewell! Farewell! Farewell my fairy fay.
> Oh I'm off to Louisiana
> For to see my Susy Anna,
> Singing Polly wolly doodle all the day.

When we reached Jedburgh Father drew in to the side of the High Street and went off on a mysterious mission, leaving me with the reins to hold. A petrifying moment. What if Flora took it into her head to bolt? I saw myself tugging desperately at the reins while she galloped down the street scattering pedestrians out of her path, knocking cyclists flying and careering over the Old Brig where I would tumble out and land headfirst in the Witches' Pool. Or maybe she would turn round and canter home to the farm, leaving father stranded and me bereft of my rugby match.

She did turn round once but only to give a whinny and look at me with a puzzled expression as if asking, 'Where's the Boss?' At which point he came back, to my great relief, mounted into the gig and handed me a bag of sweets.

'There, lass.'

'Oh, thanks!'

They were mixed chocolates, the kind I could never afford to buy for myself, quantity rather than quality governing my choice. Here I was blessed with both, some covered in silver paper, some in gold. As I peered inside the poke, the game of rugby rose even higher in my estimation.

We had to stable the pony and walk the rest of the way to the field, along with other groups aiming in the same direction. By now my excitement was mounting to such a pitch that Jessie need not have worried about the cold. If there was an icy wind blowing I did not notice it.

Father bought the tickets and we went and sat on the stand, which I still thought was a strange name, while others stood around the pitch stamping their feet to keep warm, impatient for the game to begin. I looked around at everything and everybody. Even the goalposts seemed interesting. I recognised some of the neighbouring farmers, and, hardly believing my eyes, the minister muffled to the ears in a topcoat, with a woollen tammy on his head. Not a sign of his dog-collar.

I was so busy looking at him that I almost missed the entry of the gladiators who were suddenly on the field running about in all directions, some with striped jerseys and some in plain colours. Good men and true, with bandaged heads and knees from previous battles, but all ready to fight it out to the bitter end.

Even the beginning seemed fierce enough. I thought the game had started but they were only knocking up. Suddenly the referee, an overgrown schoolboy in shorts, called them to order and blew a blast on his whistle. The crowd cheered, the minister jiggled up and down in his seat, and from then on so many things happened that I found it difficult to keep track of events. So did the reporter from the Squeaker who ran hither and thither round the side-lines like a mad grasshopper in his efforts not to miss a paragraph. It was a dangerous assignment for him, especially when a zealous player, chasing the ball, collided with him outside the touchline, sending him flying in one direction and his notebook in another. I wondered if he would include the episode in next week's report – Jedforest Scrapes Through – but for some reason he left it out.

Not that there was any dearth of incidents. I could see why Mother kept her eyes shut. I had to clap my muff to my mouth to prevent myself from gasping, 'Oh mercy me!' every time a couple of players barged into each other and I could hear their heads cracking. Sometimes one would lie dead on the field till a wee man came running on and squeezed a wet sponge down the back of his neck, whereupon the corpse suddenly sprang to life, shook himself like a terrier, and dived into the scrum as large as life.

At times the referee blew angry blasts on his whistle, pointed a furious finger at the players and appeared to be giving them a sound telling-off. But he, too, was frequently felled to the ground when he got in their way, and was limping like the rest before the game was through.

In the first half the striped lot were winning. Father was groaning and the minister behaving in a very un-ecclesiastical manner, shouting advice to the Jedforest team and abuse at the referee. Sometimes he clutched his tammy in despair and hid his face in his hands. I contemplated passing him a chocolate, but I doubt if even a raspberry cream would have consoled him.

At half-time the teams had a brief respite when they stood in separate huddles, and sucked lemons, the very sight of which drew my mouth together, though there was a caramel in it at the time. Then they changed ends and continued the fray with such vigour that one of the players was carried off on a stretcher and the referee had to run about holding a hankie to his nose to stem the bleeding. Meantime, the snow, which had been drifting down in dribbles, began to fall in earnest, though no one seemed to take any notice of it. It would have taken an earthquake at least to have stopped the match, especially near the end when Jedforest's fortunes were on the turn.

When the game was clinched by a drop-goal the Jed supporters exploded. Father cheered. The minister tossed his tammy in the air and shook hands with himself. I swallowed my sweetie, and the victorious players, ignoring their wounds, ran off the field looking modestly pleased with themselves. It was all over, except for traces of blood splashed on the snow.

We gave the minister a lift home and I was relegated to the back of the gig with his bicycle tied on with binder-twine. It kept me from tumbling out when Flora took to her heels and went speeding away home through the snowy darkness. The air was thick with flakes which froze on my cheeks as they fell, but I still had my inner warmth and the sound of 'Come on, Jed!' ringing in my ears. I felt that I had been blooded and was now an expert in the magic game of rugby.

This, of course, was big-time stuff. My own games consisted of more solitary pursuits. Skipping, swinging, playing with a tennis ball, if I could find one not already burst. When all else failed Jessie sometimes made one for me out of old newspapers, rolling pages of the *Scotsman* and the Squeaker together, moulding them into a more or less rounded object.

'It'll kep a catch,' she would say, meaning it would do for the time being, and so it did. I had many hours of pleasure tossing it up into the air and retrieving it as it came down. But a real 'stotting' ball was best, one that could be bounced against the stone walls of the house, or thrown up on the roof to come trickling down, if it did not stick in the rone-pipe. Then I would have to coax the herd to bring out the long ladder from the cartshed and climb up to rescue it.

'Man-lassie! ye're mair bother than a cairtload o' monkeys,' he would grumble, but he never refused.

There were endless permutations in throwing and catching, and a certain ritual known to all Border bairns who chanted the words as they went through the different sequences.

Plainy.
Clappy.
Roll the pirrn.
Backy.
Little ball.
Big ball.
Clitchie-clatch.
Briestie.
Birly.

The last was the most difficult as one had to twirl round while the ball was in midair and be ready to catch it as it fell down. I wondered if the rugby team went through a similar exercise when they were training, or if they just practised kicking each other on the shins.

Kick-the-can, bar-the-door, tig, and cuddy-loup-the-dyke (leapfrog) were great favourites in the school playground, but these were communal games. There was little fun playing hide-and-seek by myself, though the farmyard was a great place for such a pursuit, full of hidey-holes where one could lie undetected for hours: in the caff-hole amongst the chaff, inside an empty water-barrel, under a reaper in the cartshed, behind the harness in the work-stable, up a tree, or burrowed beneath the straw in the barn.

Sometimes I prevailed on Wee Maggie from the cottages to play but she could never find me, and grew tearful as she wandered desolately around the place. 'Where aboot are ye? Am I gettin' warm?' In the end I always gave myself up, out of pity for her. She, on the other hand, had no notion how to conceal herself and always gave the show away by giggling, or calling out: 'I'm here! Ahint the henhoose.'

My favourite solitary ploy was running with a gird, a gird simply being an old wheel or hoop which could be guided by a stick, or better still an iron cleek. There was a great art in guiding the gird to make it run smoothly and steadily without veering off to one side or another, though in my case, because of the bumpiness of the farm road, it more often ended in the ditch. But on the occasions when I ventured as far as the roadend and out on to the main road, the gird went spinning away in front of me at such a rate that I had great difficulty in keeping up with it.

Somehow, because it was so absorbing, I never noticed how many miles I ran. It was almost as good as getting a hurl.

'Are you going to walk there?' I once heard someone asking Big Bob when he had been sent on a message.

'Walk? Nae fears! I'm gaun to rin wi' ma gird.'

Big Bob's gird was his pride and joy, a perfectly rounded wheel with a splendid cleek to go with it, unlike my own dented object which became so battered and bent that it could only zig-zag across the road. In the end it called for great ingenuity to make it move at all, and I begged Jock-the-herd to find me a replacement.

'Man-lassie, whaur'll I get a wheel? Aff a cairt?'

But a cartwheel was too big and too heavy. For a time I had to be content with a small pram-wheel which went dancing and prancing away in front of me at such a speed that it was impossible to keep up with it. Then one day Jock discovered a discarded wheel from an old bicycle which had belonged to one of the hinds.

'The verra dab!' said he, straightening the spokes. 'There! that'll dae ye.'

It did me all right. Though I could never compete with Big Bob – I had only a wooden stick instead of a proper cleek – I became so attached to my gird that it was almost like guiding a live thing which jumped and jouked in front of me, with a decided personality of its own. I could have run, I felt sure, all the way to Jedburgh with it and never noticed the distance.

Parlour games could be hitty-missy if grown-ups were involved, playing down to the smaller fry and doing their best to lose. I hated when they cheated at tiddlywinks or ludo. 'Good for you! You've won again.' This was no use. I preferred a straight contest, whether I won or not, and always as a child longed to be treated rationally whether in conversation or playing a game of snakes and ladders.

On one never-to-be-forgotten occasion all the children in the district were bidden by the laird to attend a Christmas party at the Big Hoose at Edgerston. This was equivalent to being invited by God to enter heaven and play with the angels. Few of us had set foot in the mansion house before and had no idea what to expect as we wended our ways down the drive, uncomfortably attired in our best clothes and with parental warnings ringing in our ears. Dire threats of what would happen to us if we made a noise, a mess, spoke unless spoken to, ate too much, or behaved in any way normally. Had we obeyed them to the letter we would all have sat like stookies neither moving nor uttering a word.

Jessie had tried to feed me with porridge before I left home to take the edge off my appetite. 'It'll fill up your waim.' But I was far too excited to swallow a spoonful.

My hair had been brushed and combed to take all the tangles out – the 'rugs', Jessie called them – before being tightly plaited and tied with new blue ribbons at the ends. I would get murdered, I was told, if I lost them or scuffed my new shoes. Shiny black patent leather, fit for Buckingham Palace let alone the Big Hoose. Little did I know until I changed into them that they were as slippery as eels and that the polished floor was like a skating-rink. Every time I moved my feet slid from me in different directions. In the first few minutes I took several tumbles under the amused gaze of the gentry, and blushed scarlet with shame, hoping my parents would never hear of my downfall.

When I was in an upright position my attention was riveted on the glittering chandeliers that hung from the ceiling in the centre of the big room where we were assembled. Real electric light, not paraffin lamps or candles; also on the Christmas tree that stood in the corner bedecked with tinsel and coloured lights. There was a fairy doll perched on the topmost branch stretching out her gauzy wings as if poised for flight. None of us had ever seen anything like it before. We could only gaze in admiration, wondering how an ordinary fir tree grown in the Edgerston woods could possibly have undergone such a transformation.

It was quite easy to guess who Santa Claus was when he came in wearing a red cloak, a false beard and his own aquiline nose. No disguise could conceal the laird's London voice as he handed out presents to us all and said a few words to each of us. Not that we understood them. It was difficult at the best of times to know what he was saying; and now, speaking through his beard, it was impossible. But at least we all got gifts, presented with a fine disregard as to their suitability.

Big Bob, for example, was handed a dolls' teaset and Chrissie Smith, a toddler from Camptown, fell heir to a toy pistol with caps. Amongst the other items given away holus-bolus were mouth-organs, a jack-in-the-box, a teddy bear, skipping-ropes, a sewing-set, and a box of toy soldiers. When my turn came I slid towards Santa in my slippery shoes – indeed, I almost slid past him – and was presented with a catapult which I later swapped with Big Bob for his dolls' teaset. To this day I keep the cracked creamjug on a shelf, a reminder of many an imaginary teaparty held long ago in my castle on the hill, with unseen guests sipping from the cups and eating non-existent sandwiches from the miniature plates.

It was when we started playing games that I knew there was no hope for me unless I discarded my shoes, so I kicked them off and went round the Mulberry Bush in my stocking-soles. It did no good to the stockings and I paid dearly for my sins when I got home, but for the time being I felt free to gallop with the rest in the Grand Old Duke of York and Through the Needle's Eye, Boys.

At intervals the laird's house-guests, who were organising the festivities, would ask one or other of us, 'What would you like to do next, dear?' To which, when it came to his turn, Big Bob replied truthfully, 'Gang hame.'

I was sorry Sir J. M. Barrie was not staying at the Big Hoose, as he sometimes did. I had a feeling he would have had some daft tricks up his sleeve to enliven the proceedings which tailed off after a tepid game of Blind Man's Buff, during which we were afraid to move lest we crashed into any of the priceless objects displayed around the various polished tables. It was difficult to let oneself go in such surroundings. Even the fancy spread, with shivery jellies, trifles and wee iced cakes, was not to the liking of one shepherd's bairn, who, having stuffed himself with what he considered rubbish, demanded 'a slice o' plain breid'. And though it had been a great occasion, one to be talked about for weeks afterwards, we all felt a sense of relief when it was over and we were free to go home.

Organised games, I decided, were not for me. I was so used to my own solitary pursuits. Winter was a great time for sledging, sliding and snowballing. Even the hinds and the herd would scoop up handfuls of snow to fling at each other, or slither in their tackety boots down a long slippery slide, arms outstretched to balance themselves. It was great to hear them whooping like children and to know that, old though they were, they still had a spark inside them.

5. Ewe-lamb

My dream in those far off days was to be an only child, not just one of a litter. It would be wonderful, I thought, to be the sole object of my parents' care, all attention riveted on me, the most important person in the household. No more hand-me-doons to wear; every whim granted.

It was rare to find such a bairn in the Borders. The cradle seemed no sooner relegated to the garret than it was brought down again and the current baby 'shortened', so that his long clothes – the cumbersome garments into which every child was tucked and safety-pinned – could be refurbished to fit the new arrival.

'It's God's will,' Jessie would say, pursing her lips; but I felt she disapproved of the whole performance. 'Mrs Scott! She's nae sooner up than she's doon. Aye kittlin', like the cat.'

My desire to be an only child was sparked off by envy of a pupil at the Grammar School, the apple of her parents' eyes. Their one ewe-lamb.

She had a smug look on her face as if she knew she was someone special, as indeed she was. To her doting parents, at least, who could scarcely let her out of their sight. Her mother waited for her at the school gates, sometimes her father, too. Off they would go up the High Street with the ewe-lamb between them, chattering away ten to the dozen and her parents hanging on every word. Imagine being so cherished and having someone to *listen*! I wove many a fantasy about having such love and attention lavished on me.

The ewe-lamb was smaller and neater than I was. 'A dainty wee piece,' Jessie would have called her, with golden ringlets, not a hair out of place, and never a wrinkle in her stockings. I felt an inferior being in her presence, though sometimes she graciously allowed me to pick up her books or help her with her French verbs, not that I was any great shakes at them myself.

She took all homage for granted, as if she had a right to it, and every day she seemed to have a new possession. A hair clasp, a pencil case, a brooch or a bangle, and always a bag of sweets. On special occasions, such as her birthday, she would reel off a list of presents. My own birthday was scarcely noticed at home, far less celebrated with cakes, candles, parties and expensive gifts. But I was not a ewe-lamb.

One day, however, out of the blue there came the chance of a lifetime.

An invitation to spend a week of my holidays in Hawick. No other member of the family was included. They wanted *me* on my own.

Who were they? Aunt Bessie and Uncle Tom, distant relatives, an elderly couple who had once stayed with us at Overton Bush and who now wrote to say they would like to have 'the little lass' on a return visit. I had been like a ray of sunshine, they said, showing them all over the farm, being so bright and helpful that they had taken quite a fancy to me and were now looking forward to showing me the sights of Hawick. If I could be spared!

'Spared!' grumped Jessie before I could get too puffed up with pride. 'Ye'll be a guid riddance. They maun be aff their heids.'

I was nearly off mine with conceit at the thought of being singled out in such a manner. It was the first time I felt I was somebody, and for the next few days I went about with an elevated feeling, superior to everybody.

I had only a hazy recollection of what the elderly couple were like. Uncle Tom, I remembered, had a long white beard like a prophet in the bible and Aunt Bessie was small and rotund, but beyond that my memory was dim, though, of course, they must be specially nice to have noticed my good qualities.

As for Hawick I had no clearer picture of the place. I knew it was the biggest and most stirring town in Roxburghshire, proudly calling itself the Queen of the Borders. The mills were there, mysteriously turning wool into jerseys, jumpers and tweeds. And, of course, there was the monument in the main street with its strange inscription:

> Teribus y Terioden
> Sons of heroes slain at Flodden.

It was all to do with battles long ago and the gods Thor and Odin whose help the Hawick warriors had invoked when routing a party of English soldiers, returning victorious from Flodden. Revenge was sweet, and every year the incident is commemorated at the Common Riding when the Hawick folk shout out the slogan triumphantly, 'Teerie-bus and Teerie-oden', and are known locally as Teeries or Terriers.

For farming folk Hawick meant the lamb sales. I had once attended them myself, bewildered by the confused dirdum of the livestock market, with frightened lambs bleating piteously, strange collies bowfing at each other, the auctioneer rattling on nonstop, shepherds brandishing their crooks as they drove their flocks round the ring, while farmers waited anxiously to hear the final figure. As the buying and selling proceeded no money seemed to change hands apart from a luck-penny to seal a bargain. But I could tell by the look on Father's face if the price had been favourable. It meant not only much-needed money in his pocket but a feather in his cap – and in Jock-the-herd's – if Overton Bush came out on top. Something to boast about during the year.

On that occasion there had been no opportunity for me to explore the town before we had to set off on the journey home by gig. I sat in the back with Jock who had walked the sheep all the long miles from the farm to Hawick, taking two days on the job, using the drove-roads and staying the night at a friendly farm on the way. According to him, the beasts arrived at the sales in better shape than in later days when they were whisked there in an hour or so in motor-driven lorries, 'shoogled oot their wuts'.

Jock was thankful to get away from the bustle and fell instantly asleep beside me after groaning, 'Sic a steerie! It gaurs ma heid birl. Man-lassie! I'll be gled to get hame to ceevilisation.' I kept a watchful eye on him in case he tumbled out when Flora swerved round a corner. I was used to such misadventures myself, but it would be no easy job hauling the herd back into place. He was a stocky man, as solid as a rock.

Later, when the invitation came and I broke the news to him that I was about to go to Hawick for a week, he stared at me in horror

'A week! In thon noisy toon. Wumman, ye'll no' live to tell the tale.'

'I will so,' I said defiantly. 'It'll be great.'

He shook his head pityingly. 'Puir sowl! I doot if ye'll survive. A hale week!'

He made it sound like a life sentence, but nothing could dim my ardour. I was packed and ready long before the great day when father was to drive me there, this time in the motor. The Tin Lizzie. It was faster than Flora though not so reliable and we had many false starts before we finally saw Ruberslaw looming up in the distance, the rugged hill that dominated the landscape.

> Dark Ruberslaw, that lifts his head sublime,
> Rugged and hoary with the wrecks of time . . .

Why were the hills always male? I wondered. Were there no lasses amongst them?

He – Ruberslaw – had once been a great hiding-place for Covenanters who came there to worship in secret, lurking in furtive little groups on the hillside. I had heard tales of their narrow escapes from their persecutors when mists mysteriously rolled down from heaven to protect them.

It was here, too, in Teviotdale, that the Little Folk lived. Good ones and bad. Some who made crops flourish, others who caused cows to go eild (that is, cease to yield milk), or stole babies away and left wizened changelings in their place. The cure for anyone elf-struck was to gather fox-gloves, known as witches' thimbles, and make a magic potion which would cure all ills.

We saw no signs of the Little People as Tin Lizzie rattled her way into Hawick. I was to be deposited at the monument and handed over like a parcel, along with a basket containing fresh butter, eggs and home-made jam, to the elderly couple who would be waiting for me. And there they were, standing patiently beside the mounted warrior, scanning the street for signs of the Tin Lizzie, smiling and waving when it drew up beside them with a screech of brakes.

At first they seemed strangers to me, older even than I had expected, but obviously so pleased to see me that my heart warmed towards them. They thanked Father not only for the basketful of farm fare, but for letting me come. It must be such a sacrifice to him, being left without me for one whole week.

Father looked a trifle surprised at this, and at the last moment thrust his hand into his pocket, jingled around amongst the coins and brought out a fistful of silver which he passed on to me as spending-money. It amounted to almost ten shillings, more than I had ever possessed in my life before. Enough to buy up the whole of Hawick.

I could only gulp my thanks and say 'Ta-ta' when he reversed round the monument and disappeared into the distance with sparks flying from the motor. I had a sudden feeling of alarm, for I was alone now, a stranger in a strange town. Apart, of course, from Aunt Bessie and Uncle Tom, who soon dispelled my fears by taking me by the hand and leading me away up a wynd, round a corner and into their small snug house in a back street.

It was like a house in a fairy-tale, fit for the Little People themselves. Only a but and ben, cluttered with furnishings, footstools, antimacassars, pot plants and ornaments, so crowded that it was dangerous to make a sudden movement for fear of knocking over a vase or bumping into a rocking-chair. Every single space on the walls was covered with pictures and texts. Bless This House. God Is Watching. Be Sure Your Sins Will Find You Out.

There was a fierce fire burning in the grate sending out such a heat that I tried to retreat from it as far as possible, but the tea-table was in the way, spread with all the ingredients for a high tea. Meat pies, sandwiches, currant bread, rock cakes, parkins and cream cookies. We sometimes had plain cookies at home when the vanman called, or even curranty cookies with sugar on top, but these had been split open and were oozing with cream.

'A Hawick speciality,' said Uncle Tom, passing the plate to me. 'Eat up, lass.' He turned to Aunt Bessie. 'She's far too thin, isn't she, Bessie?'

'Ay, the bairn needs fattening.'

They started to talk about me as if I was not there, discussing what they would do to amuse me during the week. Uncle Tom would take me to the park, Aunt Bessie to the shops, and maybe we could visit Cousin Somebody who had a talking budgie. The main thing was that the lass must enjoy herself.

It was great being the sole object of their attention, though what with the extra food I had eaten to please them, and the heat of the fire, I began to feel drowsy. When I closed my eyes for the long grace at the end of the meal, I could happily have floated off into dreamland. But Aunt Bessie began to bustle about, clearing the table, and Uncle Tom put another lump of coal on the fire and said, 'Sit in, lass, an' get warm. Tell us all about everything.'

It was a heady feeling being the centre of attraction. For a time I opened out like a flower, elaborating on every little happening on the farm. My audience was interested in the smallest detail, prompting me to 'Go on, dearie; what happened next?' Uncle Tom kept saying, 'My word, Bessie, she's great company, is she not?'

But I could not keep it up. My head was beginning to nod, and my cheeks were burning from the heat of the fire.

'The bairn's sleepy. She's needing her bed. Light the gas, Tom,' said Aunt Bessie, reaching up to rummage for the matches amongst the ornaments on the mantlepiece. A porcelain pig, a china duck, a cracked vase containing honesty, spectacle cases, keys, and yet another text, The Meek Shall Inherit the Earth.

I forced myself to watch Uncle Tom lighting the gas for I had never witnessed the process before nor heard the hiss-ss-ss when the mantle began to glow. The gas gave out a white light, brighter than our paraffin lamps at home but less kindly. I could see the crumbs on the floor, the rust on the fire-tongs and the fluff that had collected on the mantelpiece. Aunt Bessie was not the best of housewives.

'I'll just give it a lick and a promise,' she would say each day, flicking the duster here and there; but she was nice for all that, and meek enough to inherit the earth.

I wondered where I was to sleep but the mystery was solved when Uncle Tom suddenly let down a bed from the wall. There it was, all ready for me, complete with patchwork quilt.

'Say your prayers and tuck yourself in. We'll away ben to our own room. Sleep tight, lass, and we'll see you in the morning.'

I kept coming and going all night wondering where I was, in this world or the next. The fire, though shielded by a guard, was still burning brightly, flickering in my eyes. And the grandfather clock in the corner was the busiest I had ever heard, tick-tocking the noisy minutes away and chiming every quarter. I could hear trains in the distance shunting at the station and screaming along the lines. Then Aunt Bessie and Uncle Tom snoring in unison from the adjacent room.

It was an uneasy night. I felt stifled in the claustrophobic atmosphere and flung aside the patchwork quilt, longing for a gulp of fresh air. I felt apprehensive, too, about the bed, comfortable though it was. What if it sprang up as suddenly as it had been let down, and trapped me against the wall?

When I woke in the morning Aunt Bessie was boiling one of our farm eggs for my breakfast and Uncle Tom had gone off to work. I never knew what he did; something in one of the woollen mills which kept him occupied till he came home for his high tea each evening. So Aunt Bessie and I were left during the day to our own resources.

The housework was soon over. A lick and a promise, then we were free to go out and about. This was what I was longing for. Fresh air; but it was too fresh for Aunt Bessie. We were no sooner outside the door than she began to shiver and dragged me back in again. After rummaging in a drawer she produced a woolly scarf.

'Put that round your throat, dearie, to keep the chill out.'

I was not feeling the chill, but I did as I was bid while she fixed a fur tippet round her throat, and thus fortified we finally sallied forth. I wanted to rush on ahead and see everything all at once, but Aunt Bessie held my hand and I was forced to match my steps to hers.

When we reached the main street we went in and out of several shops. At the baker's I saw cream cookies in the window and was pleased when Aunt Bessie bought some for our tea. In the greengrocer's it took her a long time to decide whether to buy carrots or onions. It seemed strange having to pay for vegetables which grew so plentifully on the farm at home, and all free.

Aunt Bessie had a purse that snapped shut, with separate compartments where the copper coins were segregated from the silver. My own money was burning holes in my pocket. I was eager to spend it but not on carrots and onions. I wanted to be free to run up and down the street, peering at any shop window that took my fancy, but I had to accompany Aunt Bessie to the fishmonger's, hopping from one foot to the other while she swithered between kippers and haddocks.

'Which would you like, dearie? Take your pick. A kipper or a haddock? Or maybe a herring?'

I was not accustomed to being consulted on such matters, or indeed on any others, and at first I enjoyed the sensation of choosing between chops and sausages at the butcher's, or brown bread and white at the baker's; but as time went by I grew impatient with the whole performance and said, 'Oh, I don't mind, Aunt Bessie. Anything you like.'

It was a strange week, the longest I had ever spent in

my life. I kept recalling Jock-the-herd's words. 'A hale week! Ye'll no' live to tell the tale.' Even at the end of the first day I felt I had been away from home for a lifetime. It was wonderful, of course, basking in the old folks' approval. Nothing I said or did was wrong. Not a word of criticism.

I was in great danger of having my head turned, and found myself acting a part so that I could receive even more adulation, colouring everything I said to make it sound more interesting. In other words, showing off. Jessie would have been scunnered with me.

The days began to emerge into a pattern. Mornings spent shopping with Aunt Bessie. Afternoons visiting some of her neighbours and old friends. Old! Everyone I met was ancient, with sunken eyes, wrinkled cheeks, and brown blotches on their shaky hands. The only bright spot was when we visited Cousin Somebody who had a talking budgie. 'I'm a prrr-rrretty wee boy. A prrr-rrretty wee boy.' But I felt sure he would sooner have been a free bird.

Aunt Bessie encouraged me to show off my talents in front of them. 'She can speak *French*,' she would tell them proudly. 'Say something, dearie.'

I felt like the budgie, and said something even if it was only '*Ouvrez la porte*' or a quotation from *Madame Lemoine chez le dentiste*. They all agreed I was a great wee character, and I began to believe it.

Most evenings Uncle Tom took me for a sedate walk to the park. There were swings there, and sometimes he would give me a gentle push to and fro. Not too high in case it made me sick. I did not tell him I had a swing at home which the herd had made for me and that I could fly higher than the treetops without turning a hair. I was getting used to acting a part, becoming a make-believe person unlike my real self.

Sometimes at night when the gas was lit in the overcrowded room Uncle Tom took down an old fiddle from the top of the press and played some scratchy Scottish airs while Aunt Bessie nid-nodded her head in time to the music. Or he would recite one of the long Border ballads which so often ended in tragedy.

> She sought him east, she sought him west,
> She sought him brade and narrow,
> Sine in the clifting of a crag
> She found him drowned in Yarrow.

'Stop it, Tom. Ye'll make the lassie greet,' Aunt Bessie would protest, drying her own eyes. 'Give us another wee tune on the fiddle.'

I did my best to be an interested audience and to take my turn when they asked me to entertain them. They never tired of hearing tales about the farm, about Bella Confectionery at the post office, Auld Baldy-Heid at the village school, or Yorkie the tramp. As for saying my poetry, I recited everything from 'Rainy, Rainy Rattle-stanes' to 'The Lord's My Shepherd', and even tried to sing one of Father's comic songs: 'I'm the saftest o' the faimly'.

I liked best when Uncle Tom told tales of his own childhood when he had brose for breakfast and ran bare-foot to school where he learned to write on a slate. Or about how he had once seen the Kelpie that lived in a nearby loch. He always ended his reminiscences with a jingle.

> That was langsyne when geese were swine
> And turkeys chewed tobacco,
> And sparrows bigget in auld men's beards
> And mowdies delved potatoes.

6. The Ragamuffin

Long before the middle of the week the novelty of being an only child, a ewe-lamb, had worn off, and I began to count not only the days but the hours till Father would come and fetch me home. We were to meet him at the monument where I was to be handed back. What if he did not turn up? The thought became a nightmare to me, and I sent off a postcard, the first I had ever written to him. With a picture of the Teribus Monument on it as an added reminder.

'Dear Father, I will see you on Saturday at three o'clock. Don't forget.' Then, of course, I lied a bit. 'I am having a great time in Hawick.' I was not sure what to put at the end. Yours truly or yours sincerely. So I just repeated 'Don't forget' and left it at that.

'What about staying on for another week?' Uncle Tom suggested.

'Oh yes!' said Aunt Bessie, beaming.

'Oh no!' I said quickly. Too quickly. Then, not to

hurt their feelings, 'It would be lovely but I'm needed at home.' Lying again!

They understood that. How could the family possibly do without me for another seven days? Uncle Tom and Aunt Bessie would just have to make the most of me, they said, for one short week.

Short! Surely no timepiece had ever ticked as slowly, as well as loudly, as the grandfather clock in that stuffy little sitting-room. I felt smothered by the heat, the suffocation of the wall-bed and the over-cossetting of the old people. Killed by kindness.

I ached for the freedom to run outside, or to sit quietly on my own reading a book. There were only three on a dusty shelf: *The Pilgrim's Progress*, the bible, and *Hymns Ancient and Modern*, but I was so starved for words that they were better than nothing. Yet it was impossible for me to cut myself off for long enough to dip into them before Aunt Bessie or Uncle Tom, fearing I must be bored, tried to liven me up by suggesting a game of draughts or dominoes. Uncle Tom always let me win. 'There! she's beaten me again. Isn't she a smart wee lass, Bessie?'

I was becoming listless and finding it more and more difficult to live up to my reputation of being a ray of sunshine when one day Aunt Bessie said, 'I think I'll take a wee nap this afternoon. Will you be all right, dearie?'

'Oh *yes*, Aunt Bessie. Can I go out, please?'

'Well – don't get lost, mind. Put on the woolly scarf . . . '

I was off like an arrow from the bow, running as if I was in a race. Away down the wynd and into the main street. Never mind the fishmonger, the greengrocer, the cream-cookie shop. I made straight for one with Confectionery above the door. Not 'Confectionary', like Bella's at the post office at home.

At last I had the chance to spend some of my wealth. There were sweets I had never seen in the window before.

Hawick balls were the local equivalent of Jethart snails, though quite different, of course. Sugar mice, bon-bons, pink and white coconut ice, nougat, macaroon bars, and dozens of others. A feast for the eyes and a problem when it came to choosing.

After much swithering I went in and bought a bag of mixed caramels, a sugar mouse, a toffee apple, and some extra-strong peppermints for the old folk, the flat pale-brown kind that were good for the wind and brought tears to the eyes. Then, making the most of my freedom, and with a treacle caramel in my mouth, I made my way to the park.

It was here I met the Ragamuffin. He was, I suppose, my first lad, though maybe it was only cupboard-love on his part, for he soon demolished the sugar mouse, the toffee apple and the rest of the caramels, and would have polished off the peppermints as well, if I had not hidden them in my coat pocket.

He had a lean and hungry look about him, like a stray dog searching for scraps. The truth was, he must have been half-starved, poor thing. A skinnymalink of a laddie with holes in his stockings, no elbows in his grubby jersey, and frayed sandshoes tied together with string. But he had a nice mop of curly black hair and an engaging grin. I liked the look of him, and he took to me, too, I think. I hoped it was not only because of my wealth.

We had eyed each other before when I was out with Uncle Tom, but *he* did not think much of the boy.

'He's just scum. Keep away from that ragamuffin,' he warned me. 'He smells.'

True enough he did, but I was used to smells on the farm. I wondered why Uncle Tom who was so fond of quoting texts from the bible – charity suffereth long and is kind – could not find a place in his heart for a ragged laddie. It was a queer thing, religion. If the boy came too near me and tried to get on to the next swing Uncle Tom put on a fierce face and shouted, 'Away you go! Keep your distance from decent folk.'

Today the Ragamuffin and I sat side by side on the swings, sucking our caramels, not saying much but content in each other's company. When he did speak he sometimes said strange things. 'I'm listening to the trees,' cocking his head to one side as if hearing voices. I understood that, for I often listened to the trees myself. Or he would tell lies. Not small tarradiddles but great thumpers, not boasting as Big Bob did, but seeing visions, I suppose.

'Ay, so I wull,' he would say, half to himself, half to me. 'Sail roond the world. An' I'll invent something.'

'What?'

'Canna say till I've invented it.' Then, 'Ma faither's got thoosands o' pounds in the bank. He's a millionaire.'

'Oh yes?' I was not sure if he even had a father.

'Ma mother's a Ladyship.'

'Likely!'

'We've got a muckle big car at hame. *Twa* muckle big cars. Hae ye ony mair sweeties in your pooch?'

When I heard the town clock striking and made a sudden move to hurry home to Aunt Bessie's stuffy little house – back to prison – he looked at me and asked, 'Are ye comin' back the morn?'

'I will if I can,' I promised, and gave him an extra-strong peppermint as a parting gift, then handed him the whole bag. I could always buy some tomorrow for the old folk.

As it happened I was back again that very evening, but not alone. Uncle Tom held me by the hand and the Ragamuffin had enough sense to keep his distance while I pretended not to notice him. It was strange living a double life. Every day when I could escape I ran first to the shops and then to the park. He was always waiting for me to receive any largesse I had in my pockets. We got on a treat, bouncing up and down on the see-saw or swaying on the swings. I never knew his name and he did not ask mine.

As a result of all the mollycoddling meted out to me during that everlasting week I took a cold in my head. Nothing I would even have noticed at home, but the old people were as alarmed as if I had caught galloping consumption and would soon be in my grave. They kept taking my temperature and dosing me with cough-mixture.

'D'you think we should send for the doctor, Tom?' asked Aunt Bessie, looking worried.

The very idea horrified me. 'What? Just for a *cold*!' I said, trying to stifle a sneeze. At home it would have to be a broken collar-bone at least before anyone took such a drastic step. 'It's nothing. I'm ever so much better.' Indeed, the cold would have taken its normal course, I felt sure, if they had ignored it instead of swathing me in shawls, sprinkling my hankies with eucalyptus and drugging me with ipecacuanha wine till I smelt as strongly as the Ragamuffin.

'I'm fine!' I kept protesting. 'Fine!'

One night, with a muffler wrapped round my head and another round my throat, they took me as a treat to a place called the Mission. I had no idea what it would be like. The pictures, maybe, or a sing-song, but it turned out to be a prayer-meeting in a hall where folk got up now and again to 'give their testimony' and tell how they came to be saved. I was terrified the preaching man would call upon me, for I had no idea whether I was saved or not. Likely not, I thought, with all the lies I had been telling lately. Be sure your sins will find you out.

Came the final day at long last. How eagerly I had waited for it. My only regret was that I would have to say goodbye to the Ragamuffin.

I managed to escape on my own to do my final shopping. A bag of cream-cookies to take home to mother – likely they would be squashed to bits by the time I reached the farm – a stucco statue of the monument for Jessie (A Present from Hawick) and a red and white spotted handkerchief for Jock. For Aunt Bessie and Uncle Tom I found a small golden angel in a shop, to put on their dusty mantelpiece. No doubt it would remind them of me. Perfect in every detail, except that I had no wings.

It was difficult to decide what to buy for the Ragamuffin especially as my money was running out. In the end I bought a bar of highly scented soap to sweeten him up and a large bag of liquorice allsorts. I had only sixpence left which I decided to give him as a parting gift.

He was waiting for me in the park, the faithful swain, hanging upside-down from one of the swings like a curly-headed monkey. All the blood had run to his head and his face was bright pink. When he turned himself right way up to receive his gifts, he sniffed at the soap and stuffed it in his pocket before devouring the liquorice allsorts one by one as if he was eating a meal. Maybe he was, poor soul.

The Ragamuffin had a present for me, too; a chuckie-stone veined in various colours. Delicate shades of pink and green and grey. He must have picked it up from a burn and spent hours polishing it till it shone like a precious stone.

'It cost a fortune,' he said, thrusting it into my hand. With a millionaire father and a Ladyship mother, he could well afford it. As for me, I valued the gift for its own sake and for the thought that lay behind it.

I could not face farewells so after a while I just gave him the sixpence, said 'Ta-ta' and went away without looking back. I never saw him again but I treasured the pebble for many a year and often wondered what became of the Ragamuffin. Perhaps he grew up to be a famous rugby player or even a Lord Provost. I was sure he would be somebody, if only in his own rich imagination.

It was more difficult saying goodbye to Aunt Bessie and Uncle Tom who grew weepy at the end. Fancy anyone shedding tears over me. For my part, I had difficulty in holding in my high spirits and was ready to set out for the rendezvous with Father long before trysting time. Would he have received my postcard and remembered to come? I was in an agony of apprehension as I walked down the wynd with Aunt Bessie and Uncle Tom, pacing my steps to theirs and curbing my desire to run ahead.

I hardly dared look when we reached the monument, but he was there before us, peering under the bonnet of Tin Lizzie who was making her customary noises, shuddering and shaking as if struck with the palsy. The relief was so great I could have rushed forward and kissed him, but of course that would never have done. He just banged down the bonnet and said, 'Hop in, lass.' Then, after a word or two with the old folk, we were off.

I looked back and waved. They seemed a lonely pair standing there in the street and I began to regret that I had not been nicer. Oh! but it was great to be free. All the way home Father ignored me, letting me sit still and think my own thoughts. I liked that. He whistled 'The Bonnie Bonnie Hoose o' Airlie' at intervals and roared 'Gee-up' to the motor when it backfired on an incline near Denholm. But not a word about what was going on at home or how everyone had missed me. Not that anyone had, I supposed.

Halfway home Tin Lizzie stuck and I got out to help with the pushing before being sent to a cottage for a pail of water to cool the engine. Everything was back to normal. I felt fine.

The farther we went away from Hawick the more I tried to straighten out the tangle of impressions the visit had left on my mind. It had enriched me in many ways. I had experienced a whole range of new sensations, some I would never want to repeat again. It was all a muddle, of course, but the one sure and certain conclusion at which I arrived was that there was nothing in the world better than freedom. Nothing!

Forever after I was to dread 'staying with people'. The scar is still there. To this day I find myself going to ridiculous lengths to avoid being boxed-in in someone else's hospitable house, preferring an impersonal hotel where I can come and go unchallenged. Kindness can sometimes kill.

Jessie was plucking a hen in the kitchen and Mother making a roly-poly pudding when I arrived home. They both stopped long enough to say, 'Hullo, you're back,' before continuing with their tasks. I watched Mother spreading rasp jam on the pudding before rolling it up, then turned to Jessie.

'That's not Jenny?' I asked anxiously as she took tufts of feathers from the bird hanging head-down from her lap.

'No, it's just a hen. Get oot ma road an' dinna mak' the feathers flee.'

She had spread sheets of the *Scotsman* on the floor to catch the fluff and feathers as they fell, and was pursing her lips in concentration. Jessie had plucked hundreds of birds in her day: chickens, partridges, pheasants, grouse, ducks and bubblyjocks, and had done her best to teach me, too. But I was slow at the job, always afraid I was hurting the poor feathered creature, stone dead though it was.

It was nice not to be noticed. I just went outside, took to my heels and ran all over the farm with no one pestering me. No Aunt Bessie to say, 'Where are you going, dearie?' No Uncle Tom warning me not to catch cold. No woolly scarf, no mollycoddling. It was wonderful to be my own self again. I sang 'Shall We Gather at the River?' at the pitch of my voice, not because I felt holy but because the rumbustious tune suited my mood.

I did everything as fast as I could. Climbed a haystack, shinned up a tree, swung perilously high on my own swing, rushed to the hill to see if the castle was still there and came home through the wood, listening to the trees. I thought of the Ragamuffin as I fingered the pebble in my pocket and wondered if he had used his scented soap yet.

Jed and Jess came sniffing towards me giving little yelps of recognition. Jock-the-herd greeted me with, 'Man-lassie!' He looked kind of pleased to see me.

'How are you, Jock?'

'Me?'

He was surprised at the question. Jock never thought how he was. He just was. I nearly asked him if he had missed me, but stopped myself in time.

He liked the red and white spotted handkerchief. At least he shook it out and examined it closely before stowing it away in an inside pocket. He seemed surprised that I had survived.

'A week in thon place! A hale week! Were ye no' fair scunnered?'

But by now I was beginning to brag a bit. 'It was rare,' I told him defiantly. 'Rare! I enjoyed myself a treat.'

'Better you than me.' The herd went off, shaking his head, and I realised I was as bad as the Ragamuffin. Telling thumpers.

It was the same when I wrote my thank-you letter to the old folk. There was no way, it seemed, of getting through life without twisting the truth.

'Dear Aunt Bessie and Uncle Tom, How are you? I am all right. My cold's away.'

That was fair enough but I had to say something else and lay it on thick. 'I fairly enjoyed myself in Hawick. It was kind of you to invite me. I hope I'll see you again soon. I am missing you both. Tell everybody I was asking for them.' Everybody being the neighbours we visited and the talking budgie.

It was not much of a letter. I could have written a better one to the Ragamuffin but I had no idea what his address was. The Park, Hawick, Roxburghshire, Scotland, the World. I doubted if it would reach him.

For the rest of the holidays I ran wild, living my own

self-contained life and not caring a button about scratched legs, torn frocks or tangled hair.

I spent whole days in the keep on the hill, not bothering to go back to the farmhouse for meals. I fed myself on books instead, eating up print as I read and re-read *Oliver Twist* or *The Mill on the Floss.* Sometimes when I came back to life I found my feet had fallen asleep and I was all pins and needles. I kept an old skipping-rope in the castle so I could jump myself back into circulation, counting up to a hundred or singing:

> Matthew, Mark, Luke and John.
> Haud the cuddy till I get on . . .

Sometimes I helped Jock with the sheep. I was pleased when he shouted, 'Man-lassie, weir that yowe through the yett.' I was becoming more knowledgeable about rams, tups, hogs, yowes and gimmers. Almost as good, so I hoped, as an extra collie. Or I went off to the fields with the hinds, acting as bondager, and rode back on one of the Clydesdales, clinging to its mane and pretending not to be terrified when the great clumping creature clattered into the steading and made straight for the horse-trough, slobbering and slavering as it slaked its thirst.

I was soon back to my normal state of disarray, tousled and tatty, speaking with a broad Border accent and earning the scorn of my ladylike elder sister who considered me beneath contempt.

'*You!*' she would say distastefully. 'You're not even fit to be a skivvy.'

'I'm going to be a bondager,' I said defiantly, aspiring to higher things.

But she could reduce me to dust with one look, so I kept out of her way as much as possible. If visitors came to tea I hid up a tree and let her take all the praise for her prim manners. She was soon away back to her Edinburgh college, and suddenly it was time for me, too, to spruce myself up, ready for my return to the Grammar School. It was a painful process.

'Ye're as tousy as a tyke,' declared Jessie as she tried to get the rugs out of my hair. 'What'll the folk in Jethart think o' ye?'

'I'm not caring.'

But I cared enough to submit to her ministrations so that I could present a tidy enough appearance at school not to be noticed one way or another. The worst part was wearing stockings and forcing my feet into restricting shoes.

The first person I met going through the school gates was Lucy, the ewe-lamb. Both her parents had accompanied her and were standing waving her goodbye with downcast looks as if she was leaving for the ends of the earth, though they would be back at lunchtime to collect her. She had a new satchel which she proudly showed me, and a wrist watch with a gold band, no less. But I no longer envied her. The silken chains would be too tight for me, though she seemed to thrive on them.

Though we were all 'Jock Tamson's bairns' born under the same Border umbrella, how varied we all were in our characters. As I turned and saw her parents still lingering at the gates for a last look at their pet I was glad to know that Mother was expecting again.

Yet when the English teacher set us the task of writing an essay on How I Spent My Summer Holiday I found myself throwing the hammer once again. The truth was not in me. What a splendid week I had spent in Hawick! The streets, the shops, the people, the talking budgie, the cosy little house, the kindness of Aunt Bessie and Uncle Tom. All was exaggerated, but no mention of the Ragamuffin. I had enjoyed every moment of it; my only regret was that one week had been too short.

The teacher gave me full marks and I was forced for my sins to stand in front of the class to read out my effusion. Serve me right!

7. Snow and Storms

The first time I made the surprising discovery that my parents were fond of me, in a sort of a way, was when I got lost in a snowstorm. I was glad I did not die or I would never have known.

It made me wonder, though, why folk kept their warm hearts so well-hidden, only showing their real feelings in moments of stress. Sometimes never at all. Borderers were seldom blate (Jessie's word for bashful) when it came to plain speaking, expressing downright opinions and giving folk their characters. Yet their tongues were tied in knots when voicing their deepest emotions. Any form of endearment stuck in their thrapples. How could one crack such hard shells?

How different from the characters in story-books who dear-ed and darling-ed each other on every page, but that, of course, was fiction. Tenderness and affection were maybe not meant for real life. Still, I thought it a pity that the hinds and their wives never seemed to give each other a glance, let alone a fond one. Even when they were courting they did not once mention the word love. No doubt it was there, deep down, but why keep it hidden? Was it such a shameful thing to do as the bible said and love one another?

I was used to it, so I grew a shell like everyone else, but I always felt there was something missing. Many a time I had the urge to throw my arms round Jessie's neck – or the herd's – and express my affection for them. I could do it to a calf or a pet lamb but never to a human being.

It was something inside me that must be curbed. Like the desire to shout 'Shut up!' to the minister when he went on too long with his dreary sermon. Thou shalt not!

It never once entered my head that anyone could love me. Except perhaps Aunt Bessie and Uncle Tom, and a little of that went a long way. At home I had the feeling I was in everyone's way, so I tried to make myself as invisible as Maister Naebody. In fact, I was a kind of *Miss* Nobody, coming and going without anyone paying any particular attention to me. 'Stand on your ain feet, lassie,' Jessie used to advise me, so I stood on them. There was no one to lean on, anyway, especially on that dreadful day when I got stuck in the snow.

The storm came on suddenly just as I was jumping down from the school bus at the crossroads outside Mary-Ann's cottage. If I had known what was in store for me I would have stayed there and begged Mary-Ann for shelter. She would have welcomed me, I felt sure, for she used to talk to me as if I were one of her hens, and often fed me with a jeelly-piece to help me on my way. Once she even offered me a handful of corn from her apron pocket.

Looking after her feathered friends was Mary-Ann's chief preoccupation. She treated them like children, fussing over them as if she herself was a mother hen. She clucked at them and knew each one by name. Maggie, Mrs Broon,

Wee Rascal, Banty, His Nibs, and the rest. According to her, they each had their own personality.

'Just like folk. See Mrs Broon! She's no' speakin' to onybody. Puir thing, she's in the pouk. Lost a' her feathers. Mebbe I'd better tak' her into the hoose. She likes sittin' on the kitchen rug.'

Later, I wished I had had the sense to sit there, too, instead of pressing on through the swirling snow.

'Watch yoursel', wee ane!' Black Sandy called to me as he turned the bus. 'We're in for a beezer o' a storm. Awa' hame at the toot. Onward Christian Soldiers!' And off he went, skidding on the icy road.

It crackled under my feet as I walked away from Mary-Ann's reminding me of the poem Miss Paleface had been teaching us at school. About the Ancient Mariner.

> The ice was here, the ice was there,
> The ice was all around;
> It cracked and growled, and roared and howled,
> Like noises in a swound.

At first it was beautiful. The feathery flakes came flying thick and fast from the sky, settling on the trees and transforming the grey countryside into what those who knew little about snowstorms would call a white wonderland. But I had been snowed in too often to waste time extolling its beauty. Darkness had fallen early, the wind was rising, the icy air growing colder. It whipped the snow into swirls, stinging against my cheeks and freezing on my hair. I had to keep blinking my eyelids to free my lashes from the flakes.

By the time I reached the farm roadend I could scarcely see a step in front of me, the air was so thick with snowflakes. The ground by now was covered and every landmark obliterated. Was I turning in at the right roadend or had I wandered by mistake into a field? I had to turn my back now and again from the force of the storm so that I could regain my breath, hoping that soon I might see the lights from the hinds' cottage windows and know that I was on home ground, but there was no lamplit glow to be seen, no sound except the wail of the wind. I seemed to be walking aimlessly in circles and getting nowhere.

Up till now I had felt a certain sense of adventure – even elation – seeing myself as a heroine overcoming all odds. After all, snow was my element. My first view of the world had been a white one, for I was born in a storm, shut in for the first six weeks of my life, and when at last I was carried outside the snow-wreaths were still there, higher than the hedgerows. Since then I had plodded through drifts many a time and experienced all the discomforts of being storm-stayed. But never before had I felt so overpowered by the angry elements, raging against me like fiends.

I tried to stem the rising feeling of panic. Be sensible! Think! If I was in a field surely there must be a dyke nearby. If I could reach it I might be able to find my bearings, or at least cower behind it from the force of the driving snow, but every step I took led me nowhere. By now I was finding it more difficult to keep my feet, and as I stumbled and fell, I realised I was in real danger.

Old tales came flooding back to my mind of tramps found frozen to death in the snow. Never mind Lucy Gray; *she* was only in a poem. These had been flesh-and-blood beings who had lost their lives in sudden storms like this. If it had happened to them it could happen to me.

I wondered if anyone at home had noticed I was missing or would they all be too engrossed in their own affairs? At least, if I was finally found frozen stiff like the tramps all my sins would be forgiven and forgotten. It was some consolation but not much.

A great desire came over me to lie still in the soft snow-bed into which I had fallen. If I snuggled down and went to sleep – a last sleep – all my worries would be over. For a second I drowsed off, before pulling myself up sharply. 'Get up, lassie,' I seemed to hear Jessie saying. 'Pit your best fit forrit.'

Which foot was my best. I had little feeling in either. By now I had lost my gloves and my fingers were dead. But through thick and thin I clung to my school satchel, knowing it contained not only my lesson-books and a library book – *Lorna Doone* – which must be returned in due course to Miss Paleface if I survived, but also some messages I had been asked to collect from the shops in Jedburgh that day. Tobacco for one of the hinds, darning-wool, safety-pins, shoe-polish and a pair of black boot-laces. Nothing heavy, luckily, or of great import, yet I had been entrusted with the money to buy them. Tam would be lost with an empty pipe, and frozen tobacco was better than none.

Sometimes I floundered in a snow-filled ditch. Was it the one near home where the red rowans grew and the little barberry bushes? Or was I maybe miles away from the farmhouse on someone else's land? Once when I fell I felt something stirring beside me, alive and warm. A sheep. If I could have seen the markings on its fleece, I would have known if it was one of ours. Perhaps I had helped to stamp the initials on its back at clipping-time when the herds shouted 'Buist!' and I ran to dip the branding-iron into the tar-pot. Would I ever hear that sound again?

The creature seemed content enough to lie there burrowed under the snow. Perhaps it would survive. I had heard Jock tell of digging sheep out alive weeks after being lost in a storm. If I lay beside it maybe I could survive, too, but I was not a sheep. No woolly covering or inner layers of fat to preserve me from the bitter cold. Instinct urged me to struggle to my feet and keep going.

Every step grew more difficult. My legs ached, my eyes smarted, my face had lost all feeling and my hair hung heavily over my shoulders, frozen into stiff plaits of ice which bumped against my back, adding to my burden. There seemed little point in going on. I had tried, and now I must give in.

The next time I stumbled I lay where I fell in a mound of snow, soft and comfortable as a feather-bed. Soon I would have a white counterpane to cover me and all my troubles would be over. I began to say my bedtime prayer, the last I would ever repeat.

> Now I lay me down to sleep,
> I pray the Lord my soul to keep,
> If I should die before I wake . . .

Was that a Willy-Wisp dancing before my eyes?

I was hearing noises. In this world or the next? A bobbing light appeared to be advancing towards me and I could hear somebody or something prodding through the snow. Jock-the-herd with his crook. Then I heard Father's voice and Jock shouting as he laid down his lantern. 'She's here! I've got her! Man-lassie . . .'

The lost sheep had been found.

I remember the herd hoisting me up from the ground and slinging me over his shoulders like a sack of corn. I was still clutching my school satchel and Father had a job to prise it from my frozen fingers. On the way home the feeling that I had caused such a lot of trouble overcame everything else, even that my ordeal was past.

'I'm awful sorry,' I murmured, bobbing against Jock's broad back.

'It's all right, lass,' my father said kindly, walking beside us with the lantern. 'You're safe, that's all that matters.'

Mother, too, was all softness and kindness when I was carried into the lamplit kitchen. Her eyes were red as if she had been crying. For me?

The next thing I remember was being in bed. Warm

blankets, a hot pig, a feeling of great comfort, and a lump in my throat as I thought of everyone's kindness.

Now I lay me down to sleep . . .

In the morning, of course, it was all different. I was no longer a heroine and nobody took much notice of me. Except Jessie who gave me a sound scolding.

'Could ye no' hae used your rummlegumption an' stopped at Mary-Ann's?'

Back to normal.

All the same, the memory lingered on. The warm feeling was there, and I decided to repay everybody by being nicer to them in future. But that, too, soon wore off. Yet I now knew for sure that I was not just a nobody in the family. I counted for *something*.

It must have been about this time that I made another surprising discovery. Jessie was not quite perfect.

It all began with the lambing-man. Every winter, the Boss, my father, hired an extra help to take the burden off Jock-the-herd's overloaded shoulders when the sheep began to lamb. The two men took turn about on night-duty, making the bothy up at the lambing-shed their headquarters. There was a trestle bed there and a fire where they could heat milk for the motherless lambs and brew their own tea. A row of sinister-looking bottles containing medicine for sick sheep stood on a dusty shelf. In a way, it was like a clinic for expectant mothers.

Nearby were the bields which the herd had built to shelter the more difficult cases brought in from the ends of the farm; but mostly the mothers gave birth out in the open, often at dead of night and in the wildest weather. It was a miracle how the lambs survived and so soon grew sturdy enough to fend for themselves. Suddenly plunged into an icy-cold world, up on their feet from the moment they were born, finding instant sustenance from their mothers, and often a helping hand from the herd or the lambing-man.

I remember a succession of such lambing-men but none more clearly than Erchie, the reason being the bothy roof had gone on fire – it was built of thatch and went up in a spectacular blaze – and Erchie was forced to stay off and on in the farmhouse, while I was relegated, as usual, to sleep with Liz-Ann, the servant-girl whom Jessie called the Cairthorse.

Liz-Ann was a great snorer, and so was Erchie for I could hear him through the wall ascending and descending the scales before reaching a crescendo and fading away into nothing as if he had died. I waited apprehensively for the symphony to restart. Sometimes he varied it with a loud whistle which made my blood curdle, especially if I was on the verge of falling asleep myself; and now and again Liz-Ann would grow restless and lash out at me with her feet, or flail her arms and hit me on the face. Often I was black and blue in the morning, but judging from the thuds and creaks from next door I would sooner have shared her bed than Erchie's.

All the same, I quite liked him. Not so Jessie.

It was like Dr Fell, the reason why she could not tell. He was an inoffensive enough big soul, with tufts of sandy hair growing straight up from his head, false teeth which clicked when he spoke, and a great desire to please but he could not please Jessie. Everything he said or did annoyed her. The way he saucered his tea, ate his food with his knife, sat with his stockinged soles on the kitchen fender, whistled endlessly under his breath.

'Can ye no' haud your wheesht?' she would say in an exasperated voice, rounding on him in a fury. 'I'm fair deived wi' "The Laird o' Cockpen".'

'Richt!' said Erchie placidly. 'I'll gie ye "Auld Lang Syne" insteed.'

I enjoyed listening to them catter-battering, like a pair of music-hall comics on the stage, though in Jessie's case it was in deadly earnest. According to her, Erchie was responsible for all the evils of mankind. Red spots of anger would appear on her cheeks as she ranted at him, but all her abuse seemed to bounce off his back. Try as she would – and she tried – she could not find a vulnerable spot.

'Dodsakes, Jessie,' he would say mildly, 'ye've got a tongue that wad clip cloots.'

'Dinna Jessie me!'

It was no longer Mr Nobody who caused all the trouble in the household. It was Erchie who lost the scissors, broke cups, upset the milk-jug and left dirty marks on the kitchen floor. No use trying to defend him, Jessie knew better. He was even accused of stealing the clothes-line when it went missing.

'He did not,' I would say in his defence.

'Did sot!'

When it turned up under the kitchen table she was convinced Erchie had hidden it there deliberately to annoy her. It became an obsession with her, so much so that Erchie used to fling his skippet-bunnet into the kitchen before daring to set foot in it himself. They never actually came to blows, only verbal ones, though Jessie often warned him, 'I'll skelp your lugs if ye dinna get oot ma road.'

Jock-the-herd had no complaints about Erchie's work. 'He's guid wi' the lambs,' and that was all that mattered to Jock.

But not to Jessie.

One day the clash of personalities reached its climax. I came down that morning to find Jessie rampaging about the place with the red danger-signals in her cheeks. The Cairthorse was cowering in the back-kitchen and Erchie sitting supping his porridge at the table, dipping his spoon first into a bowl of creamy milk at the side and then into the porridge plate, time and about.

'Impidence!' snorted Jessie, breathing fire as she lifted

the porridge pot and loomed over him as if about to spear him with the spirtle.

'What's up?' I enquired.

'Up! It's *him*. Canna ca' ma kitchen ma ain. Interferin' busy-body, that's him.'

Erchie continued to sup his porridge. Between mouthfuls he explained. 'There was naebody aboot when I cam' doon, so I just made the porridge.' A kindly enough gesture, I thought.

'It's fou o' knots,' grumped Jessie, dumping the pot on the table and giving the contents a vigorous stir.

''Tis not,' said Erchie.

'Tis sot!'

They were like a couple of squabbling bairns. It was no use acting as intermediary, so I sat down at the table and waited for Jessie to dish out my helping of porridge. She gave an angry twist to the pot and the next moment it turned on its side, spilling out a stream of boiling-hot porridge. Most of it landed on the unfortunate Erchie's hand. He gave a howl of pain and sprang to his feet, while Jessie said crossly, 'See what ye've dune noo! Cowped the pot!'

'I did not,' said Erchie, clicking his false teeth.

'Did sot!'

'Oh, Jessie!' I protested, dumbfounded.

'Haud your tongue!' she snapped at me, and began to clear up the mess on the table while Erchie rushed through to the back-kitchen, almost knocking over the Cairthorse, to run the cold water over his scalded hand, after which with a great display of dignity he went out of the house, not looking at Jessie or saying another word.

'Poor soul, he hasn't finished his breakfast,' I began, then after a look at Jessie's face decided it would be more prudent to bite my tongue. Fancy her telling such a black lie! It astounded me to discover that Jessie, of all people, had feet of clay.

All that day she went about tight-lipped. Now and again she thumped hereself angrily on the stomach. I knew the signs.

'Is anything wrong, Jessie?' I ventured to ask, when I saw her sipping a cup of hot water.

'I've got the bile. Keep oot ma road.'

So I kept out of her road. So did the lambing-man. It was his turn on night-duty, using the bothy as his head-quarters, therefore it was not till next day that we heard him stamping the snow off his boots before flinging his hat into the kitchen.

'How's your hand?' I asked him when he came in.

'Fine!'

He tried to hide it behind his back but not before I had seen that it looked raw and blistered. Jessie had noticed it, too. She said nothing but went to the dresser and rummaged in one of the drawers till she found a roll of bandages.

'Sit doon,' she ordered Erchie. 'Haud oot your hand.'

Erchie sat down and meekly allowed himself to be bandaged. No words passed between them, but I sensed it was Jessie's way of saying she was sorry.

There was no truce, though I was surprised that night to see her darning a pair of the lambing-man's socks. But soon the two of them were argy-bargying as before, each trying to score points off the other.

'Did not!'

'Did sot!'

And suddenly I realised it was a kind of game which they both enjoyed playing. Like peevers, kick-the-can, or cuddy-loup-the-dyke. Grown-ups were no different from children. No more flawless. So maybe my own imperfections did not matter all that much. I was not disillusioned with Jessie. Indeed, I liked her better now that I found she had human failings. Perfection is not a lovable quality. She seemed more like me now, though, of course, miles above me in strength of character.

As for Erchie he just went away when the lambing-season was over, still clicking his false teeth and whistling 'The Laird o' Cockpen' under his breath.

'Guid riddance!' grunted Jessie as he disappeared down the road.

All the same, I felt she would miss him.

8. Dreams and Daydreamers

Father's funny-bone worked overtime. Asleep or awake, he always seemed to be involved in some comic incident.

Sometimes I could hear great guffaws of laughter coming from the work-stable and guessed that the Boss had dropped in for a word with the men at lowsing-time while they were feeding and curry-combing the workhorses. He was not one for giving orders, only for suggesting what work might be done about the farm next day, in such a way that the hinds seemed to have made the decisions themselves. Certainly they liked his company and looked forward to his visits.

The Boss could always find something funny to relate even in the simplest daily happening, and things had a way of happening to him. Like the day his lum hat walked across the floor, before his very eyes, with the cat underneath it. It was not so much the happenings, as the way Father told them. He was a born raconteur. No one could ever be dull in his company.

If he was in the mood.

At times he could be as withdrawn as any hermit, shutting himself up in the greenhouse, his refuge from the outside world. Here he kept a private collection of odds and ends. Song-sheets, a jew's harp, seed catalogues, unanswered letters and frayed copies of the Jethart Squeaker. Often I caught sight of him through the glass of the greenhouse, watering his seedlings, sitting on an upturned tub, puzzling over an account book, playing the jew's harp, or just sitting there. But I never watched for long. There was no Do Not Disturb notice on the door, but we all knew that if the Boss was in his hidey-hole the best thing to do was ignore him.

There was little enough privacy in such a stirring household where it was difficult for any of us to find a private corner of our own. Lucky me, with my castle on the hill.

Father often went to ground when any awkward decision had to be made. He was not one for facing up to trouble or giving someone a telling-off. In any family squabble he was inclined to walk out of earshot or say, if asked to act as arbiter, 'Leave it to your mother.' In the greenhouse he was safe. Fantasy was pleasanter than facts.

More often the Boss was in a gregarious mood. He loved company, and when visitors arrived instantly became a performer. I, for one, could have listened to him till the cows came home, especially if he was recounting his dreams. Asleep, father had adventures even funnier than his waking ones.

People who record their dreams are mostly as boring as those who give chapter and verse about how they spent every single day of their holidays.

'On the Monday it rained in the morning. No, I'm wrong, that was Tuesday. On Monday the sun was shining so we walked down to the beach to look at the sea. Then in the afternoon . . .'

Similarly with dreamers. 'I must tell you about a funny dream I had last night.' *Why* must they?

Jessie cured me. I had subjected her to a rambling tale of how I flew through the air in the middle of the night and landed upside-down on the steeple clock in Jedburgh. She was not impressed.

'Keep your dreams to yoursel', wumman, or ye'll get put awa'.'

'Where?'

'In the daft-hoose.'

'Oh!' It was a sobering thought. 'Do you never dream, Jessie?'

'Me? I've got mair to do wi' ma time.'

'But you've nothing to do with your time when you're asleep.'

'I have sot! I'm ower busy sleepin'.'

Her brother, the herd, on the other hand, once admitted he sometimes had nightmares.

'What about, Jock?'

'Aboot black-faced sheep. Thoosands o' them, chasin' me ower a precipice.'

'Mercy me! What happens?'

'Nae idea. I aye wake up in time.'

Most of the dreams I heard about had no beginning, middle and end. Except Father's, and they lost nothing in the telling. I sometimes wondered if he was making them up, but maybe they were all as true as true.

He was a great one, Father, for meeting royalty in the middle of the night.

'Guess who I met last night.' Pause for effect. 'King George.'

'Goodness gracious! What was he doing?'

'Riding up the road on your bicycle.'

'The boneshaker! Never!' No wonder I was astounded at the thought of royalty riding my old rattletrap which I could hardly ride myself now that its handlebars were twisted and so many of its spokes missing. 'How did he manage?'

'He fell off,' said Father, which did not surprise me, 'and so did his crown, right in the middle of a puddle.'

'Mercy me! what did he say?'

'A bad word.'

'What?'

Father hesitated and then said, 'Dammit!'

'Oh!' Fancy the king saying a word like that, even in a dream. 'Did you say anything?'

'Yes, I said Hullo, George.'

'George! Did you not say Your Majesty?'

'Never thought of it. I asked him where Mary was.'

'Queen Mary!'

'Ay! So George said she was riding Flora up the road, wearing her coronation robes. She was right cross when she saw the king lying there. She called him a silly sumph and told him to get up and put his crown back on his head or he'd get what-for. So George said another bad word and got up . . . '

It was all so silly and yet so feasible. On and on went the story, no detail left out, till I could see King George and Queen Mary as plain as porridge in the kitchen (always with crowns on their heads), George in stockinged soles making toast at the fire while Mary tied an apron round her coronation robes and said, 'I'll just go out to milk the kye. Have a boiled egg ready for me, George, when I come back . . . '

Sometimes the tables were turned and it was Father who found himself in Buckingham Palace, dressed in his lum hat and long johns, with Queen Mary pipe-claying the doorstep – still, of course, with her crown on her head – and asking, 'Would you care for a kipper to your tea. Or a clooty-dumpling?'

Father's dreams were not always confined to night-time. I remember the day he fell asleep in church during the long sermon and began to roar with laughter until mother dunted him awake.

He was not the only one to doze off. Religion seemed to have a soporific effect on the congregation, many of whom had walked miles across country after a hard week's work. Now that they were settled down in their pews, uncomfortable though the hard seats were, who could blame them for sinking into blissful oblivion? Surely God would give them full marks for being present in the flesh though absent in spirit.

I was not much of a sleeper myself even in bed at night, so as I sucked my pandrop, I was able to observe the drowsy worshippers' efforts to stay awake. I watched Jock-the-herd nodding in the pew across the way, his head sinking lower and lower on his chest, while his sisters Jessie and Joo-anne sat bolt upright beside him, eyes fixed unblinkingly on the pulpit. I had a feeling they, too, were asleep even though their eyes were open, for sometimes they gave convulsive jerks or let out soulful sighs.

There were many strange sounds to be heard all round me, apart from the minister's monotonous voice. Suppressed snores, grunts, groans and wheezes. It was a blessing Erchie, the lambing-man, did not come to the kirk or he would have raised the roof. Big Bob sometimes took a coughing-fit just to pass the time and in the hope that someone would hand him a sweetie to clear his throat. Old Miss Eliot in the back pew gave in before the minister had finished 'Firstly' and laid her head on the book-board in front of her as if it were a pillow. I sometimes wished His Reverence would follow suit in the pulpit but he seemed to be the only one enjoying his own performance.

Up in the gallery the laird and his lot from the Big Hoose had more comfortable dreams on their cushioned seats. Red plush. When Sir J. M. Barrie was with them the wee man disappeared completely from sight for the duration of the sermon and I wondered if he was lying stretched out or just sitting hunched up like Humpty Dumpty. I wondered, too (having nothing else to do) if there were kirk mice up there or if it was too grand a place for them.

I was dying to know what had made father laugh. He told us on the way home. It was an appropriate dream for the occasion.

'All about Moses,' Father said, his eyes crinkling with laughter as he recalled the scene. 'Playing rugby for Jed-forest, belting down the field to score a try when a big fella from Hawick tackled him and tore off his breeks.'

'Gracious! What happened?'

Father shook his head. 'Your mother woke me when Moses was being carried off on a stretcher, poor soul. I doubt he had broken more than his commandments.'

Looking back, I can see that my father was no ordinary man. I felt it at the time, though I thought it was maybe only a child's view of someone I admired, but now that I have a clearer picture of him I am more sure of it. I was always bursting with pride when I heard his praises being sung. I felt no modesty about it. 'Yes! isn't he great?' I agreed.

The sad thing was, I could never say it to his face.

Fair enough for Father to dream while he was asleep. My trouble was that I daydreamed. It led me into many a pickle.

Jessie sometimes shook me by the shoulders to bring me back to reality and said sharply, 'Stop it, lassie. Ye're awa' in a dwam again. What are ye thinkin' aboot?'

I would never tell. Daytime dreams were private. They were not funny, like Father's. Mine were full of fantasy, mainly with me as heroine. The opposite from real life. I was brave, beautiful, beloved by everyone. I had the magic touch and could cure all ills. People flocked from far and near to beg for my help. I was showered with gifts. Precious jewels, pearls, rubies, sacks of gold.

Statues were built in my honour, streets named after me. I was in the history books like Cleopatra.

The great thing about daydreaming was it helped to take the tedium out of a dull task. Drying the dishes or doing the kirning. The churning. Or it could carry me into oblivion over a rough road. On the way to the village school, for example. The trouble was it sometimes carried me too far.

I can remember the time I went away past Edgerston, on and on, up towards the Carter Bar, daydreaming my way to the Cheviots instead of turning in at the school gate. I remember it specially because it was the day Bella at the post office had a new line in 'confectionary'. Toffee apples. They were new to me and as I was in funds after purchasing a jotter I spent my remaining halfpenny on the strange sweetmeat.

'What do I do with it?' I asked, holding it awkwardly in my hand by its wooden stalk.

'Sook it, lassie, or chowe it,' Bella told me. 'Use your heid.'

I used my teeth instead. The coating of toffee was sweet and crackly. In contrast the apple inside tasted sour. Still, I was not going to throw it away after spending all that money on it. So I chewed my way up the road past the Camptown cottages, through the Dark Woods and on towards the Manse and the school.

In order to take my mind off the sourness I embarked on one of my favourite fantasies. Like King Midas, everything I touched turned to gold. Hedges, fences, trees, flowers, weeds, even the stone I was kicking up the road. Mine was a revised version of the classic story. I doubt if I had even heard of Midas at that time in my life. So I let my imagination roam and transformed the whole countryside into a realm of gold, unaware that I had long passed the school gate.

With such wealth at my command how was I going

to spend it? *That* kept me going for a long stretch of steep road. A golden cradle for the baby, bracelets and rings for my mother, a splendid brand-new greenhouse for father, new bicycles for the hinds and silken dresses for their wives.

I puzzled for ages about Jock-the-herd. Would he like a gold crook or a new bowler hat to wear to the kirk? And what about Jessie? It would have to be something practical, like carbolic soap or safety-pins, but I would sooner have given her pure gold earrings, though I knew she would never have worn them.

Filling in all these details kept me fully occupied, little realising where my feet were carrying me till I heard a sudden shout which brought me back to earth with a bump. All the gold faded away in a flash and I was left with nothing but the wooden stick of my toffee-apple.

'Daursay, lassie, what are ye daein' awa' up here? Ye're miles past the schule.'

It was Auld Chuckie-Stanes, the roadman, chipping away at a heap of stones and shaking his head at me. 'Ye'd better turn aboot an' rin for't.'

I turned and ran like a hare down the road, but not fast enough, of course. The class had long been assembled when I slunk in and tried to reach my desk unnoticed. Auld Baldy-Heid was writing a sum on the blackboard, but he had eyes in the back of his head.

'And where d'you think you've been, miss,' he thundered, addressing the blackboard though his venom was directed at me.

'P-please, s-sir . . . ' What was the use of telling him I had been away in a golden wonderland? Better just to say I was late, which was obvious enough, and take the consequences. Big Bob would have done better. He had a hoard of more or less feasible excuses which sometimes fooled the teacher. 'Please, sir, the coo was calving.' 'I had to rin a message for ma granny. She canna rin hersel', wi' her bad leg.' 'Please sir, ma mither had to mend ma troosers.'

I tried my hardest not to daydream in the classroom but I did not alway succeed. Sometimes I came to my senses to discover Auld Baldy-Heid looming over me like the wrath of God.

'Did you hear what I said, girl? Answer me.'

'Yessir. I mean, no sir.'

I had to take a firmer grip on myself when I went to the Grammar School, though in a way it was easier there. With so many comings and goings from one classroom to another, and all the different subjects to learn, I was forced to concentrate on immediate matters. It was only in the Latin class that I could really let go. Anything to escape from the subject.

Mr Archie-Bald, the rector, took the class himself in his own room, and there I sat with some of the boys from my own class, also reluctantly taking this extra subject. Why we never knew. The only compensation was that Dafty left us to our own devices for long periods while he went into a dwam, and I was able to follow suit, but I had to keep a wary eye on the irascible wee man for there was no knowing when he would suddenly come back to earth and bawl, 'Get up on your feet, man, and read that first paragraph.' He called me man along with the boys, but that was the least of my troubles.

During his long withdrawn silences while he sat hunched up at his desk, I could escape, too. The boys were up to various ploys below their desks. Sometimes they made inky pellets with blotting paper and fired them at each other – or me – with their rulers, and now and again Miss Crichton or one of the other teachers would bring in a juvenile delinquent to be punished. Or the Janny would knock at the door to announce that a laddie had went and broke a windy. But apart from these interruptions there were long spells when I could let my imagination roam.

It was during these daytime dreams that I made my parents proud of me.

'Yes, that's our daughter. Isn't she wonderful?'

I saved people from drowning, rescued them from burning buildings, risked life and limb by climbing a high tower to bring down a stranded child. Or I stepped on to the stage at the last moment to take over a prima donna's part, with outstanding success, of course. My photograph was in all the papers, not just the Jethart Squeaker. It was not pride in myself that mattered. The only thing I cared about was that Father and Mother were there to revel in my success.

I used to wonder what went on in Dafty's head when he was missing from the real world. What were his fantasies? Far removed from the Grammar School, I felt sure. Sometimes he nodded his head and gave a wry smile, and occasionally he shook hands with himself as if saying, 'Well done, boy!' But more often his brow darkened and he appeared to be engaged in an angry argument. It would not have surprised me if he had opened his desk, brought out the tawse and walloped his unseen opponent.

It would have been interesting, I thought, to listen in to what went on privately in everyone's head, not that they could be a patch on Father's dreams.

When he started off with, 'Guess where I was last night,' I knew we were in for a treat.

'The moon?'

'No.'

'Where, then?'

'Davy Jones's locker.'

'At the bottom of the sea! Mercy me! what were you doing there?'

'Driving the motor,' said Father. 'I met Jonah and the whale.' He would! 'And d'you know what? Jonah was the spitting image of Jock-the-herd. I gave him a lift home . . . '

9. Facts and Fancies

'Bairns should be seen and not heard.'

How often this was said to me in my childhood; too often.

Speak when you're spoken to. Keep your opinions to yourself. Who are you, anyway, to have opinions? Do as you're told. Be obedient. Grown-ups know best. Their word was law, by the mere fact that they were older and therefore wiser. But were they?

I had begun to have my doubts and was looking at them more critically, making my own judgements, seeing their mistakes, finding their flaws. But though they were quick enough to point out my failings I would never have dared criticise theirs. I would instantly have been banished to the garret for being cheeky. There was little justice, it seemed, for the young.

Yet everyone has a need to look up to a higher being. In my case (apart from Jessie) it was a teacher at the Grammar School. The science master.

It was a pity science was one of my worst subjects, for I longed beyond anything to shine in his sight, but he had given me up as hopeless. He told me so many a time, when I came to grief with a Bunsen burner or spilt mercury on the floor. 'Oh you! You're hopeless!' Yet even that sounded like music in my ears and the fact that he had taken any notice of me at all made my heart thump. I used to dream of rescuing him from disasters or bringing off such a splendid experiment that he would say, 'Well done! You're not so hopeless, after all. My favourite pupil.' But it was only fantasy.

It was not his looks that attracted me. He was a small tubby dumpling of a man, with duplicated chins and waistcoat buttons that kept popping from their moorings. Mr Smith was his name. Fatty, the boys called him behind his back. They drew cruel caricatures of him on the blackboard, with a great distended belly, like a butter-ball, but I rubbed them out, when I could, to save hurting his feelings. I never thought of him as Fatty.

The reason I liked him so much, I think, was because of his kindly ways. Even though I was such a dolt he always opened the door for me in a gentlemanly manner (he did it for all the girls) and took the trouble to bandage my bleeding fingers when I cut them on a test tube. 'Just sit still and don't bother with the rest of the lesson. You're hopeless.'

In return I had a great desire to mother him, to sew on his buttons, mend his frayed cuffs, and shield him from the thoughtless pranks of the boys. He looked hurt and bewildered when the chalk was hidden or a simple experiment ended in a smelly explosion. His vulnerability somehow appealed to me and I wanted to protect him from all trials and tribulations. Particularly from Archie-Bald, the rector, who had a habit of sneaking into the science room when we were in the midst of an uproar. Mr Smith's face crumpled up as if he was about to cry and his stammered excuses sounded so futile that I longed to rush to his rescue.

'It was not Mr Smith's fault. He's perfect. It was the boys who did it.'

One day while I was daydreaming in the playground one of the bigger boys in my class kicked a football in my direction – his way of attracting my attention – and yelled out, 'Fatty wants you.'

'Wh-what?'

I was winded both by the football and by Willy's surprising statement. Surely he must be pulling my leg. But he repeated it.

'Fatty wants you. Get a move on; kick the ball back.'

I gave the ball the best kick I could and went off to the science room in a great state of turmoil. What on earth could Mr Smith be wanting with me? To sew on his buttons, or confess his undying admiration for a hopeless pupil? Hardly likely.

I tapped tentatively at the door. Through the glass pane I could see Mr Smith poring over a large sheet of paper, puzzling his brows and making marks here and there. Was he working out a new experiment, or writing me a love-letter?

I had to tap several times before he said 'Come in'. He turned and stared at me as if he had never set eyes on me before. 'Oh yes, you! I want you to be a witch.'

'Yessir,' I replied with blind obedience. Anything he asked. I was willing to get down on all-fours and hop round the room like a frog, if that was what he desired. But how to turn myself into a witch? Maybe I should go and look for one of the Janny's broomsticks.

'I'll need three of you,' said Mr Smith, still studying his paper.

That sounded a bit more difficult. There was only one of me.

'Get two of the other girls in your class. I expect you

can easily get yourselves dressed up as witches. You know, black cloaks and peaked hats. Oh! and you'll need a cauldron.'

'Yessir.' Then I took a deep breath and asked, 'Please sir, what's it for, sir?'

'For?' Mr Smith looked at me as if I was an idiot. 'For the procession, of course.'

It was the first I had heard of the procession but not the last. Only for Mr Smith would I have gone through all the indignities of my first, and only, appearance in the streets of Jedburgh, crouched on a tumbril drawn by a belching horse plodding its way towards the ramparts where the Provost and other dignitaries were assembled to see us pass by.

We were not the only ones. There were drays full of elves, cartloads of Ancient Britons clad in sheepskins and gooseflesh, Robin Hood and his Merry Men, Mary Queen of Scots – a spotty-faced girl from one of the upper classes – and her four Maries, a Nativity Scene complete with a flaxen-haired doll in a cradle, and the entire Jedforest Rugby team marching at the tail end. The town brass band headed the procession and played their way through their repertoire from 'See The Conquering Hero Come' to 'Abide With Me', They were loud, if nothing else.

I have no recollection of what the occasion was supposed to spotlight or why it had fallen to Mr Smith's lot to organise it, but at least it was unforgettable for one thing. The rain.

Never can there have been a wetter day since the Flood, apart maybe from the one mentioned in the Squeaker fifty years ago. It teemed in torrents, drenching us all to the skin. The elves were soaked through to their chemises, the Ancient Britons tried to shelter their bare knees with mackintoshes, even the Holy Child was awash in the cradle. As for the witches, our peaked hats gave way in the middle of the High Street and sagged over our foreheads, sending rivulets of rain running down our noses.

The only bright spot for me was that Mr Smith was riding the baker's horse by our side, togged up as some sort of cavalier in a green velvet suit, which had silver buttons on the jacket at the start of the procession but none at the end. Poor soul, he kept looking up at the sky as if pleading with God to stop His nonsense, but the higher he looked the more it rained.

We were all coughing and sneezing for weeks after, but at least we got our names and a smudged photograph in the Squeaker. And that was the end of my career as a witch.

It was Father, of course, who was the performer in the family, in great demand at local concerts and soirées where he went down a treat. How proud I was when the audience dunted their feet on the floor, clapped their hands and shouted 'Encore!' It was great basking in his glory. I would sooner have heard him being praised than received an accolade myself.

We were fifty or more miles away from real theatres: Newcastle on the one side, Edinburgh on the other, so there was no chance of seeing stage plays other than the amateur efforts got up by Father. The local performers were always themselves no matter how they were dressed up or who they were supposed to represent in the play. It was only Father who put some fervour into his part, disguising both himself and his voice, though, of course, we knew fine who he was.

'Dodsakes! if I hadna kent that was the Boss I'd never hae recognised him,' one of the hinds said, watching father strutting about the stage, brandishing a bread-knife and dressed as a burglar. I recognised the bread-knife, too. It was the one we kept in the kitchen-table drawer.

My first real glimpse of the theatre came when it was announced that Mr Samuel Somebody, a real live actor, was coming to Southdean, a village three or four miles away, to give a one-man show. No one was quite sure what that was, except that it would be a change from a whist drive, so everyone within reach wended their way to the little hall where the performance was to take place and sat on hard benches staring at the empty platform. Presently a middle-aged man with a club foot came limping forward, and from then on the small stage was crowded.

Never had I seen so many characters, all from Dickens, gathered together as clearly as if they were there in the flesh. I knew some of them already from my reading. Oliver Twist begging for more porridge, Mr Micawber waiting for something to turn up, Mr Pickwick skating on the ice. Fagin teaching his boys how to pick pockets, Little Nell on her deathbed, the unctious Uriah Heep. They were all *there*, conjured out of the air by the actor. I sat mouse-still, hardly daring to draw breath in case I missed a word, completely carried away.

I have no idea what the rest of the audience made of it, but to me it was magic. At the end when the actor limped forward and bowed I could not believe he was only one man. It took ages for me to come down to earth. I could not get over the fact that as soon as we were outside the neighbours began to speak about ordinary things like how the turnips were coming on and when the clipping would start.

I thought about it for a long time afterwards, marvelling not only at the cleverness of the actor but at the genius of the writer who had first created the characters out of his head. It gave me an added incentive to keep on trying to put words on paper myself and invent characters of my own.

The trouble was my Mr Micawbers and Uriah Heeps invariably turned out to be animals. Pigs, cows and bubbly-jocks. But at least I was getting the feel of words and the secret joy of seeing some of my inventions coming alive, if only in my own sight. And I have never forgotten that lame actor. Even now when I re-read Dickens I can still hear his sonorous voice. It seems as if he is reading the story with me.

The only chance we had as children to show our acting abilities came on April First. All Fools' Day, the day when by tradition we were allowed to let our imaginations run riot and tell lies to our hearts' content. The great thing was to keep a straight face and make the tarradiddles sound as convincing as possible. Hunting the gowk, we called it, a gowk having two meanings: a daftie and a cuckoo.

'Hunty gowk!' we cried in triumph when we caught someone napping, preferably a grown-up; but they, too, were at the game, and it was difficult not to be taken in by someone in authority when ordered, for example, to let the cat out of the milkhouse. 'She's got shut in, an' she'll lap up a' the cream, if ye dinna hurry.'

To go or not to go? Even Jessie was at it, with a face like a poker. 'Daursay, lassie, ye're no' takin' the measles? Ye've come oot in spots. Tak' a keek in the gless.' By the time I had reached the kitchen mirror, Jessie had cried, 'Hunty gowk!' and won the day.

Not so easy to fool her. I tried everything.

'Jessie! Jessie! You're wanted on the telephone. It's urgent,' I would cry, running after her as she was about to hang out the washing. It was a silly thing to say, for Jessie never answered the telephone, if she could help it. Thon noisy beast, she called it.

'Oh ay!' she would say disbelievingly. 'You answer it, lassie. If it's the king tell I'm ower thrang to speak to him.'

Try again. 'Oh look, Jessie! What's happened to that sheet? There's a great big hole in it. Look!'

But Jessie stubbornly refused to be drawn. With a clothes-peg in her mouth she muttered, 'Look yoursel'. Ye're no' catchin' me.'

If I let enough time elapse there was always the chance she might forget and I could catch her unawares, but it did not always work.

'Jessie! Jessie! The minister's on his way up the road. You're to come in and bake a scone. Hurry!'

'Tell the meenister to bake his ain scones.'

It was hopeless.

Jock-the-herd was a far easier target, but I sometimes thought he let himself be fooled just to please me.

'Jock, look out! Your pipe's burning a hole in your pocket.'

'Man-lassie, where aboot?'

'Hunty-gowk!'

My problem was how to tell when Jock was trying to gowk me.

'Man-lassie, rin for your life. The bull's got lowse an' he's in a terrible temper.'

It could be true. If so, there was no time to argue. The safest thing was to scramble over the dyke and never mind whether I was gowked or not.

Though it was all good fun April First was an uneasy kind of day, for if anything untoward did happen, who would believe it? For example, when the kitchen chimney went on fire. Jessie had been trying to clear away the soot by setting fire to pages of the *Scotsman* and thrusting them up the lum. I enjoyed watching this operation and always ran outside to see the sparks flying into the air. But today it was more than sparks. Smoke and flames came belching forth. I could hear a frenzied yell from Jessie. 'The lum's on haud. Rin an' fetch the men.'

I went tearing round to the work-stable to tell the hinds, but would they listen?

'I'm deif,' said Wull, continuing to curry-comb his Clydesdale's tail.

'Me, tae,' said Tam, who was sweeping out the stable. 'Awa' an' gowk somebody else.'

It was the herd and the Boss who finally had to come to the rescue. The hinds were horrified when they saw them up a ladder, scrambling on the roof, and rounded on me, 'Ye micht hae tell't us!'

If April First was a daft day April Second was equally full of nonsense. Paper-Tail Day, we called it in the Borders. A day when the local paper came into its own, for we made long paper trails of it and the *Scotsman*, and, armed with safety-pins, chose a victim to stalk in the hope of stealthily pinning a tail to the back of his jacket. Often blissfully unaware that we ourselves were trailing tails behind us.

This operation required great sleight of hand, for any fumbling gave the show away; and though it was comparatively easy to hoodwink our classmates, our greatest ambition was to tail Auld Baldy-Heid. We always held a council of war to decide who was to bell the cat. I can recall Big Bob slinking out of his seat and tiptoeing to the master who was writing on the blackboard, paper-tail and safety-pin at the ready. We held our breath while we watched him picking up Auld Baldy-Heid's jacket between finger and thumb. A gasp of relief when the deed was done and Big Bob was back in his seat, the hero of the hour.

It was difficult to stifle our mirth as Auld Baldy-Heid marched about the classroom with the long tail trailing behind him. Wee Maggie took a fit of the giggles and we all coughed and shuffled our feet, trying to cover it up.

'Less noise,' he reprimanded us sternly. 'Settle down and get on with your sums.'

It was when he settled down that the trouble started. In his haste Big Bob had not succeeded in fastening the safety-pin securely, with the result that Auld Baldy-Heid had no sooner sat down than he leapt to his feet, his face scarlet with rage.

'Who did it?' he roared, tearing off the offending safety-pin and the trailing tail. 'I'll murder the lot of you!'

But he knew and we knew he could not carry out his threat for it was an unwritten law that on Paper-Tail Day as on April First *we* were the ones who could get away with murder. But he got his revenge on April Third, which was an ordinary day.

Was any day ordinary?

Certainly not the one on which Jessie called out: 'There's a wee man in a kilt dancin' in the garden. Come an' see, lassie.'

If it had been Hunty Gowk day I would have known better than to look. But it wasn't, and there *was* a wee man in the garden dancing the Highland Fling amongst the flowers and nettles, with his tattered kilt swirling around his bare knees. He was diddling away to himself, making mouth-music, which came to a sudden stop when he ran out of breath. At which point he bowed to the kitchen window where we were watching, before scrambling over the candytuft to come in and get his reward.

He was a tramp, of course, but a performing one. A cut above the rest, he told us, as he accepted some coppers and a slice of bread and cheese. 'I gie value for siller. I'll do the sword dance, if ye like, wi' the poker an' tongs, ance I've got ma braith back.'

Yorky, too – one of our regulars – sometimes entertained us by waving his arms wildly and giving us a long screed. Shakespeare, he said, but it sounded more like mumbo-jumbo to us.

Then came the wonderful day when I was taken by my parents all the way to Edinburgh to see real drama in a real theatre. We were to go to something called a matinée. The word itself was fascinating enough, let alone the journey to Auld Reekie, beginning as it did with a dawn drive to Jedburgh to catch the local train, then changing along the line to the express which whirled us to Waverley.

The theatre! Never had I seen anything like it, even in my imagination. The plush seats, the rich red curtains hiding the stage, the whirls and whorls on the ceiling, the exciting sounds of the orchestra tuning up, and the audience. I wondered if the people in the boxes were lords and ladies. Even the programme sellers seemed to be part of the play, and I would not have cared if the curtain never rose, there was so much to see all around me.

But it did go up after the orchestra had played a haunting overture, and from then on I was in a trance. It was better even than listening to the lame actor at Southdean. Here were real characters living out their private lives before our very eyes, involving us all in their joys and sorrows. Sometimes I felt like an eavesdropper and turned my head away at the love-scenes. I thought we ought not to be looking and listening. There was no privacy on the stage.

The heroine, poor pathetic creature, was in a state of agitation from start to finish. I longed to comfort her as she sank to her knees, sobbing bitterly and calling upon God to help her. She carried a baby in her arms, dressed in long clothes, hiding it against her breast so that we could not see its face. I wondered if it was a real baby or only a wax doll like the Holy Child in the procession.

I cannot recollect the plot, only that the heroine had walked all the way from Scotland to London still carrying the bairn in her arms to plead with the queen for a reprieve for her sister. (Later on, I learned that the play was about Jeannie Deans and her sister Effie, from Sir Walter Scott's *Heart of Midlothian*). There was a heart-rending scene with the heroine kneeling before the throne – or was it only a chair? – where the queen sat in full regalia.

Was the reprieve granted? I hope so. All I can remember is the actress's wild hair, her ragged skirt, her bare feet and her cries of supplication as she clutched the far-travelled baby to her bosom.

There was an interval halfway through when the lights suddenly went up and we were jerked from one world to another. It was almost like being reborn. The usherettes brought round little trays with cups of tea and biscuits while the orchestra played some waltz tunes heard above the tinkle of teaspoons. All very well for us, but what about the poor heroine still stumbling along the hard road to London?

It was surprising to see how the cast suddenly sloughed off their stage-characters and became themselves when they took their curtain calls at the end. Even the dead walked, while friends and foes alike joined hands and came forward to bow. Jeannie and Effie Deans, all smiles now, and minus the baby, dropped graceful curtsies in their ragged gowns, holding hands on equal terms with the queen herself.

It was all very puzzling. Fantasy and reality merging into one. It was not till I got home and heard Jessie saying, 'Dinna mak' a slaister on the kitchen flair,' that I got a grip on myself.

She, at least, was real enough.

10. Playing a Part

But were we not all playing a part most of the time? Putting it on.

Most people's lives, I suspected, were made up of a mixtures of reality and pretence. Even Liz-Ann, the Cairthorse, had a private paradise of her own, far removed from the humdrum routine of rubbing and scrubbing. Sometimes I saw a secret smile lighting up her plain face as she polished the kitchen cutlery with emery paper.

'What are you thinking about, Liz-Ann?' I once asked her.

The Cairthorse gave a guilty start and dropped a fork on the floor. Her face went scarlet as if her most personal secrets had been revealed. 'I'm no' lettin' on,' she said and turned her head away to hide her thoughts from my prying eyes.

I felt ashamed that I had tried to probe. Our thoughts were amongst the few precious private things we possessed. Luckily, no one could tune into them like the wireless.

Ours – the wireless – frequently broke down. The aerial, trailing over a high tree, was battered by winds, or became entangled with bullocks' horns, so that all we could hear were strange sounds called atmospherics. But when it was working at full strength Father liked to share its highlights with the folk on the farm.

'That's the Savoy Orpheans' Dance Band,' he would tell them, turning it up to its loudest pitch. 'All the way from London.'

The hinds shook their heads in disbelief. It was a bit too much to swallow. A dance band playing in London and being heard at Overton Bush.

'Haggis-bags!' said the herd (which was his strongest word for 'rubbish!'). 'Thon's a terrible dirdum.' He had managed all these years without the Savoy Orpheans and saw no reason to enthuse about them now.

The men were all invited in on Armistice Day to 'hear the silence', standing in an uneasy group with their bunnets under their arms. The silence seemed to last for hours and I never knew where to look when the Last Post was sounded. The men stared at the floor, and I tried to think of the soldiers who never came marching home. Black Sandy, who drove the school bus, had been at Wypers and sometimes sang about 'Mademoiselle from Armentiers'. His French accent should have been better than mine since he had actually lived with the Froggies, but it was terrible. Miss Crichton would have killed him.

It was easy to see that Father played many roles, apart from being Boss on the farm. That, I think, was the one he liked least. Often he had to pull himself together to remember his responsibilities and would sooner have been singing 'O Dem Golden Slippers' in the Darkey Troupe.

They still talk about it today in the Borders, Father and his Darkey Troupe. There were others involved of course, but he was the guiding spirit. Auld Baldy-Heid, his face as black as soot, plonking away at a banjo. The gardener from the Big Hoose dressed in the laird's pyjamas (most working-men did not possess such garments, preferring nightsarks instead) trying to talk in a Sambo accent while telling his terrible jokes.

'Say, Boss, what am de best way to make de Swiss roll?'

'I dunno, Sambo,' Father would say solemnly, staring at him with soot-rimmed eyes. 'What am de best way to make de Swiss roll?'

'Push him down de mountainside. He-he-he!'

The audience loved it and Father was in his element.

Sometimes the hinds would chap at the kitchen door and ask where he was.

'Up in the greenhoose,' Jessie would tell them.

I would be sent to the top garden to fetch him. Maybe he would be sorting out seedlings or just sitting in a wheelbarrow amongst a clutter of plant pots, playing the jew's harp, reading the Squeaker, or just away in a world of his own.

'What aboot the Lang Field, then?' Tam or Wull would ask him once I had brought him back to life. There was no sir-ing given or expected.

'The Lang Field?' Oh ay, I'll take a look at it.'

Sometimes I saw him writing things on his cuffs. A new joke for Sambo, maybe, or a reminder about the Lang Field?

Occasionally on market days he called for me at the Grammar School gates and drove me home in the motor. I felt quite proud to be going in it instead of the bus, but there was no guarantee I would get home any quicker. Often the bus shot past us when we were stuck on a brae, with Tin Lizzie rolling back and Father shouting, 'Whoa!' as he struggled with the gears.

Mother, like everyone else, had a private and a public face. Sometimes she looked at herself in the small keeking-glass on the kitchen wall, and suddenly the harassed housewife was transformed into a young girl. Fair-haired round-cheeked, rosy-lipped, and with a sparkle in her eyes. She would pull herself up, smile at her image as if flirting with herself. 'Mirror, mirror, on the wall.' Then the clumsy Cairthorse would drop a dish on the floor, and the image, like the plate, was shattered.

I think Mother saw herself as a lady. Certainly she looked like one when dressed up in her fur coat. She always wore good shoes and gloves. And attractive hats which Father bought in a big shop in Edinburgh. I often wondered if he tried them on himself. They always suited her, and had a bit of style about them.

I can see her swathed in a motoring veil, sitting beside Father as they set off on a private jaunt on their own, This is what they liked best, to go off unencumbered by any small fry. On such occasions I felt rejected and in need of compensation. Something sweet to eat. I craved for toffee and would coax Jessie to make a boiling, or, breaking all rules, would make it myself which usually ended with the pan being burnt and the toffee uneatable.

When darkness fell I went and peered out of the dining-room window looking for the car-lights. I would stay there for ages sucking burnt toffee and seeing visions in the starry sky. When the lights at last appeared I felt a great sense of relief and shouted, 'They're coming!' Then I would settle down to my book as if I was indifferent to their comings and goings. Let them see how little I cared where they had been or how late they returned!

We were all shut away inside ourselves like crabs. What lay under Jessie's hard exterior? There must have been something there for she read Annie S. Swan's stories and gave a sigh of satisfaction when they ended happily.

'That's Alison Macrae settled doon wi' John Lindsay at last. Ay, it's a guid match, that.' She nodded her approval as she laid the *People's Friend* aside, and for a time there was a faraway look in her eyes. Was she perhaps seeing herself as Alison settling down with John to a life of married bliss? No use asking her; I would only get a skelp on the lug.

What a pity none of us ever really knew each other.

The only person who gave way to his feelings and revealed every thought that came into his daft head was Yorky the tramp. He did not care who was listening. Anybody or nobody. He wandered the countryside, swiping at imaginary enemies with his walking-stick and roaring out his ramblings to hedges, ditches, cats, dogs and people alike.

'You!' he would shout to me if we met face to face. 'A piece of rubbish. You're all rubbish, nothing but rubbish. I,' he would go on, pulling himself upright, 'I am the king of the roads. What do *you* know about anything? Nothing! Now, I'll tell you what *I* think . . .'

And he would, with so much mixed-up rhetoric that I was none the wiser at the end than the beginning, but it seemed to do Yorky good to get it off his chest. After a spout of speech he would calm down and a saner look come into his wild eyes. 'I want tea, bread and cheese and a place to sleep. You'll see to it.' He was like an overlord instructing one of his varlets. No begging or mooching. Yorky demanded attention. It was his right as king of the roads. He had played the part for so long that it was second nature to him.

What part did I play?

It varied from day to day. Mostly I saw myself through rose-coloured spectacles, a ministering angel beloved by everyone, so helpful that the world could never have got on without me. I could hear people singing my praises. 'Her! She's perfect. Never thinks of herself, always of other folk. Worth her weight in gold.' I basked in their adulation, every word deserved.

It was as well Jessie was there to push me off my high horse. 'Here, you!' slapping a wet dishcloth into my hand. 'Stop smirkin' to yoursel' an' wesh the dishes. Ye're nae ornament so ye micht as weel be usefu'.' Certainly Jessie's spectacles were made of plain glass.

I made a conscious effort to be a different person at the Grammar School, curbing my country ways and striving to keep in line with the others. I felt quite sophisticated as I strolled up the High Street at lunchtime. A townee, accustomed to traffic, more or less neatly dressed, recognised by the shopkeepers. What if they saw the real me running wild on the farm, swinging on gates, climbing trees, riding workhorses and stooking corn? Try as I did to get rid of them, there were still many rough edges.

Several times I had been invited to visit classmates' homes. Their lives were so different from mine that I would have been ashamed to return the invitations. Town households ran on smoother lines. No hitty-missy meals, no clattering sounds from the kitchen, no shouts from Jock-the-herd: 'Man-lassie, come oot an' help to weir in the soo.' No Cairthorses dropping dishes on the floor.

All the same I did not enjoy my visits. The houses were too overheated, the windows too closely shut, the rooms cluttered with furnishings. At the tea-table I could never do justice to the lavish meals, nor could I just sit still and watch, for the conversation was directed at me as the visitor. I racked my brains for something bright to say.

'The cow's going to calve.'

'Oh yes, dear?' A blank look from my hostess. 'Have another piece of pie. No? What a poor appetite you have for a country lass.'

A country lass. That was how they saw me, in spite of all my efforts to play a more polished part. What would they think if they saw the real me at home?

The day inevitably came.

It was forced upon me by none other than Lucy, the ewe-lamb, who had long been hinting that she would love to visit the farm and was consumed with curiosity to see how I lived 'out in the wilds'. She visualised it, I felt sure, as a kind of zoo with myself as one of the inmates, shut up in a cage or a pigsty.

'My dad's got a new car and we always go for a run on Saturday. We could easily come.'

I ignored all her hints. Then they became demands. 'You'll *have* to ask us. I want to come.' Lucy usually got what she wanted in the end.

One day she told me triumphantly, 'It's all arranged! We're coming on Saturday. Me and my mum and dad in the new car.'

And that was it.

There was no putting her off. I would sooner it had been Jeannie, another of my classmates, who was nicer in every way, but her father did not own a car, old or new.

'They'll just have to take us as they find us,' Mother said when I broke the news to her. She went the length of baking dropscones and a sponge-cake, but there was no setting out of the best china or the lace-edged tablecloth. It was the Cairthorse's afternoon off, and Jessie was working in the fields. So we would be left to serve ourselves with as little ceremony as possible. What would the ewe-lamb, accustomed to a maid with cap and apron, think of our common ways?

I was the only worried one. The others pursued their normal ways, Father digging in the garden in his shirt-sleeves, Mother gathering the eggs from the henhouses with a basket over her arm, and not even changed into her best blouse.

I ran about the house trying to tidy it up, straightening cushions, picking the baby's bricks from the floor, dusting the sideboard, putting a vase of flowers on the table. I wished the visitors could have seen it properly set with a snowy-white cloth and the silver epergne in the centre.

All of a sudden I felt ashamed of myself, realising I was in danger of becoming a snob. On an impulse I tore off my shoes and stockings in disgust and went about barefoot as I always did on Saturdays. Let them think what they liked. Who cared? I had a good mind to go and sit beside Grumphy in the pigsty. Instead, I found myself keeping a watchful eye on the road to see if the car was coming.

At last.

'That's them!' I cried, scurrying out in my bare feet.

'Ay!' said father, calmly laying down his spade as the car purred into sight, scattering cocks and hens out of its path. 'Hullo,' he called to the visitors, rolling down his sleeves and going forward to meet them.

'What a road!' groaned Lucy's father in an aggrieved voice, leaning out of the driving-seat to examine the mud on his car wheels. 'You should get something done about it.'

'So I should,' agreed Father evenly. 'I hope the car's none the worse. Come away in.'

They trooped out of the car and I was horrified to see Father leading them in by the kitchen door. 'It's nearer!' I felt my face flush as I saw them stare at the stone floor, the hams hanging from the ceiling, the meal-bins, the sheep-dip calendar on the wall, then at my bare feet.

The ewe-lamb was dressed to kill in a blue velvet frock, a straw hat with ribbons floating down the back, white socks and patent leather shoes. Quite the lady. Jessie would have designated her a wee madam.

'Through here,' called Mother from the dining-room. She had come in from her egg-gathering and was at the table buttering the dropscones. 'You'll be ready for a cup of tea.'

The ewe-lamb did not like dropscones. Nor raspberry jam which was in the middle of the sponge-cake. 'Run and fetch the gooseberry,' Mother told me.

'Don't like gooseberry.'

'Well, what about strawberry? I think there's a pot left in the jam cupboard.'

I went to fetch it and the ewe-lamb graciously accepted a thin piece of bread and butter liberally spread with strawberry jam. Then she partook of a chocolate biscuit, a packet of which mother had produced out of the blue. One, then another, and a third.

'She likes the taste of chocolate,' said her mother, fondly watching every bite. 'It'll do her good. She's a bit delicate, you know.'

'I'm finished,' said Lucy, licking the chocolate from her fingers and shuffling restlessly in her seat.

'Show her round,' said Mother, dismissing me from the table, though I had not sampled the sponge-cake, far less reached the chocolate biscuit stage.

The ewe-lamb followed me around the house, upstairs as well as down. 'What's that?' she asked when we came to the garret door.

'The gaol. I get shut up there sometimes.'

'What for?'

'Being bad.' Though more often I was shut in for doing good deeds that misfired.

Lucy gave me a smug look and said, 'I'm never bad.' I could see her halo shining round her head.

In the parlour she went and thumped on the piano. She could play louder than I did, but no better. Then, having poked into cupboards and presses, pulled out drawers, fingered ornaments, tugged at the bell-rope which jangled unanswered in the kitchen, she asked, 'Is that all?'

'Well, there's outside. Come and see the calves.'

She hung back.

'Will they bite?'

'No, of course not.'

But outside was not a success. She let out a scream the moment the bubblyjock came running to us on his splay feet, and turned up her nose at the smell in the byre. When a calf tried to nibble at her fingers she hit out at it angrily.

'Keep away, you nasty thing!'

There was nothing she liked. The corn-barn with rats rustling in the corner, the henhouse where a clocker was sitting on her clutch of eggs and pecked out at us when disturbed, the pigsty where Grumphy and the piglets were routing about in the swill. Even the prospect of climbing a haystack did not appeal to her. 'Oh no! Not in my good clothes.'

So in the end I gave up and left her to pick her own way through the puddles while I went and sat on the swing. I could see Father showing her parents his sweet-peas in the top garden. He gathered a big bunch for them to take home, and Mother gave them some fresh eggs and butter.

'Come again,' said Mother as they got into the car, but I could hear the false note in her voice. I waved from the swing. The wave, too, was false.

'It must be dreadfully dull for you away out here,' I heard Lucy's mother say.

'We manage,' said Father, closing the door on her.

'You'll remember to get something done about that road,' the ewe-lamb's father said as they were moving off.

'I'll remember,' Father said with no conviction in his voice. 'Safe home!'

When they had gone I wanted to rush forward and thank my parents for putting up with them. I felt proud of Father and Mother for playing their parts so well; but as usual the words stuck in my throat and I could not express my feelings. I realised, though, how lucky I was. *They* were made of the right stuff.

As Father rolled up his sleeves and went back to his gardening and Mother set about clearing the tea-table, I felt increasingly thankful that *I* was not a pampered only child.

11. Change and Decay

I cannot recall being bored as a child; it was not a word in common use in the Borders. But there were times when I desired something different to happen, just to alter the pattern of life a little. Then when it did, it was not what I wanted at all. Go back! Let everything be the same as before!

It even disturbed me at the spring-cleaning when Mother and Jessie shifted the chairs or the piano to different places in the parlour, or when they changed the curtains. I liked the faded ones best. They were old friends, and though they would not be discarded altogether, for doubtless they would be cut up and transformed into a summer frock for me, as well as cushion-covers for the sofa, it took me ages to become accustomed to the new ones.

One of the sad dirges we sang at the kirk warned us about change and decay in all around we see; but I for one kept my eyes firmly shut. All the same, I would be forced to open them soon, for whether I liked it or not, big changes were on the way.

I think I first became aware of them when it was announced that we were to go on holiday that summer to Swinside Townhead.

'Where?' I asked incredulously. For once I did not believe a word Jessie said.

'Soonside Toonheid,' she said, translating it into local language in case I had not comprehended.

'But why on earth . . . ?'

Why on earth go on holiday to that other farm away in the Oxnam district at the back of beyond, which father rented from the great Duke of Roxburghe? The farmhouse was falling to pieces and the grieve and his wife who lived in it were a fushionless pair. The ground was sour and nothing seemed to flourish on the farm. Even the cocks and hens looked peelly-wally.

Father went there once a week or so to keep an eye on things and always came back with furrows on his brow. It was always the same story. Some piece of machinery had broken down, the lackadaisical grieve had forgotten to do this or that. The whining wife with her brood of ailing children did nothing to make things better. Indeed, doing nothing was what they were both best at.

So what kind of holiday was it going to be?

I would sooner have stayed in my castle on the hill or lived up a tree like a squirrel.

It had never mattered at the village school if I could not put up my hand when Auld Baldy-Heid said, 'Hands up those who are going away on holiday.' Most of my classmates just stayed at home and ran wild. The holiday was being away from Auld Baldy-Heid.

But it was different at the Grammar School. Every hand shot up, everyone was going somewhere. One lad, a fellow-sufferer in the Latin class, was going to London to stay with his godmother. (I could not picture what kind of relative *that* was.) Others were going to the sea-side; but the ewe-lamb beat the lot of us by announcing she was being taken abroad by her doting parents. Not just over the Carter Bar into England but to the real Abroad away in a foreign land. We would never hear the end of it.

'Brussels!' she said, looking more than ever like a cat who has licked up all the cream. It was a wonder *she* had no godmother, but it was her father's cousin who lived there. 'Mum and Dad say it will be good for my French. Wait till I come back. Mary-Ann Crichton won't half get a surprise.'

I wondered where she was going. Mary-Ann. Back to her home in Aberdeen, maybe. And the other teachers. What about the science master? If he had been coming with us to the back of beyond the holiday might have been worthwhile.

I avoided the subject but when I was directly faced with it, said defiantly, 'I'm going to Swinside Townhead.'

'Is it in England?' I was asked.

'No, it's in Oxnam.'

'Goodness! you're not going very far,' said Lucy, tossing her ringlets.

Too far for me. 'Could I not just stay at home?' I asked Jessie.

'No! Ye're a' gaun. The hale clamjamfry.' No escape.

It was difficult to fathom the complicated minds of grown-ups, but I gathered it had something to do with Mother being pregnant, though Jessie would never put *that* into words, and something to do with Father deciding at last to take a closer look at what the grieve was doing, or not doing.

So, with little enthusiasm, I gathered together a few possessions and bundled myself along with the rest into the motor. My elder brother and sister, home from their colleges, were to cycle over on their own. Lucky things!

they had real bicycles with proper wheels, tyres, spokes and everything.

'Ta-ta,' I said dismally to Jessie, hovering at the kitchen door. 'I wish we were on our way back.'

'Guid riddance!' she said predictably and waved her apron, but I think at heart she felt sorry for me.

It was worse, much worse, than I had feared. Misery from start to finish. For one thing it rained relentlessly every day, adding to the discomfort of the draughty farmhouse and turning the yard into a quagmire of mud and puddles. The drookit fowls stood about pecking aimlessly in the glaur and hunching their backs, trying to find comfort under their wet feathers.

There was none for me.

Though the droopy grieve and his missis had made an effort to clean the place up – there was an old besom still lying on the sagging sofa beside a pile of unwashed garments which had been hastily tidied into a heap – the whole house smelt foosty, the cracked cups had rims of dirt round the edges, the milk was turned, the fire smoked, and many of the window panes were cracked.

'We meant to get them mended,' apologised the missis, hitching up her torn skirt and fastening it at the waist with a safety-pin, 'but himself has never had time to get round to it. He's been bad with his chest, and then the binder broke down.' On and on, always apologising.

The smoky fire gave out little heat. The sticks were wet. 'Himself forgot to take them under cover. He had to see to the sow when it got lost, and we've run out of coal. We meant to order more, but you know how it is. There's always so much to do.'

And so little done. Jessie would have had a fit if she had seen the ashes still in the grate, rust and dirt everywhere.

When it came to allocating sleeping-quarters there was no place left for me except a bumpy mattress laid on the floor of 'the room' where the windows were stuck and had not been opened for years. But that was the least of it. It was the lost feeling of being in limbo away from anything familiar or any kindred spirit that brought me almost to the depths of despair. I did not know where to turn for comfort.

It was certainly not a bookish household, except for the bible used to prop up the kitchen table. In any case, where could I have sat down quietly to read? The snivelling children swarmed after me like puppies, and the peevish baby, known as the runt (the last of a litter), was teething and let everyone know it. He was a wizened little creature, more like an old man than a baby. I wondered if he could be a changeling and if the Little Folk had stolen the real baby away and left the runt in his place. All the children, poor things, were unattractive, skinny and spotty-faced, dressed in garments handed down one to the other and seldom put in the wash-tub.

Still, it was one of them, the most unattractive, with missing teeth and a 'gleg e'e', like her father's, who helped unknowingly to set me on my road to story-telling.

Elsie always referred to herself in the third person. 'Elthie wanth a thtory,' she would lisp, dumping herself down on the dirty floor at my feet. 'Tell Elthie a thtory.'

She was a little pest but I sympathised with her in a way, knowing my own thirst for stories. It was hard going, for no sooner had I finished one than Elsie would say, 'Elthie wanth another thtory. Tell Elthie . . . '

The rest of the brood, for want of anything better to do, gathered round, too, and sometimes even the runt stopped crying.

The stories were variations of Jessie's milking-time tales, all about beasts. Others I dredged up from somewhere in my head, about tattie-bogles, bubblyjocks and real adventures like the time I got lost in the snow.

Elthie liked that best.

'Again! Elthie wanth the thtory about the thnow.'

I had to tell and re-tell the stories so often that I suddenly decided I might as well write them down. So, with a blunt pencil and pages torn from one of the children's jotters, I started off to become an Author, helped and hindered by Elsie.

'Thtop writing. Elthie wanth a thtory.'

After several disastrous meals Mother took over the cooking and I helped by setting tables and washing dishes, while the missis drooped around in her down-at-heel slippers, shoogling the peevish runt in her arms, with a dummy in his mouth to stem his whines. Now and again she said to herself, 'I must get on,' but she never did.

My elder brother and sister escaped after a couple of days. They just got on to their bikes and cycled home. I would willingly have walked it, over hill and dale, but when I broached the subject Mother said, 'You bide where you are and make yourself useful. You can peel the potatoes.'

One day when there was a faint glimmer of light shining through the rain clouds I put on an old torn waterproof which I found hanging in the lobby. Feeling that I must escape I ran out through the muddy yard up past the cottages and away to the Back of Beyond where there was nothing to see but the Cheviots, a different view from the one at home, but they were the same hills.

I had the vague intention of going on and on and vanishing into the distance, I was so fed up with everything and everybody. Who would miss me, anyway? Jessie maybe and Jock-the-herd. 'Maybe ay and maybe hooch-ay!'

Yet would it not be a pity to end my life before I had fulfilled myself in any way? If God knew every blade of grass and had bothered to count the hairs on my head, surely He must have some purpose for me here on earth. But what?

I was soon to find out.

At first I could not believe my ears when I heard the

sound of moaning, or my eyes when I saw the man lying by the roadside with blood oozing from a deep gash on his brow and his leg doubled up beneath him. His bicycle lay beside him, its wheels buckled and the handlebar twisted. It looked a worse wreck than my old boneshaker at home.

'Are you hurt?' I asked him. A silly question, with blood trickling down his face and him groaning with pain.

'It's ma leg. Canna move it. Fell aff ma bike.'

Small wonder, too, on such a rutted road.

My heart was bumping and I began to panic, wondering what was the best thing to do in such a crisis. At the same time I realised that here at last was a situation where I must show my mettle. 'Use your rummlegumption, lassie.'

The best thing, I decided, would be to run back to the farm as quickly as possible and get the men to come and help. But first I fumbled up my sleeve where I knew I had tucked a hankie. Clean for once, but soon saturated in blood when I took it out and pressed it to the man's brow. He kept hold of it, trying to stem the flow. His face was ashen and I wondered it he was about to faint, or even die.

'Wait here,' I told him. As if he could have moved! 'I'll away and get the men to help. We won't be long.'

'Thanks, lass,' he said faintly.

I sprinted back towards Swinside Townhead faster than I had ever run before, even at the Sports, splashing through puddles, never mind my pounding heart or the stitch in my side. At last I was doing *something*. It seemed miles longer than when I came along the road only a short while ago. I had no purpose in life then. Now I felt like the saviour of all mankind, of one man, anyway. The rain was pouring again. He would get his death of cold if he had to lie helpless there by the wayside for long. Run faster!

At last the cottages came in sight. The first person I saw was the grieve with an old sack over his droopy shoulders, leaning on the garden gate in conversation with Tamson, the Swinside shepherd.

Tamson was not a patch on Jock-the-herd but better than nobody in an emergency and the grieve at any time. So it was to him that I blurted out my story in great gulps of words, not bothering to make them into sentences. But he got the gist of it and said, sensibly enough. 'Ye'd better see the Boss. He's got the motor. Tell him I'll come wi' him.'

Where is he?' I asked urgently.

'Doon at the fermhoose.'

I raced the few hundred yards down to the house and there was Father with the motor at the gate, tinkering with Tin Lizzie's internals.

Once more I told my garbled story. Father, with a dirty rag in his hand, looked at me doubtfully.

'You're not making it up? It's not one of your stories?'

'No, it's not!' I cried, deeply hurt.

Was this all he thought of me? What a reputation! A teller of tarradiddles. But this was no time to take offence.

'It's true!' I insisted, fiercely. 'We'll need to hurry or the man'll bleed to death. Tamson's coming to help. He's waiting up the road.

At last Father seemed to be convinced. He slammed down the bonnet of the car. 'Right! Hop in, lass, and I'll see if she'll start. The rain's got into her.'

The motor was difficult to crank up at the best of times. I waited impatiently while Father turned the starting-handle, listening for the welcome sound of the engine puttering into life. Try, try, try again.

At last. Tin Lizzie took the tremors and began to shudder and shake. Father got into the driving-seat and we set off up the road to find the grieve still leaning on the gate and Tamson ready to shuffle into the back seat. He had brought a length of rope with him, though what he meant to do with it I could only surmise; tie the battered bicycle on to the back of the car, maybe. But it was the thought of the maimed man that was worrying me.

Hurry! Hurry! I prayed that the engine would not stall as we pressed on through the lashing rain past the cottages to the Back of Beyond.

'Just round the next corner,' I cried, shoogling to and fro as if that would make the motor go faster. The windscreen wipers were stuck as usual and it was difficult to see out. But what was there to see?

Nothing!

When we reached the spot where the man had been lying there was no trace of him, not even the wreck of his bicycle.

Could I have made a mistake? Was it round the next corner?

'No, it was here,' I insisted to myself and to Father who was banging on the brakes.

One thing was clear. He was not here now. Not a sign of him. Tamson scrambled out, clutching the rope and glowering at me as if he was about to twist it round my neck and hang me from the nearest tree; but it was Father's look and his words to the shepherd that hurt me most.

'Sorry about this, Tamson. She's a daft, lassie, always imagining things. Her head's full of nonsense.'

My lip began to tremble. 'It's not nonsense,' I protested, and then realised it was no use. I was completely discredited with no means of defending myself. Completely bamboozled, too, for how could the man have vanished and him so badly hurt? I *knew* he had been there, but how could I convince them?

I could see by the black looks on the men's faces that anything I said would only fan their anger into flames. And now I began to have doubts myself. Was I really a story-teller, making it all up? No, I was not! I felt for my hankie up my sleeve. It was not there. It was no proof, of course, but it gave me a modicum of assurance. I searched the roadside for any sign of blood, but the rain must have washed it away.

To add to the general misery the motor refused to re-start. Tamson and father had to push her to the side of the road. 'She's maybe needing petrol,' Father said. He never forgot to give Flora her nosebag but sometimes overlooked the fact that Tin Lizzie, too, required regular sustenance. 'I think I left some in a tin in the shed.'

'I'll go back and get it,' I volunteered, hoping to regain a measure of respect. Father did not indicate his approval or otherwise of my offer, so I walked back in the pouring rain like a bedraggled sparrow. The fact that I was soaked through to the skin did not bother me. I was too busy puzzling over the affair and smarting at Father's dismissal of me as a daft lassie.

How did he know what kind of a person I was? I could have analysed him, in a sort of a way, for I had watched and studied him closely. And did *he* not elaborate sometimes his dreams and his stories. But the unfair thing was that *I* had not elaborated. I had told the plain truth, though there was nobody to know that, except God if He had been watching.

As I was plodding towards the cottages I heard a familiar rattling sound behind me. Tin Lizzie chugging along like a steam roller. Father did not stop to pick me up. He did not even toot or wave, but swept by splashing up a great stream of water which caught me fair and square in the face. I was so wet already I hardly noticed it, and to do him justice he may have realised that, once he had got it started, it would have been imprudent of him to stop the temperamental motor again, and I was near enough my destination, anyway. At least I would not have to trudge back with the tin of petrol.

When I entered the untidy kitchen the grieve's children

were crawling about on the floor playing with a scabby kitten.

'Elthie wanth a thtory,' she said, clutching at my wet legs.

But I said 'No' in a firm voice, determined to live down my reputation. 'No more stories!'

12. Revelations

It was a few days later that Mother said to me, 'Dress yourself properly. We're going out to tea.' She did not say where.

Dressing properly meant putting on shoes and stockings, my one good frock, brushing and replaiting my tousled hair, seeing that my face and hands were clean, and getting myself into the right mood for company. Mother looked the part when she put on her costume and a little toque hat with a veil. Father changed into his dark suit, and we were off.

I sat in the back of the motor wondering in which direction we would go. Up past the cottages to the Back of Beyond. I averted my gaze when we came to the spot where I had left the man lying by the roadside. I was still confused at the outcome of that dark episode. It rankled so much that I tried to put it out of my mind.

In any case, I was soon kept fully occupied, getting out to open the creaky gates barring our way across the side-road. Getting in and out of the motor was easier than jumping in and out of the gig, but opening the gates always presented a problem, for some were fastened with complicated cleeks and others tied with bindertwine. It was a heinous sin to leave them open, so I had to wait till Tin Lizzie was driven through and refasten them before taking my place in the motor again. I was being useful, if nothing else, though the operation did my clean stockings no good. The ground was still squelchy, and muddy water splattered up on me from the motor's wheels.

We were aiming, I could see, for a remote farmhouse hidden amongst trees in the foothills of the Cheviots where a friend of Father's lived with his prim sisters. Nothing prim about their brother. He had the reputation of being the wild man of the Borders, especially when he had the drink taken. No opening or shutting of gates for him when he was rollicking home late at night after one of his sprees. Singing at the pitch of his voice he drove his battle-stained car at them like a battering-ram and went straight through, leaving one of his men to come and repair the damage next morning.

His exploits, vastly exaggerated, were the speak of the countryside and could have filled pages of the Squeaker each week. Everybody liked him, no matter how much they tut-tutted. His swashbuckling attitude to life gave a bit of colour to the Oxnam district.

He seemed sober and upright enough today as he came forward to greet us and help Mother out of the car. But it was not him I looked at. It was another man, one of our host's farm-hands, who came limping forward. A man with a bruise on his forehead. The man I had left lying by the roadside.

'It's *him*!' I burst out, feeling a great load falling off my shoulders, now that I could prove – if only to myself – that I was not just a daft lassie making up silly stories.

'Hullo, lass.' The man came nearer, put his hand in his

pocket and brought out my handkerchief, the bloodstains removed. 'This is yours. Mr Will, the master, came by in his car and picked me up; but thanks for your help.'

'Daft deevil!' said Mr Will, the master (as if *he* had never strayed from the paths of righteousness himself). 'His bike'll never be the same again, and he's as lame as an old horse.'

'See!' I said triumphantly to Father, showing him my hankie in case he had not understood the whole import of the tale; but if I was waiting for him to say 'Sorry!' I waited in vain.

Neither he nor Mother made any comment. I could understand them, I suppose, for company manners had taken over, and the ladies of the house had come to the door to welcome their visitors. Family affairs must take a back seat. Perhaps they would mention it later on, on the way home, but I thought it unlikely. The subject was closed, so I just crept back into my shell and shook hands with the Misses Something who each made the predictable comment, 'My! isn't she shooting up?' before ushering us into the house.

They were a 'bein' family; that is, comfortably-off, and the house showed it. Everything was good, though old-fashioned, and the ladies kept up some sort of style even though they lived so far away in the wilderness.

We sat in the drawing-room (all plush cushions, foot-stools, antimacassars and brocade curtains) except brother William who roamed around like a stray dog not knowing where to settle. When he came near me he tugged my pigtails for something to do, and now and again his sisters would say, 'Sit down, William, and take your ease,' but *they* had had more practice, I could see, at sitting still and making polite conversation.

In their young days they had been sent to a Ladies' Seminary where they had learned good manners and never forgotten them. Not so Mr Will, who did not care a button for social frills.

Sometimes he said an aside to Father about farm affairs, but it was the sisters who kept the conversational ball rolling, tossing it back and forth to each other as if playing ping-pong, with an occasional side-throw to Mother. The weather kept them going for ages. Hadn't it been dreadful? All that rain! They had been thinking of taking a trip to Edinburgh and maybe staying there for a fortnight with some cousins. I saw a 'Good riddance!' look on brother William's face, but he restrained himself from picking up the dropped ball.

When the tea came in with all the paraphernalia of sugar-tongs, slop-basin, and wee lace-edged table-napkins, he refused the delicate china cup that was handed to him. 'Tea! Can't stand the stuff!' But he did his best in his clumsy fashion to hand round the plates of food. When he passed me the seed-cake I wished I had the courage to say, 'Seed-cake! Can't stand the stuff!' but I meekly accepted it and tried to get rid of the seeds as surreptitiously as I could.

The family photograph album was lying conpicuously on a nearby table. Were we going to have to suffer *that* after tea? It was more than brother William could bear.

'Come on, John,' he said, tugging at Father's arm. 'Ben to the parlour,' where, no doubt, he kept a stronger tipple than tea.

Father did his best not to seem too eager, but went off with a look of relief on his face after excusing himself to his hostesses. How I wished I could follow suit!

Now that the men were away the ladies' tongues were loosened and they began to talk more freely to Mother. Mostly about brother William and his exploits, though I doubt if they knew the half.

'He's such a good lad, William, but a little wild, you know. Sometimes he gets carried away . . .'

Mother nodded understandingly while I watched the ladies leaning towards her as their talk became more confidential. Like hens confabbing together, clucking about the absent cockerel. After a time I did not strain my ears to listen, though the word 'baby' seemed to have entered into the conversation. The sisters were whispering something about Mother's pregnancy, too delicate for my ears to hear.

The eldest gave a warning glance at her sister and said to me, 'Would you like to go through to the kitchen, dear, and see Aggie?'

'Oh yes, please!'

I was on my feet, almost tripping over a sheepskin rug in my haste to get away. Along a dark passage past the parlour door from behind which I could hear the cheerful sounds of talk, laughter, and glasses clinking. Father and Mr Will were getting on a treat.

Aggie's kitchen was cosier than ours at home. There was a carpet on the floor, easy-chairs to sit in, and pot-plants on the window-sill. Aggie, as plump as a partridge, was sitting with her feet on the fender, with a cup of tea beside her and her skirt turned back to keep it from being scorched. She was in her good black afternoon uniform with a white cap on her head, but had taken off her starched apron while she sat at ease.

'Are they needin' mair scones, or wantin' the teapot filled?'

'No, they're not wanting anything, Aggie. I just came to see you.'

I sat down on the rug beside her, not caring whether I was scorched or not. This was my proper place. I could equate with Aggie better than with her perjinct mistresses.

'My! ye're fairly shootin' up. Hoo are ye keepin'?'

'I'm fine. How are you, Aggie?'

'Oh, I'm jacko!' (Jacko, I assumed, meant she was in

good fettle.) 'Come on, gie's your crack. Did ye hear. what happened to Pete? Fell aff his bike an' hurt his leg. Maister Will had to pick him up an' hurl him hame. A'weel, it's often happened the ither way roond . . . '

It was no use embarking on *my* story, so I sat and listened to Aggie's version. Then she asked, 'An' hoo's Jessie?'

My heart gave a lift even at the mention of Jessie's name. I knew the two had been in a 'place' together in their young days in a big house where one was a parlourmaid and the other a tablemaid, I think, though I never knew the distinction, or which was which; but they had been good friends.

'Tell her I was askin' for her.'

'Oh yes, I will, Aggie.'

A reminiscent look came into Aggie's eyes. 'The laughs we had!' said she, beginning to shake with laughter at the recollection.

'Mercy me!' I suddenly saw a new Jessie. Laughing!

'Ay, she was a great lass, Jessie. The lads were a' after her like a swarm o' bummy-bees.'

This time I was speechless.

'Thoosands o' them,' said Aggie lavishly. 'You ask her aboot Andy.'

'Andy?'

'Ay, he was the ane!'

'What about him, Aggie?'

'I'm no' tellin', said Aggie with a look of having gone too far.

Certainly she had whetted my appetite and given me food for thought for many a long day to come. Jessie laughing and larking with the lads!

'Here, wait!' said Aggie, suddenly shaking down her skirt and rising from her seat. She went through into her little bedroom and I heard her opening and shutting drawers. When she came back there were two faded photographs in her hand. This was better than the family album in the drawing-room. Brother William on his first pony, a long-ago Sunday School picnic, the whole family pictured outside the front door, a fierce-looking photograph of brother William in rugby-kit.

'Let me see, Aggie! Let me see!' I almost snatched them out of her hand, but she put one of them carefully in her skirt pocket before showing me the first. A picture of herself and Jessie in caps and aprons, their arms entwined, staring at the camera with giggly-looking smiles on their faces.

I hardly looked at Aggie. It was Jessie, the young Jessie, I wanted to see. Oh yes, that was my Jessie all right. How handsome she was. Not pretty, but something better. Dark hair with a crinkle in it, black flashing eyes, and a gypsyish look about her. But it was the smile that transformed her. I could almost swear as I peered closer at the picture that there was a dimple in her cheeks. Jessie! I could not help it. There was a lump in my throat. In another moment I would be 'bubblin' an' greetin'.'

I swallowed hard and said, 'Show me the other one, Aggie,' but while she was still fumbling for it the bell rang. Drawing-room. There was a row of them all marked. Dining-room, parlour, drawing-room, best bedroom. Aggie hastily put on her apron.

'I'll awa' an' see what the gentry want. Push the kettle nearer the fire, lassie, in case the teapot needs refilled.'

I sat there on the rug, thinking and wondering. How little one really knows of other folk. If it came to that, nobody knew *me*. But Jessie! How many more revelations were to come?

'Show me the other photo,' I begged Aggie when she came back carrying the tea-tray.

But Aggie, it seemed, had had second thoughts somewhere along the dark passage to the drawing-room.

'No, I'll no'. I daurna. Jessie wad kill me. Ye'd better

gang, lassie. They're for off.' She hauled me up from the rug. 'I tell ye what, you ask Jessie yoursel' aboot Andy.'

Would I ever dare?

The bell rang again; the signal that I had to go.

I threw my arms around Aggie and kissed her. I could never have done *that* with Jessie. But though Aggie was softer and more approachable, I knew for certain that I liked Jessie better.

There were only a few days left of the 'holiday'. The change of air, though it was only such a short distance away, had been intended to do us all good, and particularly to set Mother up for the birth of the baby later on in the year. Instead, it had been a disaster. We all looked worse. Peaky, short-tempered, and as for me I had caught 'beasts' in my hair. They had to be combed out with a small-tooth comb soaked in paraffin, a painful and degrading operation. I longed to be bald like Jock-the-herd.

Under Mother's supervision the farmhouse had begun to look a little tidier, but it was only on the surface. It would revert to a pigsty as soon as we were out of sight. I had a feeling, too, having overheard some whispered conversations between my parents, that the long-overdue chop was to come, if Father could brace himself sufficiently to administer it.

It would hurt him more than the easy-osy grieve, and I jaloused that when the time came he would dip his hand deep into his pocket to soften the blow and tide the fushionless family over their troubles.

But at least I had culled something out of that bleak holiday, if nothing else a collection of the 'thtorieth' I had made up to amuse Elsie and the rest of the brood. About Willy Weasel, Sandy Squirrel, Tommy Thrush, and wee Mary McFairy who had tartan wings and spoke with a lisp. They were to become the nucleus later on of tales broadcast in Children's Hour.

13. Crisis!

Home again!

Oh! it was great to turn in at our own roadend and rattle up the bumpy track past the cottages. Yes! there was Mrs Thing at the door shaking her rag rug, and her neighbour down on her hunkers pipe-claying the door-step. We waved to them and they waved to us, not as if they were saluting the gentry. Far from it.

'That's them hame.'

We were just them.

Now we were in sight of the farmhouse. It was exactly the same as when we had left it – what else did I expect? – with smoke belching cheerfully from the kitchen chimney and the garden a tangle of flowers and weeds. Even the nettles looked nice.

The sun which had been missing all the time we were away shone out to welcome us home, but I did not need it to make my spirits soar. The very sight of Blackie sitting on the kitchen wall and the bubblyjock chasing a banty across the yard made me want to break into song. Polly Wolly Doodle! Anything would do.

My high spirits took a downward plunge when I discovered Jessie was not in the kitchen. Only the Cairthorse clattering about in her clogs.

'She's roond at the wesh-hoose.'

Jessie had left her mark on the kitchen table to welcome us home: a freshly baked batch of toddies, fadges and dropscones. There was a savoury smell from one of the pots by the fire. Stovies.

A picture-postcard lay on the table addressed to me, with a foreign stamp on it, the first I had ever received from Abroad. The ewe-lamb had written it in French, more or less, using the few phrases she had learned from Miss Crichton.

'*Comment allez-vous?*' As if she cared! '*Je suis bon. Le soleil est chaud ici. Beaucoup d'aventures. Je suis* enjoying *moimême . . .*'

I put it aside to study later, once I had seen Jessie. My first priority. Before dashing round to the wash-house I had a word with the Cairthorse.

'How are you, Liz-Ann?'

'No' bad.'

It was as much as I expected from the Cairthorse who would never admit to being jacko, like Aggie.

'Has anything been happening while we've been away?'

'Nut a thing.'

But she would have said that if the house had been burned down and the herd eaten by cannibals. It was only when her lad, George, was mentioned that Liz-Ann showed a glimmer of animation. I always thought of him as Gorge, which was how she spelled his name in the few painfully composed letters I had helped her to write, usually making an assignation at the crossroads.

George, as far as I knew, never wrote to her, but they had an understanding, and Liz-Ann had started sewing for her bottom drawer. A teacloth embroidered with clumsy lazy-daisy stitches, and a goonie, with lace round the edges, that would have fitted a baby elephant.

'I'm away round to the wash-house,' I told her.

'Uh-huh! Awa' ye go.'

There was something in the way she said it that made me take a closer look at the Cairthorse. She turned her face away but not before I noticed that her eyes were red and she appeared to be snivelling. Was it only one of her sniffy colds or had something dreadful happened to her lad?

'How's George?' I asked her.

'No' bad.'

'Have you seen him, Liz-Ann?'

'No, I've nut. I've no' been off.'

'But you'll be off tomorrow. Will you be meeting him then?'

'I might.'

Only might!

The snivel became more pronounced. It was not just a cold. Then suddenly she turned about and faced me.

'Jessie thinks I'm daft,' she burst out. (Well! we all thought *that*. Nobody could deny.) But there was more to it. 'She says I'm aff ma heid gaun wi' a lad like George.'

'Why?'

'She says there's naethin' in him.' Liz-Ann gulped. 'She ca'd him a spindly wee runt, an' she says naebody else wad look at him twice.' Liz-Ann echoed Jessie's words as if she were repeating the catechism. 'She says I should hae mair sense than rin efter the likes o' him. It'll never come to naethin'. He's no' worth a hait.' A hait being a minute particle.

'He is so!' I cried out, thinking of the lazy-daisy stitches and the voluminous nightgown. The poor creature looked so miserable that I longed to give her some grain of comfort. 'George is all right. He's nice.' I laid it on a bit thick. 'Ever so nice!'

I had only seen George once at the crossroads, pushing his bicycle and walking more or less beside the Cairthorse, together and yet not together, not looking or speaking to each other. Right enough, he was undersized and plain as porridge, but Liz-Ann was no raving beauty herself, and if they were fond of each other what did it matter? I thought of Mr Smith, the science master, with his wispy hair and bulging waistcoat. He was no Sir Galahad, yet how willingly I would have met *him* at the crossroads.

For the first time in my life I felt my birse rising against Jessie. She was wrong. Instinctively, I knew it; and though I felt a traitor, talking against her behind her back, I said so flat out.

'She's wrong! Don't you listen to Jessie, Liz-Ann. It's your business. It has nothing to do with her. Never heed what she says. George is all right. He's better . . .' Better than nothing, I was going to say, but stopped myself in time.

The Cairthorse began to knuckle away her tears as I continued with my advice. 'Just you go and meet him tomorrow. You will, won't you, Liz-Ann?'

'Ay, I wull.'

She gave a great sigh and stopped snivelling. Good for me, I thought! At the same time I felt guilty about Jessie.

'She'll likely be needin' mair sape,' said the Cairthorse, handing me a large bar of carbolic. 'Will ye tak' it roond to her?'

I took the soap and rushed away round to the wash-house, forgetting everything except the joyful prospect of seeing her again. Jessie! Jessie!

There she was, my anchor in life, the same yesterday, today and forever. No hugs or kisses, though I longed to throw myself into her arms. A look was enough. At least she gave me that; a long steady look that said everything, and then she went on with her work.

She was possing the clothes in a big tub, thumping the dirt out of them with a woden poss-stick as if she was giving them their licks. 'Take that! And that!'

She had been using the scrubbing-board, too. I could see that her hands were soft and wrinkled from immersion in soapy water. Nearby some sheets were boiling and bubbling in a pot which spilled over now and again, sending trickles of hot suds along the floor.

The wash-house was only a shed in the steading which the hinds used for odd jobs during wet weather. The turnip-cutter stood in one corner and the cross-cut saw in another beside Jessie's mangle. Sometimes the men came here to make straw ropes, but not if Jessie was in residence. Today it was her domain.

Having recovered from the first upsurge of pleasure at seeing her again, I stood back to take a closer look at her, trying to recapture the young Jessie I had seen in the faded photo. Yes, she was there all right, the same in essence, though her hair was steel grey and the soft look had given way to one of rigid repression. What matter that her cheeks were no longer smooth? I knew and loved every wrinkle in her face.

'What are ye glowerin' at, wumman?' she said, aware of my stare.

'I'm just looking.'

'A'weel, hand me the sape.'

She went on possing, while I stood there in one of my half-dwams, pondering on what might have happened if she had married her Andy, and why she hadn't. Maybe someone had turned *her* against him, as she had tried to do with the Cairthorse.

'It's God's will,' she often said, all planned from above.

'Nonsense!' I cried out, emerging from my dwam and suddenly realising it was not God who made a mess of folk's lives. It was folk themselves. Even splendid folk like Jessie.

At that moment I saw the light, and my life was changed for ever.

The wash-house was my Road to Damascus.

That moment of re-birth is so firmly etched in my mind that I have only to smell soapy-suds and I am back there hearing the thud-thud of the poss-stick and the bubbling of the boiler. A hen who had been cackling in the corner came half-running, half-flying past me on her way out to the yard, exuberant after delivering her egg.

Not as exuberant as I, suddenly relieved of a thousand chains that had been binding me, stultifying my young life till I was not myself but merely a pale shadow of everyone around me, especially anyone in authority. But from now on it would be different.

I would be *me*.

There is a time for everything, the Good Book tells us. This was my time. Why it should have happened now I had no idea. It must have been building up inside me for long enough, brought to a head perhaps by the dreary holiday at Swinside and by poor snivelling Liz-Ann.

It was not just that, it was everything in the past, all the times I had been put down by my superiors and made to feel inadequate. A daft bairn with no rummlegumption. Suddenly in a split-second I saw myself inside-out. Flyped, as Jessie was flyping one of Father's shirts before shoving it into the tub; and inside I was no worse than anyone else. No better, maybe; but as good as. Why had I never thought of it before? There was no time now to think it out properly, to pull the thread through the needle. I would have to go away by myself, straighten it out and tie a knot at the end; but the difficult part was over. I had found the needle and inserted the thread through the eye.

Meantime I tried to put my new-found confidence into practice.

'Jessie!'

'Ay, what?'

I took the plunge.

'He can't help being a spindly wee runt,' I burst out. It was not the Cairthorse I was defending as much as trying to pit myself against authority.

'What are ye bletherin' aboot?' said Jessie, not taking much notice of me.

'George.'

'Whae?'

Jessie gave me one of her looks but I stood my ground.

'Liz-Ann's lad.'

'Her!'

'Yes, her!' I said defiantly. 'She's a human being.'

'She's a human disaster. D'ye ken what she did the ither day? Spilt a hale pail-fou o' milk on the clean kitchen flair, an' she's broken the back-kitchen windy an' an ashet, forbye.'

'No point in breaking her heart, too.'

Jessie paused in her possing to take a closer look at me.

'What's up wi' ye, ye silly lassie? Are ye no' feelin' richt?'

'I'm feeling fine.' Never felt better!

'A'weel, ye're no' lookin' it,' declared Jessie. 'Ye're peely-wallier than ever. A dose o' castor-ile's what ye're needin'.'

I knew I was not tackling this in the right way, but I persisted. Tackle it I must.

'Jessie! what if it had been you?' You and Andy, I wanted to say, but I could not go as far as that.

'Me?'

'If it had been you and George.'

'Him!' She blew the lather from her hands – the graith – and continued, 'I'd hae mair sense than look the road *he's* on, a shilpit wee cratur like thon.'

'But what if he had been somebody else? Somebody you liked?'

She wiped her hands on her rough brat and said impatiently, 'I've got nae time for riddles. What's got into ye, lassie? Is the black dog on your back?'

'No, Jessie.' I urged myself to go on and make my point, however feebly. 'I'm just sticking up for Liz-Ann, and for myself. I've got as much right to an opinion as anyone else.'

'Maybe ay an' maybe hooch-ay!'

'Big folk are not always right,' said I, bracing myself. 'You're sometimes wrong, Jessie! Me, too, of course,' I conceded, 'but not all the time. So from now on I'm going to make up my own mid.' As a parting shot I added, 'And you can keep your castor-oil!'

She was at the scrubbing-board now, rubbing for dear life as if scrubbing out all my sins. She whipped round for a second. Was she going to give me a clout on the ear? I felt the colour rushing to my cheeks in anticipation of the blow, but she held her hand.

In that brief second during which our eyes met I tried to tell her everything I was feeling. I could not say the words right out.

'Jessie, I love you! You are my shield and strength, from whence cometh mine aid. But you are you, and I am me. The time has come for me to loosen the chains and go on in my own way, so that I can find out who I am. Always looking back in gratitude to you for setting me on the straight road. Do you understand, Jessie?'

I wonder if she did? There was just a flicker in her dark eyes as they met mine. Then she turned back to the scrubbing-board and said, 'Get oot ma road. It's high time ye lairnt some rummlegumption.'

'I've learnt it, Jessie,' I said, and ran off to my castle on the hill to think it all out.

14. A Fresh Beginning?

I could see father in the greenhouse perched on an upturned pail, playing the jew's harp. He, too, had retired into his shell in search of solitude.

I climbed the crumbling walls of the old keep, moss-covered and with ferns growing from the crannies. I sat there for a long time looking towards the Carter Bar, not seeing the hills or anything around me, stunned by what had happened to me.

I sensed that I had passed a milestone. Gained something; lost something, too. I could no longer take the easy way out, merge into the background, believe everything I was told. Bairns should be seen and not heard. Life would be more difficult now; more exciting, perhaps. But I would still need Jessie as an anchor. Maybe more than ever now; but on different terms.

I came to no great conclusions with all my thinking, except that I knew I had found myself. Was I worth finding?

A skylark singing overhead echoed my feelings. 'Free! Free!'

Flora, the white pony, came galloping by, nickering with joy at being alive. Things had changed for her, too. since the motor had taken her place. Did she regret losing her chains? She lay down on the grass and rolled over and over, kicking up her heels. 'Free! Free!'

A bright butterfly settled on the castle wall beside me. It reminded me of a poem Miss Paleface, the English teacher, had read to us at the Grammar School. She had a book called an Anthology out of which she read now and again at the end of a lesson, picking the poems at random. I think she liked hearing the sound of her genteel voice, but it was the poems I liked.

> The tulip and the butterfly
> Appear in gayer coats than I.
> Let me be dressed fine as I will,
> Flies, worms, and flowers exceed me still.

So who was I to be thinking so much about myself? A mere article, as Jessie would have said; but an article with new-found faith in herself. I'll show them! I'll do something with my life! You wait!

'Man-lassie, ye'll tummle doon, if ye dinna watch oot.'

Jock-the-herd had come stravaiging across the hill with Jed and Jess at his heels. He was leaning on his crook, *his* strength in time of need, while the dogs lay panting on the grass. The herd blended into the background, as if he were part of the Cheviots himself.

'Hullo, Jock.'

'Ye're back.'

'Ay, I'm back, Jock.' But I'm a different me. Do you not notice the change? Not him! Perhaps if I had turned into a black-faced yowe he might.

Jock never wasted words, so I thought that was the end of the conversation, but I was surprised when he spoke again, and almost fell off the castle wall when I heard what he had to say.

'She'll be pleased to see ye back.'

'Who, Jock?'

'Jessie, of course. She's missed ye. She's been doon in the plook.' Down in the mouth, he meant.

I was astounded, not only at the thought of Jessie being doon in the plook because of me, but at the herd noticing it. When he and Jessie met face-to-face in the farmyard they never even acknowledged each other's presence.

There was more to everyone than met the eye.

The skylark was still singing overhead and I wanted to sing with it, elated to know that Jessie had missed me and that my feelings for her were not just one-sided.

I wished the herd would go on, but he had reverted to normal and was as dumb as a drystane dyke till we heard a tinny bell ringing from the distance. The dinner-bell calling me home. Sometimes I took note of it, if it came up my back, or if I was hungry.

I felt hungry now. Toom in the waim. I could almost smell the stovies. So I slithered down from the castle wall, dislodging a stone or two, and ran away home, forgetting all my introspective thoughts. I was only a starving bairn in need of sustenance.

Jessie was dishing the meal when I came in. The castor-oil bottle stood on the table beside my plate, but I took no notice of it. I knew, and I think Jessie knew, too, it was only there as a gesture. The cork would not come out.

She did not look at me but ladled a helping on to my plate.

'Eat up your stovies, lassie,' she said in her usual sharp tone.

'Yes, Jessie, I will. They smell good.' My tone was warmer.

Her hand lingered near my cheek. Was she going to

touch it? Give me an unexpected little pat perhaps? No! she changed her mind and gave me a slap instead. A wee skelp.

It stung for a moment, but it was almost as good as a caress.